An American on the Western Front

An American on the Western Front

The First World War Letters of Arthur Clifford Kimber, 1917–18

PATRICK GREGORY
AND ELIZABETH NURSER

The
History
Press

To *the memory of*
Naomi Kimber Marshall

First published 2016

The History Press
The Mill, Brimscombe Port
Stroud, Gloucestershire, GL5 2QG
www.thehistorypress.co.uk

British Library Cataloguing in Publication Data.
A catalogue record for this book is available from the British Library.

ISBN 978 0 7509 6052 6

Typesetting and origination by The History Press
Printed and bound in Malta by Melita Press

CONTENTS

ACKNOWLEDGEMENTS

Many people have helped in the production of this book: directly and indirectly, people from the modern day and from years past; and we would like to thank them all. To begin with, Mark Beynon of The History Press for commissioning *An American on the Western Front*; and Clara and George Kimber for their original and vital work after the First World War, work upon which we were able to build.

But we would also like to thank a great many historians and experts, past and present, for their scholarly research. Among them are the late John S. D. Eisenhower and James J. Hudson for their important military and aviation histories of America's war effort in the First World War; likewise the late Arthur Raymond Brooks, official historian of the 22nd Aero Squadron; and the aviation expert Jon Guttman for his diligent proofreading and suggestions for additional detail to be incorporated in our work. Grateful thanks also go to Blaine Pardoe of the League of World War I Aviation Historians for his research notes and help; and to the AFS Foundation for its invaluable archive.

We would like to acknowledge the support of Professor Andrew Wiest of the University of Southern Mississippi for his scholarly introduction to this book and Mark Taplin, the United States' former chargé d'affaires at US Embassy Paris. It was Mark who commissioned the mission's 'Views of the Embassy' project in 2013–2014 which focused on the work of American diplomats and volunteers in France following the outbreak of war in 1914: work which was then carried out so ably by Dr Lindsay Krasnoff of the Office of the Historian of the US State Department.

I'm indebted to Lindsay for her invaluable research and a later invitation to collaborate in a State Department webinar on the subject.

We would like to acknowledge the help of the staff of the British Library in London, including permissions manager Jackie Brown; the Imperial War Museum; the Service Historique de la Défense in Paris; the Smithsonian Institute in Washington DC; the Submarine Force Museum in Groton, Connecticut; library staff of the Texas A&M University in College Station, Texas; and also, and importantly, Conrad Berger of the Library of Congress in Washington DC.

Thank you to cartographer Barbara Taylor for her excellent original artwork and for making our vague map-making ideas reality; and also to the railroads writer and consultant Ken Kinlock who provided valuable advice on otherwise unfathomable century-old American railway timetabling.

Personal thanks go to Elliot Ross for his assiduous end-noting of this book and for his website design, to friends Paul and Denise Wright for their encouragement and help in pursuing the project over these last years; and most especially to my wife and family, Isabelle, Thomas and Elizabeth for all their constant support.

Patrick Gregory

We wish to acknowledge the help of other descendants of Clifford's brothers who added snippets of information from family memories, in particular Dr Clarissa Kimber, another of George's daughters. His youngest daughter, Naomi Kimber Marshall, sent the remaining archive, including a number of pictures used here, which had been retained by her mother. Naomi's death shortly afterwards sadly precludes her seeing the completed book. Anne Kimber, a granddaughter of his elder brother John, sent genealogical information of great interest, and Ghislaine Shelley also added her efforts in France. Michael Over, archivist at Kent College, Canterbury, was able to confirm information about Clifford's time there. All these, we thank.

We have attributed the ownership of pictures in their captions, and thank all those who have kindly allowed us to reproduce their illustrations in this book. Most of the photographs were taken by Clifford at the front. Thank you to Darren Lusty of The History Press for his skill in enhancing those very old and fragile prints.

Elizabeth Nurser

PREFACE

Arthur Clifford Kimber wasn't the first American to serve in France in the First World War, nor was he the last to die there. He wasn't the first person, American or other, to write his thoughts from the Western Front in the form of a diary or letters, or in prose or poetry, nor did he achieve particular distinction in military service while he was there. But what is striking about the letters of Clifford Kimber is the size of the canvas he left behind, one on which we can see not only the portrait of a young man, but also manage to glimpse an image of the United States as it gathered itself for its first proper foray on the global stage and prepared to walk out on to it.

In order to explore these two stories as fully as possible, and flesh them out for the reader, Elizabeth Nurser and I have used a variety of different methods and resources. Small fragments of these letters have been aired once before in extracts contained in the book *The Story of the First Flag*, compiled by Clifford's mother shortly after his death. It focused heavily on one aspect of Clifford's time in France – his mission to carry the first official flag sanctioned by the American Government to France at the beginning of the war – before turning to some other snippets of his life in service there. We are indebted to Clara Kimber for her work, but felt that the time had now arrived to share the letters more fully, to flesh out Clifford's story and to give it a proper beginning, middle and end as well as put it in context.

In the time that has passed since Clara sat down in 1919 and 1920 to record something of her son, these letters as well as bits of memorabilia and photographs gradually came to be scattered around the world, stuffed in boxes and trunks, in attics and garages and under beds in homes in the United States and Britain, alongside the letters of Clifford's brother, George. The approaching centenary of America's involvement in the Great War marked a fitting time to begin sifting through them and compiling them, to publish a representative sample of letters and photographs.

Thus *An American on the Western Front* sets out to tell these two stories in tandem: that of Clifford's life and America's war effort, and in essence mixing the personal and the public. I have attempted to do this primarily through the letters, which Elizabeth and I have edited; but also through a narrative structure that puts Clifford's story in its place within its historical context, explaining how the country readied itself for and applied itself to the war effort in Europe. In order to help achieve this I have borrowed from a wide range of sources, both academic and private, and I have acknowledged these in endnote and bibliography form and elsewhere. I have not included all of Clifford's writing, but large and strictly sequential extracts. Nonetheless, partial or not, I hope we have allowed him to tell his story all these years on and that a proper balance has been struck between his letters and the narrative I have fashioned around them.

A century on, we can see afresh the world Clifford left behind so suddenly. We can share a young man's thoughts and feelings during the last eighteen months of his life as he grew up very fast, during extraordinary times, moving from everyday and humdrum concerns to the sudden realities and brutalities of war. It is, necessarily, the story of a life only part lived, of hopes and dreams cut short. But his letters allow us a vital worm's eye view of the war, where we can follow his story and that of America from the sunny optimism of springtime California in 1917 to the dank mists of northern France in autumn 1918.

It has been a privilege to share this young man's life and it is in his memory and that of his colleagues, for their bravery, that this book is written. I would like to thank Elizabeth for her unstinting work and her editing skills and for her agreeing to participate in the project in the first place. I hope the book will be of interest to the general reader as much as to the academic scholar, whether he or she chooses to read it in full or skims through it for certain episodes or facts. Either way, I hope it will add some understanding to the overall picture of America's role in the Great War and that others may borrow from it in the years to come.

Patrick Gregory
London, 2016

Please keep all my letters carefully. I shall number them and will write the story of my time when I return.

This book is a selection of those letters, sent by Clifford Kimber, a young Stanford University student, to his mother and two brothers, on the 'adventure of his life'. He wrote 160 letters home, from leaving California and his departure from New York for Europe in May 1917 to his death in September 1918, weeks before the Armistice and the end of the war. Other letters to friends have not survived.

Clifford's story begins in April 1917, when he was entrusted with an American flag (now in the archives of Stanford University) to present to the French commander of the unit to which he would be attached as an ambulance driver.

American volunteer ambulance units had first developed in the older universities of the east coast as a way of helping the Allies in a non-combatant role while the United States was still neutral. By late 1916 a pro-French fever had spread to colleges on the west coast, and ambulance units were formed at the University of California at Berkeley and Stanford University. Young men like Clifford, already convinced that the Allies, and in particular the French, were fighting for liberty and Western values, threw themselves into the fray.

By the time Clifford's unit left for France, the United States had entered the war. The flag that had been entrusted to Clifford in April became the first American flag to be raised in the European conflict. However, the ambulance units were still civilian, officially attached to the French Army. As America reorganised its armed forces during 1917, most of the young volunteers joined one or another of the services, and Clifford eventually became a pilot.

Arriving in Liverpool after the Atlantic crossing, Clifford posted a batch of letters as soon as the boat docked. It had been an exhilarating journey across the Atlantic, with boat drills, sightings of flotsam and jetsam from sunken vessels, and dodging submarines near the Irish coast. He exhorted his family back home to type up his correspondence as soon as it arrived, to preserve what he hoped would form a complete journal of his wartime experiences. He expected to edit this journal himself and produce a book when he returned to California.

Clifford wrote completely frankly to his family, just as he would have spoken to them. Early published reports of an exciting experience that he had in New York, protecting the 'Stanford' flag from a hijacking by the University of California *ambulanciers* who were travelling to France at the same time, had resulted in embarrassment:

> *Please don't let anything I say in my letters get published at all unless I give permission, or you ALL (not one) really think it all right. I have changed, and I assure you I was thoroughly ashamed of that Times clipping. I have absolutely no desire for that kind of publicity. PLEASE TAKE NOTE.*

In telling his story, he not only wanted to capture what he saw in writing, but also in photography and sketches. The letters are peppered with references to drawings, most long lost, and photos which he used to explain or support events. Most of the photos taken before he joined the American air arm were collected and turned into an album by his brother George. Unfortunately, almost all of those taken during his flying days have disappeared. Whether they were lost in transit from France to California when his effects were dispatched by his commanding officer, or later, is unknown – probably unknowable. (We know the photographs once existed because he directed that the 'plates be sent to his mother in the event of his death'.)

Nonetheless, what does remain of Clifford's record has been enough – from the perspective of 100 years later – to piece together the story of a boy who jauntily went off to war with romantic idealism and a certainty that he would return, but who after eighteen months had become a man with no illusions about the grimness of war and the possibility of death. The fact that he was not able to edit his story himself means that we have probably lost much that would have interested later generations (he was a keen observer of people, events and, especially, machinery!), but it has allowed us to be with him in the most mundane, as well as terrifying, experiences. We can feel the boredom, the fun, his homesickness, the carefree pleasure of travel on leave, small humiliations, and the thrill of flying and combat in the air.

The remarkable survival of so many letters is due to the conscientious typing up of the letters as they received them, by his mother and his younger brother, George. At least four copies of the letters were made and bound in leather. There is some variation in the text of the letters, but not of sufficient importance or extent to affect the extracts here. Everything relating to Clifford was jealously guarded by his mother and on her death by George. But somewhere along the line, most of the original letters were lost – perhaps they were discarded as redundant when they had been transcribed. How the photographic plates disappeared is a complete mystery. (Other photographs, some of which are printed here, come from a variety of sources. Where known, we have made appropriate acknowledgement.)

In 1999, shortly before her death, George's second wife, Josephine, packed up Clifford's effects (which she had inherited) and sent them to me in the United Kingdom. I am George's second daughter; I had come to England as a student, then married and settled permanently. Josephine could think of no one in the United States who would be sufficiently interested to take them *in toto*. Like Clifford's mother and brothers, she hoped that someone eventually would publish an edition of the letters to fulfil Clifford's intention. I agreed to try, but during the last fifteen years personal matters have intervened and it looked as if more years would pass before there was a proper attempt. Clara E. Kimber, Clifford's mother, had already published extracts from some of the letters in 1920 as *The Story of the First Flag*, a beautifully written tribute of a mother to her son. But there is much more in the letters that deserved publication and another version was needed.

Rescue came in the form of my son-in-law, Patrick Gregory. He could conceive of no better time to publish this book than in the centenary of the involvement of the United States in the First World War, and he suggested we collaborate. This book is the result of that collaboration and without his enthusiasm, knowledge, skill and perseverance it would not exist. Thank you, Patrick.

Elizabeth Nurser (née Kimber)
Sudbury, Suffolk, UK
2016

INTRODUCTION BY PROFESSOR ANDREW WIEST

On the morning of 6 June 1994 a telltale roar prompted the crowd around Sainte-Mére-Église to look to the skies. Parachutes popped open all around as 1,000 men tumbled from their aircraft towards the landing zone below. Led by thirty-eight veterans who the French press had dubbed the '*papys sauteurs*', or 'the jumping grandpas', the paratroopers drifted to the ground, with only one of the grandpas sustaining a minor injury. The spectacle gave way to ceremonies and speechifying by a glittering assortment of queens, crown princes, presidents and prime ministers from countries both large and small. The 45,000 veterans in attendance were treated like the heroes they were.

The events surrounding the 50th anniversary of D-Day formed a year-long cottage industry in France with more than 350 events, ranging from a Second World War themed jazz festival to the construction of three new major military museums. The 50th anniversary tide of historical memory had arguably begun to swell the year before with the 1993 release of Steven Ambrose's *Band of Brothers*. And the 1994 ceremonies, as it turned out, represented only the leading edges of the Second World War wave that struck America's collective consciousness. The full force of the wave did not crash ashore until the 1998 release of the Steven Spielberg movie *Saving Private Ryan* and the publication of Tom Brokaw's *The Greatest Generation*. Next followed Tom Hanks' and Steven Spielberg's collaborative effort on the HBO miniseries adaptation of *Band of Brothers* in 2001. The tide of remembrance receded only slowly, marked by the opening of the National World War II Memorial in 2004.

April 2017 marks another watershed moment in America's military history – the 100th anniversary of the entry of the United States into the cataclysm that was the First World War. Much as the famous Normandy American Cemetery and Memorial sits atop Omaha Beach at Colleville-sur-Mere and stands as silent witness to the brutality of war, the Meuse-Argonne American Cemetery and Memorial sits near Romagne-sous-Montfaucon, keeping silent vigil over a landscape that had once been cut by trenches during the carnage of the final stages of the First World War. While the Normandy American Cemetery, with its nearly 10,000 crosses, still hosts throngs of visitors and pilgrims every day, the Meuse-Argonne American Cemetery, with its nearly 15,000 crosses, lies almost silent as only a tiny trickle of visitors pause to honour the fallen.

The Second World War transformed the United States and the world in myriad ways. Within that historical avalanche of events, the campaign in Normandy stands alongside Stalingrad, El Alamein, Kursk, Midway, Guadalcanal and many others as a pivotal moment. Certainly Normandy, and the titanic war of which it is a part, is deserving of historical fame. But in many ways the American experience in the First World War was even more transformative.

It was with its declaration of war in April 1917 that America first took its place on the world stage, a place it has never relinquished. It was in the First World War that America came of age, muscling its way to the international table to sit beside its European and Asian rivals. It was the beginning of what many historians now term the 'American century'. There is now a widely accepted school of thought that views the First World War and the Second World War as integral parts of the *same* conflict. In that view the Second World War, for all of its ferocity and carnage, merely continued and propelled forward changes that had their beginnings in the First World War.

The First World War was, perhaps, the most important single event, or series of events, of modern times. Within that war, the Battle of the Meuse-Argonne stands out as the pivotal American moment. Led by General John 'Black Jack' Pershing, the American Expeditionary Force (AEF) sought to expel the Germans from a vital sector of their Hindenburg line of defences. The battle, involving over 1 million American military personnel, raged from 26 September until the end of the conflict on

11 November 1918. After bogging down amidst the formidable German defences and suffering from critical logistics breakdowns, the American forces eventually made great gains – but at a tremendous cost. More than 26,000 US soldiers were killed and over 110,000 were wounded, making the Meuse-Argonne far and away the most costly battle in terms of lives lost in American history.

Given the importance of the conflict, the intensity of the fighting and the tragic losses incurred, the history of the First World War in the United States is sadly obscure and intellectually incomplete. A trip to any major bookshop will reveal shelf after shelf of books on all aspects of the Second World War, while the few books on the First World War languish in a small, dusty corner. Americans remain fascinated by the towering personalities of the Second World War and find the First World War to be oddly unsatisfying. Perhaps it is because the First World War was such a slow-moving affair that resulted in such a short-lived and ill-advised peace. Set against the evil of Hitler, the menace of Stalin, and the stubborn resolve of Churchill, the leaders of the First World War, men like David Lloyd George and Woodrow Wilson, seem stodgy and in over their collective heads. Perhaps some of the problem lies in the communications technologies of the time. The Second World War can be experienced in sharp film images, some of which are even in colour. First World War images, though, are herky-jerky and mute.

Europeans and their historians take rather more note of the First World War, where it is often still termed the Great War. The heightened public and historical awareness of the events of 1914–18 across the pond is in part because the conflict had such an outsized effect on the course of Europe's collective future. The Great War shook the foundations of Europe that had been centuries in the making, shattering the Russian Empire, destroying what had been the Austrian Empire, leaving embittered nations in Germany and Italy that were susceptible to the rise of dictatorial regimes, weakening France, and crushing the Liberal Party in Great Britain.

The historiography surrounding the Great War in Europe has followed an interesting pattern. First there was a great flood of books published mainly by the wartime participants themselves, taking credit for successes and laying blame for failures in the largest single series of events that the world had ever seen. After the coming and going of the Second World War, the study of the Great War fell out of favour with the few historians remaining, labelling the earlier conflict futile, its participants bumbling and its tale less than compelling.

As the Cold War frightened the modern world, the Great War seemed ever more antiquated and less worthy of historical attention, other than damning its leaders as hidebound and uncaring. Only in recent years, with the complete opening of document collections and archives, has the study of the Great War undergone something of a mini renaissance. Without societal axes to grind, modern scholars have shone a much more careful light on the events of the first two decades of the twentieth century and have utilised methodologies varying from gender history to cultural studies to advance our understanding of the First World War. Sadly, although the Great War is at last something of a B list celebrity in Europe, there has been no corresponding rise in prominence on the US side of the Atlantic. There is a small group of American historians toiling away on research concerning the First World War, from Michael Neiberg to Mark Grotelueschen, but their numbers pale in comparison to the army of US historians who work on the Second World War.

What makes the situation all the more difficult to understand is the remarkable literacy of the First World War. Almost all of the untold millions of officers and men who took part in the conflict could read and write, and many were inveterate correspondents, diarists and poets. From Field Marshal Sir Douglas Haig's diary, which lays bare the mind of a strategist, to collections of vivid letters penned by humble enlisted men and sent home to loved ones, the vast archive of written source material on the First World War is a historian's dream. Researchers can access the treasure trove of historical raw material at archives big and small, from the US National Archives to dusty and seldom used local collections in France and Germany.

The new work being done on the First World War in the US and Europe is fascinating and in many ways represents history at its best. The focus of that work, though, tends towards the strategic. Was the war futile? Were the commanders of the First World War innovative, or stagnant in their thinking and actions? Was the war a true international turning point? While questions such as these are certainly worth a good historical pondering, the lowest levels of conflict have received even less reconsideration. What was the Great War really like for its young practitioners? Why did young men go to war, and how did violent combat interact with their humanity?

In the immediate aftermath of the First World War several veterans of the conflict penned testaments to their experiences that still stand as classics of the genre, including Erich Maria Remarque's *All Quiet on the Western Front*, Frederic Manning's *The Middle Parts of Fortune* and Siegfried Sassoon's *Memoirs of an Infantry Officer*. Since those early days, though, too few writers have turned their pens to the real, gut-level experience of the war. For the laundry list of reasons catalogued above, the First World War from the standpoint of the regular soldier remains something of a historical unknown. And the case is even worse regarding the lives and times of United States soldiers. Other than the famous few, the historical anomalies like Sergeant Alvin York, the US serviceman toiling for his country in the American Expeditionary Force at St Mihiel or the Meuse-Argonne remains, sadly, historically anonymous.

Patrick Gregory and Elizabeth Nurser's *An American on the Western Front* marks an important first step to fill the historiographical lacuna of the experience of American soldiers fighting and dying in the trenches of France. The study is based on the extensive letter collection of Arthur 'Clifford' Kimber, uncle of Elizabeth Nurser, an early volunteer, an avid correspondent and a true man of his time. Blended with a deft editing hand of historical background, Kimber's wonderfully written letters make for compelling reading. Gregory's narrative history is detailed, accurate and well written, but it is the letters themselves that really set this study apart and make it so indispensable for both laymen and field experts alike.

Through Kimber's many letters, readers are able to access the human level of war – the essential humanity of a young Californian with great dreams, thrown into a maelstrom of events that would eventually take his life. Kimber's letters are full of texture and nuance, ranging from wondering about his life's goals, to meetings with the famous and near famous, and efforts to spark and receive love. Here we see the full picture of an American Great War soldier – from his pre-war decision to enter the military, to train journeys across the country with his mother, to his petty squabbles with friends, to his decisions to join the flying corps, to the nearly endless boredom and to questions of his eventual mortality. Here we see war as it really was rather than the type of war that we so often read about.

An American on the Western Front forms a compelling story that allows modern readers to access the First World War for what it really was – a war fought by young men with real lives and dreams. A war of puffing locomotives, boundless patriotism, scheming officers, bad food, fleeting glimpses of love, personal foibles, rivalries great and small, distant families, endless boredom and training and eruptions of death and destruction. This work by Patrick Gregory and Elizabeth Nurser allows us all a fascinating window to a dimly understood past – a past that has lain historically dormant for too long.

Professor Andrew Wiest

I

BANTHEVILLE, OCTOBER 1920

The farmer posed proudly in his tractor, staring out over the freshly dug earth at the two Americans. The men were both grimy and sweating from their exertions in digging the heavy, debris-laden mud. It had been a long day for them, only partially successful, and the light was beginning to fade. The farmer hadn't used his tractor to help them – it was too delicate a process for that, he knew – but he'd been on hand to advise and encourage them nonetheless, to help them move some of the heavier earth. Now, at his request, one of the men was taking his picture. A memento, perhaps, of a successful day yet to come, a day when the man with the camera might find his brother.

George Kimber had only recently arrived in Europe, the first time on a continent he hadn't quite made it to as a 10-year-old boy. But this was different. Then, a family holiday in England, after a year's schooling for his elder brothers in Canterbury, had ended with John and Clifford having an extended adventure with their father in mainland Europe, while young George had accompanied his mother back to Brooklyn. But now here he was, back in his own right, in Europe to study. A botanist by training, he had taken up the offer of a scholarship at the University of Brussels, the guest of an organisation which was a hangover of the recent war in Europe, the Commission for the Relief of Belgium. His work under Professor Rutot was as enlightening as it was challenging: he was enjoying his time, enjoying the rigours of the study; and he liked Brussels and Belgium.

But he wasn't in Belgium today. He was standing in what once had been a garden, now strewn with rubble and weeds, in a small village in north-eastern France; and the reason he was there had nothing to do with botany, with the possible exception of the tangle of weeds beneath his feet. Part of what had brought him to Europe in the first place, and this village in particular, was unfinished business with one of his brothers. It wasn't about his regrets at not accompanying him when he was a boy: this time it was to find his body. Because Clifford had not just travelled to Europe once without him: he had gone back again as a young man in the service of his country, and that second time he hadn't returned. His big brother was frozen in time as a 22 year old, just George's age now.

The village of Bantheville and its surroundings were still recovering from the war: the evidence of the war's ravages was still around and about. Two years on, give or take a few weeks, and its after-affects were still to be seen and touched, the detritus under his feet and some remaining mementoes in the ground which sloped above him up to the churchyard, twisted metal reminders of a conflict which had claimed so many. The many in this area had included local French men and women, of course. It also included the German battery which had operated from the village, and it also numbered the young American pilot who had tried to silence the battery.

It had been the opening day of an offensive in this Romagne area of north-eastern France, part of a wider Franco-American push to break the resolve of the German forces here at the end of September 1918. Arthur 'Clifford' Kimber had been sent in sometime after 11 o'clock on that misty morning, following the line of the road up from Grandpré to Dun-sur-Meuse. At Bantheville, focusing in on a target on the ground, Clifford had begun to dive. But artillery fire from the ground caught him, his plane exploded, stopping him forever, the wreckage plunging down to the ground and the village.

George remembered the letter his family had received at the time from Cliff's commanding officer. 'He was an excellent flier', Captain Ray Claflin Bridgman had said, 'made a good record while with the squadron and gave his life for a noble cause'. But what ate at George was the fact that his brother's body had never been recovered – and there was an actual body, he was sure of that. A body which had been buried, and somewhere here; he had ascertained as much from various sources. But the question was, where? There was no concrete information from the various sources he had contacted as to where exactly a grave might be, and no obvious clue on the ground here, no marker certainly, and in terms of intelligence only conjecture from the locals. So this was a new chapter for him, trying to fit more pieces into the jigsaw of information that he and his mother had assembled over the last couple of years. Now he was digging into the earth beneath him to see if his belief could be vindicated.

Before setting out for Europe, George and his mother Clara had managed, through various intermediaries, to contact a member of Clifford's old 22nd Aero Squadron unit, a former airman who, they had heard, might hold a clue. Lieutenant John A. Sperry had been shot down and captured by the Germans somewhere near Bantheville days before Clifford's plane was destroyed and had seen an ID tag in the possession of a German officer – Oberleutnant Goerz – and he recognised it as Clifford's tag. If a tag had been found, perhaps it had been recovered from a body. Also, Sperry had been told, a body had been recovered and buried somewhere nearby. Armed with these snippets, and once settled in Brussels in the autumn of 1920, George had written to the German authorities in Berlin. But the information he had received back from the Deutsche Militär Kommission – a numeric list answering his various queries – had been dispiriting:

There was no information available on his query from the German Central Records Office in Berlin.

The warden of Bantheville cemetery says there is no grave there belonging to Arthur Clifford Kimber.

Oberleutnant Goerz has no information. He burned records after the war.

Re: the shooting down of Clifford's plane – It has been ascertained that a Spad plane was brought down by the anti-aircraft battery no. 721 in the western section of the Meuse, behind the German lines, on September 26th, 1918, according to a notice contained in the war diary of the Commander of the Anti-Aircraft of the 5th German Army. As the aforesaid battery had taken up position in the vicinity of Bantheville at the time when the Spad airplane was shot down, it is supposed that this plane was that of the 1st Lt. A.C. Kimber.

So George now found himself in Bantheville in the fading light of an October day. He had to determine for himself what the parameters he was searching within were, what the area looked like, where the obvious places to look might be, how many clearly unmarked graves there were to contend with. He needed to see who might give him some clues, to ask locals what they remembered. Before he set out from Brussels he had written ahead to the local authorities at the American Graves Registration Service who, since the war, had been assembling the nearby American Cemetery at Romagne-sous-Montfaucon. He asked if anyone might help him search and, also, if they could recommend anywhere to stay nearby. They had replied promptly, assuring him that someone would be on hand to assist him when he arrived and that rooms were available in the Hostess House of their local YWCA. So George had set out, travelling, as was his wont, with two suitcases, one full and one empty, the latter to be filled in the course of his travels with dirty clothes.

The man from the cemetery delegated to help him was Captain Chester Staten and, after making contact with him at Romagne-sous-Montfaucon, the two set out towards Bantheville. A quick inspection of the graveyard of the church there bore out what George had already been told: there were no plots bearing the name of Kimber. So they began chatting to some of the locals: what did they know? Did they have any leads or suggestions? Rather curiously, the first thing they discovered was that they weren't the first Americans to visit the village recently looking for a body. An American officer had come from Germany, from Halle, to look for the body of a fellow serviceman, an American lieutenant, an aviator. The officer had been looking, on the locals' suggestion, in the very area George now stood – the garden between the church and the road.

The officer, whoever he was, had apparently found nothing when he looked. That didn't deter George: he wanted to do his own searching and his own digging. George and Captain Staten got to work with spades, turning over the ground as carefully as the soil would allow and throwing rocks and debris to one side. It was hard going. The ground was heavy and frosty and after several hours of labour their work showed only glimmers of hope. Human remains were there all right, and even then, not one but two bodies, but these were not their fellow countrymen: they were the bodies of two German soldiers, possibly simply buried in the ground where they had fallen two years before. The two men decided to suspend their dig for the time being, mindful that in turning over this lumpy ground they might be disturbing and cutting through more bodies – German, American or French – than they were uncovering.

'It was best not to work over the garden too thoroughly,' George wrote later in a letter to his mother, 'for fear of obliterating all traces of graves, until we have more definite information.' They decided to wait some months until springtime when, it was hoped, the ground would be more friable and easily sifted.

But their earlier search of the ground up near the church had proved more fruitful. Among the detritus of metal and other tangled remains left over from the war, they managed to uncover – rather surprisingly, given that it was now two years since the war had ended – the parts of two aircraft, including the two engines. The wreckage of the first was above ground, the second partly buried in the soil. Carefully removing a marker containing a number from the first, Staten then dug down into the earth to see if he could find any clue as to the make and origin of the second, eventually retrieving a metal plate with a serial number. These could, George hoped, prove to be vital clues.

2

LETTER-WRITING

29 October 1920

Back in Brussels, George wrote to the Headquarters of the American Forces in Germany in Koblenz, reporting on what he had pieced together thus far. Could they, stationed in Germany, uncover more information on Clifford from German records? It had been a German garrison after all, so could those records provide a clue as to who might be buried there, and where? He said he had heard of several cases of new records being found in the German war offices, apparently previously overlooked, concerning the graves of Allied soldiers who had been buried by the Germans. He had been told as much at the cemetery in Romagne and on a recent visit to Paris.

He also asked the Koblenz office for information about the officer who had preceded him to Bantheville, the one from the American base in Halle. Whose grave was he searching for? Where had he obtained information that there was the grave of an aviator? George told them he was certain that Clifford's body was somewhere to be found in the village. He had the word of the Red Cross for that: they had stated 'definitively' to that effect in a letter to him two years previously. He and Captain Staten had also now found plane wreckage at Bantheville which he thought could be Clifford's; and there was that third piece of information to go on – the testimony of Lieutenant Sperry.

In terms of possible locations the area to concentrate on, he told them, in a phrase he was to find himself writing time and time again over the next year, was the patch of garden or grassland between the road and the church in the village. He wanted to leave them in no doubt about that: that was the area to be concentrated on, where a thorough search must be undertaken. Yet in private correspondence home he was more muted, conceding that his conviction was based more on a balance of probabilities: 'From the stories told me by the peasants [locals in Bantheville] who, unfortunately, are not always in accord, and from the more positive information I have regarding the circumstances of my brother's death, I am inclined to believe that his grave is in the garden.'

23 November 1920

George wrote to his collaborator in the search in Bantheville, Captain Staten, at Romagne-sous-Montfaucon. He had another piece of information for him to pass on to his Graves Registration Service colleagues there. George had written to his mother in Palo Alto back in California to check on a letter she had received eighteen months before. The Adjutant General's Office at the War Department in Washington had written to her then with some details of how Clifford's plane had been shot down, and the letter had contained some technical specifications of the plane he had been flying: a Spad XIII (pursuit plane), number 15268, engine (Hispano-Suiza) number 35529.

George was excited. The number tallied with what they found. George wrote:

> It seems therefore that the airplane which you and I concluded last month was my brother's, the one from which you took the plate near the church at Bantheville, was, in fact, my brother's machine. I think that we may assume for the present, in the absence of any information to the contrary, that the grave in the garden, between the church and the road, if there be the grave of an aviator in the garden, is my brother's.

He also mentioned, in case a body was uncovered, that by way of possible identification Clifford normally carried around a leather pocket chessboard.

George asked Staten if he had managed to do any more searching in the meantime. 'As one of the peasants was so positive that the grave was in a certain location, although digging there at the time did not seem to promise very much, have you looked into that location further?' He also enclosed the photograph he had taken of the farmer in his tractor and developed back in Brussels. Could Staten find his way to leave it for the farmer in the local café in Bantheville? A little 'thank you' for his time.

24 November 1920

To be on the safe side, he followed up his letter to Staten with another one to the head office of the American Graves Registration Service in Paris. He told them about Sperry's confirmation of the ID tag and the fact that locals in the village believed an aviator was buried in the garden. This belief – or was it speculation? – may have been further heightened by the recent appearance of the unnamed officer from Halle. He had been specifically looking for the grave of an aviator in that patch of grassland. How many aviators had been removed from the locations around Bantheville to the Romagne cemetery? Also, did they know who the Halle officer had been – a Graves Registration Service person? Why had he gone and why did he think there was likely to be a grave there?

30 November 1920

For good measure, George also wrote to the adjutant general and the Chief of the Air Service in Washington, giving information on his searches thus far and requesting information on the officer from Halle who had visited Bantheville. Where had he got his information from?

Something occurred to George, a name he remembered from the past: an officer in the American Air Service, a Captain Fred Zinn who had written to his mother some eighteen months before. Zinn had passed on information he had obtained from the German authorities at the time, some of which had since been restated to George in letters from Berlin. Was Zinn the officer from Halle? George also gave the Air Service command the engine numbers on the remains of the two planes he and Staten had found.

2 December 1920

A rather flat response arrived from the American Graves Registration Service in Paris two days later, one of many such messages George would get used to receiving over the months ahead. This was perhaps a reply to both his letter to them and the one he had sent to the HQ of the American Forces in Germany at Koblenz – maybe Koblenz had forwarded his letter to Paris. The Graves Registration letter was brief and to the point. There was 'no further evidence' of burial and 'no further information' had been received from German authorities.

The weeks passed by, and in the absence of any further correspondence from authorities in Germany or France or the United States George concentrated instead on his studies. It was approaching Christmas and he had been invited by a friend, a fellow botany student in Brussels, to spend the holiday period in Switzerland with his family. Fernand Chodat knew that George did not have any family in Europe and besides, he wanted George to meet his father Robert, the professor of botany in the University of Geneva and director of its alpine laboratory. In Geneva, George would also meet Fernand's mother and three sisters, twins Isabelle and Emma, and their elder sister Lucie.

22 December 1920

But before he left on his Christmas holidays, George had time for another quick exchange of letters to and from Washington. The Chief of the Air Service's office had written back. Information, the letter said, would be sent to him at the earliest moment. Yes, it was Captain Zinn. He had made an 'exhaustive tour in the endeavour to locate information as to the fate of a number of missing pilots and observers', said the letter, adding somewhat doubtfully that 'much of his investigation was guided by hearsay and statements of local residents'. But rather more bafflingly for George, the Chief of the Air Service's office went on to venture that it was 'doubtful identification could be made of the planes' that George had mentioned. As a statement it seemed a little odd. George knew that he had, at the very least, located Clifford's plane. That much could not be gainsaid.

23 December 1920

George replied to the air chief's office by enclosing the letter forwarded by his mother: the correspondence they had received some time before from Clifford's colleague, Lieutenant John Sperry, setting out in more detail what had happened to him. He, Sperry, had been shot down and taken prisoner on 4 October 1918, south-east of Grandpré, not far from Bantheville. George now realised that this was some days *after* and not before Clifford was killed, although it changed little. Sperry went on to detail what he had witnessed after being captured by German forces. He said that he had seen Clifford's ID tag in a German flying observer's quarters in the town of Montmédy, behind German lines. It was in the possession of an officer called Goerz, a lieutenant from Burgfeld in Germany.

'This office had a large collection of such tags,' said Sperry:

as it was their business to keep an account of all American airmen shot down in that section. He [Goerz] told me that it was his intention to return all of those tags at the end of the war to the relatives or their owners. I was especially interested in it [Clifford's ID tag] because [he] was in my squadron as you probably are aware. I was taken away from this officer shortly after and I never had an opportunity to speak with him again. I do remember, however, that he said that the body was buried but that he could not tell me just where.

George set out later that day for Switzerland with Fernand, the two young men travelling by train down to Geneva. It was an enjoyable break, a family time, and one made still happier for George by the time he managed to spend with one of Fernand's sisters, Isabelle. Three years younger than he was, Isabelle had made an instant impression – a student in fine art at L'École des Beaux Arts de Genève. George determined to go back to see her the following summer. But in the meantime it was back to Brussels. He returned a fortnight later to his apartment in the Rue de la Loi, focused on the twin-track of his studies and the search for his brother.

7 January 1921

The first letter he received in the New Year promised little. It was another, rather bald, note from Washington, from the War Department Office of the Director of the Air Service, telling George what he knew already. 'The records of the Berlin Central Records Office show your brother to have been killed in action September 26th 1918 and to be buried in Bantheville.' It was hardly worth sending, he thought.

2 February 1921

A month on and George was itching to get back Bantheville to renew his search. He wrote again to the authorities at the cemetery at Romagne-sous-Montfaucon, addressing his letter to the commandant there to check what progress, if any, had been made. He thought it best to go over the details of his case once more, given the thousands of records they dealt with. 'Last October when Capt Staten and I were searching we both of us felt the strong probability that the grave was in the garden between the church and the road in Bantheville.'

He explained again how the two of them had decided that to have conducted a more thorough search back in October, given the condition of the ground, would have risked 'obliterating all trace' of a body or bodies. Better to leave until February, by which time 'the grass and weed covering had been beaten down by rain, wind etc., thus exposing the actual ground'. So now, here he was. Had Staten already begun the search again? Was Captain Staten still at the cemetery or had he been transferred to other work? Or, conjuring up another name he remembered from the previous October, what about Lieutenant Denny? George said he would like to go down to Bantheville in two weeks' time to recommence the search. Would the Hostess House of the YWCA be open?

3 February 1921

The following day, he wrote to Dame Adelaide Livingstone at the British Embassy in Berlin: a Colonel Thomas at the American Embassy in Brussels had suggested he get in touch. He wondered if she could help with any official German war records from her position in Berlin? He said that the only information he had been able to obtain thus far from the Berlin Central Records Office (complete with a few typos of his own, and errors in the German records) was:

List 28122/W
Kimber A.C. Lieut. Flieger
Beirdigt: im Bautheville
Gem. v.d. Inspektion de Fliertrup

'I am writing to you in the hope that you can offer some suggestions,' wrote George. 'I do not wish to leave a stone unturned to find the grave.'

3 February 1921

The same day he wrote – in German – to the German officer named by Sperry in his letter, asking for any information he could provide. It was addressed simply, and in the hope it might eventually find its intended recipient, to 'Lieut. Goerz, Burgfeld, Deutschland'. It was a long shot, he knew.

4 February 1921

A day later Captain Adjutant W. E. Shipp wrote back to George from the American Cemetery in Romagne. Neither Captain Staten nor Lieutenant Denny was still there and no, the body had still not been found 'but', added Shipp, 'it is believed that the present season is as favourable as any other for searching for bodies'. If George wanted to assist, a searcher would be sent out with him to Bantheville 'and all other possible assistance will be given in this search'.

5 February 1921

Back in the US, the office of the quartermaster general of the War Department in Washington had written to his mother in Palo Alto. It might have been something or nothing – it might have been the authorities wishing to plan for the future, to have some information to hand in case something did turn up. Or, perhaps, in fact, they knew something. The person writing to her, Captain M. N. Greeley, Executive Officer of the Cemeterial Division, asked Clara if she could provide dental records for Clifford, ' … chart of all dental treatment … to include filling, crown, bridges etc. as well as any fracture of bones prior to entry into military service'. The information was 'to be used in matters of identification', although no further information was forthcoming.

7 February 1921

Adelaide Livingstone replied to George's letter from the British Embassy in Berlin. The Americans had now established a Missing and Enquiry Unit of their own in Berlin, she said, and they would be better able to offer assistance. She suggested a name – Captain E. M. Dwyer, US Cavalry.

28 February 1921

The trip to Bantheville had yielded nothing. Back in Brussels George was trying to get on with his own work, but he was impatient with the lack of any progress in his search. He had received nothing for weeks, not since his mother had told him about the request for Clifford's dental records. So he took to his typewriter again. Thus far he had concentrated on Americans in Washington and Americans in and around Europe; French locals in Bantheville; Germans; the Red Cross; the British, and on any sources he could muster in Belgium. Time now for the French authorities. But who to write to? He didn't know, but in the end he decided to go to the top – to the hero of Verdun and France. Writing in French, better than his rather rusty German, he sent it to 'Monsieur le Maréchal Pétain, 4 Boulevard des Invalides, Paris, France'. Pétain could always ignore it if he chose to, but George didn't want to leave any stones unturned.

28 March 1921

Something and nothing – the American Forces in Germany, HQ of the 2nd Section of the General Staff, Koblenz, wrote to him, and the Central Records Office in Berlin had written to say that they were investigating and that as soon as any information was available they would be in touch.

4 April 1921

Surprisingly, a reply came from Pétain's office in Paris, from 'Le Maréchal de France, Vice-President du Conseil Supérieur de la Guerre'. Perhaps something had piqued the interest of the man who famously didn't let them pass at Verdun. The letter said that Pétain had written to the general commanding the Verdun Sector to ask him to investigate the case. He said that the central administrative body in Paris now also knew of the request and would follow it up. 'At this stage research is continuing and the Maréchal will not forget to send you on the results.'

10 May 1921

Back in California, the US Army Cemeterial Division had written once more to Clara. Captain Charles J. Wynne said that a search party had gone back to Bantheville armed with a sketch that George had provided them of the village. The party found the area George had searched but merely concluded that 'the area was covered by stone and debris: although locals said it had been a garden prior to the German departure and was only covered over after. Either way, no body was found.' Captain Wynne suggested that perhaps Clifford's body had been brought, unrecorded, to the Romagne-sous-Montfaucon Cemetery nearby as an unknown, though searches would continue. 'The spot indicated on [George's] sketch as the location of your son's machine is inaccurate. The machine was found about 150 yards north-east of the spot and was buried in the ground'.

George seemed further away than ever from unravelling the tangle.

3

COMING OF AGE

The young Arthur Clifford Kimber had only been in California for five years when he went to Stanford University in September 1914. He was following in the footsteps of his elder brother John and looked to the experience as yet another in an already long list of adventures they had had together. He began to find his way around the college campus and enrol for classes but, as he did so in this happy and positive environment, the first battles of a savage war were already being waged 6,000 miles away in Europe, a war in which he would later become involved.

The conflict was, in all senses, a world away from the one Clifford, as he was known to his family, enjoyed in the sunshine of Palo Alto. The family had moved west when his father, the first Arthur Clifford, a clergyman, had died suddenly in the summer of 1909 in the apartment above the church he had established in New York. It had been a terrible loss for a still young family: for his widow Clara, at 42

Reverend Arthur Kimber. (*The Days of My Life*, © Kimber Literary Estate)

Sketch of St Augustine's church, New York, around 1880. (*The Days of My Life*, © Kimber Literary Estate)

more than twenty years Arthur's junior; for the eldest boy John, who was 14 years; and for Clifford, 13, and George, two years younger.

The Reverend Kimber had been a dynamic and inspiring figure, not just to the family who looked to him as a guide and for love and support, but to a large body of parishioners in downtown New York. Thousands of men and women, many of them recent arrivals to the United States, flocked to his mission church in Manhattan's Lower East Side. He was the vicar of St Augustine's, an Episcopal church in the city's Bowery area: an area which acted as a magnet for the city's dispossessed or newly hopeful. St Augustine's offered spiritual, and some practical, support on the way. A devout man, he passionately believed that his Anglican tradition constituted a modern manifestation of the true church of the apostles, and through it he wanted to do what he could to help the people who came his way.

The mission was an offshoot of Trinity church, Manhattan, located on Broadway and Wall Street, the main Episcopal church of New York and the wealthiest parish in the United States. Trinity church had served the area since the late seventeenth century, a place of worship for some of the city's celebrated figures over the years, and at the time of Kimber's ministry the Sunday home of many powerful and rich New Yorkers, including members of the Astor family.

Arthur Kimber was appointed in 1872 as the first Vicar of Trinity's new mission church of St Augustine's and energetically set about designing and supervising its construction. A large and imposing building on Houston Street, not far from the berths of the boats which carried them to America and the tenements which housed these new immigrants, it grew as both a church and a community centre with an associated complex of teaching and meeting rooms and an apartment for its new vicar on the top floor.

It was a church which soon buzzed with activity. On top of the religious services and Sunday schools, carpentry classes were set up, tuition in leathercraft and tailoring was offered, housewifery lessons and sewing tuition – all skills passed on to prepare the members of the congregation for a productive life in the New World. Kimber also provided English lessons to those who wanted them; and to make doubly sure that the Word did indeed get out, he took care to translate the *Prayer Book* into several European languages with a printed weekly service sheet allowing his flock to follow his services. Even Yiddish was catered for, ever hopeful as he was of possible converts from the Jewish faith.

Another aspect of Kimber's social activism saw him working with New York's public authorities to try to find other practical as well as religious solutions to the city's problems and attempting to tackle some of the problems at source. During the mid-1890s he sat on the city's Police Board working with Teddy Roosevelt, then police commissioner for the city. The two had something in common and wanted to address the same issue, albeit for slightly different reasons: to keep drinking in the city under control. Kimber's aim was to save souls and keep families together, while Roosevelt wanted to keep drunken brawling off the streets and the hospitals uncluttered with A&E casualties. More people might be kept in productive labour and for longer.

It was a pragmatic arrangement and Kimber did his bit to lend his help to Roosevelt and his supporters who wanted to take on some of these problems on the ground, curtailing drinking hours on Sundays and limiting the size of glasses in which beer was sold. In the face of opposition from Tammany Hall, Roosevelt succeeded and the reforms stuck, or at least for the time he remained as a Republican commissioner in a notably Democrat city.

After Arthur and Clara's children were born in the mid to late 1890s, a family life developed which revolved in part around the church and Kimber's public affairs, yet private time together was still jealously guarded. That life was divided between a large house in Brooklyn and one Kimber had originally built just before his marriage out in Bayville Beach on Oyster Bay, Long Island. The latter effectively became their summer residence, as Arthur had two curates on whom he could lean. But life in the city was also a

Clara Evans Kimber on her wedding day, June 1894. (*The Days of My Life*, © Kimber Literary Estate)

comfortable one, as the boys put down their roots in Jefferson Avenue in Brooklyn, attending local schools and playing among themselves and with neighbours' children. When their father was there they would watch and 'help' him in the workshop he had made for himself at the top of the house, Clifford in particular studying him as he busied himself with various woodworking and mechanical projects. In his time, Arthur Kimber had patented several ingenious devices, largely for his own pleasure, including a fold-up travelling bath, and at one stage – and somewhat more improbably for a clergyman – even inventing a form of rudimentary torpedo.

Clifford inherited this love of mechanical contraptions from his father, but he was also the most daring and adventurous child of the three and would often get into scrapes and trouble. When he did so, Arthur Clifford Sr would be called upon to dole out the necessary punishment – in typically Victorian or Edwardian style with a big stick – although Clara felt her husband secretly admired and enjoyed his son's exploits.

Clifford, as ringleader, would sometimes persuade his brothers to join him in going out to play on the roof of the house. This was strictly off-limits for obvious reasons, but didn't seem to deter Clifford from leading

The Kimber brothers in around 1905 (left to right): George, John, Clifford. (*The Days of My Life*, © Kimber Literary Estate)

the others up to the fourth floor near their father's workroom-study and using an access door to climb outside. Once there, they would jump on to the roofs of the neighbours' houses to play. On one particular occasion, and for whatever reason, Clifford also decided to borrow their mother's flat iron to take with them. The iron he proceeded to drop down one of the neighbouring chimneys, making a sound below, which he deemed satisfying enough, and causing a good billowing of soot up on to the rooftop. Clifford was happy with his handiwork: it had fallen hard and fast and had made a good metallic thud when it reached the fireplace far below. Unfortunately for Clifford, though, the startled neighbour in her sitting room seems to have been able to identify Mrs Kimber's new iron easily enough. The crime was uncovered, with the familiar result that their father was called upon to do his bit. Arthur duly gave his son a hiding, but later reported to Clara that he could scarcely keep from laughing at the youngster's outlandish explanations.

Summers saw the boys enjoying more freedom still, given the run of the countryside and coastline around them on Long Island. They had a little boat which, with permission, they were allowed to take out on to Oyster Bay. The Roosevelts also holidayed nearby and Arthur would see his old ally from time to time when he was in residence, although by 1901 Roosevelt was already United States President and had other calls on his time. On one occasion when he was there, as family memory happily recalled, a flotilla of warships had sailed up the sound by the president's house. From the balcony of his house Arthur Clifford Sr normally enjoyed watching the comings and goings of the bay through a telescope he had bought some years before. But on this particular day he managed to pick out something he had not expected. Apart from the warships, far out to sea he could make out a small and distant figure in a small boat. Clifford had taken the rowing boat to follow the ships and was now standing up in the middle of it, smartly saluting the officers on the bridge as they in turn gave the salute to the commander-in-chief on the shore.

The Reverend Kimber's sudden death, when it came, rocked the family. Used to the happy security he had brought them, Clara felt bereft and agonised about the best course of action to take for the boys. After several months she came to her conclusion: they would leave the city and move out to the West to have the support of, and be closer to, members of her own family living in California.

Eastleagh Cottage, Bayville, Oyster Bay, New York. (Kimber Literary Estate)

She and the boys duly set sail for this new life in November 1909, taking a steamship out of New York Harbor bound for New Orleans and then onwards by train to the West. There they settled for a period with her parents and sisters, living on their small farm near Hanford in the Great Valley of the state. When their possessions finally reached them from the east coast they moved into the town of Hanford itself, where the children were entered into the local schools and Clara began to teach music. A gifted pianist, Clara was also interested in pedagogy and designed a music syllabus for beginners. But ever restless and seemingly never satisfied that things could be good enough for her family, she judged the schools in the little country town were not good enough for her children, moving the boys next to the university town of Berkeley, home of the University of California.

Clara was a driven and intense woman, but in some respects the restlessness and insecurity she now began to display harked back to an earlier time, and stemmed from her own straitened circumstances in her teenage years and as a young adult. She was originally from upper New York State and had had a reasonably settled early life on the family farm near Bainbridge. Things changed when there was a family dispute about the ownership of the farm. Her father cast around for a better life, investigating possibilities in the West, various teaching jobs in West Virginia, and eventually fetching up running a boarding house near Parkersburg. But it was a desperately precarious existence and the family nearly starved.

Clara, at 16 already an accomplished musician, began to teach to supplement the family income. She decided to set off on her own, and took various residential jobs in Virginia. Eventually she took advantage of the training available in shorthand at the Chautauqua Correspondence School and prepared herself as a secretary. By 1886 she had fetched up in New York City to work for the charity The King's Daughters and Sons, a Christian body which had been established to help the impoverished of the city's slum areas. It was there that she met Arthur Kimber, a man who had gone on to provide not only material comforts and a family life with her but the security and status she had always wanted.

Now, with that security gone, she determined once more that education alone held the key to her future success and happiness and that of her sons. She wanted her sons to have as first-rate an opportunity in education as she could muster for them, so settling in a place where they could progress from high school to college was an important consideration. Berkeley seemed to fulfil that need, at least at first. Yet even Berkeley, when she reached there in 1910, proved only to be another stopping point. Barely two years later the family would be upping sticks again and moving on, this time to the South Bay Area of San Francisco and Palo Alto. She bought a smallholding, Kodina, outside the town in the Santa Clara Valley.

Kodina gave the boys a taste for farming and for the purported riches to be gained from what they liked to talk of as 'scientific farming', which was enjoyable for them, if not Clara. They also began to explore the hills and the California countryside around them as they settled into their new life. The previous few years had been a rocky time for them. The loss of their father, the worries their mother had over money and years of upheaval around the West had all left their mark. Yet they appear to have been determined to keep what happy family life they had and become an ever-tighter unit. The boys were there for one another and Clara became at once both the head of the household and the focal point of its support. Devotion to their mother – to her health, to her happiness and her financial well-being – became entrenched dogma for the boys and would surface time and again in later life. It was a recurring theme of the letters Clifford and his brothers would write over the years. Worries about 'Dear Mother' and her health and financial situation would never be far from their thoughts.

The Kimber home, Tennyson Avenue, Palo Alto, California, around 1916. (Kimber Literary Estate)

The Palo Alto School of Music around 1916. (*The Days of My Life*, © Kimber Literary Estate)

In time Clara plumped not for the countryside around Palo Alto but the town itself, and she eventually settled the family there. It was to be their final move as a family. She collected what assets she had available to her from her husband's estate in New York and ploughed it into a plot in the town's Tennyson Avenue. She built a house on the land and set up a music school, the Palo Alto School of Music, and from that point onwards the family's life appears to have been relatively comfortable, even if grumbles about money did continue in the years ahead. The boys settled at the local high school in Palo Alto and from there went on to the town's university, Stanford. Both in school and college, Palo Alto represented the 'good start' in the boys' lives Clara most coveted. It was still a small town and life there revolved around the university, and arriving barely more than twenty years after the university had opened its doors they soon found themselves part of its community.

So it was that, in time, Clifford found himself enrolled at Stanford in the autumn of 1914. For the next two and a half years he applied himself to anything and everything that came his way, including, but by no means overly fretting about, his class work. He got on with his studies it was true – he had inherited something of his parents' work ethic after all – but

he also found time to explore the Bay Area, going on walking tours and bike rides with his brothers. He helped the family finances with weekend and summer jobs and maintained the interest in music inherited from his mother, serving as business manager as well as playing in the Palo Alto Symphony Orchestra, which his brother John established in 1915. That year was also the one where Clifford was to meet his best friend of college years, Alan Nichols,

Arthur Clifford Kimber as a student. (Kimber Literary Estate)

The Palo Alto Symphony Orchestra, conductor John Kimber. (*The Days of My Life*, © Kimber Literary Estate)

someone who was to play an important part in the next years of his life and to whom he was to look for guidance. They would study together, become energised by events in Europe together, and ultimately serve alongside one another in France.

The war in Europe had raged on from 1914 into 1915. The United States, under President Woodrow Wilson and a Democrat-controlled Congress, maintained the country's neutrality. Wilson did not wish the country to be dragged into a bloody conflict in which, Wilson argued, the US had no strategic interest. There was little to be gained from entering on one side or the other: it wasn't 'our war'. Besides, and as he was aware, there were many in America who, through family ties and ancestry, bore differing allegiances to the warring parties of Europe. There were those with strong national ties to Germany or Russia, Italy, Poland or Britain, or the many nationalities of the Austro-Hungarian Empire.

But Wilson's doctrine of so-called 'strict neutrality' was to be sorely tested by the sinking of liner RMS *Lusitania* in May 1915. German U-boats had adopted a new policy at the time – by targeting shipping in the waters near Britain – a policy of unrestricted warfare against all vessels they found in and around the British Isles, in an attempt to strangle Britain of its lifeline of food and supplies from around the world.

'Unrestricted' in this instance meant the decision to target any and all shipping, of merchant fleets and other crafts approaching British shores, irrespective of whether they belonged to warring nations or were neutral. It was under this policy that a U-boat took the decision to torpedo what it knew to be a passenger liner in the seas off the south coast of Ireland. The result was the loss of 1,198 passengers and crew, including 128 Americans. In the weeks leading up to the sinking, the German Embassy in the US had placed notices in dozens of American papers warning of the danger posed to shipping. The advertisements advised, 'A state of war exists between Germany and her allies and Great Britain and her allies; that zone of war includes the waters adjacent to the British Isles.' Formal notice was given by the Imperial German Government that 'vessels flying the flag of Great Britain, or any of her allies, are liable to destruction in those waters and ... travellers sailing in the war zone on the ships of Great Britain or her allies do so at their own risk'.

Nevertheless, the attack when it came caused huge shock in America and strained the sinews of Wilson's doctrine. The debate that followed forced him into a concerted defence of his policy of neutrality, but Wilson stuck doggedly to his line. At home he argued that nothing was to be gained from entering the conflict now, privately fearing the civil discord which could be unleashed in America, while demanding in communications with the German High Command that they reverse their notion of unrestricted warfare. Eventually, in September 1915, came a partial retreat, Kaiser Wilhelm II issuing an order to the effect that Germany would refrain from sinking passenger ships without warning.[1] Yet the arguments continued to rage between politicians of the left and right in America, between Wilsonian Progressives and those of the Preparedness movement, between Republican interventionists like former president Teddy Roosevelt and pacifists who opposed all armed conflict.

It was not a debate confined solely to the political classes or opinion formers of the east coast or the industrialists there or in the Midwest. The south and the west coast were just as alive to the arguments going to and fro in the country. In California the students at Stanford and Berkeley were increasingly energised by the arguments of whether or not to intervene in this ever bloodier conflict.

Already, since 1914, hundreds of young recruits from across America had joined what they saw as an idealistic and just cause on the side of the Allies, volunteering to serve on the front line in an auxiliary capacity. Some had been involved as early as the war's first Battle of the Marne of September 1914 and ambulance corps like the American Ambulance Field Service (later the American Field Service or AFS) were soon formed to help the war effort on the Allies' side. In time they were organised into sections of twenty-five or thirty men, mirroring the regular sections of ambulances in the French Army to which they would become attached, and put to work as distinct units within it. Each section would be assigned to a particular division of the army and by 1916 could be found dotted across the Western Front and down into the Balkans.

So it was in the autumn of 1916 that, as part of an awareness-raising initiative and to see if more volunteers could be sought, the American Ambulance Field Service went to the Stanford campus to give a presentation. Two members of the audience were Clifford (or 'Arthur' as he was still called in official life) and Alan Nichols. The effect of the talk on them was electrifying, as Clifford recalled when looking back on that night a year later in a letter to his family from the front in France. It is from this point that we can begin to see the world through his eyes and tell the story in his own words as he wrote to his mother and brothers:

> You all know why I came to France ... That lecture that was given in the Stanford Univ. Hall early last fall started things. Previous to that time I had just followed the war in an interested way; of course my sympathies were with the Allies, but I had hardly felt the seriousness of it all and the need for getting into it and doing my part. In fact no inclination or desire to go to Europe till the war ended had ever come to me. Afterwards, I had hoped to travel in war-torn Europe simply as a matter of curiosity. Well, as I say, that magic lantern lecture describing the work of the American Ambulance Field Service in France, quite woke me up. It brought the war home.
>
> Shortly afterwards it was announced that a Stanford Unit of the American ambulance was to be organized. Immediately the spirit of adventure, prompted in part by a desire to help the Allies, came upon me. Investigations always precede or at least always should precede decisions. Everything seemed indefinite; too good to be true; and more or less of a false stir. But work went on and gradually it looked like business. Still I was sceptical.
>
> Then many questions arose. Should I go before finishing college? Could I raise $150, the necessary amount of money? And most important of all, had I a right

to leave Mother whom I loved beyond words, and wanted to see happy and comfortable and above all well. She would worry herself sick. Then did I really want to go after all? Joe Eastman took my name. He assured me that as far as he was concerned I was accepted. The Christmas holidays came. The final selection had not yet been made. One day I received a letter informing me that in making the selection the Friends of France had not included me. No reasons were given. What a shock and blow.

The winter had been hard; mother was not at all well; John and George hated to advise me, but intimated that they felt it my duty to stay at home. I then definitely decided not to go with the first Stanford unit, but I determined to know why I had not been included. I thought there was something personal and that Joe had just taken a dislike to me for some reason or other. Maybe I was right and maybe wrong. A lot has been uncovered since then. Experience is a hard and bitter nut, a valuable teacher.

Up to that time I had promised to only contribute $100. Alan had signed up for $150. Could I go higher? I felt I had no right to borrow or take hard-earned and much needed money from you three. You were all giving me sympathy because you realized how terribly disappointed I was, but in spite of it all you seemed glad that I was going to stay with you, and I don't blame you, especially mother. You are very brave Mother dear.

Registration day for the Spring semester had arrived. Joe asked me if I would come through with $125. I said 'yes.' He would let me know by 11 o'clock. Dr. Elliott said registration fees would be returned if I left before two weeks. I paid my registration fees and signed up with Joe, deciding to be on the safe side either way, especially if the unit did not leave for France and their plans fell through. Was that double playing really fair?

Preparations went on apace. Was studying French and getting ready to leave. I was studying away, determining not to lose in my University work in case I stayed and convinced that a little extra learning would not be wasted time.

In the meantime I was fighting a tremendous battle within. 'Go, you may not get another chance. What if the war is over before you finish in College? You will then miss seeing it,' said one voice. 'Mother will be all right; besides your brothers are able to take care of her and keep her happy.' And the other voice said, 'Stay. There is still lots of time. Mother cannot spare you now. Your duty is to stay; finish your College course and do all you can to preserve the home.'

Oh, what a struggle it was. Wanting to go and wanting to stay. I could not concentrate on my studies; I became selfish it seemed; crabby and hot tempered. My lack of real character made itself manifest. Each time I decided to go my conscience *hurt me. Yes, Mother, John, and George all consented and said 'Go'. It was hard for them and the words of Dr. Willis came to me. 'It is always harder for those who stay behind at home.'*

Finally my better nature asserted itself and I gave up Europe, telling Joe so someone else could immediately take my place. As soon as that was done I began regretting again, and thinking of all that I was missing. Falsely proud (I hate to confess it) I dreaded what my friends would think of me after I had said I was going. They would call me 'yellow'.

Gradually I became reconciled to remaining; it was hard, and I believe now that I was not a game sportsman for disappointment, and sourness at everything around me showed out. What a spirit. What a rotten character.

In the meantime circulars and letters arrived from the New York office of the Ambulance Service. Mr. Sleeper offered to pay part of my expenses. Finances seemed to clear up. By working hard in the summer and saving, I could raise enough money to take care of all my expenses to and from France and while there. At that time the necessary $450 and $500 seemed a fortune.

Mother wanted me to finish College before going to France. It was my duty to consider her wishes and requests, and apart from my 'duty' I wanted to comply with what she wanted out of love alone. Yes, by going to summer school at Berkeley and Pacific Grove, and carrying the maximum number of hours during the Spring and Fall terms at Stanford, I might be able to graduate by Christmas 1917 instead of with my regular class of 1918. But to lose any hours would crash all the plans. You know I am not a natural student, and hate to be bound down with studies and courses I don't like. Well, it was the only manly thing to do.

So Clifford postponed his plans for now. He had reached this uneasy truce – with himself, with his mother and family and with those of his classmates taking the lead to France – with a heavy heart. He resolved to make as good a fist of it as he could, seeing out his academic career. He set Christmas 1917 as his cut-off point and went about his studies 'hammer and tongs', in his own words, to finish his classes. He intended to get to France by 1918, assuming the fighting continued. But diplomatic events were to intervene to foreshorten that wait.

4

THE RUSH TO WAR

Events unfolded surprisingly quickly. A war which was eminently avoidable for America – and Woodrow Wilson had gone to some lengths to avoid it – suddenly became, in the space of a few short months of 1917, inevitable.

The president had campaigned throughout 1916 on his platform of neutrality. 'He Kept Us out of War' – the slogan of his re-election campaign against Republican challenger Charles Hughes referred less to events south of the border with Mexico and the revolutionary wars there, than to the war in Europe. In the case of Mexico, a so-called punitive expedition led by Major General John Pershing, had been sent into the country in March that year to try to capture the revolutionary leader Pancho Villa, who was harrying border areas and citizens of the United States. It was necessary to stop any such cross-border raids and face down a man deemed a menace to security. But as keen as he was to see Villa punished, and he did send Pershing's force, Wilson was also keen to see the operation brought to as swift a conclusion as possible. By early 1917 he had withdrawn American forces without a definite outcome.

War in Europe, meanwhile, was something Wilson was even more determined to avoid if at all possible. Under his presidency the United States had so far not found itself dragged into conflict there, and if the judgement of the ballot box was anything to go by in 1916, the people of America endorsed his position, albeit by a small majority. It appeared that he was in tune with the instincts of enough of the electorate. Broad sympathy for the Allied cause, with some notable exceptions in the population, did not extend to actual involvement.

The election in November was indeed a close-run thing. Wilson edged his opponent by only 600,000 votes in a combined popular vote of over 17.5 million. After some days in the balance the counting finally ended in the western states. The decisive Electoral College votes of California pushed Wilson over the line. Like his father before him, young Arthur Clifford Kimber was a Republican supporter and was disappointed by the slim 46.7 per cent to 46.3 per cent with which the Democrat president had taken the state.[2]

Wilson's deliberate approach had won the day and appeared to be vindicated by the savagery of events in the world outside, with 1916 witnessing casualties of more than 1 million dead or injured in the Battle of the Somme. Matters appeared to be reasonably under control for the newly re-elected president in the early weeks of 1917. Wilson addressed the Senate on 22 January in a speech where he even dared look to the future, asking members of the upper house to help him in his quest to forge the 'foundations of peace among the nations', once conflict was at an end.[3]

There had been only one major threat to the uneasy equilibrium reached with Germany since the autumn of 1915 and that had been contained. This was the sinking in March 1916 of a passenger ship, the SS *Sussex*, sailing in the English Channel between Folkestone and Dieppe. Up to eighty passengers and crew were lost, including a number of American citizens, and it had sparked a fresh wave of diplomatic activity at the time. The United States demanded immediate abandonment of Germany's submarine warfare against passenger and freight-carrying vessels.

Eventually, on 4 May 1916, the German Government replied, following intense discussions within military circles in Berlin. Yes, it agreed – or agreed in part – to rein in the U-boats' activities. Germany was prepared 'to do its utmost to confine the operations of war for the rest of its duration to the fighting forces of the belligerents'. Yet, in an important caveat, it also noted that the German Government should not be expected to restrict the use of an 'effective weapon' at the behest of a neutral power. It should be expected if the enemy were at the same time 'permitted to continue to apply at will methods of warfare violating the rules of international law'. The United States had fired off another missive – this time unacknowledged by Berlin – tartly notifying the 'Imperial Government' that it would not entertain any suggestion that the rights of United States citizens was contingent upon conduct of any other government, 'Responsibility in such matters is single, not joint; absolute, not relative'.

But that, save for the last diversion of opinion, was where matters had rested for nearly nine months, and there had been no flare-ups. Then suddenly, on the afternoon of 31 January 1917, little more than a week after President Wilson had set out his vision for future peace in front of the Senate, the German ambassador to Washington, Johann Heinrich von Bernstorff, called on Wilson's Secretary of State Robert Lansing at his offices in the State, War, and Navy Building not far from the White House, to deliver a letter setting out a sudden *volte-face* in the German Government's policy. Lansing recalled:

> When he entered my room at 10 minutes after 4 I noticed that, though he moved with his usual springy step, he did not smile with his customary easy assurance. After shaking hands and sitting down in the large easy chair by the side of my desk he drew forth from an envelope, which he carried, several papers. Selecting one he held it out saying that he had been instructed to deliver it to me.

Unrestricted U-boat warfare was to be resumed. The 'brutal methods of war' of the Allies had forced their hand, the letter said. Germany would meet the Allies' illegal measures by targeting all navigation, that of neutrals included, around Great Britain, France, Italy and in the eastern Mediterranean.

Lansing recalled:

> It was therefore with real amazement that I read the note and memoranda handed me. I can only account for the premature announcement of indiscriminate warfare on the ground that the food situation in Germany had reached such a pass that the Imperial Government had to do something to satisfy public opinion.[4]

Lansing went to see Wilson at the White House that evening and the two men spoke in private for almost two hours. They had little choice in what to do, they concluded, and they must sever diplomatic ties with Germany. Wilson went back to Capitol Hill on 3 February, this time to address a joint session of both houses, the first of three such trips he would make in the next three months. On this first occasion it was to review those events of the previous year and what had been said then, and to read out the contents of von Bernstorff's letter.

'This unexpected action of the German Government, this sudden and deeply deplorable renunciation of its assurances' had left him, said Wilson, with 'no alternative consistent with the dignity and honour of the United States' other than to sever ties. Yet even then, Wilson held open the possibility that matters might yet not escalate. He refused to believe, he said, that it was the intention of the German authorities actually to proceed to destroy American ships and take American lives. If his 'inveterate confidence' should prove unfounded he would return before them to ask for authority to protect United States' interests.[5]

Events speeded up through February. Two more American vessels, the *Housatonic* and the *Lyman M. Law*, were lost to German U-boats in British waters and the Mediterranean respectively. The fact that there had been no loss of life – the crews had been evacuated at gunpoint before the vessels were sunk – did not cut any ice. Commerce was suffering because so many American vessels were refusing to cross the Atlantic.

Public opinion was further inflamed by the emergence of a telegram, seemingly from the German Foreign Minister Arthur Zimmerman, offering military assistance to Mexico in the event that the United States entered the war on the Allies' side. The proposal from Zimmerman, through the German Embassy in Mexico, was a straightforward one, written in a most to-the-point fashion. 'Make war together, make peace together', said Zimmerman. If they did, generous financial support would be made available to Mexico to reconquer lost territory in the United States: in Texas, New Mexico and Arizona. 'The ruthless employment of our submarines', said Zimmerman, would compel England to make peace in a few months.[6]

Was it real? Did he actually send it? Some detected a cynical motive behind it, from those on the Allied side who had an ulterior motive in wanting to get America into the war on their side. In fact, it had initially been intercepted by British Intelligence who were circumspect about admitting that they knew. But either way, the telegram's chilling use of language, when made public, could have had only one effect. In spite of initial doubts as to its authenticity, opinion moved steadily against Germany. Talk of re-conquest of previously held Mexican territory played particularly badly in the southern and western states of the Union. The fact that Mexico had little intention of acting on the offer did not matter: a spectre had been conjured up which would not easily be laid to rest.

On 26 February Wilson returned to Capitol Hill to seek to strengthen further his administration's official policy from that of a simple breaking off of diplomatic ties with Germany to a new position of 'armed neutrality' for American shipping against the threat posed to it. Precisely how the new policy was to be implemented Wilson was careful to avoid specifying, but he wanted Congress' authorisation for defensive arms to be issued to merchant ships. The ships could use them if they felt they needed to repel aggression, although Wilson believed there was a wider principle at stake:

> I am thinking, not only of the rights of Americans to go and come about their proper business by way of the sea, but also of something much deeper, much more fundamental than that. I am thinking of those rights of humanity without which there is no civilization. My theme is of those great principles of compassion and of protection which mankind has sought to throw about human lives, the lives of non-combatants, the lives of men who are peacefully at work keeping the industrial processes of the world quick and vital, the lives of women and children and of those who supply the labour which ministers to their sustenance.[7]

Through March the mood grew for intervention on the Allied side. In Russia, the Tsar had been forced to abdicate in the face of food riots and political upheaval: the Russian war effort was crumbling on the Eastern Front. Then closer to home on American soil there was an explosion at the Mare Island Naval Shipyard at Vallejo in the Upper Bay Area of San Francisco. Barges loaded with naval munitions blew up killing six people and wounding thirty-one. It was deemed to be sabotage and linked to a German naval officer, Lothar Witzke, who was later arrested.

Finally on 29 March, ending any lingering doubts, had any remained, as to the authenticity of the Zimmerman telegram, the author himself dispelled them in public. The German Foreign Minister addressed the matter in a speech, admitting that its contents were true, even pressing home and justifying his argument with reference to the 'hostile attitude' of the American Government, which was seeking to 'set the entire world against us'.[8]

So it was, on the evening of 2 April, that Wilson found himself once again before a joint session of Congress. It was to be war. With a profound sense of the solemn, tragic step he was taking, he said that Congress should declare the recent course of the Imperial German Government to be nothing less than war against the government and people of the United States. Armed neutrality had been ineffectual. It had proved impracticable in defending shipping against attack from 'outlaw' German submarines. The submarines had to be dealt with on sight. America would not choose the path of submission. He said:

> We have no quarrel with the German people. We have no feeling towards them but one of sympathy and friendship. [But] the right is more precious than peace, and we shall fight for the things which we have always carried nearest our hearts – for democracy, for the right of those who submit to authority to have a voice in their own governments, for the rights and liberties of small nations, for a universal dominion of right by such a concert of free peoples as shall bring peace and safety to all nations and make the world itself at last free.[9]

Two days later the Senate voted in favour of Wilson's resolution, and two days after that it was endorsed by the House of Representatives. Later that same day, 6 April 1917, the president signed his official declaration. America was at war.

In spite of the uncertainty and danger unleashed, Clifford looked back at this time – both personally and what was happening publicly – as an exciting one, suffused with optimism and promise. Writing from the front six months later, the vibrancy of California in April 1917 was still fresh in his memory:

> *Spring came. Our home and grounds blossomed out. Mother was stronger and much happier. The tennis court was put in, and home developed into one of the greatest and most binding family ties. We all took an interest in the 'place' and worked on the lawns, pulling out weeds and watering plants. Shrubs were gotten from Mrs. Coryell's Menlo Park place. Looking back, one of my greatest pleasures and pleasantest memories was driving Mother up to Mrs. Woods' on Saturday. We were a happy family and Mother seemed so much better. Never since Pap died had we been so comfortable and happy with the possible exception of when we lived on the ranch. But then it was too much of a strain on Mother and we boys were too young to really appreciate her cares and needs, and the responsibilities of the place. HOW DELIGHTFUL WAS THE SPRING OF 1917.*
>
> *Then early in April the United States entered the war on the side of the Allies. Immediately all was excitement and everybody was talking about what they were*

going to do and what everybody else should do. President Wilbur announced that all students who left the University because of the war to go to France or into military training, etc., would be given full University credit for the term's work, the only conditions being that their standing was good at the time of their withdrawal.

It seemed as if all the men quit their studies to enter the service of their country in some form or other. There was a general exodus from the Quad to the Stanford Officer's Reserve Corps under Major Bugge. We three boys were all there. Some men were suspected of doing this to get their hours easily without any more mental effort. Well, if that was the case they were unpleasantly disappointed; for the squads drilled and drilled and drilled, until at the end of the day's work everybody was tired out. But most of the men were governed by patriotic motives. My duty called me to France.

5

READINESS

'PRESIDENT SIGNS DECLARATION OF WAR. US ARMED FORCES SEIZE GERMAN SHIPS IN ALL HARBORS AND DETAIN THE CREWS', boomed the evening edition of the *Washington Times* on 6 April. The paper carried the president's declaration of war in full, alongside news reports of the impending war. 'Whistles Proclaim News to Cheering Crowds as Nation Enters War', added a patriotic subheading, along with the blunt 'Germans Warned to Keep Their Mouths Shut', paraphrasing comments from the Attorney General Thomas Gregory to German nationals living in the United States. More to the point was another subheading: 'Army and Navy Advised'.

The first steps were being taken to put the country on a war footing, but in truth it would take some time to make this a reality. Numbers in both the standing US Federal Army and the volunteer, state-based National Guard were still tiny by comparison to the numbers mobilised by the belligerent armies of Europe. Troop numbers and the readiness of America's armed forces for combat had formed part of the backdrop to political arguments over the preceding three years. Republicans and members of the military establishment, most notably former president Theodore Roosevelt, had argued for years that whether the US was involved in conflict or not – and some had indeed urged such a course – the numbers of the federal army and navy and the equipment which they could use needed to be massively boosted.

This argument of the Preparedness Movement had some powerful backers, and had been heard loudly in the 1916 presidential election campaign. Gradual moves had been taken by the Wilson administration to address the issue, most notably with the National Defence Act of 1916 which aimed to boost the army to 165,000 and the National Guard to 450,000 in five years;[10] but critics still continued to protest that this was not enough. A pro-naval lobby gained the upper hand in the Senate and secured a more rapid increase in the build-up of different classes of warships and armaments, including naval aviation.

But by the time war was declared, troop numbers were still stubbornly low: only some 121,000 federal soldiers and 181,000 National Guard could readily be called upon.[11] It wasn't enough. Wilson had held discussions with his Secretary of War Newton Baker in the preceding months to ask him to look at options for boosting these numbers as the threat of war loomed. Now the man charged with the task of leading the American Expeditionary Force to France, Major General John Pershing, was looking to Wilson and Baker for just this thing, asking for 1 million men to be put at his disposal.

Wilson was instinctively opposed to the idea of outright conscription and had thus far shied away from it, not least because it was a political hot potato. He still held to the belief that volunteerism might yet save the day. This he now abandoned – volunteer numbers were still stubbornly low, he realised – and he asked Newton Baker to proceed with an approach they had dubbed 'Selective Service'. This approach and the legislation which Baker now brought before Congress outlined a plan whereby men aged between 21 and 30 were required, as a first step, to register for war service in their local precinct. For this purpose, over 4,500 civilian boards – and they were, importantly, civilian not military – were established across the country.

Once registered, men were eligible, if selected, to proceed for a medical; if passed fit they could enrol for military service. But while mandatory to register, it was still not the case that these young men would automatically be pressed into service. A 'draft' of a certain number of men would have to be determined by means of a ballot, with everyone registering being allocated one of a series of numbers. If a subsequent lottery draw matched the numbers these young men were holding, they could be drafted.

The Selective Service Act was aimed at mobilising a large number of men of a fighting age quickly and was passed into law on 18 May. But although the various steps had been taken and necessary administration put in place, it would be a further two months before the first draft number was drawn, and more before troops in any large numbers would begin to come on-stream for Pershing's American Expeditionary Force.

For his part, back in California in April 1917, Clifford wanted to resuscitate his plans for joining the American Ambulance. He had followed all the twists and turns of the war debate of preceding months and had watched as his friend Alan Nichols and the 1st Stanford Unit had departed for France in February. But now that Wilson had fired the starting pistol he was impatient to get to the front, and to get there quickly. The American Ambulance seemed the best and most logical way of doing so:

> About that time I thought of organizing or attempting to organize a second Stanford unit of the American Ambulance. Letters from Mr. Sleeper of Boston [Henry D. Sleeper, one of the leading lights and principal organisers of the AFS] showed that he was very enthusiastic about the plans. Dr. Wilbur, Pres. of Stanford, thought it was a good plan, but in spite of all his professed patriotism, he did not go out of the way to help (that is, at first). He simply sat back in his chair and stated his sanction and presidential approval. Oh, yes. He did give me letters of introduction to W. C. Crocker and W. B. Bourn of San Francisco.

The W.B. Bourn Clifford mentioned was William Bowers Bourn II, a wealthy industrialist whose fortune had come from mining and utilities in California: the Empire gold mine; gas and electricity interests in what had become the Pacific Gas & Electric Company; and he was the owner of the Spring Valley Water Company which supplied San Francisco with its water. He was a well-known figure and one who attracted his own share of publicity and controversy given his dominant position in the provision of utilities in the state.

But for Clifford, Bourn was a link to the world he wanted to volunteer for. He was the president of the Friends of France, a campaigning group dedicated to the cause of the country where most of the fighting was taking place and which they were pledged to help. The Friends worked alongside the American Field Service in maintaining the latter's ambulance service and voluntary organisation in the field in Europe. Clifford set to work organising as he could, writing and speaking to any and all who could help in his rush to set up this second unit. ˙

Then, in a passage which betrayed some of the petulance which Clifford was prone to, a sudden burst of anger. Seemingly unaware of the hubris he was displaying, he gave vent to his feelings of dismay that the organisation he was trying to establish was slipping out of his hands. Chicanery was at work, he divined. He felt hard done by, even now brooding on it as he looked back at the episode six months later from France. Having missed out on a chance to go as part of the first wave on volunteers in February, he saw others muscling in on his act:

> One night just as I was preparing to issue the call for volunteers, the phone bell rang and Frank Taylor '18 inquired for Arthur Kimber. He said Dr. Wilbur had told him to see me about going to France as an ambulancier, and invited me up to lunch at the Frat. house next day. Ha. Little then did I realize that he and Clem Randau were going to pump all the information they could from me, and then for their personal aggrandizement and prestige among the students, gently but firmly take the organization out of my hands. Well, they had the inside dope on Bourn and the Friends of France, and on Sleeper and the American Ambulance. After several days, during which time the call was issued and write-ups secured in the D.P.A. and Times, etc., I saw what they were driving at. How can men be so selfish at the expense of the feelings of others. If it had been some other and less important and patriotic affair, I would have played my hand and fought them to the last ditch. But as it was, there was only left one thing for me to do — quietly withdraw ... But the disappointment, not of losing the leadership, but of being rudely squeezed out without the slightest thanks for all the secretarial and investigating work I had done, was sharp and keen.
>
> However, having already been accepted by the American Ambulance and my financial condition being greatly improved, I decided with the advice of Mother, John, and George, to go on ahead; try to make a mark and amount to something, by the time the unit of which I was technically a member, should arrive in Paris.

So he got on with it. Recruitment at Stanford was rapid, as it also was 30 miles away at the University of California in Berkeley. A fortnight after war was declared three units, each with twenty-one volunteers, had been formed: Clifford's 2nd Stanford Unit and two more from Berkeley.

To send the volunteers on their way a ceremony was arranged in San Francisco, organised by the Friends of France along with the recently formed American League of California. The three units gathered for the leave-taking down at the harbour, by the Ferry Building off the

Embarcadero waterfront. They were joined by 2,500 more students from Berkeley, 1,500 of them cadets, and a further 1,000 from Stanford, plus detachments from the US Army and Navy. The assembly marched away from the harbour and through the streets to the Civic Auditorium. Thousands more were packed inside the arena to greet them for a rousing and patriotic display of pride, anthems and flag waving.

The background to the stage in the auditorium was a giant Stars and Stripes. In front of it were other smaller flags of Allied countries with banners proclaiming messages of humanity and fraternity. In the middle hung a large, booming declaration: 'Duty to God and Country'.

The sixty-three young men on the stage drank in the cheers as 'America', 'The Star Spangled Banner' and the 'Marseillaise' were sung. They were joined by dignitaries from church, army, politics, their respective universities, from the Friends of France and the American League of California. The crowd gave a rousing reception to the French Consul General Julien Neltner and then came speeches and presentations.

William Bourn stood to address the crowd:

> The greater battle has been fought. The victory is won. The soul of America is triumphant … You carry to France the flag of our country, for our country, for humanity. Our flag, the flags of heroic France, of martyred Belgium, of dauntless Britain can not be furled until liberty, honour and justice are made the law of mankind.

Flutes and drums summoned Boy Scouts up the aisles carrying the banners of Allied countries: France and Britain, Belgium and Serbia, Italy, Japan and Portugal. Brassards were fixed to the arms of the volunteers bearing the insignia of the Friends and, finally, a flag ceremony: four Star Spangled Banners were presented to the men, gifts of the American League.

Mindful that it would be some time before American combat troops would be in action at the front, the American League had written to the War Department seeking authorisation for the flags to be presented as the first official flags of the country to go to France. The first of these flags was destined for the 1st Stanford Unit and, because that unit was already in service at the front, it was decided that it should have the honour of unfurling this inaugural flag. It would be brought to them in France by the 2nd Stanford Unit. The flag was made of heavy silk, the staff bore a silver plate bearing a dedication to the unit.

After the ceremony, Clifford's colleague Clem Randau – the young man whom Clifford had previously felt piqued by – approached him on behalf of the new unit. Would Clifford take the flag ahead to France as quickly as possible in advance of the rest of the volunteers? Randau followed this with an official note on 27 April. 'Dear Mr. Kimber', his fellow student began formally:

> in entrusting to you the care and delivery of the official flag to be sent to the First Stanford Unit of the American Ambulance Field Service, we feel certain that the mission will be safely executed. It was the wish of the Friends of France that this flag be publicly presented to the representatives of the First Unit upon your arrival in Paris. Mr. A. Piatt Andrew, founder of the American Ambulance Service, will no doubt be glad to arrange the details of the presentation for you. You are hereby instructed to convey to the First Unit the greetings and best wishes of the entire Second Unit. As advance guard of the Second Stanford Unit, you are carrying with you the hearty fellowship of those soon to follow, and whom you will join in Paris. Very sincerely yours, C. J. Randau, Corps Leader.

It was arranged that Clifford would travel across country to New York, to a further ceremony there, and onwards to France. The following day, 28 April 1917, he set off, accompanied for the first part of the journey by Clara.

> *Plans having been made, Mother found it possible to accompany me to New York. Oh, how glad I was that she did it. The only arguments against it were expense, a considerable item, and her health. The trip would be a tremendous strain. Never think I didn't want it. ... I DID. But I felt that it would be much harder for her to say goodbye finally in New York than in San Francisco; and then the trip back to California alone would be very hard on her. Thank goodness things turned out as they did.*
>
> *Never will I forget the send off that San Francisco gave the two U.C. and 2d Stanford units that last week in April. Little then did I realize just what it all meant. But the mothers all knew. I could not understand then why Mother looked so sad. Everything seemed so fiery and full of spirit. We all sat up there on the platform before the thousands in the audience, and felt very much amused that we who were going on a simple adventure, inspired partly by patriotism, of course, should be exhibited and made a lot of on that platform. It was then that the flags were presented, and the 1st official U.S. flag for service to the first Stanford Unit already serving at Verdun.*

And several days later the new leaders of the 2d Unit, learning that I was planning to leave early for France, thinking that possibly they should show me some consideration after what they had done or, more likely, realizing that the flag should be sent to France as quickly as possible, bestowed the flag honor of carrying it, on me.

The next day Mother and I left for New York, and John and George accompanied us as far as San Francisco and the Oakland Mole where the transcontinental train started. I was a fool. My head had been turned by the unexpected honor. Clem and Frank had asked me to give the flag publicity in the East, that I did in full measure. But like an ass I decided to start at home and interviewed the SF Examiner reporter, who the next day credited me with saying a great deal that I didn't say and putting in an article about Stanford–U.C [University of California, Berkeley] rivalry about getting their respective flags to France first. The U.C. units were to leave the next week. Well, it was somewhat of a race, but it should not have been advertised. That article cost me many a regret but all said and done I am very glad now for the lesson it was and its results have bought me. The best teacher is experience, but a dear one indeed.

6

SETTING OFF

The whole family set out from Tennyson Avenue together as a unit, at least for the first part of the journey. The Transcontinental Railroad Clifford and Clara were to catch actually left from Oakland, further up the Bay Area, so they first had to head the 30 or so miles north from Palo Alto, up the west interior side of the bay to San Francisco. From there they caught the ferry across the bay to Oakland and the Oakland Mole railway, wharf and pier complex which bore its name. The family made the journey and the day as happy a time as possible – difficult, given the foreboding which played at the fringes of their conversation. The family talked gamely about the future, about their plans and the different ideas and opportunities they saw ahead. For Clifford, the adventure that he was embarked on was just that: an exciting promise of a life out of the ordinary, an experience, an opportunity to see the world. For Clara it was different, and difficult. While she had accepted his decision to go to France, and took pride in what he was doing, it was difficult to see beyond what for her was the cold reality: the loss of her son to a life bordered by uncertainty and danger.

As the eldest brother John did his best to act as a broker, reassuring his anxious mother on the one hand, while offering words of encouragement to Clifford on the other. He knew that Clifford still harboured moments of uncertainty, when the instinct he was following, and which answered his quest for both adventure and 'duty', gave way to doubt and reflection. Was it right? Was it his duty to go out and help a cause in which he believed? Or was Clifford abandoning his family and causing his mother needless heartache? No, said John, he should stick to his course and answer his calling.

John would miss him, but they all had their own roles to play. For his part, now that he had finished at Stanford, John was going to redouble his efforts to try to get to Harvard Law School; and for that he first had to find the necessary funds to pay his way and his tuition fees. He had recently signed up as a salesman for a household wares firm, travelling California selling aluminium pots and pans; anything to raise the funds.

This left George. At 18, soon to be 19, the youngest was torn between them all; he felt keenly the loss that was coming. He was devoted to his brother and wanted more than anything to go to France with him, but he knew equally that his studies at university beginning that September were his priority. That, and being by his mother's side, was especially important if John was going to spend so much time away from home, on the road.

The family congregated until the last moment inside the railway station, chatting together as gamely as possible, but when the time arrived, and as they had previously agreed, it was only John and George who made their goodbyes. It was a difficult moment for the young men, George in particular feeling Clifford's imminent loss keenly, but the brothers had made earnest vows to write to one another on a regular basis with all their news and views, to keep their little unit together as best they could over the forthcoming months and miles.

For Clifford and Clara this first part of the journey promised to be an experience in its own right: a week-long trip across the breadth of the country, stopping here and there in the Pacific North-West, West and Midwest, before fetching up in New York. Chicago and Detroit had been earmarked by Clifford for brief visits on the way. An opportunity, he hoped, to give the flag and his Stanford unit some publicity and to capitalise on some of the war fever that was sweeping the continent. He would see what interest he could garner, which newspapers might send a photographer or reporter. The pair of them also planned to see family members.

The train pulled out of Oakland into the California night, heading north for the railroad ferry at Port Costa, a giant paddleboat which operated across the Carquinez Strait between Port Costa and Benicia in Solano County. From there it was on to Sacramento and beyond, up to the old volcano of Mount Shasta at the southern end of the Cascade mountains and the steep route into Oregon.

Clifford had promised that he would start his letters on the train, to detail the journey as the first part of what he hoped would form a war journal. George had said he would begin the process of typing the letters up as they arrived, to help keep the record in a permanent and legible form.

Clifford began the next morning, Sunday, although this first letter bore the previous day's date, 'Shasta Route, April 28th 1917'. They were already some way advanced on the journey up through northern California.

Dear John and George,

We have just arrived at Edgewood, and I am taking advantage of a change of scenery that is less interesting, to drop you a line. Neither Mother nor I slept very well last night after leaving the Oakland Mole. I was so hot (ventilation was rotten until I opened head window) and restless, because we were continually stopping, and the engine kept blowing and blowing. Mother told me that the reason she didn't sleep was because she was so tired. You have to get used to these old berths. I couldn't stretch out, even diagonally, without hitting my head, or cramping my feet. Alan must have had an awful time [when Alan Nichols had made the journey in February 1917], having two in a berth. Mother also didn't sleep in the beginning because of worry. She would come to a logical reason for not worrying, and then would worry and have to think it all out again.

We passed over on the big ferry. I thought we would never start again. I looked out of the window at Sacramento, where we backed and backed. There was a man packing the mail in a large netted truck. The old senators get a lot, for they had at least six or seven station wagons heaping with mailbags.

Forty cents apiece got us a pretty fair breakfast, two eggs and drinks. We ate lunch at Dunsmuir. The scenery at this point is very much like that from Merced to el Portal, only it is much prettier, more magnificent, and instead of being covered with brush or nothing at all, is thick with pines and cedars. The river is large, too. We were all put in a state of 'preparedness' for points of interest, by a man, regularly employed by the Railroad, a magazine seller, who has his speech memorized, and yells it out in an awful sing-song, always accenting the wrong words, and hurrying over the important ones.

We got our first glimpse of Mt. Shasta, covered with snow, then it was lost to view for an hour or more. In the meantime we saw National Guards at all the tunnels and bridges, 'the real dope'. As we ascend 2000 to 2500 feet, the mountains are covered with snow all around us. Finally we arrive at Shasta Springs, where everyone gets a cup of soda water right from the Springs, – O.K. too just like vichey, only stronger and more bubbly (is that the way you spell it?).

The highest we go is about 4000 feet, as high as the floor of the Yosemite Valley. Sisson, the town, is 11 ½ miles from Mt. Shasta, and is 3554' high. Mt. Shasta seems within a stone's throw. It seems hard to believe it ascends two miles above us. It is magnificent, – covered with snow, and its peaks lost in the clouds and indistinguishable from them, it is truly worth seeing. My, but this train shakes, with its two engines and eleven cars. Near Mt. Shasta is an extinct volcano and cedars on it, and some patches of snow. Now we are crossing a fairly large plateau, broken by rounded hills, and surrounded by blue and snowy mountains. A tourist, returning from San Francisco, tells me that only last week it was covered with snow three inches deep. Mt. Hood (Grandma's painting was of Mt. Hood) appears in the distance when the train turns right, and looks like a huge, broad cone. It is snow covered, too, and seems quite near, altho in reality it is dozens of miles away. You know at this height the atmosphere is very thin and clear. (We are not yet in Oregon.)

Have just arrived at Montague, elevation 2541, and 375 miles from San Francisco (about halfway to Portland). This is certainly a trip worth taking, especially in such fine weather. Mother is having a fine time, and is now taking a nap on the seat ahead of me, with her coat and my coat and the shawl over her.

Whenever the opportunity presents itself, be sure to take the Shasta Route, you, especially, John, when you go to Harvard. Now that I see what it is, I would not miss it for anything. The state highway comes right thru here, and is in pretty good condition. We have just passed a Goodrich road sign. The scenery is wonderful and I only wish you were here to enjoy it with us. Don't miss it if you ever get the chance.

I am not studying much right now, because I prefer to see the sights. The wide plains and the broad, expansive, and I hope smooth ocean, will give me plenty of opportunity. However, when I see an object, the name of which I want to know in French, I open Prof. Seward's dictionary, and there it is. After doing this enough, I ought to remember such words as rateau, montagne, etc.

Now the plateau is breaking and is becoming rocky and rough. It is funny what supports the occasional towns. 'Buffalo Lager' seems to be the most popular kind of beer advertised and consumed, and Barnes's Circus seems to take first place in the field. The train man, who has the wrongly placed accent, says that the towns are very prosperous, and are supported by cattle and grain. Mother is still asleep. I will write again from Portland. Believe me, I will constantly think of you both. Don't forget to write, Care American Ambulance Field Service (I sleep with the FLAG every night, of course).

Believe me, your loving brother, Cliff

∽

Portland Station.
April 29th, 1917. 5.30 P.M.

Dear John and George,

We have seen Uncle Milton and Aunt Clyde and Harriet Josephine. [Clara's brother and family.] All are in fine condition and send love. Uncle Milton is enthusiastic about moving east and buying a farm. His reasons seem O.K. and the change will be for the better. No need to worry about his finances. He says that Vancouver [Vancouver, across the Columbia river from Portland in Washington State, not Vancouver in Canada, is now part of the Portland-Vancouver metro area] was too small for three banks, and that he forced the other bank to buy him out at a pretty fat figure. It seems to me as if he got out at the most opportune time. He is O.K. Harriet has grown considerably, but is still a little girl eight years old. Fine disposition; exceedingly well pleased with our coming up.

Last night, after mailing your letter in the last mail box at our disposal in California, we crossed the border into Oregon. At Ashland we had a chicken dinner, price 50c apiece. It was all prepared and ready in a big dining room in the station. At Siskiyu we were over 4000' high, nearly a mile, and then we began our descent to Portland, elevation 25'.

As you know, sleeping cars are stuffy and have poor ventilation. The only way I can sleep is to open one of the windows. After turning in last night, I opened my window as usual. At midnight we passed the second longest tunnel on the Shasta Route, and we were near the end, and the window was hard to open. It took about an hour for the smoke to clear out so I could sleep again, and then, as I was nearly doped, I had little trouble.

Uncle Milton says for me to get before the public all I can, for unless a man thinks he is somebody, no one else will. We phoned for the Portland Oregonian editor (biggest paper north of San Francisco, with about 100,000 or more circulation) and he came up to the Vancouver mayor's house, and took 'his honor', the ambassador to France, six times, with the FLAG, and twice by himself, for insert use. Also quite a bit of dope for feeding the public with.

After dinner I sat down and wrote three letters to eastern papers: the Chicago Tribune, the N.Y. Times, and the N.Y. Herald. I told each editor that upon my arrival at their respective cities I would phone them, so that their reporter and photographer could come up to my hotel, and 'I would take great pleasure in giving them a little of my time'. That gets by——? I will let you know. And what with the Oregonian, and the above papers, besides Hearst's news service, I ought to be pretty nearly ready to run against Wilson in 1920; especially after a triumphant return from France, after a public presentation of my FLAG in Paris.

I also wrote Dr. Sleeper and told him that if he had any plans for the reception of the STANDARD in New York, I would be on hand the later part of May 5th. (I may still parade in Trinity.)

Mother thinks it is best to cut out Niagara so as to be in New York early. We will have a day and night at Chicago, and we will spend a day or so at Detroit. I guess Niagara can wait if it has to. It has waited quite a while already, and it can't get any grayer.

Well, boys, Oregon is a great country; the scenery is magnificent, with firs and firs and firs, instead of redwoods. Wherever you look and wherever you are, there are trees, trees, trees. One reason I like it so well is because it is new. Wherever we go the milk is rich and fine. Cattle prosper, and dairying is an important industry. Portland is quite a city; it has several factories, a little ship-building, and quite a lot of commerce.

I saw the good old 'Beaver' in dock today. We leave here 7 p.m. arrive at Chicago 9 p.m. Thursday. Leave Detroit 6.20 p.m. Friday and arrive at New York 3 p.m. Saturday.

I want George to open all mail that comes for me, and with the aid of John answer it. Please make a list of all the letters I receive, and tell me the news of the important ones, without forwarding me unless very important, or unless I ask for them. If any letters come from the East, from American Ambulance Field Service, and have anything in them which you think would be of use or service to the Second Stanford Corps, please copy the parts of importance to the corps, and notify either Clem Randau or Frank Taylor, by sending them the copy or phoning them. Please file away my mail for future reference, and reading over by me.

Have just received news that berth from Detroit to New York costs $5 each. I guess that means sit up Friday night, our last night – thank the Lord, our last night.

Well, boys, I must close I will write to you often, and expect a stack of letters in New York. Don't forget the papers. I have asked Uncle Milton to send you copies of the Oregonian. As Weeks always says to me, 'Be good'.

As ever, your loving brother,

Cliff

P.S. I can't find words to express my gratitude to you for the kind and generous self-sacrificing way you helped me off.

7

THROUGH THE WEST

The train travelled east out of Portland, on through the night, striking north up into Washington State. Around seven in the morning they pulled into the city of Spokane near Washington's border with Idaho. The old trading post and centre for the fur trade was now a large mining and timber centre – 'some city,' thought Clifford – and they were able to stop off long enough to have breakfast. It also gave Clifford time to send his letter of the previous day and dash off another quick note to his brothers, enclosing a university library card he had forgotten to leave behind with them in California. Then it was back on board for the three days and two nights which would see them through the states of the West and Midwest to Chicago, and their first proper stopover:

Climbing the Divide, Past St. Marie, 9.40 a.m.,
Monday April 30th '17

Dear John and George,
    We will cross the continental divide tonight at about 6000' and over. I am writing as we go, so that the description will savor more of reality and accuracy.
    We have been following the Spokane River, and skirting the Lakes that feed it. Pine and fir forests cover the mountains. It is no exaggeration to say that even when the lumbermen have gone thru and demolished the forest, new forests of little trees here spring up, four and five feet high, and nearly everywhere they are as thick as brush, and a most beautiful green. I wish you could both be here to see the sight.

Sometimes we are above the snow, but generally it is above us, but always in sight. If the train would stop long enough I would eat some. Mountain streams are running everywhere; it is raining too and I think trying to snow but it is too warm.

Now we are going thru a great lumber waste. It is a shame. Rotting logs and stripped trees everywhere. Forest fires thru carelessness, etc., and patches of snow around us. The rain is melting lots. We are not yet in the High Rockies. This is a great lumber district; and after cutting the trees, the logs are chucked into the river on our right. There are piles and piles of lumber at St. Marie, the river is quite wide, and very swift, although I have not seen any rapids yet. (Really, the Columbia headwaters.)

I have just bought 10 colored postcards for 25c. Will send you a couple. This careless and wasteful lumbering is a disgrace and is getting on my nerves. I have just been passing thru magnificent green forests, and here all is burned or cut. We are now traveling on the Chicago, Milwaukee & St. Paul, electrified for several hundred miles either side of the Divide. Our electric engines will hitch on at noon for about 24 hours. George, you may remember that illustrated lecture at Stanford last year – moving pictures, you know; well, I'm seeing the real thing. It is almost impossible to write on a train that is zig-zagging and rushing its way thru the mountains. I haven't seen any real gorges yet, only steep tressels over ordinary ravines 75' or so high. Mother calls them 'gorges'; the real things are still hours away. Must now study French. I know the first verse of the Marseillaise. Will continue later.

En Route, 1.40 P.M. Monday.

We have just passed thru a snow storm in the real mountains. All the mountains around us were covered and are still with a snowy mantel. First time I've been in a snow storm for eight years. At an altitude of a mile or two the air is clear and snappy, not too cold, and pure. Not working, it is not hard to breathe. But mountains and gorges and ravines, etc., get quite tiring after hours and hours and hours of them at a stretch.

Every time we come across a bridge or a tunnel, we see Montana militia boys. The train stopped to put off some mail and a couple of boxes at one of their camps. One fellow complained, saying 'Is this all the grub we get today? Where's our grub?' He looked at me; I laughed and said 'Oh, Cheer up.' He replied half joking, and half in earnest, 'Well, wait until you have been here awhile,' and I guess he was right. Bleak mountain tracts, beautiful, but monotonous, cold and chilly, snow half succeeding in falling, a train twice a day, elevation a mile and far from home and friends, and above all NOTHING TO DO, and no prospect or immediate chance of being mustered to service or sent where there is real service, or being promoted. It must be, 'Well, wait until you have been here awhile.'

We have crossed a ridge, and the snow is not falling where we are now. The train is descending Eastward, but still has to climb over the Divide, – that tonight. Thousands of little pines, about 18 in. high, are springing up where the forests were burned four years ago. It is a great moral demonstration to see how patient Nature is slowly proceeding to repair the damage man has deliberately or carelessly wrought. But to think of fifty years before the forest is once more, is somewhat discouraging. I don't know where this letter will be posted. As usual, Mother sends love. She and I have a standing understanding on this point. We are now at Henderson, a petit village, I don't think it is even on the map; it's another lumbering town. Your loving brother, Cliff.

P.S. This car stinks like tin cans, too many babies.

Tuesday, May 1st, 9.15 A.M. Mountain time
3 hours more in Montana
En Route to France

Dear John and George,

We are now completing our last leg in Montana. The steam engine picked us up last night at 3 A.M. the Electric returned to the mountains, and – immediately – cinders and smoke. It was delightfully refreshing to breathe clear, crisp air at a height of 6322' above sea level. We crossed the Divide last night just east of Butte at 10.15 P.M. and are now hustling down the headwaters of the Missouri. And what a difference in the surroundings. But before I go on, I want to tell you how delicious it is to lie in your berth and look out of the open windows at nothing but snow, snow, snow. How I wanted to eat some, and I didn't get a chance. It was not cold at all, just sharp and snappy, crisp and a little chilly.

Now we are in cattle and stock country. It does not seem good for anything but grazing and none too good for that. The valley is perhaps two or three miles wide and bounded by low, jagged hills, the kind you see in so many Indian pictures. Cattle and horses very numerous.

HAVE JUST REACHED MILES CITY.

Sorry for the interruption; my fuzz has been growing ever since I left Paly. As my razor is ze good old-fashioned kind, I don't dare use it while train is in motion. They might arrest the porter for cutting my throat, when he would be perfectly innocent.

Ten minutes at Miles City sufficed, and now I am once more clean (?) shaven. Another flat-topped Indian hill comes in sight. Just before we reached Miles City we had a regular Wild West thrill, good for the movies. A man was walking behind two horses pulling a rake. I don't know why he wasn't riding. The horses took fright at the train, the superior 'iron' horse, and started off on a run. The man tried to hold them back. He ran, too, pulling away for all he was worth. Suddenly he tripped; first he was dragged along on his back, then he rolled on to his stomach, and skimmed the ground, awfully pretty too, for about 50 feet. He soon decided that the horse couldn't go as fast with him as without, so he wisely let go. The runaway team with the rake just tore thru the fields, into the pasture, scared another team hitched to a heavy wagon which the driver controlled, and demoralized the horses and cows. It was at this point of the route that the film ended, for the train moved out of range of the fotographer. Such a thing as this occasionally lends color to our trip.

You see there is very little green now, men are putting in their grain, and the fields are just recovering from their winter snows. They are still brown. The clouds are wonderful; the enormity of all is appalling. After having passed thru the Coast Mountains, the Sierras, and the Rockies proper, and then coming out on the Plains or Plateaus of Eastern Montana, one is very much impressed with, what a large and expansive country we live in. I can appreciate how small California really is. Think of the toils of an early transcontinental journey, when it took a day to go as far as we go in half an hour. It was a wonderful thing to build this railroad and all the others — one cannot help being impressed.

Now we are right on the bank of the river again, now about 100 yards wide. It has grown: is muddy and sluggish, and almost quiet. The trees that line its shores are just beginning to bud but as yet show no green. What a contrast to sunny California, and the Santa Clara Valley, garden spot of the world, where everything is in perpetual bloom, and they have already cut the hay crop, and are planting other things. Here they are just beginning to sow their first spring crop.

I think geologists would call this whole country a lava foundation. From the way the hills are cut away, there should be no difficulty in telling. I wish I had had some real practical geology. Mother is feeling in fine spirits; she says this is the first transcontinental trip she had really enjoyed.

Lovingly, Cliff

The train continued its journey through the West, winding through Montana and across the state of North Dakota, on through the night into Minnesota. Clifford and Clara woke early in the morning as the train prepared to pull into Minneapolis-St Paul. There was a brief ten-minute stop in each station, allowing Clifford time for a snatched view of the twin cities; and it gave his mother the opportunity to say hello to her sister-in-law Fanny, who lived in the area and whom she had not seen in some years.

It was an encounter which he himself avoided, knowing that he had already been committed by his mother to spending time with his father's other sister, Annie, in New York, something to which he was not looking forward. He and his brothers looked on Annie and Fanny with a degree of suspicion: they were unhappy with the treatment, as they saw it, that their mother had experienced following their father's death eight years before. The issue now at stake was their financial settlement, as responsibility for Arthur's estate lay with Annie. Money, whether to their mother or themselves, was not as forthcoming as they would have wanted.

Clifford and Clara arrived as planned in Chicago that night. Clifford had been looking forward to sleeping in a bed for the first time in six days and they had booked into the city's Southern Hotel. He wanted a good night's sleep ahead of what he hoped would be a busy and productive day, and on the Thursday morning he set off for the first of several visits he had planned for Chicago and Detroit. It was part of a promise he had made to Clem Randau and Frank Taylor before he set off from Stanford – to try to get whatever publicity he could for their unit and flag – and to this end he wanted to see if he could talk his way into some of the Midwest's bigger businesses and factories.

He was aware that he was visiting Chicago just a day ahead of Marshal Joseph Joffre, the commander-in-chief of the French Army. Joffre had come to the United States as part of a war commission, alongside a British delegation, to raise the tempo of political, public and industrial life for the war effort to come. So it was an opportune time for Clifford as well. Maybe the captains of industry in this industrial heartland would help him get his message out? Perhaps a picture in one of the city's newspapers?

He was a young man on a mission, with a cause to promote and a flag at hand, and buoyed by his sense of purpose and with something of a dash of self-regard, he set off for Chicago's two giant meat-packing plants, Swift & Co. and P.L. Armour. Swift and Armour were among the nation's biggest processors of beef, pork and sheep meat and as well known as any companies he could think of who might help him get his message out. However, it was to be a mixed day:

Southern Hotel, Chicago, Ill. May 3rd, '17

Dear John and George,

This is a poor hotel. We went thru Armour's plant today; had an awful job doing it, but did it all the same, and it was great. All the meat houses and stock markets are closed to visitors now, by order of Uncle Sam, but since he is a relative of mine, too, I worked it. You see they are afraid some pro-German crank will poison the soup, or the contents of the large vats.

Following Father Gleason's advice, we first went to Swift & Co. We pulled all the wires we could but to no avail. We could not play on their sympathies or anything; to tell the truth, it was some-what discouraging. Then we tried Armour's. I inquired for Mr. Armour and found there were four of them. P. L. Armour, whom I then asked for, was in New York to see his sick mother. Watson Armour happened to be in. I wrote on my card, Mr. Kimber wishes to see [Mr. Armour], nature of business, Stanford, '18, from state of California, on way to France, wishes to speak to Mr. Armour. (IMPORTANT.)

His secretary came out and I had to tell him all. You remember the letters Randau gave me? Well, they were at the hotel; but the story sounded quite plausible, and the secretary, Mr. Diffendaugh, returned to Mr. Armour and told him what I said. He came back with Mr. Radford, who said it was an hour to take us through. He had worked there 12 years, and knows the business from one end to the other. Their rules were therefore laid aside for the Ambassador to France. You see Joffre comes to Chicago tomorrow.

You will be interested to know the organization of the stockyard, etc. Armour & Co, Libby, McNeil & Libby, etc., are separate companies, with plants near the stock yard, the stockyards are run by a separate organization. They buy the cattle, sheep, hogs, etc., from all over the country, then these packing companies bid for the different stocks. Radford says that sometimes they get stung, but on the whole are pretty clever bidders. They buy by the day, and cattle bought one day are killed the next, or even the same day; after being purchased they are driven to different corrals; they have elevated driveways, so as not to interfere with traffic.

I cannot go into all the details; of course nothing is wasted. The operations are so quick there is little time for smell. Sheep are stabbed in the neck, and hogs in the heart. Cattle have to be hit on the head, or 'beaned' first. You should see them cut and quarter the hogs, etc. A man with a big axe, sharp as a razor, cuts a whole hog in half at a blow. The carcasses are slid around without the slightest effort. Peanut butter is another interesting commodity. There is an awful lot of help, you can imagine. Wish I could tell you more about it, or you could see the whole process yourself.

Chicago is a great city, seems now as if New York were in sight. Mother and I both feeling fine. With love, Cliff.

8.45 P.M. Thursday, May 3rd 1917
via Michigan Central

Dear John and George,

Have just been breaking the monotony of a night ride on train by sketching passengers. Rather shaky, of course, but this paper is swell to draw on. It worked O.K. as long as I drew the backs of their heads. Then Mother wanted to stretch out on her seat so now I am riding backwards opposite her. It's a different proposition sketching passenger's heads face to, especially if they are pretty females and happen to notice you. – I gave myself away, and now that game is up for the time being. The lady whom I was honouring hid behind her escort's coat when she saw what I was up to. It created quite a laugh. It is fun to watch people, more so than to study French. A young girl was several seats ahead of us, – alone. A young man sat down in seat back of her. Both were good looking. I thought I would wait awhile and watch, and then possibly drop in for a howdydo. You see when one travels quite a ways on the 'choo-choo' car, society and social propriety stretch with the distance.

Well, I waited and was glad I did. After a while Mr. X took the step I had been considering, and took the seat next to the dark beauty in the silk patch dress and the scarlet coat. No, she wasn't fresh from the drug store or the paint factory – they started a seemingly perfectly proper discourse. A little later he edged up closer and then 'Put your arm around me, dearest', or perhaps sweetheart, whichever it ought to be, and we saw a rather stunning or striking or 'catching' picture or pose for such newly met young'uns. Well, that settled it for me. Soon he got off. Now the young lady sits alone. If she had behaved she might have had real company. Thus Heaven takes care of us.

Another station, another wait, Detroit 2 hours off. We got there 10.55. You know how it feels to get on the theatre train; well, we feel that way, plus 2 hours, plus start all over again, and a trip back again. We speak of hours now as tho they were minutes out West. We've gone so far, the rest must be easy.

Chicago pleased me. It presents quite a nice appearance yet seems to lack certain features that a person brought up in New York or San Francisco is apt to look for in a large city. I didn't expect to find so many wooden shacks. It is easier to remember and tell about them than to describe in writing; besides I had only an hour or so to stroll about in.

Well, we will soon be there. Good luck, au revoir, be good. Love from Mother, Your loving brother, Cliff

P.S. When we reach New York, I will try to see Teddy [ex-president Theodore Roosevelt], *and get him to give me a letter to the Kaiser or Poincaré or maybe King George. Nothing like trying. This interviewing great men, or at least trying to and sometimes succeeding, is the best kind of fun I know.*
Cliff

8

NEW YORK

The final stopover on their rail journey was Detroit, planned by Clifford around a visit to the city's Ford motor works. It was only a brief tour of the factory but satisfied him for now that he had at least done his 'duty' towards his fellow members of the 2nd Stanford Unit in attempting to garner some publicity. He had not found his way into any newspapers in the Midwest, no opportunity to pose proudly for photographs with the flag as he had in Oregon, but he was looking forward to the opportunity afforded him by the week ahead in New York.

It would be a busy week, both socially and in terms of public tasks. They were to stay with one of Clara's cousins, Dora, but visits had also been planned to a host of old family friends from their days in Brooklyn and Oyster Bay – the Doughtys, the Farrars, the Phillipses, the Zabriskies, the Sayres – all families Clifford had grown up with, and whose children he, John and George had played with. Then, of course, there was Aunt Annie. The latter did not know it yet, did not even know she was in New York, but Clara was determined to see Annie, and determined to take Clifford with her.

Mother and son had also agreed to take the flag to St Augustine's, this the most solemn of tasks for Clara to return to her husband's church with Clifford before he set sail for Europe. Clifford understood the need and had agreed to go with her both to St Augustine's and Trinity, but for him the week ahead held two priorities. The first of these was to prepare for a march that the American Field Service (the 'American Ambulance') wanted him to help lead down Fifth Avenue carrying the flag. He needed to find out more about this and the other duties they had assigned, including the ordering up of a second commemorative plate for the staff of the flag. The second task was a more personal affair: he wanted to attend a speech being given in the city by his political hero, former president Theodore Roosevelt, and if at all possible effect an introduction to the great man himself.

The former president, however long out of office, was still an active and influential public figure across America, a driving force behind the cause of preparedness for the conflict. It was a career Clifford had followed since he was a child. Although he had never met him, he remembered his father talking to him about some of the work he had done alongside Roosevelt during his time as the city's police commissioner in the 1890s.

He had also often been teased by his family over what had come to be known as 'the watch incident', when a young Clifford had gone out into Oyster Bay in their little rowing boat to stay on 'watch' for the president and his naval ships. Later, at high school in California, Clifford had decided to run for the post of student body president, buoyed by a series of speeches made by Roosevelt through the West. He was much taken by the larger-than-life image projected by 'TR', as the latter boomed his way through speech after speech during his 1912 'Bull Moose' presidential bid.

'When you see an elephant think of me!' bellowed Clifford in imitation of his hero, not quite taking to heart TR's maxim of speaking softly and carrying a big stick. His friends Francis Bergstrom and David Elliott tried to talk him out of it, but Clifford persisted in his one-man attempt to take on the school's system of appointed student body president, challenging his would-be opponent to a public debate on school issues.

It took the intervention of Principal Templeton to finally rob Clifford of his political dream, telling him that that was not how the school was going to proceed. It was an affair he would laugh about in his later college years – albeit insisting that democracy had been thwarted – but he was still earnestly set on aping, as much as he could, the career of 'the great man'. Clifford hoped Roosevelt would remember his father's work of twenty-odd years earlier, were he to meet him. But first of all he had to work out a way of securing such a meeting.

The TR task was one for another day, however. The first thing he had to do on arrival that Saturday morning was to make contact with the AFS and its co-ordinator in New York, Henry Sleeper:

Brooklyn, N.Y., May 6th 1917.

Dear John and George,

I have not written to you for several days, due as you may well suppose, to my being exceedingly busy with many things, calls and sightseeing. As soon as we reached New York we went to headquarters at 14 Wall Street. Met Dr. Sleeper, and he is a regular Bostonian, a perfect gentleman, and as kind as he can be. He has made arrangements for me to see Mr. Pottell, who will attend to the publicity in New York, regarding the flag. I will see him at 10 A.M. tomorrow, Monday May 7th, and he will order a plate with inscription. Dr. Sleeper says it is a 'beauty'.

Sat. went to Cousin Dora's, where we had lunch and supper. She lives three blocks from our Brooklyn house, just above Lewis on Hancock. In the afternoon walked down to Abraham and Straus, and got one pair B.V.D.s [underwear] and 2 pairs of pyjamas. In the evening called on the Farrars and Doughtys. Grace is a regular American girl, you know what I mean, a la A.H., and Redmond is a bright, sporty, polished gent, very pleasant. One can easily see that Mrs. is older than Judge Farrar. Doughtys were glad to see us too. Miriam is pleasant and attractive and quiet, and another ordinary American girl. Of course they were awfully glad to see me.

Mother wrote Miss Banister that we were coming, and she delayed in replying until late yesterday. Of course her letter was not delivered, and I will not get it until tomorrow. Then she got scared and spilled the beans by phoning to Aunt Annie, confound it all, and gave the whole thing away. I wanted the fun of watching Aunt Annie's facial expression. I phoned A.A. as soon as L.B. told me. She is excited and up in the air, had not even heard of my coming. My. But I will have fun with her tomorrow afternoon and night when Mother and I go up there for dinner.

Roosevelt speaks in Kismet Temple in Brooklyn, Tues. night and Judge Farrar is going to try to get me a ticket that I may hear him. I want to make an appointment with T.R. and I am sure he will give it to me when he learns that I carry the First American Flag to France.

We are now at Mr. Phillips's. They were awfully glad to see us. We stay tonight and return to C.D. tomorrow night. Herbert wants to go to Plattsburg but not being a citizen they are letting red tape stand in the way. He may go as a private. He and I went to Coney Island today, and then to the Berralls where we called on old Mrs. Berrall and Kate and Isabel. They were old friends of Pap's, and were of course delighted. Bertie is certainly a big-hearted, kind and noble fellow. Mr. and Mrs. Phillips are fine, and all send love.

Our sailing has been postponed till the ———. Can't get a convoy for the 12th. Am not allowed to give exact date, and I don't know it if I wanted to.

*We went to St.Augustine's this morning.Went in the door, we were late, and asked
Mr. Dobbin if he would take charge of my umbrella and satchel. He didn't recognize
Mother or me.When Mother said, 'This is Clifford, Mr. Dobbin,' you should have seen
his astonished look. Dr.Anthony preached a good sermon, but the 'holy' man is too
full of himself. He has a special (2nd) Cross to precede him into the Anteroom off
the Chancel, and does not consider it worthwhile to march down the main aisle.
He sings the service, too. Well, I am keeping the Phillipses waiting, which I don't
like to do.Will write tomorrow. Hope you are well.All send love.Au revoir, a present.
Vous [sic] frère, Cliff. Keep all our letters private.*

Brooklyn, N.Y. May 7th, 1917.

Dear John and George,
*   It is 11.25 P.M., now, as I start this letter, but so much of event and interest
is happening that if I don't write now, much will be forgotten and never written.
Yesterday we went to St.Augustine's as I told you in my other letter, and then to the
Phillipses.Today we saw Aunt Annie.*
*   Mr. Phillips left with me, and we went to New York together. He is a Grand Old
Man. I got the Flag from the American Ambulance headquarters, and took it up to Mr.
Emery Pottell. He wrote a letter to Tiffany & Co., asking them to add a new plate with
the inscription 'This banner, blessed by the Bishop of California, is the first American
Flag flown in France with the Official Sanction of the United States Government.'*
*   He wants me to carry it in a parade down Fifth Ave., on Thursday. We will have
several Bands, etc., and regiments of regulars and marines, and the U.C. men of
course. Their flags will follow Stanford's. I am to be included with the U.C. boys in
entertainments etc., to follow.We will have lunch at Sherry's, and in the evening at
9 P.M. will be the guests of the California Committee at the theatre to see 'The Lilac
Time.' Friday will see us at the Ritz Carlton. Movies will be taken. I have not seen the
reporters, and following George's excellent advice do not intend to do so.All publicity
will be left to others. I then took the flag to Tiffany's. It will be done Wed. afternoon.
The parade starts Thurs. 11.30. Fifth Avenue presented a sight I will long remember.
Thousands of fine flags were hung out from the buildings, presenting a most beautiful
and impressive sight. New York is not upset, but it is certainly taking the war seriously.*
*   As soon as I got to Central Park, I read my mail, which the office girl at 14 Wall
St. gave me, and was delighted to find a letter from you, George. Congratulations.
If I could write letters like that was, I should be worthwhile. It was excellent, and*

right here let me say it was to the point and contained some splendid advice which I intend to follow. You are right when you say you have little news to tell me, and therefore it is not worthwhile to write more than twice a week; and that I have a great deal. Therefore I am trying to write once a day.

We had a very pleasant hour or two, and lunch at the Zabriskies. Both the boys expect to enter the sub-chaser flotilla. Then we went to Aunt Annie's. We got lost half a dozen times, but finally arrived at 4.30 when we should have been there at 3. Aunt Annie seems just the same, and as if she would live another 25 years. Cousin Kate is now retired on half pay; Cousin Arthur is bald, but just as much an American as ever. I know my description is crumby and you want narrative, so here goes.

Preliminaries:
'Hasn't changed a bit. Tall, but thin, not yet filled out.' Then Auntie suggested that I go with Auntie to the BAKERY. I went; and she told me how she had sacrificed more for us than any other human being, and how MUCH she loved us (nix). It is useless to go thru all my talk and her beating around the bush. Here are the results I uncovered:
1. Will pay me $50 now as an advance allowance, not sure about summer allowance.
2. Will give me a steamer rug SHE used, if I will not give it to anyone else.
3. Will NOT pay John's carfare to Harvard.
4. Will NOT pay tuition.

On those last two, I got her to say she would consider. She WILL possibly pay tuition. She talks pessimistically as if the Estate could not afford it. I want to be careful not to antagonize her lest I be unable to find out the true condition of the Estate. I hope to go thru the books, etc., and find out, first, how things stand. Real estate is not selling well now because of the war, but she hopes the slump will be temporary only. SHE HAS HUNG ON TOO LONG. You can't wait till I have seen her again before forming your final conclusions. There is a ring of jealousy of Mother in everything she says or does, and I am going to sail into her if she gets too beastly in her remarks about the person who has done more for us than any other person in this world.

I have been very anxious to meet Mr. Roosevelt. He speaks tomorrow night in Brooklyn. Mr. Doughty, who seems to have the inside track on Brooklyn politics, has been very nice to me, and has made it possible for me to meet 'our foremost citizen'. Tomorrow, Tues. night I am going to be introduced to U.S. Senator Calder, at the Montauk Club in Brooklyn. Roosevelt is his guest for dinner. He has promised to introduce me to T.R., and I am then going to ask for an appointment maybe at Oyster Bay. I am hoping against hope that I may be invited by Sen. Calder to dine with him.

I am awfully excited, and as it is 12.15 P.M. I must get my sleep. Love from Mother. Cliff

∽৹

Thurs. Night, May 10
New York.

Dear John and George,

Mother got sick of being my secretary today, so I must write myself. The last three days have been very eventful, but today has been exciting. Tuesday morning we went to Governor's Island where we saw Dr. Smith. He met us and took us into the chapel. He was awfully nice; said some prayers for us and showed us all the old flags in the Chapel.

On our return to Manhattan we saw an English cruiser steaming up the Hudson. It looked like business, too.

We then went to 14 Wall Street, where the Oregonian [the newspaper Clifford had posed for with the flag in Portland] awaited us. I look like a gorilla in the insert. Then I went to Aunt Annie and Mother back to Brooklyn. After a chronicle of the past three days' events, I will tell of my interview with her. After seeing Aunt Annie, I rushed back to Brooklyn to the Montauk Club, where I was introduced to U.S. Senator William Calder. He is a fine man thru and thru. I snatched a bite by buying some zu-zus [snack-food], and met Cousin Dora and Mother in front of Kismet Temple, where T.R. was to speak. We waited in line till 8.30 from 7 P.M. when the doors were closed and we were shut out.

I noticed that one important looking man kept taking society people up to the door-keeper and letting them thru. I went to him and told him who I was, where from and what for, and he said I ought to go in. I asked if Mother and Cousin Dora could also come, and he graciously beckoned Mother and Cousin Dora to follow, and marching up the steps, ENTER.

Col. Roosevelt made a wonderful speech. Mother is going to bring a complete copy of his speech, so I will not do more than to say it was minus hot air and egoism and noise, but right to the point. And although it tingled of sarcasm of the administration, was so American as to be beyond criticism, and only deserving of respect and careful thought. It was GREAT. We all walked back to Cousin Dora's and stopped as we passed the old Brooklyn 464 house on Jefferson Ave., and admired it in the dark.

Wed, I got up very late and went to Senator Calder's Brooklyn office where I got the letter introducing me to Col Roosevelt. His secy. was very kind, and he and

I wrote the letter together after which Senator Calder's signature was attached. I
will meet Mr. Roosevelt at his office Friday 12 M. Appointment has already been
made. The letter reads as follows:

Col. Theodore Roosevelt,
Office Metropolitan Magazine,
New York City.

My dear Colonel Roosevelt,
   This will serve to introduce Mr. Arthur C. Kimber of Stanford University, California,
who is calling on you relative to a matter in which he has a deep personal interest.
Mr. Kimber is leaving here in a few days to carry to France the first American flag
to be officially sent to France, and which he is taking to the First Stanford Unit of
the American Ambulance Field Service now serving at Verdun. He is a young man
of excellent character, and I am deeply interested in him.
Believe me, Sincerely yours,
Signed William M. Calder.

I then went to St. Augustine's Chapel to see the Tablet [a plaque to the Rev. Arthur
Kimber in the church he founded]. It is beautiful, and a fine memorial. But whom
do you think I saw? Harry Heckner was talking to Mr. Dobbin as I entered the
Church proper. He had not been to St. Augustine's for over a year and a half, and
it was quite a coincidence that we met. He was full of reminiscences as you may
suppose. Mr. Randolph was not at Grace Church. He is now in Pennsylvania. At four
o'clock I went over to Tiffany's to get the flag. By appointment Aunt Annie was there
to see it and give me $200; $100 to pay note to IST National bank so you boys
need not worry, and $100 for other expenses. I just got $100 from Dr. Sleeper in
Boston today so you see I have about $290 from New York on – a safe margin.
The flag had been taken to Tiffany's by me at the suggestion of Dr. Sleeper and Mr.
Pottell. I rushed home to dinner, I mean Cousin Dora's. After dinner Dr. Fairbairne,
the Doughtys and the Sayreses called to see the flag. Of course they were delighted.
I asked Miriam to the theatre and she can go Sat. night, if I do not hear before that
time; then back to Sayres where I slept well.

Clifford had also taken part in the parade that day, Thursday, 10 May. It
was one of a number of processions down Fifth Avenue in the course of
the week. The thoroughfare had recently been renamed the 'Avenue of the
Allies', in part to herald the arrival in the city of Allied war commissioners

who had come to America for discussions with political and business leaders, but also to help rally the American people behind the war effort.

Marshal Joseph Joffre of France and British Foreign Secretary Arthur Balfour took their turns to join the parades on different days, their motorcades processing slowly through the city as they waved at the crowds: Joffre on Wednesday 9th and Balfour on Friday 11th. The avenue was festooned with flags and banners of all types, but with three standards of blue, red and white most in evidence – the Stars and Stripes, the Union Flag and the French Tricolour. The days and scenes were ones which were captured for posterity by the American impressionist Frederick Childe Hassam as part of his 'Flag' series of paintings.

The centre of Manhattan was a riot of colour and noise, thousands upon thousands of people thronging Fifth Avenue. But as he prepared himself for the march down the great thoroughfare, it became apparent that not all was well with his UC (University of California, Berkeley) colleagues taking part in the march with him. Perhaps irked by Clifford being the sole representative of his Stanford troupe while UC were there in number, or perhaps unhappy at the glory going to their California rival, some of the UC students began to act up:

Thurs. Night, May 10
New York.

This morning, Thursday, I got up with a day of event and excitement before me. Mother and I went over to the Waldorf Astoria where we waited for the U.C. men to come down before starting the parade. They seemed exceedingly interested in me, and asked many questions regarding where I was staying and when going to sail. I didn't answer direct, but changed the subject. I am glad now. We went to 59th St. and 5th Ave. where the parade was to start, and then it happened.

Mr. Pottell wanted me to head the U.C. men. First a photographer insisted on taking a group picture of us all, including me, and some of the U.C. fellows got sore. The picture was taken. Suddenly, as I was getting my flag ready, they rushed on me. It was right at the head of 5th Ave., too, and there were thousands of people around. 30 to 40 men overpowered me right before everybody, grabbed the flag, put it in a taxi and rushed off. I fought like the dickens. If I could have hit the number of jaws and noses I aimed at, the U.C. crowd would be a sorry looking bunch now. I fought my way clear and rushed for the taxi. It was speeding up Central Park drive with the Stanford Flag. I grasped a fine auto passing by, but the U.C. men dragged me off. Fighting my way clear again, I started to run from them towards the disappearing taxi. In spite of the fact that I had my overcoat on they could not catch me and I jumped on the running board of a fine car – I don't know whose. The man was dumbfounded but I ordered him on and scolded him because he did not go full speed. We picked up a policeman and he commanded the driver to open his throttle. I guess the 'cop' thought a murder had been committed. The red taxi was still in sight.

We finally caught it just after it left the 23rd Street entrance at Central Park West. One U.C. man was aboard, and believe me he was scared as the angry 'cop' asked me if I wanted him arrested. We drove back to where the parade was to start and they were waiting. On the way the U.C. man said they were going to send it back to Stanford by Wells Fargo. They nearly did it, but hereafter when I am around that bunch I will be armed with a Colt automatic, nor will I be afraid to use it. 42 men on 1. Some sports. I had more respect for them, but what can you expect from U.C. If they expect to keep our flag from France they are going to get STUNG. I got into my car escorted by Mr. Myles, a Yale '18 man. Two liveried chauffeurs sat in front. Some car too. The U.C. men there were at least RAZBERRIED.

There were at least 100,000 people to watch the parade. Fifth Avenue was decorated at its best and the streets were packed all the way down. After the parade Myles and I motored to his mother's Park Ave. apartments where we left the flag. I have the key to the closet in which it is locked; then we went down to Sherry's, the fashionable place for lunches, dinners and dances. I didn't get much chance to eat. The U.C. men did, but that's about all they got. Myles introduced me to a young girl, Miss Viola Flannery 600 and something 5th Ave., and we had lunch together. A regular 5th Ave, society girl, O.K. too. U.C. men looked on; then after a number of speeches the orchestra struck up. Ah. Right in front of the U.C. men who sat in bunches minus ladies, we did a fox trot. Several other couples were dancing too, but all New Yorkers.

Then we saw Movies of the battle of the Marne. Again the U.C. men all sat together in a pack. Miss Flannery sat between Myles and myself, and we chatted all thru. Of course there were other society belles, but they were escorted by New York men. There were lots of older society men and women there too. Some of them smoked cigarettes as well as men. Mrs. Anthony Drexel was there [most likely Mary Drexel, heiress and philanthropist, part of the Duke tobacco family of North Carolina].

Miss Flannery told me that she had just had her coming out in New York. How's all this for me – a book agent and 'hasher'. She invited me to call on her. I don't know that I can seeing I have left my dress suit in Palo Alto, but I certainly shall *write. She will answer, I am sure. Well, I will let you know when I sail. I don't know absolutely yet. Tomorrow I meet the greatest and best known and respected man in the world, Col. Theodore Roosevelt. I am awfully excited. I am going to tell him of the Flag incident; he may lend me his 'big stick.'*

Now for my interview with Aunt Annie, and the condition of the Estate. I am enclosing a set of suggestions, and if you are in favour of them please type them off, but do not act until Mother comes home.

The Estate has depreciated to $39,242 and probably less. I have secured a list of all property except personal. There is no use ringing that in now, when the time we shall get it is so near. This includes real estate and buildings, 1st mortgages and cash. My lists are not as clear as I would like, but I have been so pressed for time that I have been unable to copy them off. I am sure you will have little trouble in deciphering them.

Clifford went on, in some exhaustive detail, to outline the present position of the estate looked after by Aunt Annie and what he thought ought to be done with it in the future. He wanted to address what it meant for the three of them now and in the years ahead, and what money would be left. The older ones had been through college, or almost, but there still remained George. He also had a question over finances for John were he to get into Harvard Law School. But what would remain of the estate after that, if, as he thought, Aunt Annie continued to mismanage it? It was a theme he would return to time and again in his letters from France.

In the meantime there were more pressing concerns. The day of his departure was fast approaching and he had a number of other tasks to accomplish in New York with Clara before he could leave.

9

LOOKING BACK

The next time Clifford put pen to paper he had boarded the ship that was to carry him and his precious cargo to Europe. He and his fellow passengers were bound for Liverpool in England, the first stop on his journey to the front in France. Their ship was the *St Louis*, a passenger steamship which had previously seen military service in the Spanish-American War nearly twenty years before. In the intervening years the *St Louis* had reverted to its civilian role, ploughing the liner route from America to Europe and even continuing its regular trade during the war years. But recently, given the unwelcome attention of the U-boats patrolling the Atlantic, it had become the first American vessel, merchant or passenger, to be fitted with naval guns and to sail for Europe in this newly armed state, under the stewardship of Captain Herbert Hartley.[12]

Clifford settled down in his cabin that first night in the middle of May 1917 to begin another letter, a long letter which he was to write in fits and starts over the next ten days, sending it eventually from Liverpool and enclosing a note for the attention of any interested censor that he or she was to skip most of the contents, that all but the last two pages were personal and that they were not to waste their time.

Now, although he was on board the ship bound for his new adventure, he used the opportunity to look back on his last few days on American soil:

U.S.M.S. 'St. Louis,'
Monday night, 9.40 P.M.

May 14th, 1917.

Dear John and George,

   We are practically off, but have not yet put out to sea. The St. Louis is riding at anchor in Lower New York Bay. We are outside the submarine nets, but still in an American port. The Captain intimated that the ship would probably leave U.S.A. tomorrow morning. After all my promises I have let four long days go by without writing, but they have been just chuck full of calls and business engagements. Nights were nearly always occupied, and when they were not I was so tired with the day's work that writing was impossible. A rule has been made that no mail be sent after sailing, so you will have to wait three or four weeks before getting this letter; therefore I write it in diary form, not forgetting the four days that have passed. Please excuse this lengthy introduction.

   Friday was a very eventful day, and meant a great deal to me. Mother was kind enough to accompany me throughout, and you can believe I enjoyed it and was tremendously glad. We left Brooklyn as early as possible, and went to New York via the Fulton Ave. elevated. It took us right to Park Row. The walk down town was short and sweet, and we arrived at 2 Rector Street about 9.20. The passport office was not open upon our arrival, but in a short time the clerk came and let us in. A passport is quite a document; ask Mother all about mine, I am sure it will interest you. Just as Mr. Galbraith of San Francisco said, it was waiting for me when I got there. Mother and I then rushed to 14 Wall Street, where there was some mail. The main object of this visit was to get letters to the French and English Consuls.

   Mr. Hereford did not at first see the idea of my taking the St. Louis a week ahead of time, but after a short explanation he enthusiastically sanctioned my plan. He was certainly 'sore' when he heard the details of the flag escapade of the day before. He said that the U.C. men had been generally misbehaving, and that that was not the only thing he had against them. Myles was there and I asked him to soothe Mr. Hereford, so the U.C. men would not get it too hard. He must have had some effect, for I learned afterwards that all the U.C. men got was a very severe lecture.

   While waiting in the outer office for the promised letters to the Consuls and so on, Myles drew his chair up and chatted with Mother and me. Then to my undisguised delight, he handed me a book 'Friends of France' the one we borrowed from Miss Kimball to read, and he autographed it. I was most grateful. Incidentally, Beverly Russell Myles, 875 Park Ave., New York, Yale 1918, is a man worth seeing when you come to New York, John. I am awfully glad to have him as a friend, because he is such a nice, clean, manly fellow. He says that maybe the American Ambulance Field

Service will be able to use me in New York, after I have served in Europe several months; I certainly do hope so.

The letters came and I was exceedingly glad to leave the office and proceed with my business. The French and English Consuls visaed my passport. We saw the English Consul, but the Frenchman kept himself locked up in his private office. But later on he gave me a most charming and courteous letter to the French Consul in London. This will help me in getting through England without delay. The English Consul talked to us; believe me, he acts as though he owned the earth, and almost as if he were immortal, looking down upon us poor humans. He asked me when I was to sail, and I answered: 'On the St. Louis, Saturday, May 12th.' 'Monday, May 14th' he contradicted. 'Well, the man in the office told me Saturday', I ventured. 'I say Monday' he repeated, and that ended it as far as I could see. He was right, but most peremptory and important.

It was nearing 12 M. so as Mother and I had an appointment with the Ex. President of the U.S. we hurried up town to the Metropolitan Magazine headquarters. Nor can anyone say it was not early, as we arrived about 11.35. While we were waiting I could not help remarking to Mother upon the good looks and pleasing ways of the office girl. She had two most attractive dimples and an awfully pleasant way of smiling. Not at all flirtatious, but just sweet and kind. She seemed to keep everybody good-natured, and there were lots of persons waiting, too. It takes tact to manage so many people, and, believe me, she had it. I went up and told her I had an appointment with the Colonel at 12 M. and asked if there were many people before me and if I would be delayed long. She seemed very much amused; the same question must have been asked her dozens of times by dozens of people, and she replied, 'Oh, he tells everybody to come at 12 M.'

A French Red Cross Nurse preceded me. She seemed very anxious to meet Mr. Roosevelt, and I am sure she was DELIGHTED when she came out. Finally, Mother and I were asked into Mr. Roosevelt's outer office. The walls were decorated with Metropolitan Magazine original illustrations, and pictures of Teddy. A stenographer jabbed away at a typewriter so fast you could not see her fingers; it was fascinating to watch her. We were called into the inner office just as Mr. Roosevelt was shaking hands with the nurse. She was thanking him for the interview and blushing with joy. My heart was fluttering, too. Senator Calder's letter had worked fine, and I can never repay Mr. Doughty for what he did in getting the senator interested in me.

Mr. Roosevelt shook hands warmly, first with me and then with Mother whom I introduced, and then said, 'Pray be seated, Mrs. Kimber.' He was most cordial and seemed quite interested in us. He was autographing some books, and talked to us absentmindedly while he wrote his name, and about the most commonplace things, too. When he had finished this he gave us his attention, and then it was that his personality began to be felt. He has a most suave and confident yet frank and interesting way of talking. I described my mission, told him where I was from, where going, when and why. He seemed deeply interested, and said, 'Fine, fine.'

Mother said she did not like her boys to go, naturally, but would not hold them back when duty called. 'That's the attitude, Mrs. Kimber. You are just the right kind of an American mother. I will tell Mrs. Roosevelt about you. My four boys are entering the service in one form or another. I want to go too, so I can say, not "'Go'" but "Come."' Mother then told him that he knew Dr. Kimber. 'Let me see, where did I meet Dr. Kimber?' he thoughtfully said. 'My husband knew you when you were Police Commissioner. He was Vicar of St. Augustine's Chapel, 38 years.' 'Oh, yes, that's right, when I was police commissioner, Jake Riis* introduced me to Dr. Kimber, and we did some work together. I remember how glad I was to meet the Doctor. Yes, yes. That was years ago, when I was Police Commissioner'. The watch incident was then recalled, and seemed to create quite an impression upon him. Then I asked him if there was any possibility of my joining his division in France. He asked my age and some other questions, and said I was just the kind he wanted. 'But it doesn't look as if they were going to let me go,' he said, and although he was smiling and covering up his feelings, one could distinctly see that he felt hurt and sad that the U.S. Government was so unpatriotic as it then appeared. Roosevelt has no selfish political motive. He is ambitious, but because he feels he can be of real service. He is not looking for self-glory, but for National honor and success. He wants to see American citizens act as Americans SHOULD. He then said that if they let him go, all I had to do was to write him, and he could use me and some of my friends, and would be glad of our experience. 'Be sure to mention the fact that your father, Jake Riis and I knew each other when I was Police Commissioner of New York, and that Senator Calder introduced you to me, and I will do all I can for you. And please don't hesitate to ask me if you need me. Also recall the watch incident.' He explained that otherwise his secretary might never show him the letter.

After that, he wrote in my book, and you will see the original: 'Good luck to Arthur Kimber' signed 'Theodore Roosevelt. May 11th, 1917'.

You can imagine how happy I felt. The book is indeed a precious treasure now, but how invaluable was that interview, in which dear Mother and I met America's greatest citizen and statesman, and one of the foremost men, in fact, the best known and most respected man on the earth today.

---

* Jake Riis had been a prominent campaigning journalist and social reformer in New York at the time.

Roosevelt is not just what I expected. He seems older and more careworn. His strenuous life is beginning to show; remember, he is a grandfather now. His hair and moustache are gray, but his teeth are just as fine as ever. One could tell he was 'Dutch at a glance'. His cheeks are rosy; he has all the old fight, but less noise and more seriousness and earnestness. He is quieter that I supposed he would be. He is all a man and a fine model to follow. May he be our next President.

Mother and I took the Subway up to Bronx Park, where we got a duplicate copy of the book for the Estate as kept by Aunt Annie. Mother will tell you of our call, and BE SURE TO ASK HER. I opened up and gave her a piece of my mind when she started to run down Mother to my face. When we left I made her feel good by kissing her several times; but she has no children to fool with now, and SHE KNOWS IT TOO. We talked about the storage; ask Mother for the details.

We went to the Phillipses for dinner. While waiting, Bertie and I read the Britannica article on Roosevelt. What a wonderful career that man has had. Mine is very much like his so far. He went to Europe when 14; I ditto. After graduating, he entered politics. Quit studying law and was never admitted to the bar. Europe when 22 years. I am 21, and I have a big opportunity right now in this world war which he did not have. Of course he had a wonderful personality which I lack, but I'll bet I have just as much enthusiasm though; by the time I am 59, the United States will know who I am. Wait and see.

We said goodbye to the Phillipses and hurried to Cousin Dora and Mrs. Sayre's house to bed. Perhaps you are getting bored. Cheer up, I have told of one day only. This is a regular Dickens novel; I am growing quite literary, you see.

Clifford recounted how he had gone with Clara and Dora to the theatre on the Saturday to see the musical *The Love o' Mike*, where, he confessed to his brothers, he was much taken with the star, Peggy Wood. He had shown a picture of Wood later to Clara and Dora, who had apparently felt the star's eyes to be of the 'come hither' variety. 'Now Mother is worrying for fear I propose to and marry an actress before I get home. Cheer up, the Lord will guide my actions.'

On the Sunday morning, though, it was up early again for a return to the city. He had with him the flag and, accompanied by Clara, was bound for Trinity church on Broadway and Wall Street where a special service had been organised, a leave-taking ceremony in which he would take part. It would honour the task ahead not only for Clifford and his American Ambulance colleagues but the ranks of servicemen who would now follow them to Europe:

Mr. Boyd, the sexton met me and placed the flag next to the choir stalls just opposite the Trinity flag. Quite a few shook hands with me before the service. I was an acolyte for the day. It is quite an experience to march in procession in robes, and sit in a choir, looking down on an Old Trinity congregation. The service was most beautiful and inspiring. I was awfully glad things were just as they were. Dr. Manning used most fitting words when he spoke of the flag, and announced to the congregation that it was the first American flag to be carried to the French front with the official sanction of the American government. Quite a few people went up and touched it. Three sisters kissed it. Many people were impressed, and during Sunday a great many people saw it. It remained for the other services. Monday an article appeared in the New York Herald, and many people made a special trip to Trinity to see the flag. After service, Mrs. Phillip Brown took a pin of the U.S. flag off her coat and pinned it to mine. She was awfully kind and I was much impressed. Mother will tell you about this, remind her. We waited a short time for Dr. Manning, and then all went up to his house for dinner. We met his daughters; the younger one is most attractive, but the older one seems more earnest and serious and is equally attractive, though not so girlish or pretty. We had a very nice visit. Dr. Manning says he knows Roosevelt quite well and meets him often and that next time he sees him he will speak of me. He is very kind and wholehearted. I am certainly glad he is one of my friends.

(It is now 12 P.M. Still at anchor in Lower New York Bay; may weigh anchor any minute.) Goodbye for the present. Will continue tomorrow, and write of today then. God bless you, and goodnight. Cliff.

May 15th, 1917, 12 M. Noon.

Dear John and George,

We are now at sea, headed for the submarine zone but still far from it. Yesterday we embarked, but I must trace its events before discussing the present. Monday morning a great deal faced us. Several things had to be bought, and quite a few details of the voyage had to be tended to. I got up early and had breakfast with the Sayres. They bid me goodbye and I hurried over to Cousin Dora's. Mother made arrangements for a taxi to carry us to the boat at 12 P.M. Then we took the Putnam Ave. car to Bedford Ave. and started to look for the Bedford Bank. That institution has moved and also changed its name. When we finally found it we had two checks cashed on Mother's signature. Now there are only a few dollars to my account at the First National Bank of Palo Alto. But doesn't it seem wonderful to think that a bank will honour checks when they have not seen the signature for 10 years, by comparing Mother's signature with that of 10 years ago?

We hurried to New York and paid for my ticket across the Atlantic. I was to room with a young lieutenant. At 14 Wall St. I sadly said goodbye to Myles, who thanked me for calling in. Letters from you and Mr. Randolph awaited me, and honestly, they were very welcome.

It has been always one of my ambitions to go up the Woolworth building. Mother didn't want to go at first, but I persuaded her to undertake the adventure. Looking up from the sidewalk, the top of this massive hive is lost seemingly in the clouds. Express to 26, then local elevator to 59; tickets, 50c, were collected at this point. Then we were put into an elevator ascending the tower or pinnacle, and surrounded by spiral stairs. The elevator was just large enough to hold six or seven people, and, just think, it was round. The views from the observation gallery were wonderful. All New York unfolded itself. We could not have had a better day. People looked like ants; autos, wagons, trains and trolleys looked like tiny toys; the whole was a dream. It must be wonderful to go up in an aeroplane. Mother felt a little sick and nervous; she was tired and excited. I felt fine, not a bit dizzy. It was some drop to the first floor; the air in the elevator shaft roared by – we were going so fast. Mother is bringing illustrated booklets of this trip.

We then had a light lunch at one of the Child's establishments. We went to Trinity to get the flag; many people were there praying, and seemed very much impressed. Incidentally, Mr. Sleeper suggested the other day that after the war the flag be placed in the museum at Washington with the other relics of the war.

I got some American dollar bills changed to English pound notes. They are funny pieces of paper, white, and only printed on one side in black letters. They don't seem like real money, but I guess they are. At any rate, they and the $100 French draft are safe in my money belt, next to my digestive organs; they are not yet converted into food, but they will be. We stopped at Abraham and Straus on the way home, and bought two pairs of gloves, two dozen film rolls, shaving brush and bandanas. Later on I got some 'blue jays'. The taxi was waiting when we reached the house. It did not take long to pack things on board and Mother and I started off on the last trip we were to take together for quite a while, but NOT our last trip. The driver was wonderful in the way he dodged and gained on the other machines. I asked him to drive past St. Augustine's and shall never forget it. Thus we got to the dock, pier 62. Who do you think was there? A– A–. Thus Mother and I were denied a last hour together. I can never forget or forgive it. Poor Mother was so brave and there was a third party to cut us out. Unasked for, uncalled for and uninvited. She gave me a box of chocolates but that was no compensation for dear Mother's tears. How I wished I could talk to Mother alone that last hour, and try to comfort her.

I soon got on the boat and we pulled out. Many an anxious look did I cast toward Mother, and she met me smiling bravely through her tears. May God bless her, I do hope she gets home safely. Write immediately. The boat pulled out on time, 4 P.M. sharp. I gazed long toward the end of the pier where several hundred people were waving to us; I could not spot Mother, but I knew she was there, and I watched till the pier was cut off from my view. It all seemed like a dream. We were off; slowly the St. Louis steamed down the Hudson River; buildings passed; New York unfolded itself in panorama – a wonderful sight. To think of all those people living in that hive of offices. Goodbye, New York.

So we steamed down New York Bay. As I said before, all seemed like a dream. Nearing the Narrows we met a Flotilla of Torpedo Boat Destroyers; they were a pretty sight. Most of them were lying at anchor, but those that were steaming full speed or even half speed were really beautiful. Of course they were painted a dull gray, but that only made them harmonize with their surroundings. The U.S. Gunners on the St. Louis waved in passing, and they were answered by cheers from Uncle Sam's ships of the line. There was also a Monitor at anchor. They are awfully funny looking craft, very low with a high rakish mast. A speedy launch kept pace with us, and almost did circles around us. Every now and then the owner waved his arm in farewell. The Narrows are well protected from submarines, by a series of large steel nets suspended from kegs. The entrance is marked by buoys and is not more than a couple of hundred yards wide, easy to guard with torpedo boats.

The St. Louis steamed down Lower New York Bay a short distance, and then turned and dropped anchor. It was a surprise and disappointment; but she was not to stay long. We had dinner at anchor, and at least no one could say we did not have every opportunity to enjoy our first meal. I met an Irishman named Ferguson. He knew the Captain – by pulling strings he managed to secure seats for both of us at the Captain's table. The Captain is a fine man; he is quite young but in spite of his age has the reputation of being one of the most daring yet competent Captains on the Atlantic. He is awfully good natured, and when he laughs, he shows a splendid set of teeth fully equal to T.R.'s. He is tremendously handsome, so makes a hit with all the passengers. Last night I didn't get to bed till 12.30 A.M. because I was writing to you, catching up for days I was behind. Before going to bed, I walked out on the deck. The sea was calm (of course we were in Lower N.Y. Bay) and we could see a wonderful sight in the lights of New York City and suburbs – that was worth seeing.

10

AT SEA

Clifford settled down to life on board, gradually finding his sea legs. But he wanted to get into a routine to give his days some structure. Some hours, he planned, would be spent in bookwork, persevering with his efforts to learn French and writing his letters; other parts of the day were allocated to getting to know his fellow passengers and taking part in the ship's activities and social scene.

It did not work out exactly as he had planned it – it was not always interesting, nor was it particularly productive – but the rhythm of daily life he and fellow passengers duly established mixed the leisured experience of an oceangoing liner with something more edged with danger. Had anyone needed reminding of the curiously different circumstances they now found themselves in, they only had to look out on to the promenade deck for a hint of what might lie ahead of them in their journey across the Atlantic. It had only been two months since the ship had been kitted out for its new role and the *St Louis* now looked the part. It had been furnished with five heavy guns of different diameters, dotted around forecastle, quarterdeck and stern and an armed guard of two dozen US Navy personnel: enough, it was hoped, to help her in the event of enemy attack. It was a necessary precaution. In the months ahead – and even before the liner was officially co-opted once more into military service as the newly renamed USS *Louisville* – the *St Louis* would become one of the principal carriers of troops in the first phase of military deployment to Europe.

'Allies Day May 1917' by American artist Frederick Childe Hassam. (Courtesy of the National Gallery of Art, Washington DC)

A watercolour by Clifford of a *Zouave* soldier, Nice/Marseilles, September 1917. (Kimber Literary Estate)

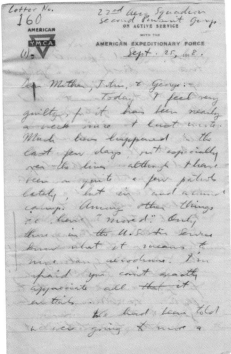

Clockwise from above: A scrap of map from one of Clifford's last patrols, south-west of Verdun, September 1918. (Kimber Literary Estate); Clifford's last letter home. (Kimber Literary Estate); Arthur Clifford Kimber's grave, Meuse-Argonne Cemetery, Romagne-sous-Montfaucon, France. (Kimber Literary Estate)

The first flag today, Stanford University, Palo Alto, California. (Courtesy of Stanford University)

The first flag – a detailed close-up shows the service ribbons 1918–19. (Courtesy of Stanford University)

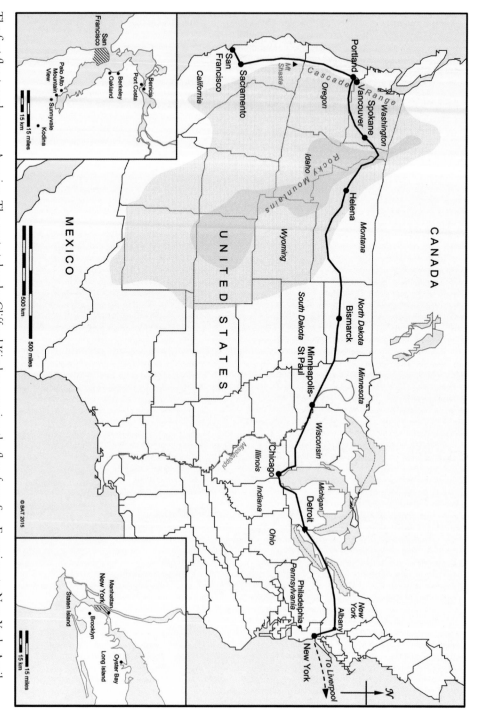

The first flag travels across America. The route taken by Clifford Kimber carrying the flag, from San Francisco to New York, April–May 1917. (©BAT 2015 Barbara Taylor)

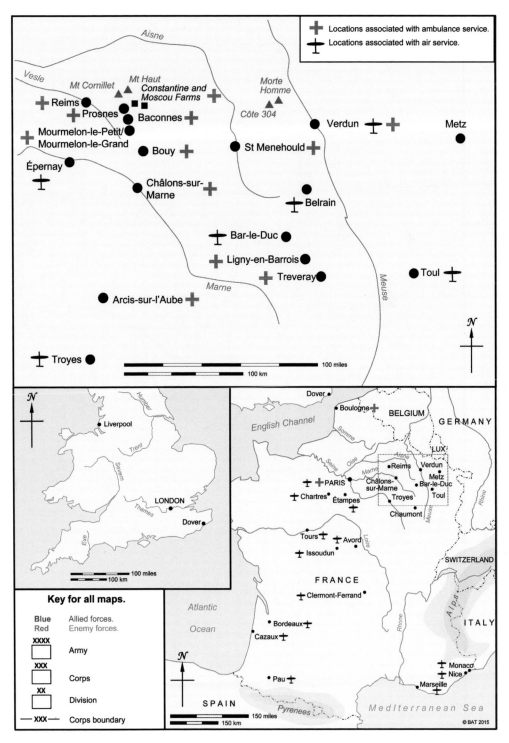

Clifford's service with the American Ambulance and French & US Air Services, 1917–18.
(©BAT 2015 Barbara Taylor)

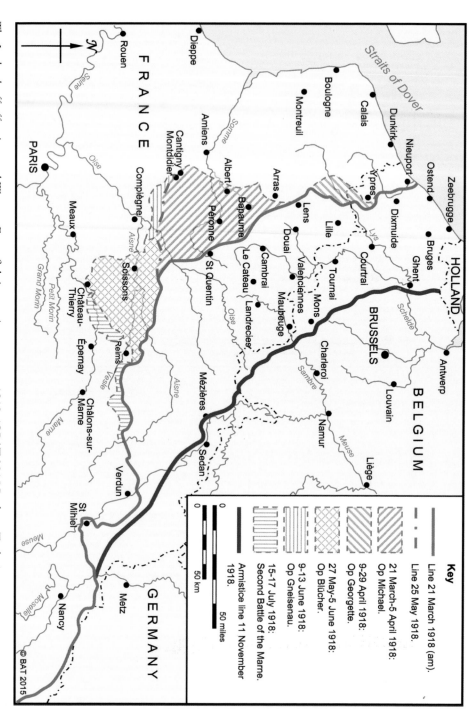

The Ludendorff offensives and Western Front fighting, spring–summer 1918. (©BAT 2015 Barbara Taylor)

Key

Line 21 March 1918 (am).

Line 25 May 1918.

21 March–5 April 1918: Op Michael.

9–29 April 1918: Op Georgette.

27 May–5 June 1918: Op Blücher.

9–13 June 1918: Op Gneisenau.

15–17 July 1918: Second Battle of the Marne.

Armistice line 11 November 1918.

0   50 km

0   50 miles

© BAT 2015

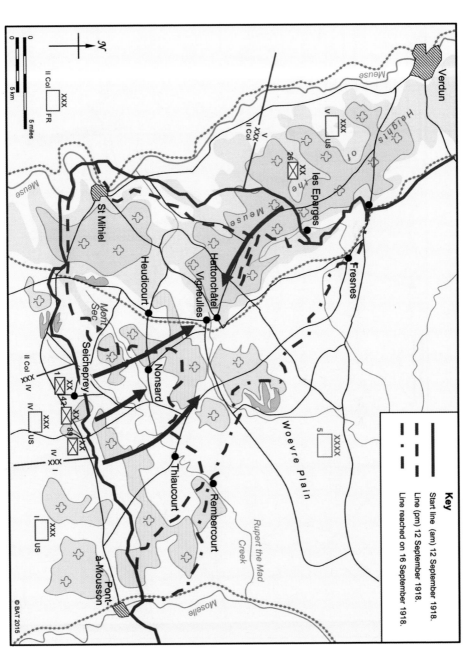

A battle map showing the positions of key army units, St Mihiel Offensive, 12–14 September 1918.
(©BAT 2015 Barbara Taylor)

Key

Start line (am) 12 September 1918.

Line (pm) 12 September 1918.

Line reached on 16 September 1918.

Verdun

Meuse

Heights of the Meuse

Îles Eparges

V
XXX
II Col

V
XXX
US

XX
26

Fresnes

St Mihiel

Heudicourt

Hattonchâtel

Vigneulles

Mont
Sec

Seicheprey

Nonsard

Woevre Plain

XXXX
5

Rupert the Mad Creek

Thiaucourt

Rembercourt

II Col
XXX
IV

XX
1

XX
42

XXX
IV
US

XX
89

XXX
I
US

XXX
I

Pont-à-Mousson

Moselle

Meuse

XXX
FR
II Col

N

0   5 km
0   5 miles

© BAT 2015

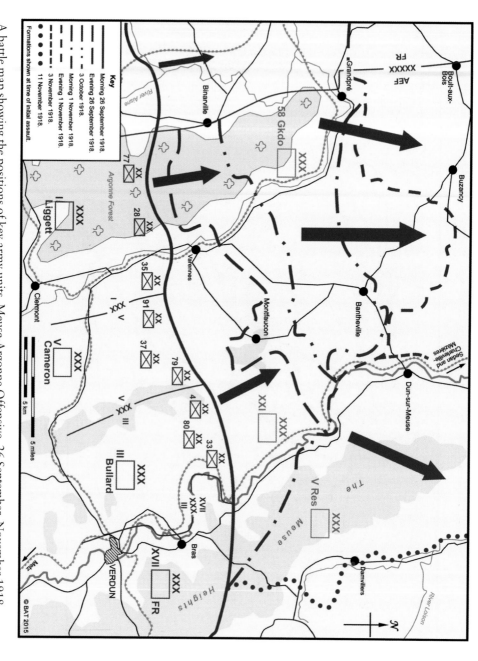

A battle map showing the positions of key army units, Meuse-Argonne Offensive, 26 September–November 1918. (©BAT 2015 Barbara Taylor)

Key

———	Morning 26 September 1918.
—·—	Evening 26 September 1918.
—··—	3 October 1918.
—·—·—	Morning 1 November 1918.
———	Evening 1 November 1918.
-------	3 November 1918.
••••••	11 November 1918.

Formations shown at time of initial assault.

Binarville

River Alsne

Grandpré

AEF XXXXX FR

Boult-aux-Bois

Buzancy

58 Gkdo

XXX

77 XX

Argonne Forest

Liggett I XXX

28 XX

35 XX

Valennes

91 XX

I XXX V

Clermont

CAMERON V XXX

5 km

5 miles

37 XX

Montfaucon

Bantheville

Sedan and Charleville-Mézières

Dun-sur-Meuse

79 XX

4 XX

80 XX

V XXX III

33 XX

XXI XXX

V Res XXX

The Meuse

Bullard III XXX

XVII III XXX

Bras

Damvillers

River Loison

N

Meuse Heights

VERDUN

XVIII XXX FR

Metz

© BAT 2015

So began Clifford's journal of on-board life.[13]

This morning I did not get up until quite late; you see breakfast is served till ten o'clock. I have an outside room, but it is of no advantage to me, as all the portholes are screwed tight, and closed with light screens. Persons are forbidden to strike matches on the deck at night or use electric flashlights. Just before breakfast, the St. Louis weighed anchor and put out to sea. We passed an English Cruiser, but were in turn given the laugh by an American Torpedo Boat Destroyer bound for Europe. It was going very fast, although I am told it was only going to make 16 knots after clearing the coast as that speed is much more economical. I had a good breakfast, and so far have held it down. The pilot dropped off about 4.30. His boat was picked up and hauled out of the water like a toy by the pilot steamer that met him. My, but those men are nifty in handling a boat.

This morning I spent a good deal of time in walking around the decks and talking. The sea had been smooth all day and was very blue and pretty. While we were finishing dinner, the gunners held target practice. I will tell you about our guns; there are four four-inch guns, and one six-inch gun. The former are about 15 foot long, and the latter 20; they are firmly mounted [here three lines are rubbed out by the censor].

I am going to sketch some of them later on, and maybe take pictures, but before I do that or study French, I must get written up to date. Passengers are not allowed in the gun deck (promenade deck) during practice or engagements, but we could see the results of the fire from the saloon deck. The shots were sent at a target a couple of miles away that had been dropped off; the St. Louis turned; they were pretty accurate; the reports were deafening. You know these were big guns, the biggest I have ever seen. The shells screamed as they whizzed through the air. In a few seconds they would hit the water near the target and then skip another mile. Sometimes they would skip as many as two or three times. They shot up a big column of water.

About three P.M. we had a life drill. We all put on life preservers and lined up on deck. We were given instructions as to how to proceed, in case we heard the guns shoot. Everyone is ordered to the saloon upon the first shot, and then must await orders. This afternoon I walked some more. I feel I must get in and keep in condition. My cold is much better; the sore throat has entirely disappeared. I still have sniffles, but the salt air does a lot of good, and they will be soon gone. Dr. Kennedy, one of the American Red Cross doctors gave me a smallpox vaccination a few moments ago, so now I have met all the requirements of the service. Goodbye again, love, Cliff

⧖

Wednesday 16 May

Dear John and George,

Today I have been thinking – how under the sun can I trust such a roll of letters on one ship? If she goes down, all my past history is lost. I will have to send a couple of sheets to an envelope, and a few days apart; that will keep up your excitement, and make receiving part of them if not all of them, a certainty. One of my greatest dreams and hopes was shattered today, and I accepted defeat with a heavy heart and a wobbly stomach, although I am not yet seasick; feeling fine, but the swell is stronger and I don't know how long I can last. Heaven is merciful, though and seems to be working up a resistance gradually as the waves rise. Well, my disappointment lay in this; just before getting on the boat, Mother and I saw and heard a lady and her daughter, whom I pronounced to be French. Mother agreed with me; right there I saw my French professoress. I was going to converse with her and wiggle my shoulders, and wave my arms as she surely must do. She sits at the same table as I do – the Captain's table (I will describe all my table mates later on,) and all her actions and manners seemed to strengthen my hopes; She and her Mother must be French. A U.S. Navy Lieutenant and a Harvard student returning to England to enter the war, both had their suspicions about her being French. Schuyler, the Lieut. said she was a too delicate and retiring princess to be French, and Smith, the English student, said she didn't powder right for a French mademoiselle. Today I met her on the deck; I have seen her before, but have not attempted to talk with her, she is one of the slowest persons on board to get acquainted with, and I asked if she would help me learn to talk French. 'I am awfully sorry' she replied, 'but I don't know a word of French.' I nearly fell over, the deck was slanting greatly. 'Perhaps after two years in France I can help you; do you know if it is hard to get around in France if you can't talk the language?'

I was dumbfounded, what could I say or do? I thanked her. As I walked away I thought of how mean fate is, and how uneducated she must be – think of a GIRL, not knowing how to speak French, can you imagine anything worse? This ended my dreams. There are two or three real Frenchmen on board, but I hesitate to ask them to help me; you see my dream called for a delicate princess. When I told Schuyler and Smith about it, they roared. 'Cheer up, she'll only wish you to wait two years.'

What Clifford didn't yet know, and only found out some days later, was the actual identity of his dream girl, the erstwhile and would-be 'French professoress', although even when he did find out, he did not dwell on it in his diary. Perhaps it was down to some embarrassment on his part – evidenced by his haughty or humorous reaction to her capacity with French – that he and his two companions had failed to recognise her. She turned out to be the actress Lillian Gish. In the letters covering his voyage to England he only made mention of her by name on one other occasion, when they had reached England and he made his goodbyes to Gish and her mother. It was left until more than a year later before he talked about her properly in a letter home.

Was interested to read that you saw Lillian Gish in Hearts of the World. What do you think of her? Meeting her on the boat I never dreamed that she was a Movie Star. Didn't discover it until three or four days out of New York. She was very quiet and nice and except for a certain amount of powder which I suppose is excusable with Movie Stars – she was absolutely natural. Yes, I thought she was French when I first saw her and I expected to make the most of an opportunity to parlezvous but it developed that she didn't know a word of that language.

Gish was travelling to England at the behest of the American film director D.W. Griffith. The two had already made a number of pictures together, including 1915's *Birth of a Nation* and the film *Intolerance*, which Griffith had been in England in part to promote a month before, attending the film's London premiere on 5 April, the day before America had declared war on Germany.

But Griffith's mission to Europe had another purpose, and that was very much connected the war effort – a forthcoming propaganda offering, *Hearts of the World*, which he wanted to get to work on. He had toured parts of the Western Front in France looking for suitable locations for filming and in Britain had held talks with a number of prominent public figures, including Prime Minister Lloyd George.

Now he wanted his leading lady to come to Europe to prepare for the project. This she was now doing, taking the first opportunity available to travel after Griffith had contacted her, by sailing on the *St Louis*. Gish was accompanied on the voyage by her mother Mary and some weeks later the pair would be joined by her sister, and co-star in the film, Dorothy. Together they would witness the effects of war in England: blacked-out London, the wounded servicemen returning from France and the damage wrought by the bombing raids of German balloons which were beginning to menace the capital.[14]

On the journey to England though, and as Clifford described it, life on board was a mixed bag of the humdrum alongside reminders of the dangerous waters they were sailing towards.

Today we played shuffleboard a little, and deck golf, in which the same sticks and round places of wood were used. It was quite a bit of fun; at least it broke the monotony of doing nothing. You know all a man can do on a ship is to eat and sleep. We all say we intend to read and write and study, but nobody does. It is easier to talk and promenade. But I am getting in some French study. Today I got a shave at the barber shop; it cost me two bits but it was worth it; I know I am getting extravagant. There goes the bugle for supper, a regular Cornet march; cheering follows. The ink is all over my hand and I must wash up. Some passengers go in in evening dress, etc., with stiff shirts; it is as much fun to watch them as to eat. Goodbye for the present; I've strung a lot of bull, but that's all there is to write about.

Sunday, May 20th 1917.

Two days more gone by without a note; why? Because nothing exciting has happened. Friday we met the White Star Liner Adriatic; some boat; but believe me she was pitching gloriously. [Here five lines censored] *I am proud of myself, here I have been six days at sea, and I haven't missed a meal yet. Yesterday and the day before we were in about a 20 foot swell, but seeing that we worked up to it gradually, few people were affected.*

Last night the order was passed around that anyone going on the guns at night would be shot. The gunners all have automatics and the Lieut. in charge means business. As I understand it, this order is necessary because last voyage some poor German 'nut' wrecked the 'Sights' on one of the guns. This morning nearly all the passengers attended service in the saloon – the purser read it. Church of England hymnal and prayers were used. Everybody was earnest and sincere if able to be judged by the facial expression. They are beginning to realize the seriousness of the situation we are about to face. No one has acted foolish so far, although one woman who has lost six near relatives due to submarine attacks and mines has not undressed yet. A good many have life suits, long rubberized bags with legs and arms, and a hole for the head. They are supposed to keep people warm as well as afloat, and they say that six people can be kept afloat by mean of one of these sacks. The American Line ticket man tried to sell me one – $60 – Goodnight! At any rate, since nearly all the women here have them, and the capacity of the ocean is unlimited, all we have to do is to throw them overboard and ourselves get into the boats.

The suits are unsinkable and it is claimed they are as complete and comfortable as a downy bed; but they are so big that six persons wearing them would fill a good-sized lifeboat. CHEER UP. That service this morning was good. We sang 'Onward Christian Soldiers', 'Travelers by Land and Sea', and wound up with the tune of America. As there were nearly as many English as Yankees on board, no one knew what to sing, and it was a jumble of 'My Country, 'Tis of Thee' and 'God Save the King'.

I want to tell you about this man, Smith, with whom I have struck up quite a friendship. He is as Englishy as they make them and has had two years at Harvard, so is quite Bostonian, although he denies this, saying that Boston and Harvard are two entirely different places as they are, to be sure. His father is a self-made man and very successful, and I should judge extremely wealthy. He had built and installed printing presses that are in use by all the big book publishers and papers in the world, including the N.Y. Times, Herald, etc., places in Boston and Chicago, Paris, London and Berlin. Evidently a big man. Smith is a fine chap – he has a great deal of good honest common sense and is very broad minded. He is quite a contrast to Lieut. Schuyler of the American Navy, who, like most Military men, is exceedingly narrow-minded. He has travelled considerably, although he had never been West of Chicago. He speaks French very well, having lived in Paris over six months, and having been well trained since a child. He is a good student, having had a splendid foundation in English boarding schools. He is only 18 years old, although he has the maturity of a man 23 or 24.

He and I have talked a great deal, and he shows that he has more than a superficial knowledge of the subjects he discusses, which, by the way are varied. After having been away from home (his folks live in London) for a year and more, you can believe he is very anxious to land in Liverpool. His family is quite separated, due to the war, it seems; his father being in Paris, his brother in Belgium with the British artillery, and his mother and sister at home in London. He is planning to enter the aviation service, and will certainly make a good aviator. He has been up many times. The only fault I have to find with him is that he is so wealthy he doesn't seem to know the value of money. If he had to earn all he spends he would spend less and be more saving. Of course he has such ability he will have little trouble in earning a great deal, once he starts. It is very interesting to hear him tell of his social activities in Harvard and New York. He and I are going to ride to London together. He says that if I am in England several days he will show me the interesting places in London. He is very generous and quite polished – not at all stuck up – although he couldn't see it very far when I sat down in the entrance hall next to a steward and got the story of the sinking of the Lusitania first hand.

This steward jumped off the stern just as the Lusitania went under. He was in the water 4 ½ hours and was unconscious when picked up. His story was graphic and fascinating. There is another steward on board the St. Louis who has made every voyage the St. Louis has made up to date. He shipped 22 years ago, and is still on board; nearly 300 voyages, round trip. Thus we are amused day after day. The worst is yet to come; the last two nights I will be prepared, believe me. We are all kidding ourselves along, I don't think the danger is very great anyway. If I was born to serve in France I wasn't born to drown, at least on this trip.

I said I would describe the persons at the Captain's table; this is just to show you what an interesting group of individuals we have on board. We are seventeen in number and a happy lot. Not one of us has been sick yet, although Miss M— did not come down to breakfast the other day because she said she was lazy and wanted to break the monotony by oversleeping. As I have said before, I haven't missed a meal, and have sent down to my cold storage such things as hors d'oeuvres, pickles, olives, plum pudding, fish of all kinds, pickled artichokes, asparagus and everything else calculated to start a volcano, including ice cream and nuts. I am feeling fine and dandy, as an attractive girl would say.

Well, to begin – No. 1 is an Irishman named Ferguson. He is going back to Ireland to get his sweetheart, so he informed me. It was due to him that I got a seat at the Captain's table. He is an interesting fellow to talk to, and has some very pronounced views on religion. He says he believes that no one can get to heaven, unless he be born again, that is, unless he becomes Christianized. I told him Christian is that Christian does, and that I believed that Socrates has as much chance to get to heaven as St. Paul. He believes every word in the Bible, and although interesting to argue with, he is hopeless to convince. He has some mighty fine ideas. He likes to read biographies, especially of early exponents of the Gospels. Always cracking jokes, he is a typical Irishman, not lacking the brogue.

No. 2 is a genuine Englishman, with a monocle. He has it tied on a black thread string, and puts it to his left eye whenever he looks at the bill of fare, then he lets it drop and blinks and smiles. He is quite stout, and like many fat men has a jovial disposition. His face is very red, and always smiling whether there is something to laugh about or not – that makes no difference. Every other day he orders pale ale with his dinner. I had a talk with him the other day, and learned that he was a woollen merchant with American markets. He says that the war is cutting down his business to beat the band. He has crossed the Atlantic six times since war was declared in 1914. So you see he must be 'some boy' with some business. Two years ago, when German submarines began to operate, he bought a rubber vest which he wears day and night. He showed me the tube and mouthpiece that he uses to blow it up and which he carries in his pocket like a fountain pen. Of course he is so fat he couldn't sink anyway, but his preparedness scheme relieves his mind so he can sleep. The most interesting thing about him is when he puts his glass to his eye, and when he laughs; as I sit directly opposite him, I get the full benefit.

As the ship is rolling like the dickens, and as I want to get my dinner, it will be necessary for me to stop at this point, wash my hands and take a brisk walk. I am getting used to the constantly moving decks, but writing on a rising and falling deck is sickening.

∽∾

Tues. morning, May 22nd, 10.10 A.M.

Dear John, George and Mother,

Yesterday, everything was hurry and bustle in preparation for possible disaster. The lifeboats which had been hung out upon leaving New York were lowered to the promenade deck to facilitate loading them in case of necessity. There is one large launch, so we need not worry about drifting. In the afternoon we had another life drill and lecture in the dining saloon. About 5 P.M. we passed some bales of cotton, and barrels of oil from some wrecked ship. Last night, Monday night, was the most dangerous of the trip because of our being right in the zone. Many people sat up all night, and few of them took off their clothes. Lieut. Schuyler, Smith and I played some games until ten, talked until 11 and then turned in. We were all going to get up at three and see the sun rise. Smith called me and can testify that I slept soundly, and he had quite a job waking me, and that I was entirely undressed and in my pyjamas. They both stayed up and are now sleepy. After a couple of hours I went to bed again, undressed, too, and then did not get up until 9.45. Nearly all the nurses on my deck (below the saloon deck, which is in reality the main deck on the St. Louis, making now the Lower deck, although they call it the upper deck for satisfying the whimsical nature of the passengers) slept either on deck, or in the saloon. It was awfully funny when I returned to my room at 4.30 A.M. and passed thru the saloon, to see ladies lying on the sofas, and in the main entrance hall men fully dressed, lying on the floor. Those who stretched out on the deck, not only nearly froze to death, but stiffened themselves for days to come.

This is the way I figured: it takes from five to twenty minutes for a ship to sink after being torpedoed. As the torpedo or mine strikes 15 or 18 feet below the water line, a man stands the same chance on the lower deck as on the upper deck. If there is not time to dress, there is not time to put out the boats, and it is just as warm in the ocean in a pair of pyjamas, as with several sweaters and an overcoat, and much safer too. If he has ten minutes he can dress and put on his life preserver, and be ready almost as soon as the person already dressed. If I was born to drive an ambulance in France I wasn't born to be drowned on the St. Louis. This idea of sleeping dressed in the upper decks is all 'bunk'. People need their sleep; destiny will take care of them. I never dreamed that so many people would act so foolish, but I suppose they start each other.

This morning at about 4 we sighted an American T.B. Destroyer. About 9, so I am told (I was asleep), we passed an open lifeboat from a victim of the submarines. No one was in it, and the name could not be read. About 10.30 [four lines washed out by censor] we could see the mainland. Liverpool is now about 30 miles off, and we will get in late tonight if they don't get us first.

Smith and I are going to go to London by train. He is awfully kind in his offer to show me the city. I will get to Paris as soon as I can, and by the time you GOT my telegram, I hope you ceased worrying. I only wish you are all right and I could know it. FLAG IS SAFE. Goodbye for a while. Lovingly, Cliff.

11

ENGLAND

The next letter, during his penultimate day at sea, was the last Clifford would write home from on board the *St Louis*. He wanted to continue these recollections at a future time, and write other notes and cards to friends before he disembarked, but he was keen to finish this memoir for now. He wanted to package and address the correspondence properly so that he could get rid of the letters as soon as the boat docked – he trusted safely – in Liverpool.

He was anxious to send them off to his family back home, so they could continue typing them up and preserve what he hoped would form a complete journal of his wartime experiences. But in terms of this journal, the next contribution was one which the censor reviewing it did not seem to feel completely comfortable with, to judge from the number of excisions he or she made in the text:

Tuesday, May 22nd, I P.M.

Dear John, George and Mother,

The announcements that I made in my first four pages were not the official returns. Lieut. Schuyler was wrong about our [two lines out] that throws our schedule back eight or nine hours. But, good news, we are safe. About I I A.M. we sighted several trawlers off the Irish coast which is constantly in sight. It is a bold rocky coast with many little Gibraltars, covered with lighthouses. No one on board knows [four lines out]. Little later on we sighted an English freighter about 3500 tons. As we drew abreast of her we hoisted our colors and she did likewise. The Stars and Stripes, absent for days, now fly at our rear halyards on a gaff. Whether this British boat is a patrol boat (we passed quite close and did not see any guns) or an ordinary freighter, is more than I can say. But best of all we sighted two T.B. Destroyers, AMERICANS, flying our colors. One of these is escorting or convoying us in, so we feel absolutely safe. Of course you know there are many U.S. boats over here now, relieving the English of patrolling and convoying duties. I don't think the censor will mind if I say that one of them is the [here washed out] and the other [here washed out]. Know in America that both those boats are here. As the first Destroyer came abreast of the St. Louis, the passengers on board the latter gave rousing cheers. Signals which few understood were exchanged from the bridges. The destroyers looked awfully pretty as they cut through the waves, rolling and pitching gracefully and more than one would expect considering how smooth the ocean is at present. I can see the second one now as I write; again she sprints out of sight.

We are now about at the spot where the Lusitania went down, but she was unarmed and unconvoyed. If all goes well, as it undoubtedly will, we shall arrive in Liverpool early tomorrow morning or very late tonight. The first 'Land Ho' sent a thrill through me. I have already mentioned passing an empty lifeboat early this morning, also considerable wreckage, etc., some life preservers were seen and two or three bodies were spotted from the bridge. Some poor victims of the German U-boats.

The bugle blew for dinner 20 minutes ago, and I must eat. Do you remember that cartoon in the San Francisco Examiner, of the sower, with the California bear trotting along beside him, saying 'a man must eat'? After dinner I am going to write several letters and quite a few cards, besides walking around a bit. Au revoir at present. I don't know any more French than when I started. Love to all, Cliff.

When he next took up his pen to write home it would be from Paris the following weekend. Five days had passed in the interim, during which time the *St Louis* had successfully navigated the submarine belt around British shores and docked safely in Liverpool. Clifford and his fellow passengers were happy and relieved to have made land and bade the ship's crew a grateful farewell, clambering down from the ship to reclaim items of luggage being piled on the quayside.

This, one of the first voyages of the *St Louis* in its new guise, had been a happily uneventful one for Clifford and his cohort, in spite of the dangers lurking around and beneath them. But in the months ahead – and even before being taken into official military service by the Cruiser and Transport Force – the ship was to have many more nerve-racking journeys and encounters. A near miss with a sea mine in December 1917 destroyed a nearby, accompanying pilot vessel just off Liverpool. Two other close shaves before then, in July, saw a torpedo fired at the ship which somehow missed and a gun battle with a nearby surfaced German submarine; and a month later, a curious incident when the *St Louis* had an apparently unwitting collision with another U-boat, scraping against the latter's conning tower and removing some 18ft of the protective rubbing strake covering the vessel's keel.[15]

Once disembarked, Clifford resolved to see a little of Liverpool before he and other fellow passengers had to catch their train down to London. He wanted to make the most of his time in England. He was fascinated by what he saw both in Liverpool and on his journey: the expanse of the Mersey and the sprawling docks; the sight and sound of so many and varied people from across the world; the 'beautiful country' the train passed through; but then, finally, by the obvious privations of wartime London. The latter were the first tangible glimpses Clifford had had of the effects of war, still far as he was from the front-line trenches.

After two days in London he was on the move again, to France and the headquarters in Paris of the American Ambulance Field Service. It would be his stopping-off point before travelling to the front to present his precious cargo – the flag – to the 1st Stanford Unit of the American Ambulance. It was from a desk at the AFS offices in the Rue Raynouard that he recommenced his journal, looking back on what he had seen and experienced in the preceding week, beginning with the last days at sea:

May 27th, 1917, rue Reynouard 21, Paris,
Care American Field Ser.

Dear Mother, John and George,
I am awfully sorry to say that hereafter I do not see how I shall be able to write more than one or possibly two letters a week. However, I will take notes from day to day, and my letters, although arriving less often, will not lack anything in the way of news. Of course you want to know how and when I got into Paris, but you will have to read the letter from the beginning, and save the 'finale' till the end, and where it naturally belongs.
Tuesday night was the most trying of the whole trip. We were in the most danger- ous part of the Irish Sea, and in spite of being convoyed by one U.S. Destroyer No. 54, everybody was nervous. I went to bed and undressed as usual, but not without some misgivings. Before turning in I tied and roped my trunk, packed my bag and

got ready for the morning. The steward had been very nice so I handed him a $3 tip, which was nothing extra, I confess. Although I got into bed at 11.30 I did not get to sleep until after 1, for nervous women were making so much noise assuring and reassuring each other that we would soon be in port, that sleep was impossible, until I was nearly exhausted. I slept soundly, because the ship was rolling very little and was quite steady, but by five o'clock people were making too much noise packing their trunks, etc. (which they did all night).

After walking around several times on deck, Smith and I sat down. We were over the bar and up the estuary, but the bowtender informed me that not a man on the ship was in or over the bar. It was impossible to see land although we were very near, because of a low thick mist. All was safe, though, for the gunners were chatting with the passengers and no one was on the watch for submarines. The little gun captain was pacing the deck, receiving the congratulations of the passengers. He was tired out, for he had been on the bridge without rest for 50 hours.

The Estuary was smooth as glass with hardly a ripple. Not a person was absent from breakfast and all enjoyed a hearty meal. I figured that ten shillings was all I could slip the steward, but that seemed to please him. Smith went $5 on all his important tips. We met the deck steward on the stairs, and slipped him a dollar each. He was one of the nicest acting and cheerfulest men I have ever seen, a real gentleman.

About ten A.M. we got our first glimpse of land. Up to that time everybody had been cracking jokes about not being able to find England, is the little Island lost, or had the Germans blown it up with a shell? Of course there were lots of small boats on the Mersey, including fishing smacks with red sails, small steamers and trawlers, dredgers and lightships. The Channel, which is all the time being blocked by sand drifts and therefore must be constantly kept clean by dredgers, is well marked by all kinds of buoys and lightships. The lightships look very funny with their two masts and lighthouse in the middle. As you can imagine this was quite a novelty to me, and I still don't see the idea of building the tower like a lighthouse. Still, there are lots of things I don't see.

All through the morning we had been steaming very, very slowly, not more than 4 or 5 knots, but the Channel was narrow and irregular. A small steamer, flying the British Naval Reserve Flag, came near and lowered a boat. A man with a suit case came on board; he was not the pilot, I am sure, for our Captain took us in. I think he must have been some kind of immigration official, come to examine the privates who were third class. And, by the way, they were a bunch of fellows that deserved to go first class, College men, etc.

Seeing the British flag with the blue field aroused my curiosity. This was what I learned: the flag is called the Union Jack for the union of England, Ireland, Scotland

and Wales. When mounted on a red field, it stands for the merchant marine, and is the flag generally taken as the British flag. On a blue field it means the Naval Reserve and is flown by pilot boats and patrol boats. On a white field it is the flag of the actual navy as such, flown by torpedo boats, battleships and all ships of the line.

Liverpool and the towns around it would be united if they were in America, and called by some one name, but the English are great at keeping the old names. The right bank of the Mersey going up, is residential, while most of the business is carried on in Liverpool. It presents a beautiful front to the traveller up the river. Fine red brick houses with blue slate roofs, all built to conform with each other, and following one general artistic scheme, line the river for several miles. In front of them is a fine drive and then a magnificent beach. The whole is unmarred by railroads or any general traffic. The roofs of the houses are nearly all peaked and each house has several very high and large chimneys. Few of the houses were more that 3 or 4 stories high. Just below this residential district was a fine Light-tower, several hundred feet high and artistically proportioned. As I remember it was in a fine large park. The red and blue colors of the houses blend nicely with the rich and verdant greens and give the whole a very pleasing effect. Above this district to the East was the town hall, a fine building, very beautiful, and surrounded by magnificent lawns and now used as a hospital. One of the most striking things the visitor notices is the fine lawns and magnificent hedges, which are so lacking in America. Believe me, the whole South bank of the Mersey presents a beautiful sight, and unmarred by any act of man. The only billboard that I saw there was one big one, saying SPRATT'S DOG BISCUIT and it was a real blight to the otherwise fine effect.

Turning to the left or Northern bank, we could see all kinds of shipping; docks and funnels and masts, derricks and cargoes. Liverpool does a tremendous lot of shipping, and she looks pretty well prepared for it. A thing that a New Yorker or San Francisco man immediately notices is the small, inferior ferryboats. To me they were a joke, as a good many more things are, but then England does not want our heavy fine equipment. George probably remembers the big Liverpool landing station, which is huge floating dock. As we drew up to the dock we saw lots of soldiers, and gallantly clothed officers; some Highlanders were there, Hindoos, Irish, Welsh &c. who presented quite an interesting appearance.

It was then that we heard some very discouraging news: we were told that Col. Roosevelt was not to be allowed to bring over his contingent, and that he had gracefully withdrawn; but that Pershing, who took six months to run over Mexico for Villa, and then couldn't catch him, was to come over right away with 40,000 regulars. Of course, the fact that America was going to come now pleased us, but why couldn't

Teddy have come too. We also heard that two nurses had been killed on board the Mongolia, which left New York a few days after we sailed. They were on deck during target practice, and a gun exploded. They should have been below; our Captain kept us below and the Captain of the Mongolia should have done likewise.

We had to go thru an awful lot of red tape before they would let us off the boat. The Red Cross unit got off quickly, but they made us ordinary and special passengers all wait quite a while, while each one was questioned and examined. They gave us little numbers and as our number was called, we stepped to the front. I showed the plate on my flag and some letters and went right through; some of the others had to wait a long time. The customs officer simply opened my valise and glanced at it a moment; he asked me if I had any tobacco, and I said 'No' so he checked me off and I was free in England.

Once off, and on to English soil, Clifford took the first opportunity he could to post the letters he had written on the *St Louis*. He also sent a telegram home to Palo Alto to tell his family he had arrived safely. Then it was on to a bus with some of his fellow passengers to travel from the docks into the railway station at Lime Street. He saw this as an opportunity for a sightseeing tour and asked the driver if he could 'ride with him' before going up to sit on the top deck:

The streets of Liverpool are quite crooked and irregular. Like most of the streets in Europe they are cobbled, but the stones are so well fitted and placed that the surface is really quite smooth. There are many hills and the whole city has a rolling appearance. The buildings are all low, few more than three or four stories, have peaked or gabled roofs and are made almost entirely of stone. There seems to be very little life in the city, and business is very dull, due of course to the war. The persons one sees are mostly women, children, old men, wounded or crippled, and a few soldiers off on leave. Right now the main means of transportation are the cabs, hansoms, old taxis unfit for service at the front, and queer trolley cars. These latter are quite interesting; they are short and stubby with a queer shaped fender running entirely around them, four wheels, and a double deck. One thing I was glad to see was that there were no trolley wires, which are substituted by a third rail through a crack in the street, like New York. They look just about as clumsy as I have drawn them, maybe not quite so high. Liverpool has few very large buildings, but this class would include two which were really quite noticeable. One was St. George's Hall, which is the Court House. It is a striking and magnificent building. The other was the Leefer or Leever building.

How do you suppose Liverpool got its name? There used to be some birds in the vicinity called Leefers. They frequented a marsh or pool near the river; this was called Leefer's Pool. As the town grew this pool was filled in, and buildings erected over it. Gradually people came to call the vicinity first Leefer's Pool, then Leever Pool, and then Liverpool. The Leefer Building is right over this pool, or where it was. Isn't that interesting?

When I got to the station I started to look for my trunk but could not find it. It evidently had not yet arrived, so I decided to go to lunch, but the trunk was more important. After a lot of confusion and two hours of waiting and hunting, it turned up. Then got my ticket for London, and checked my trunk, and that left me about ten minutes for lunch.

I had lunch at a third class refreshment room. I sat at the same table with three English privates; they were only boys and weak ones at that; we would call them 'runts'. It shows to what England is reduced, and France and Germany, too, for as I saw later, I found it was quite typical. One was about the build of J.H. Smith but not half so strong; think of sending a fellow like that? to the trenches to do our fighting. The war can't last much longer when men like that are used on both sides, if the U.S. gets in a million huskies. When they get up to leave I wish them good luck. There was such a crowd on the ordinary train, as they call it, that I decided to take the Red Cross Special for the St. Louis Unit which was to leave a little late.

As I looked at the passengers get on the 2 P.M. train, I saw scenes which were really heart-rending. Many soldiers were getting on the train to go back to the trenches after a leave of absence, and their mothers, sisters and sweethearts were saying goodbye to them. The men tried to be brave and not show their emotion, but the women were one and all without exception breaking down and weeping. It was a genuinely sad sight. Not a family in England that has not been robbed of someone. In France the soldiers talk little to their wives and sweethearts. There is no more saddening thing than to see a 'poilu', a married man with a family, enter the station with his wife and womenfolk and children and, his pack on his back, take a seat at a table, sitting sidewise, so he can get in the chair, and silently look at his loved ones. The whistle blows and he takes a last long lingering kiss, another look and silently gets on the train. His wife stands by motionless and expressionless until the train pulls out, and not until then does she break down and cry. Few men can stand by and watch a scene like this unmoved.*

---

* Clifford had apparently just witnessed such scenes involving French *poilu* soldiers and their families in some of the stations he passed through on the way to Paris. He had only been in France for forty-eight hours when he wrote this, but was already commenting on it as if it were a sight he was familiar with.

*It was 2.05. Our engine blew its whistle, and I hopped on board. I had a compart-
ment all to myself practically all the way to London 4 ½ hours, and I thoroughly
enjoyed myself. At first there were a couple of doctors in the compartment but
they soon moved to another one to smoke. Believe me, it was a most fascinating
ride. Two things were most striking and caught my attention. First practically all the
buildings were of red brick, with steep gable roofs covered with tile or slate. Second,
everything was rich green and the fields were marked off and bordered by hedges.
THE REAL THING. There were lots of trees spread over the country which was
rolling and anything but monotonous. The train passed several canals. Occasionally
we saw a canal barge pulled by a horse. Do you remember the little tow paths? The
bridges are all well built and very artistic. Sometimes we could see thatched barns
which were really quite quaint in their surroundings. The country through which we
passed was mostly given over to grazing, and there were lots of sheep and cattle
grazing. All were plump and well fed, the wool on the sheep being especially long.
Oh, how I want to cycle over that beautiful country, and I hope John or George
or both can be with me, when I do it after the war. In the meantime, George, you
can do nothing better than to go on with your College work. I am looking out for
an opportunity for you over here, and believe that I can find it for you right in our
office 21 rue Reynouard. As soon as I know, maybe in several weeks, I will write
you or even telegraph you.*

*About 3.30 we passed a beautiful green on our right; on it some boys were play-
ing cricket. It was a 'master's' game, and they all looked very pretty in their white
clothes. We passed by so quickly though, that I couldn't watch much of the game.
I saw one ball bowled.*

*The usual English or Continental train has disconnected compartments, but
the Special was called an American Special, and it was possible to walk from one
end to the other by opening about a thousand doors. There were an awful lot of
doors to open, and besides they were low. The English trains are awfully light and
have a great deal of waste room. The passenger cars have four, and the big ones
six wheels, the wheels are light and almost toyish in appearance. The freight cars
have four wheels and are very short and light; the whole system seems to me like
a miniature railway. They call them railways, not railroads. The engines are equally
light and funny, they are just like the toys you buy, and have no cow-catchers, but
a sort of hook fastened in front of the forward wheels. The freight cars are very
light, and only about ten feet long. I saw a man pushing one with one hand, no
exaggeration, either, left hand at that. The bumpers are very funny, too, and almost
ludicrous. You know how heavy the American bumpers are; the English are a little
out of proportion.*

The first stop of this London and Northwestern Railway Special was at Rugby. We passed the ordinary train at an earlier hour and reached Rugby at 4.30. It was quite an imposing station, a long track approach and quite an engine shelter and boiler house. All the buildings were of brick. The school was far to the right and impossible to see. I saw no castles up to five o'clock and I am not sure I saw one then. One thing I don't like about European or English trains, is that one can't open the window at all because of the tremendous amount of soot. Oil burners are the thing, but they have no oil here to speak of.

I saw several picturesque old manor houses with their courtyards and their hedges. Incidentally, while I was in Liverpool, I saw three soldiers walking together, each with a leg off and on crutches. That is just a sample of what the war has done all over. England and France feel the war and are near exhaustion; but what must Germany be.

The train pulled into London at 6.20. P.M. I strolled around until 6.45 waiting for the ordinary train in order to meet Smith again and say goodbye to him. I will not write of all I saw or took note of, because I know you are tired already. When the train arrived I met Mr. and Mrs. Smith who were waiting for Norman. I also said goodbye to Schuyler, Murphy, Miss Mutton, etc., and Miss Lillian Gish and her mother. You know Lillian Gish is the Movie actress that starred in Intolerance. Looking at her no one would think she was a very successful Movie girl.

I had an awfully hard time getting accommodations in London. Nearly every hotel was filled with relatives of wounded and regular patrons. After going to the Regent Royal Palace and several others, I finally located at the Norfolk. 7 & 6. It is situated half a block from the Thames, and I took several strolls long the waterfront in the short time I was there.

Every foreigner who visits England in time of war is supposed to register with the police. I spent a lot of time hunting up the police station after I arrived, but when I finally found it the registration office was closed. I had supper at a small restaurant. Our bill of fare was the following: 'Public meals order, 1917. No meal can be served which exceeds in cost 1/3'. 30c isn't much, nor do you get very much in the line of eats.

I took a walk around the Strand and neighbouring streets. Everything was dark and quiet. Only a few street lights were burning, and they were dimmed from above by sticking on a big shade. There were a great many soldiers on leave, walking up and down the streets. The queeners were numerous; maybe many were lovers, but the biggest bunch were bums. Before leaving London I learned to distinguish many soldiers by their uniforms and hats. The men wear colored pieces of cloth to mark the regiment from which they come.

Late Wed. night I went down to Charing Cross Station and saw some wounded arrive. There was quite a crowd and they were cheered heartily. Then an ambulance brought out the badly wounded the crowds no longer made noise for fear of disturbing the men, but quietly waved, and the game soldiers smiled and made feeble efforts to wave back. London is a regular morgue; dark and quiet at night, it is almost gloomy; in the day it is quiet and dead.

Thursday morning I went to the French Embassy, presented my letters – I had one from the French Ambassador and Con. Gen. of New York – argued my case and insisted that I could not wait the three days that they wanted me to. The Embassy was very nice, and secured me passage on a troop ship from Folkestone to Boulogne, a most rare privilege for a civilian.

While in London I bought some maps of the war zone, and will send you duplicates; they are excellent. I took the 2.55 for Folkestone and on the way saw some beautiful English homes and mansions. I will not describe my trip in detail, for it would take too long and might bore you.

I crossed the Channel in one of the six troop ships, and chatted with veterans all the way over. The morale of the British troops is excellent. A regiment of Scotch sang and laughed and joked as they double-timed down the quay. One cannot help admiring them for their cheerful attitude. Surely these men must realize the gravity of the situation and the danger with which they enter the trenches. They were home on leave and have ten days off in twelve months; most of them go home to see their folks.

We were convoyed across the Channel by destroyers and aeroplanes. Mind you now few persons other than troops come the route I came which took I hour and 15 minutes. Most civilians go via Southampton and Dieppe and spend 6½ hours on the boat.

When I got to France I had quite a time to make my way and get my transportation to Paris for nothing. One of the English officers helped me out; he took me to a French official and put me through in fine shape. Just as the train was about to start, a French Red Cross private came up to me and asked if I had had any dinner? I had not, so he gave me 2 sandwiches and a bottle of water which he had planned to eat in the middle of the night. Wasn't it kind of him? I had some night ride to Paris. Left Boulogne at 9 P.M. and got in at 5.45 A.M., and there was no sleeping car service; got about one half hours sleep; Frenchmen in the compartment laughed and talked and drank and snored all the way over. I was mighty glad when I finally reached Paris, and, believe me, I was just about all in.

I will describe our headquarters later on, as I will be in the office six weeks waiting for the 2nd Stanford Unit. I am to be in the office to register the California men when they come. That will be great after that New York affair. My uniform will be finished Wed. 11 A.M. and I will leave for the front almost immediately after that with Mr. Andrew [A. Piatt Andrew, the founder of the American Ambulance], to present the flag to the 1st Unit. Because of war conditions they of course cannot come in, and could only send representatives after many days' delay. We feel that they should not have to wait for the flag. But at any rate I have practically delivered the flag in spite of U.C. and I will forget the incident when they arrive.

I am fairly well quartered, and am absolutely well and happy, but would certainly like to hear from you and know if Mother got back from New York safely. I will do my very best for George and the chances are I can land him a job out here. At any rate, here's hoping. And go easy on the Estate. Don't spend too much or A–A– will sell some more real estate and lose a lot, and please write often.

12

PARIS

Clifford and his cohort were of course only the latest in a growing line of young Americans who had come to France to serve; young men drawn in by a 'righteous' cause or spurred by a sense of duty and attracted by the idea of action and excitement. Volunteers had fetched up in Paris offering their services in one form or another, in ones and twos, and then on a more organised basis to hospitals and military offices from August 1914 onwards, often as *ambulanciers*.

One of the first major encounters of the war, the first Battle of the Marne in September 1914, had acted as an early recruiting sergeant for these young men, but just as important was the work of the American Embassy in Paris and that of the expatriate American community there. The latter's was a careful balancing act, especially in those first months of the war. The embassy attempted both to maintain the neutrality adopted by its government and to put in place institutions which would prove of longer term worth to its French hosts. In this, the work of the US Ambassador at the time, Myron Herrick, is worth some scrutiny.

At the time war broke out in early August of 1914, Herrick, a Republican, was actually preparing to leave Paris, to be replaced as ambassador by William Sharp, a man more in tune with the sensibilities of the Democrat president back in Washington. But war altered those plans, at least for a period of months. Cables went back and forth between Paris and Washington in early August. It was agreed that Herrick would stay for the time being, to try to guide his office and successor through some uncharted waters, and to set about establishing some of the parameters of the non-aligned stance America was to take on the ground.

His responsibilities increased in the first days of September when the Government of France, its capital threatened, opted to relocate temporarily to Bordeaux. With the government went a large number of the foreign diplomatic missions accredited to it. But Herrick, with the blessing of French Prime Minister Raymond Poincaré, opted to remain in Paris to protect not only US interests and citizens but also to act as an honest broker in everything from representing the interests of German and Austro-Hungarian prisoners of war or civilians interned in France, to protecting Parisian monuments and museums.

As other diplomatic missions in the city remained boarded up through the autumn, the US Embassy became a focus of activity, official and unofficial, as partnerships developed to provide financial relief and medical aid to those in France affected by the war. One of these initiatives came in the form of the American Ambulance Hospital in Neuilly in the western suburbs of Paris, which opened its doors on 9 August 1914. This was a private initiative funded and staffed by US volunteers, established ostensibly to treat wounded soldiers from both sides of the conflict. It was accepted in this capacity by the French Government as an independent military hospital, although it would go on in its later development to play a more directly supportive role in the French war effort.[16]

Herrick's wife Carolyn, President of American Ambulance's Women's Committee, had an early and influential role helping the new hospital find its feet. She used her friendships with French and American women to raise funds and garner volunteers. Aided by other embassy spouses like Ellie Sherman Thackara (daughter of celebrated Union general William T. Sherman in the American Civil War), Mildred Barnes Bliss and by Frederica Berwind Harjes, who was married to the banking magnate Herman Harjes, and with the support of the American Chamber of Commerce in Paris, the operation got underway, with young recruits found to staff it and a number of other relief efforts.

Some of the volunteers who came to Paris had ties of family or friendship with France or Britain and others had found themselves in Europe at the beginning of the war, interrupted in their 'grand tour' of the continent. Many had Ivy League or other established college backgrounds, but whatever those backgrounds or motivation, they began, through the tail-end of 1914 into 1915, to find their way to the capital and to form into distinctive new ambulance groupings.

The first two of these units was the Harjes Formation – named after the senior partner of the Morgan Harjes Bank in Paris – and the second, Richard Norton's Anglo-American Corps. These developed separately and worked as distinct units for over a year before eventually merging under the banner of the American Red Cross. But it was a third ambulance grouping that grew out of the American Military Hospital and would grow into the largest and best organised. This American Ambulance Field Service, as it became known, was in large part the work of Abram Piatt Andrew, someone who Clifford was to encounter in his early days in France.

Piatt Andrew had arrived in Paris at the turn of 1914–15, and like others before him joined as a volunteer. Yet his background was slightly different to the majority of those serving. To begin with, he was not in his early twenties but his early forties, and he already had a notable career in academia and public life behind him.

A first job had been as an assistant professor of economics at Harvard, a post he held for nine years; after this came stints as Director of the United States Mint and the Assistant Secretary of the Treasury in the Taft administration, after which a tilt at front-line politics in his own right. But, following a defeat in a congressional primary contest Andrew had contacted the president of the American Hospital's board, Robert Bacon, offering his services in Paris. Bacon accepted, albeit on the understanding – that is Andrew's understanding – that the only work on offer was whatever ambulance driving needed doing at the hospital. That was enough for Andrew. It was a fresh challenge and a way in.[17]

Within weeks of arriving in France Andrew had taken stock of the challenge. He was there to drive, certainly (that was, after all, what he had agreed with Bacon that he would do), and he had got down to the nitty-gritty of obtaining a driver's licence and getting out on shift. But the hospital, with a still-limited number of ambulances, had recently taken the first steps in sending some vehicles out into the field to serve smaller regional hospitals.

Andrew was a resourceful and politically savvy operator and he identified what he thought needed to happen next. It was a two-fold approach: firstly he would expand the service in terms of size and scope, in numbers of men and ambulances available; but secondly he wanted to address the issue of where these men would operate. He thought they should get closer to the front itself, offering immediate assistance from the battlefield, not busying themselves with the more humdrum business of ferrying less acute or more stable cases from railway stations to hospitals – the front line would hold more interest for his eager young volunteers.

For the first months of the war, French military policy was to keep any American volunteers away from the front, for them to do ambulance driving and relief work at a safe distance from the battlefield. The authorities' thinking appeared to have been governed by wariness about the possible motivation of these 'neutrals'. Could volunteers have divided loyalties, perhaps harbour pro-German sympathies, and prove a danger if left to wander freely near the front line and Allied troops?

Piatt Andrew thought otherwise, and set about persuading the French military that this was a risk worth taking. His American Ambulance organisation would recruit able and properly motivated volunteers and vouch for their good conduct. He persuaded them to offer his men a trial on the front line in the Alsace region, to test them closer to the fighting and working directly with French troops.[18]

It did the trick. The work was deemed a success and quickly led to the proper incorporation into French fighting units of these new, young *ambulanciers*. From April 1915 onwards American Ambulance and other Norton-Harjes/Red Cross units found themselves in a new, more advanced role. Their numbers swelled. By summer–autumn 1917 Norton-Harjes units had over 600 ambulance drivers and 300 ambulances and the American Ambulance could boast 1,220 ambulances spread out over thirty-one sections and supporting a total of sixty-six French divisions.[19]

Meanwhile, arriving as he did in late May 1917, Clifford settled into his new life and new surroundings, temporarily stationed in the American Ambulance headquarters in Paris:

21 rue Raynouard, Paris, France, May 28

Dear Mother, John and George,

I am beginning to learn the streets of Paris now, and can find my way about much more easily than before. I have a splendid book of maps and am making excellent use of it. I am also beginning to understand what people say when they talk in French, and to quickly choose words to answer them. This actually talking with French people makes the study of their language not only more interesting, but exceedingly enjoyable. I have an opportunity to learn, and believe me, I am going to take it. Wait till I get home.

Late yesterday afternoon I had a job thrust upon me which made me late to the second sitting of dinner. But I gladly accepted it, and have decided to do all I can in the office, outside, or otherwise, to aid and expedite the work for the Field Service, for I not only give myself good training and a desire to work that may make a good impression on my superiors which will possibly stand in my stead at some later date, but I help the cause of the ALLIES by doing my utmost.

The men are not paid, and some think for this reason that it is their duty to do as little work on the place or in the office as they can and then take the rest of the time off, and go down town or loaf. About 25 to 50 per cent of the men take a disgraceful attitude toward what they should do, but the rest are splendid fellows; then there are black sheep everywhere, and our bunch is no exception.

When I arrived there were near two hundred men; now there are about 100, the rest having left for the front as Ambulanciers or Camion drivers. You know the reputation Paris women have, and some of our men are their equals, sad to say. Men will be accosted on the boulevards and avenues at night, and will carry on disgracefully. Morals in Paris are very low, and the war makes them worse than ever. But on the whole, our men are a pretty good lot, with exceptions.

After I finished my late job (clerical work which was a rush order and had to be finished and forwarded to Bordeaux that very night) and had dinner or rather supper, I took a walk down to the river, and then northwest along its banks. I crossed from side to side as I reached the bridges, and got many views. Many soldiers were out walking and other people, too, as it was Sunday, a holiday, and I had a chance to observe them very closely. The average French private on leave in Paris is pretty poorly clad from the standpoint of looks. Of course his clothes are comfortable, warm and service-able, but they look as if the soldier had had a hard time. Black corduroy trousers or breeches, and a light blue-gray coat and cap, dark or blue puttees, and heavy black military boots, the whole not very tidy looking or attractive, constitute the uniform of the French 'poliu' it seems. Some veterans have the famous red breeches and cap which proved so fatal to many in the early part of the war. Few of the men look happy; they seem tired and careworn, dogged and yet melancholy, almost discouraged, as if they believed the war was never going to end. They need something to cheer up and stir up their pep. They should be supplanted by husky American troops and given a much needed rest. And they know that their poor families are practically starving for want of food and clothing, yet they cannot buy it for they are paid practically nothing. France is nearly exhausted. The U.S. has entered at the 11th hour. American troops and flags are needed to rehearten the French 'poilus'.

As it was getting late, about nine o'clock, I decided to return by the river steam-boat, built very low in the water. When loaded heavily they look as if they would swamp, and would, if there were waves as high as a foot. They have two decks and are very novel looking. Their smoke-stacks just miss the bridges by a few inches.

I got off at the Passey landing, the nearest stop in our locality, and then strolled along thru the Trocadero park grounds. (You may begin to wonder how long it stays light in Europe: in the first place clocks are set ahead an hour here for daylight saving, but it seldom gets dark until 10.30 by our time. We get up at 7 our time, 6 yours, and retire about 11 ours, 10 yours.) The park is very pretty and quite restful for persons wanting a quiet stroll or a place to sit down. I kept going till I came to the Trocadero proper, which stands on a high hill right across the river from the Eiffel tower, and has a magnificent view. The door was open so I went through and out into the balcony. I had a fine bird's eye view of the prettiest part of the Seine, the Eiffel Tower, Les Invalides, Notre Dame, etc., etc. A French woman came out. She had charge of the Buffet, and pointed out the important and interesting places. She didn't understand a word of English, so I had to use my French. She was about 55 years old, but in spite of her age she was very quick to 'savez' my poor French. But that is the way for me to learn, and I talk with everybody I can.

But Paris is a great old city, and there are many wonderful sights and buildings. I am going to sketch a lot of these and send them to you first chance I get. I will have about six weeks in Paris, so, take it from me, I will know Paris well, and hope to speak French passably.

How are things coming on in Palo Alto? I am awfully anxious to know. I suppose in a month or so many of our boys will join the army as conscripts. It is horrible, but if you could see the results of the German atrocities over here, you would be glad that at last the U.S. has awakened to the need of fighting for the rights of humanity. We ambulance men have been having quite an argument over who started the war, how it will end, and why the U.S. entered it. All hot air, of course.

I suppose John is now off on his agency. As regards our business etc., at home, I have so many really important things to think about here that I give it little attention. Being right in France is opening my eyes, and I am getting a life lesson. After I have served my six months in this service, I will probably enter the regular U.S. army, or air service. Write me what you think about it. The French have given the men here a chance to enter their service, and later on transfer to the U.S. service when our troops get on the line. The opportunity is wonderful and way ahead of the U.S. Aeroplane service. Several of the boys are going over to it. THINK OF THE GREAT TRAINING. Don't worry about me, though, I won't enter it right away, and probably not for several months. Write me what you think about it. I feel that I can do more than operate an ambulance; but I will not act now or right away; lots of time. The war will last several more years without any question.

You are of course interested to know what they give us to eat. Breakfast: coffee and French war bread in warm milk. Very filling and all we want of it. Dinner: some sort of boiled meat, all we can eat, often roast and sliced meat, potatoes and one other vegetable, and a custard, fruit or pudding dessert, and all the bread we want. Supper, soup, meat, vegetable and dessert. The ambulance service has a good water supply, so we get water, not wine or beer in Paris, unless we want to buy it. It is not served or kept in the quarters. And by the way, men must be in by 12 P.M. and a roll call is taken every morning. But we get all we want and can eat, and although not very elegant, it certainly is nourishing and filling. I am happy, well, contented, and industrious I hope.

I want to finish some typewriting for Mr. Ewell in the office early tomorrow morning, so I am going to go to bed. Love to you all and God bless you. Will look out for position for George. Have not yet seen persons to whom I have letters; too busy. Goodbye take care of yourselves and DON'T WORRY. We have a song as follows: (it is sung in the trenches and took the place of Tipperary).

*Pack all your troubles in your old kit bag
and smile, smile, smile.
While there's a Lucifer to light your fag
Smile boys, that's the style.
What's the use of worrying?
It never was worthwhile – so
Pack all your troubles in your old kit bag
And smile, smile, smile.*

This is a good song for John on his agency. It has an awfully catchy tune, too; that's just the chorus. Good luck and love to you all; please write often.
Lovingly, Cliff.

The Field Service headquarters was a constant hum of activity. Volunteers who had left for the front a few days before had been replaced by a new wave of men, including the contingent from Berkeley whom Clifford knew. They had docked in Bordeaux the previous day and travelled up to Paris by night train.

Now it was Clifford's turn to move on. On 1 June Piatt Andrew asked him to start for the front, to join the 1st Stanford Unit. He was to stay with them for perhaps six weeks, until his 2nd Unit arrived, but it meant an early opportunity for him to present the flag. Excited, he gathered his belongings in his trunk and set off for the Gare de l'Est to catch his train.

The first flag reaches France. Clifford Kimber joins the 1st Stanford Unit of the American Ambulance, SSU 14. (Kimber Literary Estate)

Somewhere in France
June 3rd, 1917

Dear Mother, John and George,
   I am with the 1st Stanford Unit of the American Ambulance Field Service,
Number 14 in the service. I have been here one day, and am having a great time.
   I had quite an exciting time catching the train, but got it all right. I met a French
Red Cross Nurse on the way out to the front. She was very nice and helped me get
my bearings etc. She spoke English quite well. She said she had three brothers at
the front; she wrote her name in my address book; Mlle. de Soucy. Her family has a
house in Paris, and a Chateau in Normandy, where they go in the summer; but it is
now broken up, due to the war. Afterwards I expect to see her at her Chateau (don't
worry, she is over 30). I showed her the inscription on the Flag, and she seemed
quite happy to have the opportunity of riding in the same car.
   It seems awfully hard for me not to be able to mention places. Alan and Doc
Spears [Alan Nichols, his friend, and Spears had come out with the first unit]
came to the town where I got off the train, but missed me. I started to walk to the
little town where the section was located, about ten miles off. [This was probably
Ligny-en-Barrois.] *With four miles to go they overtook me and picked me up.*

'Our swimming pool' at Ligny. (Kimber Literary Estate)

A 55th Division cook feeds refugees and local people in the vicinity of
Mourmelon-le-Petit, June 1917. (Kimber Literary Estate)

Saturday we went after my baggage in an ambulance – lots of fun. (My letter must sound awful but I have anything but an inclination to write today.) Alan was awfully glad to see me, at least he appeared to be. He is certainly a fine fellow and I cannot say too much in praise of him. We have a fine bunch of men, good natured and good sports; the only objection I have is the language most of them use, but that is typically American. Of course they do not all let out blue streaks, but most of them do, lickity split.

Our section is now on repose, but we are expecting to move to the front any day. I am in a section of the country that is most beautiful. One would scarcely think that within a few miles the Germans have lost 800,000 men and have failed in their attacks. It is an awfully hard fought section, and has been for three years. I wish I could tell you where we are, but I can't. The boys all go swimming in a neighbouring canal, which was started by Napoleon. It is great. The locks make a regular swimming pool about 20 feet deep, 10 feet wide and 150 feet long; lots of fun.

Our food is well cooked and plenteous. We are comfortable and warm at night; will send pictures of our quarters as soon as I can. The flag presentation has not yet taken place, but will in a day or so with all the military splendour that I could have hoped for. A French military band will play; companies of French soldiers will march, and I will hand the flag over to the French General in charge of the Division, after

First Communion, children in the village of Ligny-en-Barrois, June 1917. (Kimber Literary Estate)

making my speech, and he will present it to our Lieutenant, both making proper addresses. I will write you more about it when the ceremony comes off. I will also send you pictures.

This morning the girls and boys of the village in which we are located had a first communion in the cathedral. It was most attractive and spectacular, and we took several pictures of it and the children individually. There was a lot of mail for nearly every one this morning. Alan got John's letter, and let me read it. I wish I could write like that. Today I can't write a thing; I think the real reason is because there is so much to say and I don't know how to say it or where to begin.

I am trying to take notes of all I can, but there seems to be so much to do and see. Most of the fellows right now are sick of hanging around, wanting to go out to the front again; but it is new to me, and I am learning a lot, and having a wonderful time. Some of the boys are going to enter aviation, but I have definitely made up my mind not to consider it.

We are going in swimming pretty soon, and are going to have some races. Alan is a peach of a swimmer.

How do you like the aluminum selling, John? Wish I was out with you. As for your coming to France to do office work in Paris with Mr. Beatty or American Field Service, George, I should strongly advise you're not doing it, for I know you would be very disappointed. They can use you, but I know you wouldn't want to be used the way they will use you. Save your money; wait till after the war, and then come over to hike and canoe on the canals with me. I think Alan and Jack will be with us; but stick to College now, for it will pay you. Don't think, though, that I am not anxious to see you, for I am. Dear Mother, how are you? I do so want to hear from you, and now a long time has gone by. Write me often, Love to you all. (Our work is not dangerous as John thought, some of the boys are almost ashamed of doing so little and being so safe.)

13

THE FLAG PRESENTED

As Clifford had recorded in his previous letter, the ambulance unit he joined, and with it the 55th French Infantry Division to which it was attached, was then currently 'at ease' (*en repos*) in a quiet setting away from the front line, some 150 miles east of Paris. It was part of a pattern of rest and recuperation afforded the troops as often as circumstances permitted in between periods of duty. The 55th's Regulars had been through a lot in the previous three years, seen a lot of action, a lot of fierce fighting and bloodshed, their ranks decimated along the way. Veterans of the First Battle of the Marne and First Battle of the Aisne right at the beginning of the war in September 1914, the division had then fought through two campaigns in the Artois Sector the following year, before playing its part in 1916's battles around Verdun.

Now, after this brief period of rest in the early summer of 1917, the division would be moving to the Champagne area to occupy a sector east of Champagne's main city, Reims, recently the scene of fierce fighting. The Battle of the Hills, as it came to be known, had been waged over the previous two months to try to seize back an area of high ground, the Moronvilliers Massif, stretching between Reims eastwards towards the Suippe River and north of the main road (the present day D61) leading out between Reims and Verdun.

The hills themselves – Mont Haut, Mont Cornillet, Mont Blond, Le Casque and Le Téton among them – reached skyward no more than 260m, yet they dominated the plain below, affording the Germans a crucial observation point and the opportunity of tactical superiority in the area. By late May, as a result of a concerted French offensive, most of the main objectives had been secured in recapturing the hills. It would now be the 55th Division's task to hold its section of the area for as long as it was there and to protect French lines against the sporadic bombardments and raids which were set to continue through the summer.

But for now, Monday, 4 June, this last day of rest before moving to the Champagne Front, a goodly number of the 55th's ranks had been assembled for a ceremony near the small village of Tréveray, not far from where the American Ambulance had been staying at Ligny-en-Barrois in the Meuse department, about 50 miles south of Verdun. The ceremony would finally see the handing over of the first official American flag to be flown on the front and Clifford, unsurprisingly, was in his element:

Somewhere in France, June 4th [Ligny-en-Barrois]
S.S.U.14– B.C.M.

Dear Mother, John and George,
    What a relief. The FLAG has been presented. The presentation came off today, and I am going to tell you all about it. Last night after dinner, Lieutenant Boudrey, in charge of our ambulance unit, informed me that the presentation would take place Monday morning at 9 o'clock (today).
    I had a general idea of what I was going to say, but not expecting that the presentation would come off until Wed. or Thurs. I was not completely ready. I didn't get to bed until after 11 P.M. for I was busy formatting what I was going to say. For three hours I sat in Alan's ambulance, and when I finally turned in I felt absolutely confident and happy.
    The General of the Division to which we are attached was not able to be present, for he had to go to the place that the Crown Prince has been so anxious to capture for the last three years, and where we are soon to follow. Colonel Collon was put in charge of the ceremony; two French regiments were to be present; and right now let me say that never before has such an honor as we received been conferred on any American force in France. Stanford is greatly honoured not only to carry the first official flag but to have had such a welcome from the French army.
    We got up at 6.20 this morning and started to get ready to go to Treveray where the presentation was to take place. Two men left early to go to other towns for the standards of French regiments on repose there. They also took to the meeting place the French color bearers and guards of honor.

Lt. Boudrey [Boudrez], Mr. [Peter] Fischoff who served as French–English interpreter and I in the staff car at 7.30 AM. We were driven by a splendid French army chauffeur who kept up a constant speed of 35 to 40 miles an hour around corners and through villages and past all kinds of vehicles and obstructions. It was thrilling the way we skimmed by wagons at that speed not missing them by more than an inch and all at that devilish speed. The complete ambulance unit crowded into five of the ambulances followed us but at a much less reckless speed. They were soon lost to view.

Our car arrived at Treveray about 8 o'clock. I met Colonel Collon and through Fischoff our interpreter I told him about what I expected to say and received directions as to just how I was to proceed. And when I got out on the field of review I was mighty glad to have received my instructions. The field of review was on the top of a high hill overlooking the valley and village, and with a wonderful view in all directions. As we approached we could see company after company of French soldiers manoeuvring into position. They all wore the steel helmets and had bayonets in place. Wait to see the pictures.

Clifford makes his speech, preparing to hand over the first flag. Alongside him, Colonel Collon, commandant of the 55th French Infantry Division. (Kimber Literary Estate)

130

First Collon reviewed the troops by riding up and down the lines in front of them. Then he took his place just in front and I marched with a French guard of honour to position. And the staff officers and guards took their places in our rear. Right in front were Alan Nichols, Doc Spears (to be official color bearer after presentation of the flag) and [Walter] Snook. S. and A.N. are now escorts to the colors. Behind them were the French flags and regimental standards with their guards of honour, and behind them the band. The Stanford boys lined up in back of them; to either side were the two regiments and the two mounted officers.

At a signal from the Colonel I started my speech. As far as I can remember it, it was as follows:

Colonel Collon, Lieutenant Boudrey; Members of the 1st Stanford Unit of the American Ambulance Field Service; Soldiers of the French Army and other persons present;

'A few days after war was declared between the United States and Germany, and the United States of America became one of the Allies of France in this great world struggle which we all are now witnessing, this flag was dedicated in California to be carried in France as the official standard of the 1st Stanford Unit of the American Ambulance Field Service and was presented to the Second Stanford Unit to be carried to the men already serving at the French front. These dedicatory services took place April 24th 1917, in San Francisco's new civic auditorium with more than 14,000 persons present. It is the first American flag to be carried in service at the French front and was officially sanctioned by the United States Government.

'The Stanford men in whom this valuable confidence was placed felt it to be their duty to get the flag to the men at the front with the least possible delay and yet utmost surety. They tried to make arrangements to send the flag on ahead but they were met with disappointment. Finally rather than wait several months they selected me to bear the flag to France and I assure you I deeply appreciated the honour bestowed upon me. I believe it is altogether fitting and proper upon this occasion for me to read you two letters which I was given upon leaving Palo Alto, April 28th 1917. (The letters from the Secy of War and the Stanford Unit number 2 were read.)

'My instructions were to bring the flag as quickly as I could and that I have done to the best of my ability. You all know the history of this flag, how it was dedicated and blessed in California; how it led a parade in New York down Fifth Avenue before thousands of persons and how it was saluted and cheered by that vast multitude; how an attempt to capture it was frustrated; how it reposed in the chancel of Old Trinity Church New York and was there seen and prayed for by hundreds; and how it was carried to England on its way to France.

Colour party of 1st Stanford Unit, SSU 14, prepares to accept the flag. (Kimber Literary Estate)

The flag is handed over. (Kimber Literary Estate)

'Mr. A. Piatt Andrew was unable to make arrangements for a public presentation in Paris as the organization known as the Friends of France had hoped, and he told me when I left that great city that he keenly regretted the fact that he would be unable to be here at its presentation today.

'Fellow countrymen, I feel greatly honoured to have been selected to carry this flag to you, and I assure you that it is with a very deep feeling of pride and relief that I complete my mission and hand the flag over to Colonel Collon who will present it.

'My Colonel here is the flag.'

My speech went off without a hitch; it was not memorized. I knew what I wanted to say and I felt what I said. You will be surprised that I did not feel at all confused before all the thousands present. The occasion was so solemn and impressive that I thought only of what I was saying and not how I appeared.

Immediately upon finishing my speech I handed the flag to Colonel Collon and he made a very eloquent address and presented the flag to Doc. Spears, now the official flag bearer. As the Colonel spoke in French it would be very hard for me to tell you what he said but I hope to get a translation of his speech and send it to you.

Then the band struck up The Star Spangled Banner, and ended with the chorus of the Marseillaise. (Before, while the troops were marching into position, they had played the Marseillaise.) One of the Stanford boys afterwards told me that the Stanford men were just on the verge of crying, and that tears came to his eyes during the ceremony, speeches, etc., but that when the band struck up our National Air right in back of them shivers went down his body (and other men said they felt the same).

Just stop and think. It is the first time in the history of the world that French fighting troops have turned out in such an impressive review in war times to be present at the official presentation of the 1st U.S. flag to be officially carried in France. It is the greatest honor that any American force has ever had in France and so far no American organization of any kind has had such an honor in this war. And just to think, that in five days the Croix de Guerre will be presented to the section and pinned upon this beautiful flag, for our unit has been cited for its splendid work and it has officially been announced that we have a Croix de Guerre coming: hasn't Stanford a right to be proud?

The whole presentation was GREAT. It was a fitting climax to all that had preceded, and the Croix de Guerre pinned on the FIRST UNITED STATES FLAG will be the finishing touch. Oh, how I wish you could have been present – I can never forget it; it was much more than I ever dared to expect; and to think I was one of the central figures – the only other speaker being the Colonel.

We are now back in camp at — [Ligny-en-Barrois]. Alan has just been talking to me, and he has told me something that makes me feel very glad. By a system of all the men sending their films to Paris for developing and printing, every picture taken is printed in an album and catalogued; then any man can order any picture by number in series. Over one hundred pictures were taken this morning, and out of them many must be excellent. I am going to order a lot, and a lot of other pictures of other things too.

By the way, the Mayor of the town near which the presentation took place, was there sketching the whole. He made an excellent drawing and is going to try to make me a copy; I am just dying to get it.

Well, I want to go in swimming now, so I will say goodbye temporarily, and if anything interesting happens before sending this letter, I will tack on a postscript. Good luck to you, John, in your agency; that was a fine letter you sent Alan, and I hope to get many like it while I am in Europe. Goodbye, George, and look forward to being with me after the war; and as for you, Mother —
What's the use of worrying?
It never was worthwhile
Pack all your troubles in your old grip bag
And smile, smile, smile.
Get the music to this on the victrola or piano, it's great. Remember me to all I should be remembered to. Alan sends his regards. Lovingly yours, Cliff.

Somewhere in France, S.S.U. No. 14
June 7th, 1917 (Thursday)

Dear Mother, John and George,

Greetings. Did not George say that I might finish by driving a staff car? Well, if he did he was right, for that is what I am doing. Our section has a new Ford touring car only two or three weeks in the service, and Lieutenant Boudrey has appointed me the driver of it. Lots of fun, too, when the section is moving in convoy as it did yesterday; the staff car darts in and out to the front from the rear, and vice versa, and you know how I enjoy that.

While at —— the town I went to first from Paris, I had the pleasure of seeing, first, my first glimpse of an aerial destroyed house of which I took several pictures; and second, the first action of anti-aircraft guns that I ever witnessed, and also of hearing the guns at the front. Alan and I took a walk and heard these latter from the top of a hill in back of the village.

Late Tuesday night (5 June) it was so hot that Alan, Doc Spears and I, who were out walking, decided to cool off by taking a swim in the canal. We returned to camp

Clifford Kimber with staff car, June 1917. (Kimber Literary Estate)

and were just on the point of leaving with our tights (8.30) when one of the boys came running to announce that Lieut. had just received orders to move to the front, and that we were to get ready that night and have a 4.45 A.M. breakfast next morning. You can imagine the excitement and rush. Orders were to take on enough gas to go 180 kilometres. Just to think that we are now within a few miles of one of France's most wonderful cathedrals, which is now in ruins.

It started to rain just before we left, and kept it up for about 25 miles. It was good, too, for it settled the dust. We had a great trip to —— [Mourmelon-le-Petit], where we are now located, and I enjoyed myself thoroughly in spite of the strain, because of the excitement and fun of driving my machine at racing speed with the Lieut. as passenger. He is a typical Frenchman, very changeable and excitable.

Just as we were sitting down to supper last night, there was a typical thunder and lightning storm. My, but it rained. After it lulled up a bit for a short time Alan and I and several others, moved our cots which had been placed in the open and had had full benefit of the rain, but had been somewhat protected by canvas and put them in a room that we were given. Believe me, we all slept well Wednesday night.

Yesterday, Wednesday morning, I was called at 6 A.M. for Lieutenant wanted me to drive the Medical Division in the Staff car. He kept on delaying and we did not get off until 9.30. We passed the French sausages (observation balloons anchored

135

to autos) advanced quite a ways beyond the French batteries, and right up to the advance poste for the ambulances. The Germans were right over the hill; recently the French forced them over the crest. I was surprised at the seeming inactivity; big guns and 75s were firing over our heads both ways, and we could hear the singing of the moving shells but none landed near us naturally enough. The two villages through which we passed were absolutely in ruins. I will send some pictures later on. German devastation is awful. I saw many interesting things, including trench systems, abris and barbed wire entanglements, it was all very interesting. I will take photos next time I go through; that is better than describing them.

I had to wait at one of the posts for the Medicine Divisionaire. We were just ahead of a concealed French battery of 75s and they barked away in a most commonplace and methodical manner. Bang — Bang — every 7 seconds, for three or four rounds, and then a lull of about a minute. They gave me a steel casque to wear out. It was quite heavy compared to the hats I am accustomed to. They look something like a policeman's hat.

Yesterday afternoon I cleaned up and washed my car and I have just put on the finishing touches this morning. I am quite proud of it. I just received your first two letters last night from Philadelphia and Pittsburgh. Was awfully glad to hear from you. I have dropped A- A- a card and that is all I expect to send her for quite a while.

I will keep your letters for future filing; as for my keeping a complete diary, I have no time. I am keeping notes of movements and places; as for events, anything worth keeping I am writing you about.

Last night we saw an aero duel between a French and a Boche; they were way off and dodged and dropped like birds. Finally they disappeared in the distance, and we were denied the finish. Love to you all, write to me. Cliff.

After thirty-six hours' service on the front. (Kimber Literary Estate)

The work that Clifford and his contemporaries were carrying out consisted mainly of three different types of duty: acting as *ambulanciers,* most commonly driving the ambulances; being *camion* (truck) drivers, ferrying equipment to and from the frontlines; and driving the staff car, something Clifford was now beginning to do. It was no longer what had been referred to in the early days of the war as simple 'jitney' duty, with volunteers moving the wounded between hospitals or from sanitary trains to hospitals. They were indeed operating in advanced, often dangerous, circumstances. Yet just as often their work was interspersed with long periods of inactivity.

A new lexicon was learned and used, with Clifford quickly slipping into it in his letters home. He and his colleagues might temporarily have to take cover on the front line in *abris* – shelters or dugouts – when a German bombardment began. They would evacuate *blessés* or *malades* – injured or sick – from the forward positions. Badly injured troops would have been given immediate, rudimentary treatment at a first-aid post in the trenches, but after that they would be brought by *brancardiers* (stretcher bearers) to the advanced dressing stations, ideally less than a mile from the front trenches. It was at these dressing stations, or *postes de secours,* where they would be met by the ambulance drivers and evacuated to a triage hospital, usually under an hour's drive away. The man in charge of the medical operation within the division was the *médecin divisionnaire* (or Med. Div.) who was often ferried by the men around the front for tours of inspection and driven to and from conferences.

These first few weeks of his time on the front come across in his letters as some kind of odd *Boy's Own* existence, as Clifford got used to the realities and privations of war, with its sudden bursts of shocking violence, while learning to amuse himself during the long periods of downtime. The harsh winter of 1916–17 had given way to a summer which was often hot and sunny and the American volunteers could find themselves swimming and relaxing or busying themselves with their hobbies not a million miles away from the fighting on the front.

That the work itself – when they were on duty – held its dangers, was obvious. But the other feature that the men now had to learn to contend with was the inevitable flip side: the routine and boredom of war when bullets and shells were not crashing down. This boredom was perhaps magnified because they were non-combatants at this stage, and it would not be long before Clifford and his colleagues would be dreaming of other theatres where they thought they might be more actively involved.

14

BEARING WITNESS

The boredom and routine that Clifford experienced, and to which he now began to refer in his letters, nonetheless failed to dampen his enthusiasm for recounting in detail what he saw around him when he wrote home. He was still excited by the rawness of what he saw: the machinery of war in action; the sight and sound of battlefield warfare; men operating in extreme circumstances.

At reserve post near Prosnes: Bill Losh and Clifford Kimber. (Kimber Literary Estate)

It was new and still thrilling for him in spite of its brutality. He was conscious of witnessing events that were strange, events from a different world to the one inhabited by his family back in California, and he wanted to record it for them. 'Movements and bombardments generally come at night', he told them, 'so thrills come at that time rather than during the day.' But in telling them his story, he not only wanted to capture what he saw in writing, but also in photography and sketches. The letters are riddled with references to drawings (most long lost) and photos which he used to explain or support events. After the presentation of the flag, a good many of these photographs and sketches now concerned planes and flying, a clue to where his interest was beginning to turn:

Somewhere in France, S.S.U. 14 [Mourmelon-le-Petit]
B.C.M. June 10th 1917

Dear Mother, John and George,

The poste de secours [Prosnes] that we serve is very much exposed being located about 50 feet from a crossroads that the Germans constantly shell. At night the Germans bombard the French roads a great deal in an attempt to stop the steady movement of troops, munitions and supplies. But such a location shows French efficiency and organization which is rotten and this is just a little example of which there are many. But because of the danger, only one ambulance advances to the poste at a time. The others stay a couple of miles to the rear on a somewhat sheltered road. Four ambulances to a shift.

Therefore as soon as Bill [Losh] and I arrived at this waiting place we stopped to wait for the ambulance at the advance poste to return with its wounded. There was a French 75c.m. anti-aircraft gun nearby and so to kill time we walked over to where it was. We sat down and watched with the soldiers for the appearance of a Boche avion. Way off and high over the advance lines three French machines were circling around and around just like hawks. Suddenly a German plane appeared near them and it looked as if the French were chasing it. Immediately all was bustle around our gun. The chief gunner sighted and looked at the Boche with a range finder. Two shots were fired and both missed, but they came awfully close. All four aeroplanes were so high and far away that it was very hard to see them. They soon disappeared in the clouds, the German evidently beating a very hasty retreat. That was all we saw. The anti-aircraft gun was mounted on an automobile truck which was raised off its wheels by means of jacks. This made it much firmer.

An *abri* and trench near Prosnes. (Kimber Literary Estate)

The entrance to a dugout. (Kimber Literary Estate)

An ammunition convoy passing through Livry. (Kimber Literary Estate)

About eight o'clock Pete Fischoff came out in his machine. He was carrying French war bread and pinard* out to the advance poste de secours. I thanked Bill for bringing me that far, jumped on Fischoff's car and started the last lap out.

We went thru a demolished village on the way. Enclosed is a picture of the ruined church. Note the torn-up and confused graveyard.

All along the road were little piles of French shells. You would be surprised and disgusted if you see the way they waste 37s and 75s. When they advance they do not even collect those that they have piled in readiness on the ground near the guns. They must think that shells are easier to make than to pick up; it is disgraceful.

When we reached the poste, Carl Randeau and several 'Brancardiers' and Red Cross men came out to talk with us. As the Germans had not yet started bombarding the poste and all was quiet, we stayed out of the abri for an hour or so until dark.

We wandered around what were the first French line trenches on the 14th of April. They are awfully desolate looking places. I would rather do anything than live in them, and least in the French trenches. They are bad enough now, and just think what they must have been like in the winter. I hope to have the opportunity of going

---

* The common term for the cheap red wine drunk by the troops on the front, which was watered down.

141

The destruction of an ammunition dump. (Kimber Literary Estate)

out again soon, and in the daytime when the light is good, so that I can take some pictures. There are hand grenades all around the trenches and the ground near them; the fellows seem horribly afraid of kicking them and sending them off, but I can't exactly see the danger of that. I am going to get some pictures of trenches and barbed wire entanglements later on, and will send some to you. The prints I send will be solar prints and will not look as nice as velox. Velox is too expensive here, and we have no facilities for printing with it ourselves. I don't want to risk any of the films; I will send you many sun prints though.

Some French aeroplanes kept circling above us to keep off the Boche avions and observe the enemies' lines. After a while it began to get really dark, and as it did so the Germans began shelling the cross roads, and believe me, our poste de secours gets its share. You may wonder when it gets dark here; the clocks are set an hour ahead and we are much farther north than you so we have light till ten or later. Well, we were mighty glad to get into the abri after those German shells started to come and burst our way. They make an awfully weird sound as they whistle and scream over your head, and when they burst — GOOD NIGHT.

We started back to — with three assis and one coucher [three wounded able to sit and one stretcher case], *who had arrived between 10 and 12.45. This trip back was quite exciting. When we got out of the shelter to crank the car, we found it covered with dirt and debris, an inch deep, that had been hurled up by exploding shells. The machine was not hit, and when we got back I was mighty glad, I assure you.*

All are standing around waiting for dinner. Alan has discovered the flageolet [a musical instrument, a type of recorder, which Clifford had brought with him] and is creating quite a stir; lots of fun. This evening (Sunday June 10) I am going to develop five films. Goodnight, Cliff

June 11, 1917

We developed the films and they came out fine. I have some quite rare pictures. Oh, how I wish I had taken pictures on the way over on the St Louis, etc. The first ones I took were after I left Paris, and now I regret it greatly.

After supper last night Alan and I took a walk for about two miles north of town. We passed an ammunition dump where there were thousands of 75s stacked up and later we came to the hangar of one of the French sausages or captive observation balloons. The soldiers in charge then explained everything to us. Later on we hope to get some pictures and maybe a flight. Don't let this worry you though, as the chances are very very slight.

An ammunition stack near Bouy. (Kimber Literary Estate)

Concealing a 'French sausage' (observation balloon). (Kimber Literary Estate)

The basket for a balloon, with SSU 14's Allan Muhr to the right. (Kimber Literary Estate)

A French observation balloon in the air. (Kimber Literary Estate)

Ambulance quarters at Mourmelon-le-Petit, sheltered by trees. (Kimber Literary Estate)

Little groups of men and horses are constantly passing us, either going to the front or returning. All the French seem so tired and even the horses reflect the weariness. When the poilu asks how long we think the war will last, we all say only a short time, for if we tell him the truth about it, he seems absolutely broken in spirit.

L'Illustration has just arrived, and has an excellent front page cut of the presentation of the flag. Alan shows up fine. Colonel Collon is seen handing it to Doc. Spears, our standard bearer. Snook, on the left, is cut off by the General's hand. The picture is very clear, and worth your getting. The three French flags show up fine too.

I don't feel much like writing letters; this 'do-nothing' life is getting on my nerves. When we are busy it is great, but we loaf so much while waiting to work. I ought to write to Myles, Sleeper, Rogers and Smith. How many sets of aluminum has John sold yet? How's the selling game?

Clifford was stationed with the American Ambulance in north-eastern France but was, because of censorship restrictions, careful to avoid using exact place names. Sometimes at the beginning of his letters he would simply record the name of his section or 'Somewhere in France' via the 'B.C.M.', *Bureau Central Militaire*, which organised postal delivery, and he began to refer to the towns in which they were operating by single initials.

The unit he had joined, the 1st Stanford, had been reclassified as Section 14 and served in the French Army as *Section Sanitaire États-Unis 14* (SSU 14). Before Clifford joined the unit it had spent three months split between an area further east near Verdun, which was then reasonably quiet, and the Toul Sector further to the south-east of Verdun. Now SSU 14 was stationed in the Champagne area south-east of Reims, near the village of Mourmelon-le-Petit. In due course, Clifford expected to rejoin his original 2nd Stanford Unit which by now had arrived in Paris. But in his letters home he was already looking ahead and discussing leaving the Ambulance Field Service entirely once his agreed volunteering stint of six months was up, with his interest in flying increasingly coming to the fore. In the letters he also wanted to discourage his brother George from following his lead, urging him to continue with his studies until such time as he might be called upon to fight and be enlisted in the regular US armed forces.

Although stationed near the front line and beginning to serve its wounded, Clifford was still a novice to the ways in which the war was being prosecuted. He was only beginning to scratch the surface of what was going on and was eager to learn more of what was happening across the battlefields. He wanted to find out as much as he could about the mores and practices of the soldier and airman involved in fighting, and what lay ahead in terms of the war's advance. Part of this involved keeping an ear to the ground and listening to the gossip: plugging in to the rumour mill, where news and opinion (fact and fiction) and propaganda were often tightly interwoven.

Clifford had difficulty in disentangling tall tales from reality, if the following account is anything to go by. What comes across in the letter is both his naivety and his readiness to fall back on rather unfortunate broad brush depictions of the nationalities involved in the war, their strengths and weaknesses:

Somewhere in France, June 13th 1917

After dinner we were all entertained by an American and member of the Foreign Legion. He was a young fellow, 19 years old; he ran away from home two years ago to see the war and the trenches, and now he says he has had enough. His eyes watered as he talked of his home in San Francisco, and at the mention of familiar San Francisco names. He told us a great deal about the war, and his stories were thrilling in the extreme. Of course he has the Croix de Guerre; practically all in the Foreign Legion have earned it.

He says the reason the F.L. fights so well is because of the race rivalry. Spaniards, Italians, Americans, Russians, etc., all claim to be the best fighters and so they try to prove their valour to their comrades. The French army uses the F.L. for starting an attack. Seldom are they in the trenches for more than 12 hours; they give no quarter and ask none. The Germans fear them above all their enemies. This man says when they start for an attack, they discard guns and coats, and make a rush with four sacks of hand grenades, long knives and revolvers. The grenades make a great deal of smoke and blind the enemy. They knife and shoot with their revolvers all in the way, and rush on trench after trench. They never turn back or hesitate, and every man in the F.L. tries to outdo his comrades. This young soldier says that the greatest trouble with the Frenchman is that he hesitates and turns back, or shudders when he uses the bayonet, and so does not stick hard enough, and that he is excitable and too easily rattled. The Spaniards and Italians are excellent at the start, but they weaken and tire. The Anglo-Saxons are best because of fearlessness and endurance.

You may be able to understand why the Germans fear the husky Colonials. It is said they won't fight the Australians, and that it takes two and sometimes three of them before they will stand against one Canadian. The French are too nervous; but look what they have been through. They deserve great credit, for they stopped the Germans.

I asked him why no quarter was given, and he said it was too much work, and it was a waste of time; besides, the more prisoners taken, the less food for the victorious soldiers to eat. He confirmed one rumour that we have been hearing of late; the Germans tie their machine gun operators to their weapons by means of chains; then they can't run back as the Allies advance; they know they will get no quarter and will be killed anyway, so they see how many men they can mow down before being killed. Doesn't all this seem awful? But the Germans started it. Of course in big attacks, when thousands of men are taken they are spared; but the soldiers are more and more getting in the habit of refusing to let the other side surrender, but kill them anyway.

After the Foreign Legion makes its advance, the French follow. They have a bunch of men called 'trench cleaners' who are armed with long knives. It is their duty to butcher every man they see, and throw grenades down the dugouts to kill the men taking refuge there. Believe me, unless sent ahead, I will be satisfied to visit the second line and abandoned trenches. Only to die like a rat in a trap is not one of my ambitions, and thank the Lord I don't have to.

Before this dare-devil soldier left, I gave him some armour, which I had secured to keep as a souvenir. He was awfully glad to get it, and said it would help him a lot. It covers the abdomen, thighs and privates, and is a big protection: made especially for certain French soldiers; mine had been picked up on the field. When he left we wished him good luck, but few of us envied him. He said 'We are going to V-, where we will start another attack; that means some more fun.'

Tuesday the 18th was a fine day, and I took the Medecin Divisionnaire out to a post near the front. While waiting for them, several officers and soldiers talked with me. I took their picture and will send them a copy. They were at the old French line trenches (1st) and showed me all over them. Very interesting. Took some pictures and also one of a group of soldiers at mess. They all seemed delighted. The stories of not taking any more prisoners than they had to (you can't kill a whole regiment) were confirmed. The other day nearly a hundred Germans surrendered in this section; they were immediately lined up and put out of trouble, so this officer told me, one said they had a little fun first when they took prisoners. They gave the Boche a good meal, made them feel pretty good and sing the Marsellaise, then they shot them. You must fight the enemy with his own weapons. Germans have been known to inoculate prisoners with tuberculosis bacilli, and to make English and French prisoners sleep next to lousy Russians. Officers are seldom executed, it is usually only the men. I don't know how much of this will get by the censor, but it just refers to German atrocities, and retaliations necessary and just.

Incidentally, one of the boys got a letter in which was enclosed a Times clipping saying that according to a letter I wrote to my brothers the U.C. men tried to get the flag in New York. The article sounded awful. Possibly I was entirely to blame, but please don't let anything I say in my letters get published at all unless I give permission, or you ALL (not one) really think it all right. I have changed, and I assure you I was thoroughly ashamed of that Times clipping. I have absolutely no desire for that kind of publicity. PLEASE TAKE NOTE.

Some of what Clifford recounted does make him appear a little credulous, although these were still early days and he would in time learn to view with more scepticism the varying stories and reports he would hear. But battlefield executions and executions of enemy prisoners of war have indeed been documented in the First World War, not least at the time of point of contact on the battlefield. In the heat of battle, prisoners were not taken who might otherwise have surrendered. Those gaining the upper hand in hand-to-hand combat might literally have 'taken no prisoners' in the course of an attack and clearance of enemy trenches. Professors

Joanna Bourke[20] and Niall Ferguson,[21] among others, have reflected upon the practice of enemy executions in varying guises, and there appears little doubt that summary executions did take place on the Western as well as the Eastern Front. But quite whether one should give credence to Clifford's report of nearly 100 prisoners being killed in one (seemingly casual) fell swoop remains a moot point. Either way, Clifford himself seemed to find it necessary to be clearer in what he was reporting when he next wrote home:

> *I will qualify what I said in my last letter about the warring armies not taking any more prisoners, but only in large lots. They do not bother with small groups or individuals. This from French officers in the regulars.*
>
> *Somewhere in France, June 16th, 1917*
>
> *Our friend, the Med. Div., during the night suddenly got a notion that he would like to go out and look over his postes in the early morning. Sergeant waked [Leslie Scott] Shipway who was to drive the camionette, a two-passenger Ford repair and general utility car, and me. We were cranked up, and on the way by 4.30 A.M. Mr. Muhr [Allan Muhr, Head of Section 14] went along with us and two of the Med. Div.'s aides. Cook was great and gave us some bread and jam and sardines and cold coffee for breakfast.*
>
> *That was some trip. The roads on which we travelled were constantly under German fire. I drove the Staff car just as fast as I dared, but every now and then it was necessary to slow down to avoid debris and shell holes in the road. It was the most exciting trip I have had yet, and thrilling is no word for it.*

Left: 'Our Médecin Divisionnaire'. (Kimber Literary Estate). Right: 'Bread for breakfast' – showing volunteers Shipway, Fox, Snook and Randau. (Kimber Literary Estate)

A '220' at Moscou.
(Kimber Literary Estate)

Clifford's ambulance
beside the damaged
church at Prosnes.
(Kimber Literary Estate)

We first stopped at M. [Moscou], where the Med. Div. examined the poste. The French batteries replying to the German fire were not more than 50 yards off (of course they were all along the line) and concealed in a dense wood. They would give loud barks, the reports echoing back and forth, and then we could hear the shell screaming into the distance. You can always hear the German shells approach, for they give a loud shriek, and you have plenty of time to drop on your stomach in a trench to avoid the éclat. Of course if the shell landed near enough to do any damage, it would not make any difference whether you were standing up or lying down sprawling on the ground.

Then we went to P. [Prosnes], that poste located near the crossroads. We waited a long time for the Med. Div. and aides, who ascended the hill to the French lines. Then they came back and we started on our last and most exciting lap. This was thru the village of P. and home.

Just as we left the poste C. [Constantine] the Germans began bombarding P. where are located some French batteries. The poor little village is all shot to pieces now. During the night it had suffered steady shelling and the roads were wretched. We were going full speed and bouncing like anything in the staff car, with Shipway and the camionette following as fast as they could travel. Just as we were about to enter the village, a big shell burst right in the center not more than a hundred yards ahead of us. It sent up a column of smoke and dirt at least a hundred feet and blotted everything from sight. To stop and turn was out of the question so we sped on ahead. The little staff car did nobly, and we skidded around the curve marked XX, and climbed up the hill the home side of P. without slowing down a bit. Mr Muhr said afterward he certainly thought we were going to turn over on that turn. Dust, shell holes and fallen trunks of trees all did their best to stop our progress, but to no avail.

When we got to the reserve poste we slowed down, for we felt comparatively safe. We looked around to see how Shipway was, but, good gracious, he wasn't even in sight. We waited a few minutes, and then Mr. Muhr jumped in, he had stepped out of the car, and sped back to the danger zone full speed. He refused to let us accompany him. My, but we were excited.

After a while Shipway came leisurely along with Mr. Muhr following in the staff car. He had broken two spark plugs in P., and had calmly gone up the long hill on low rather than stall his motor, for he knew he could never start it again if once he stopped. Then S. went home in his camionette, by home I mean camp, and the rest of us in the staff car visited several other postes in the direction of the arrows. We got home a little after 11, and mighty glad too.

That was some trip and one that was full of excitement. It is seldom that we get so many thrills in one day. They are rare and far between as a rule. The rest of the time it is just loaf, loaf, loaf. I got some good pictures on that trip, three films. In the afternoon I went to B. – [Bouy] six kil. away, to see the aero parc. This is a base for French aerial operatives. I got in with the mechaniciens by chatting in French. They introduced me to their lieutenant, and the captain is going to take me up in one of the planes tomorrow morning, between six and seven A.M. I don't know what type of plane I will mount the air in. There are Moranes, Dorands, Farmans, Nieuports, Sopwiths (English make) and Spads and Caudrons. Alan is going to go down to the parc with me and he may get a flight too. He will snap pictures of me in an avion. The cook is going to call us at 4.30 A.M.; it is an hour's walk. I will not send this letter till I land, and then I will add a second part, so you will know I am safe. Love to all of you, Cliff.

15

FIRST FLIGHT

Clifford wasn't a complete novice to flying, and his interest had not come from nowhere. While he was growing up – first in New York and then on the west coast – the Wright brothers and other early pioneers were experimenting with the new science of flight. The Wrights had made the first powered, sustained, controlled, heavier-than-air flights in December 1903. But they and other competitors worked over succeeding years to make the planes they flew more practical, capable of travelling greater distances and remaining in the air for longer and longer durations. The idea captured the imagination of Clifford and his father and brothers just as it fascinated a whole new generation in America and around the world.

The spring and summer of 1908 was an important time in the development of flight, as the Wrights' biographer Tom Crouch records in the Smithsonian Institution's National Air and Space Museum journal.[22] With contracts for the sale of aeroplanes to a French syndicate and the US Army lined up, the Wrights were test-flying their latest model in the Kill Devil Hills near Kitty Hawk, North Carolina. But others were also taking to the skies: Henry Farman flew his Voisin Farman I in a 1km circle to win the 50,000 franc Deutsche-Archdeacon prize; the Aerial Experiment Association, founded by Alexander Graham Bell, built and flew a series of three aircraft that spring and summer. It culminated in the flight of Glenn Hammond Curtiss in his biplane 'June Bug' at Hammondsport in upper New York State in July. But eventually the way was clear for the Wrights to make their first flight in public in August. It came in Europe, in France, when Wilbur Wright took his eponymous Wright Model A craft up over the Hunaudières Racecourse, south of Le Mans. It was a runaway, fly-away success and he followed it with scores of other flights across Europe in the next year, as he, later joined by Orville, wowed the crowds and the great and good in equal measure. The new masters of the skies became instant celebrities.

Among the enthusiasts in the crowds in France was a 12-year-old Clifford, who was on holiday with his brother John and father in Europe. The two boys had spent the school year of 1907–1908 in England, boarding at Kent College in Canterbury following a family holiday in the country. Their mother had lived nearby with young George, while their father returned to New York. But Reverend Kimber had come back in the late summer of 1908 to take the older boys on a short tour of continental Europe before their year was out; and it was in keeping with his love of mechanical contraptions and technology that he now took them to the Le Mans racecourse.

The demonstration, if it wowed the crowds in Europe, certainly made a lasting impression on Clifford. Within a few years, and following the sudden death of their father and the family's relocation to California, Clifford had taken to building his own gliders. Wright-style powered craft were still beyond him economically as well as technically but he was able to save enough in 1910 to build his own unpowered craft and take to the hills around Berkeley. He and his brothers and friends formed a little club and poured what money they earned into the materials needed to build the gliders.

His mother Clara, in a self-published memoir many years later, recalled Clifford's taking off in one especially large glider and flying it from Cragmont in the Berkeley Hills, and crashing further down the slopes. He was largely unscathed, if $10 the worse off. One local newspaper, the *San Francisco Call*, gave a breathless account of the incident where Clifford was said to have been 'hurled to the ground by the wind' and how his 'machine' had fallen on top of him amidst a 'mass of wreckage'. Other reports appear to have gone that little bit further, publishing erroneous and untimely accounts of his death.[23] But either way, the budding 14-year-old aviator had his attentions focused less on a supposedly near-death experience and more on better plane design. 'Young Kimber declared that he would begin work', said the *San Francisco Call*, 'on a biplane glider which he believes will be more stable than the single plane kind.'

At Bouy with a Nieuport 15 plane. (Kimber Literary Estate)

A Dorand AR plane. (Kimber Literary Estate)

Now, six years on from his own amateur efforts, Clifford found himself up in the air once more, albeit in a fully powered and much faster aircraft. But the thrill was back. It all seemed so right, so natural:

Somewhere in France, June 17th 1917

The captain met us in his office about seven. We talked about fifteen minutes and then went back to the field. He showed us his machine – a Dorand – and then said in French: je cherche un pilot.

The mechanicien helped me mount into the cockpit, and the pilot took his place. An assistant turned over the propeller, and the motor started to bark. Slowly at first, then it turned into a roar, and a tremendous stream of air blew past me. He slowed down for them to remove the blocks from the wheels, then with the aid of the mechanicien he steered the avion out of the crowd of machines, opened the throttle and we were off. Faster, faster, in jerky bumps; then suddenly all seemed smooth, and the ground fell away. We were mounting rapidly and within five minutes we were several thousand feet high and moving northward. It was like a dream; no longer the motor seemed to bother us. We floated along as steadily as it is possible to imagine. A stiff breeze but absolutely no lunges nor jerks, and such wonderful scenery. The earth thousands of feet below us looked like a gaily painted map all in greens, and villages looked like the models you have seen in Expositions; the whole was wonderful.

Before starting and while waiting for the machine to be got ready, I had been awfully hot. I knew I would need it, and so I had put on my sweater under my coat. And they gave me a woollen hat and a tremendous fur coat, warm as toast. As I say I was standing on the ground and sweating, almost ready to suffocate.

But after ascending I was glad of all that rigamarole. We headed north and flew nearly 30 kil. in that direction. At that time right under us was a large town, R. [Reims], and we could distinguish the wonderful cathedral quite clearly. Not far off were the German lines. Bursting shells stirred up little puffs of smoke and dirt. The enemy began firing shrapnel from 75s at us, but of course it all flew wild. I got a very good picture of bursting shrapnel, and the accompanying puffs of smoke. As we returned we passed over a barren waste, once 'no man's land'. Trenches looked like zigzag lines, drawn or scratched on a flat surface. Roads were little streaks; canals and rivers glittered far below. In all, between the hours of 6 and 9 A.M. I took 30 snaps, and believe all will turn out fine.

We were in the air 45 minutes and during that time climbed about a mile. French sausages below us looked awfully funny; I have been accustomed to looking up to

The view from the cockpit
– 'First Flight'. (Kimber
Literary Estate)

Standing in a plane – 'First
Flight'. (Kimber Literary
Estate)

*them. The thing I noticed about the descent was how much warmer the air got. The
landing was fine, the bounces and shocks were about the same as an auto going
over an ordinary road. It was quite tame to get out and walk. Alan was waiting for
me when we landed, and the captain has agreed to let him go up Tuesday, so we
will both go down early in the morning.*

*I believe I would make an excellent aviator, but don't worry for I won't enter for
a long time, and it is safer than any other branch of the war service. Reports are
always exaggerated – I experienced no uneasy feelings, was not at all dizzy; it was
GREAT. 'BULLY' as T.R. would say. They have only lost six aviators here in the later
spring offensives, and they were fighters and all brought down by the Germans;
none of them accidents. I will be an observer and photographer if I enter, and
absolutely safe (five months from now).*

*Alan is awfully glad he went down with me, and I think he realizes that for some
reason or other things come my way. He calls it luck. He may realize some day
that it is initiative – enthusiasm. Yesterday afternoon in the broiling sun I walked
ten miles, round trip, to meet these officers, etc., and that is why I went up today.*

*The sun was very hot and when we got back to M——, our headquarters, we
were just all in. At 4 P.M. Mr. Muhr is going to take six of us to a canal several miles
off, for a swim. Goodbyes and good luck to you all. God bless you all. Lovingly, Cliff.*

*P.S. Will send John a copy of Excelsior too; keep this. In section 1, I am the 'officer'
making the speech.*

So began in earnest Clifford's determination to get up in the air for himself.
Soaring into the clouds, with the wind, the speed, the earth below laid out
before him, it was all a heady mixture for a young 21-year-old in search of
excitement. He took, by his estimate, more than 100 photographs at the
parc and in the air, marvelling at the sight of Reims cathedral seen from an
altitude of 2,000–3,000ft and how some of his pictures looked like maps.

From this point on a major element of his photography and his photo
album would be taken up with pictures of Morane-Saulniers, Dorands,
Farmans, Nieuports, Sopwiths and Spads. The bug had bitten properly
and he began counting off the months until a possible release date, all the
while earnestly reassuring his family back in California how it was, in
reality, all very safe stuff indeed.

But work still had to be done in the here and now. For all the time
the volunteers had off, amusing themselves around camp (or 'loafing' as
Clifford described it disapprovingly) and for the times on duty when there
was no fighting, there came periods of intense activity when the effects

A wrecked house at Moscou. (Kimber Literary Estate)

of bombardments made themselves felt. In a letter at the end of the same week he looked back on what he had witnessed on different days and nights, beginning with a visit to the front with the medical officer:

With S.S.V. 14, par B.C.M.
June 22nd, 1917.

Dear Mother, John and George,

 At one o'clock Tuesday morning [Allen] Tucker's alarm clock woke me up, and dressing quickly I cranked up the Staff car for the Med. Div. wanted to go to the front on a tour of inspection. We stopped for a moment at C. and then went on to M. These two postes, according to our leader, Mr. Muhr, are the two worst and most dangerous ones that the American Ambulance has yet served. The darkness and the unfamiliar trenches, etc., at M. gave us quite a problem in finding the right abri or poste de secours. At last we saw a diamond light and entered. Blocking the doorway was a dead brancardier, head and chest where he had been shot, all covered with an oiled cloth. A few moments later three other brancardiers, with stern and set faces, carried him out. Everything was so dark and damp and gloomy, it was horrible.

An ambulance, *camionette* and staff car at Constantine *poste de secours*. (Kimber Literary Estate)

The *poste de secours* at Constantine, 'Villa San Francisco'. (Kimber Literary Estate)

[Wednesday] *a dead man was carried into C. on a stretcher. Both legs had been shot off, and he was a sorry sight. They put him in a dugout about 50 yards off, and sent for the coffin; then we went back into the abri and started to wait – wait – wait for blessés. It was drizzling outside and very disagreeable. During the night the Germans had started a 'tire de barrage' preliminary to an attack. It was wonderful; the French batteries replied, and made a regular curtain of fire in back of us. A German incendiary shell hit a big pile of rockets and made the most glorious sight that I have ever seen with fireworks. All during the night both sides sent up rockets, star shells and red white and green lights; it was wonderful. As morning broke the hill was covered with smoke and dirt thrown up by the shells; the gunfire sounded like a tattoo, it was so fast and regular. The boys had never heard such barrage fire before; yet the result gained was only a few trenches and about 100 French pousares*. If they did all that for such a little attack, what must have the British offensive have sounded like.*

Believe me, we were mighty glad when our 24 hours were over, and we got back to M. to sit down and eat a nice warm meal which our cook had saved for us; we turned in immediately. [Friday] I was rudely awakened this morning, Friday, about 2 or 3 o'clock by a great commotion in camp. Motors were buzzing and the lieutenant was giving orders in a very excited way. The results of the German attack were just being felt, and wounded were pouring into the postes in large numbers. All the machines except the five which had just returned from duty (including mine) were ordered out. Ours were held in readiness, but we were allowed to sleep.

At dinner today we learned that one of the boys in section XXVIII near us, which had just arrived the other day, had been killed by éclat that same night; they were serving further up the line. That has made us all serious. Believe me, when I get killed (I hope I won't) it won't be in the trenches, or driving an ambulance, but I will fall to earth like a wounded eagle. But cheer up, there is little danger. Five months more in this, and six months training in aeroplanes before being sent to the front, and by that time the war will be over. Love to you all. Cliff.

June 24th, 1917.

Dear Mother, John and George,
    Tonight I am on duty and am writing this letter while daylight still lasts, at the poste de secours that I am serving. It is near an artillery station and the French

---

* He might mean *puisard*, an individual pit designed to channel and drain water.

guns are constantly barking away about 50 to 100 yards to our rear. The departing shells make a shrill whistling sound, but this is quickly lost as they speed on their path of destruction. Naturally enough the German answers the French salutes quite regularly. When we hear a German shell come whizzing along, everybody ducks to avoid the shrapnel, which is apt to come our way as soon as the shell bursts. Then it goes flying overhead; of course, if a shell bursts very near to you, near enough to kill you outright, it makes little difference whether you duck or not.

The worst thing about this war as far as I can see it, is that it keeps so many men who might be doing useful work, quite idle. They must wait and be ready in case they are needed and so it is necessary, but most of the time they are doing absolutely nothing.

I must correct something I said in my last letter. That S.S.U. 28 boy was not killed; at least he has not died yet. It was at first thought so, but after his death was announced, he didn't seem to like the idea, so he just 'hung on'. He is much better now and his chances are good, although it was necessary to amputate the poor boy's leg. This is how it happened: Section 28 had been just two days out from Paris, where they were sent on duty near us. Mr. Andrew, who seems to be disliked by everybody, including Mr. Muhr and all others, sent for Mr. [William] Wallace, leader of the section to come to Paris. He had not yet had time to inform the boys how to act. The boys had received no instructions as to how to behave under bombardment; therefore when the shells started bursting around, they stood still instead of throwing themselves flat upon the ground. One of the boys was foolish enough to seek his car, at which the Boche were probably aiming, for protection. The boy cranking the car miraculously escaped. The side of the car was practically blown away, so those who went to M le G [Mourmelon-le-Grand, sister town to Mourmelon-le-Petit] to see it say it is a wonder the chap was not killed outright. You cannot blame anybody but the Boche and Mr. A. Piatt Andrew.

But why the mention of A. Piatt Andrew in this angry way? Why was he suddenly to be singled out for criticism? According to Clifford, this industrious and resourceful founder of the American Ambulance was 'disliked by everybody' and was to be held directly to blame for the effects of enemy action. What had gone on?

There can be no doubt that some anger and irritation was directed at Andrew by others in the unit. When things go wrong, the boss is usually blamed, especially if he is not on the spot. But for Clifford in particular the answer, and it was a relatively petty one in the grander scheme of things with a war raging around them, stemmed from the pique Clifford was beginning to feel about his position after some weeks at the front. It arose from what Piatt Andrew probably thought of as a minor administrative change. It had been his original plan to send Clifford only for a short period to the front to link up with the 1st Stanford Unit, the Section 14 with which he was currently serving. He would present the flag there and work with the unit for some weeks before returning to Paris to join Clifford's 2nd Stanford Unit, once the new arrivals finally reached Paris.

But Andrew had revised his plans, maybe thinking that there was little need to rearrange rosters already up and running on the front with Section 14. Besides, he had other, weightier matters on his mind. General John Pershing had recently arrived in France with the first contingent of the American Expeditionary Force (AEF), and Andrew was considering the future of his Ambulance Service: would it be subsumed into the AEF or retain an independent identity as a separate unit in the United States Army's table of organisation? In the event, later that year, the AFS and other ambulance units were incorporated into a new and larger US Army Ambulance Service.

For now, however, serving on the front and quite ignorant of these high matters, a young and restless 21-year-old was left nursing a sense of betrayal that he would not get to work alongside those of the unit he had helped gather together. With perhaps a little too much time on his hands, Clifford elevated Andrew in some of his more intemperate letters to the status of 'villain' or 'crook'. But at heart, apart from his disappointment at this slight, there lay a more general problem for Clifford.

For all his complaints of the idleness of others, the 'loafing' and inactivity which he decried, he himself had succumbed to some of its side effects. Grumbles, pettiness, worries and dissatisfaction with his situation began to intrude in his diaries. With time on his hands, and in spite his best endeavours to remain busy with his photography, writing, chess, sketching, music and brushing up on his French grammar, he began to see and take slights. The situation wasn't helped by his having received very few letters from home, from the family and friends to whom he had written so assiduously for two months.

To keep his spirits up, he wondered in his letters about life back in Palo Alto, of his family, their 'beautiful blooming home', friends locally and those they knew at the university. All the while, though, he looked up to the skies over France:

Buzz – buzz – buzz, etc. we can constantly hear the hum of the aeroplane motors over our hands. It is nothing to see 14 to 16 machines in the air at the same time. The other night we could count 14 machines, Boche and Francais, and 11 Boche sausages, besides the French observation balloons. Tonight an E— flew right over us, only about 50 feet from the ground, and later on a Nieuport within a hundred yards; a glance up now and five are in sight.

And can you blame our ambulanciers for wanting to be aviators? Think of it – there is no chance of being mangled; you either live or die, and if you do you fall like a wounded eagle; and you are buried whole, not in parts or not at all. But the danger is slight; not a Frenchman has been lost in this district since we arrived. A Boche was brought down near B. today, although we could not see him in his forced descent. When bombing, raiding and observation machines go out they nearly always do so in floats convoyed by fast fighting Nieuports or S. or S. etc. It is an awfully pretty sight to see as many as fifteen or sixteen machines in the air at once. So far nearly all of the fatalities have been due to gun fire and not accident and losses are small in proportion to infantry and artillery, etc. As soon as I finish this letter I am going to get under cover in the abri and leave the trench, as it is getting dark and the Boche are bombarding more than when I arrived.

It was up there that he belonged, he was sure of that. He had now applied to join the aviation service and had written to Paris, to Edmund L. Gros, a San Franciscan of French heritage, who was the medical director of the American Ambulance.

Gros, a physician, managed to combine his medical duties for the American Ambulance with a different role: that of the de facto organiser of early American aviation efforts in France. He had helped create the so-called *Lafayette Escadrille* (French Squadron 124, or *Escadrille* 124, the original unit of American pilots who flew with the French Air Service from 1916) and the 'Lafayette Flying Corps' (later American foreign legionnaires who would fly with a variety of other French squadrons). Both were home to volunteer American pilots, and he facilitated the squadrons' relationship with the French authorities. Clifford wanted to be part of Gros' effort and wrote to him in Paris. But almost as soon as he had sent in his papers applying to join, another opportunity presented itself – another potential distraction in a different theatre of war.

16

STUNG

The problem facing Clifford stemmed from a reorganisation and reassignment of members of his old and new units. The headquarters in Paris had determined that the original unit he had been part of, the 2nd Stanford, was to be sent to the Balkans as its first posting. Furthermore, it was going to take eight to ten more men from the unit he was currently with, the SSU 14 '1st Stanford'. The contingent was due to relieve Section 10 of the American Ambulance, who had been in service on the Macedonian Front, working in theatre with French forces from the previous January. The Stanford men would follow in their footsteps, sailing to Salonika in northern Greece and travelling overland to the Balkan Front in Albania, taking up their base quarters and the section's vehicles in Koritza (modern day Korçë).

Clifford's dilemma was whether he should aim to go with them, or to stick with his plan to fly. He had already been encouraged in his ambitions to join the Lafayette Flying Corps by Edmund Gros, but he was still waiting to see if that would translate into something more concrete. His friend Alan Nichols had already been accepted. Might he be next? The main thing he wanted to avoid was to be left with nothing. He longed for fresh excitement. Ought he to hedge his bets and apply for the Balkans expedition but hope that any acceptance was countermanded by a subsequent order to be included in the flying corps?

As is apparent in his next letter home, his options had already been narrowed down for him. Matters regarding the former had been taken out of his hands, and not in a manner which would make him feel any better:

With S.S.U. 14, par B.C.M.
June 26th, 1917.

Dear Mother, John and George,

I must see Dr. Gros at any cost and it will be impossible any other way. The first Stanford section is as good as broken up now. There will be no fun staying with a new bunch of fellows.

Yesterday I was at the poste on duty as I wrote you Sunday. In the early morning they brought down some dead Germans from the lines; they were going to inter them Monday night. When I left they were turning black, and were beginning to smell and were being eaten by the flies. The boys who came in tonight say they are still there and beginning to stink quite badly. They were an awful mess. Some had crushed skulls; some were minus legs; one had no head and no legs. C'est la guerre.

I was at the poste 24 hours straight; not a man to carry in; under bombardment most of the time. My, but I had a swell French lesson. The priest there talked with me for two hours, and had me read aloud and drilled me on pronunciation; a fine man.

Piatt Andrew came out today and absolutely repudiated his promise about letting me join my own section in Paris. That poor boy in section 28 died last night. Mr. Andrew came out to attend the funeral which will take place tomorrow. We are all going over to be present.

The boys have been talking about the Salonika proposition. By a little system of grafting Carl Randeau [brother of the Second Stanford leader Clem who had already left the service to go into aviation], who has been chosen leader, I don't know by what means, has selected seven of his friends, and has not included me. I guess I am stung again, but now I must remember that little song 'put all your troubles in your old grip bag and smile, smile, smile'. The Lord will take care of me whatever I do. Mother dear, the only reason I don't want to enter aviation is because you will worry; but I assure you it is fairly safe, if a man is careful, and at any rate I won't be an ambuscader.

Alan is a fine chap, but I think he is somewhat inconsiderate of others at times. It was due to me entirely that he got his flight in an aeroplane. He is now in Paris. Before leaving he promised to find out all details of entry into aviation for me. He has written two of the other fellows and has used his influence to get one of the others in. Not a word for me and not a letter to me. Well, I have feelings like any other person.

I received a letter from you today, Mother. It was dated May 29th. You don't say whether or not you had received my telegram sent from Liverpool the 24th, and

Dead German soldiers at
Moscou, the *poste* & *abri*
in the background. (Kimber
Literary Estate)

Walter Malm standing near
the body of a dead German.
(Kimber Literary Estate)

after my letters arrive, please answer them referring to them and don't forget to type them.

I am awfully glad to hear that John still has pep. He must keep it up though; it is hard, but it will pay. Tell him to never get discouraged. But he has my sympathy. And George, cheer up about that job you are trying to get; we all have our troubles. I am having my share now. Do they pay you cash or hash for waiting on tables? Never mind about the S.P. job or the Chautauqua. Jobs are hard to get but the experience of getting turned down a dozen times is worth more than getting the first job you ask for.

I try to be optimistic all the time; right now it is hard, but my next letter will be breezy I assure you. Everything comes to him who waits. My biggest worry is about you, Mother dear. Love to you all; write me often, all of you. Lovingly, Cliff.

Clifford appears to have been a young man who wore his heart on his sleeve and who took offence reasonably easily and often. The letters he wrote are peppered with references to various injustices and slights to which he feels he was subjected. He also tended, albeit in the privacy of his own letters, to carp about others' behaviour and to find fault in colleagues and masters alike. Very likely he was the author of much of his own misfortune: his own attitude and personality may have alienated others.

Guns stacked outside the church while soldiers attend Mass, Mourmelon-le-Petit, June 1917. (Kimber Literary Estate)

It seems apparent, from the moment he began the process of setting up the 2nd Stanford Unit in California and the leadership of that group was wrested from him, that others did not consider him an easy companion. He now found himself something of an isolated figure, out of step with the two units with which he was associated: the 2nd clearly did not want to include him in its plans for the Balkans, and the 1st Unit to which he was officially attached contained men whom he found uncongenial. By many of these he was doubtless judged a prig and even a snob.

The relatively sheltered world he had inhabited up until this European adventure was centred on a close-knit family, dominated by a clever, self-educated mother who had determined that her boys should only mix with 'the best of society'. He did not fit in easily with a group of men, a number of whom were older, who may have behaved or spoken in a way he considered bawdy or inappropriate, and he certainly appears not to have gone out of his way to keep their company. It did not occur to him that he would get the reputation of being stand-offish.

When he wasn't working at the *postes de secours* on the front, he was busying himself with his various activities and hobbies, especially photography and, of course, his writing. He was not an easy mixer with the bulk of the men with whom he was billeted; and when he did seek company it was with a small number of people he considered of like mind. A young man who now was making little secret of his desire to leave to join the flying corps was not going to be rewarded with inclusion in his colleagues' future plans.

Whether or not he was blind to any possible shortcomings on his own part, Clifford was, to his credit, at least prepared to try to be stoical about it – 'we all have our troubles' as he said to his brothers. Besides, he realised that there were more serious realities to be faced in the theatre of war:

With S.S.U.14, par B.C.M.
June 27th

Dear Mother, John and George,
We just got back from M le G where they held the funeral of that Section XXVIII man Osborne. It was very impressive and something I will never forget.
We started about 8.05 A.M. Many of us rode in the camion (inside) and we were just about jarred to pieces. My, but we bumped.

As soon as we arrived at the old aviation parc where there is an outdoor chapel, we all lined up in military order. Doc. Spears carried the flag. Practically all the men in section XXVIII were there wearing steel casques [helmets]. Altogether there must have been nearly 100 Americans present, for sections 12, 14, 19, 27 & 28 were well represented. There was also a large number of French. One armed squad was there and acted as a guard of honour. Brancardiers, stretcher-bearers, carried the coffin. We all lined up in front of the Chapel, thus: Osborne's brother, a member of the camion service, reached M. just a short time after his brother had a relapse and died. He stood out in front and bore up fine. After prayers etc. had been read, one of the ambulances from section 28 backed in and the brancardiers lifted the coffin in. Osborne was not the first dead man our ambulances have carried. Then slowly, with the hearse leading, the procession formed and started to march toward the graveyard. This was right near the old aviation parc, and it was necessary to cross the field to get to it. Slowly we marched past the sheds of Henry Farman, then the Ecole Nieuport, and finally the Voisin hangars, then out into the field to the open grave. Several more prayers and the body was lowered to rest. The whole was very, very impressive. Few of the men spoke until it was all over; all were very deeply affected.

Afterwards I shook hands with Osborne's brother. One of the men not in line had kindly taken some pictures for me with my camera. I told Osborne I would send him some for himself and parents and he thanked me warmly. I am mighty glad I had my camera and was able to record in pictures that military funeral. Thank goodness we had an American flag today – Osborne was buried under his own colors.

Well, the boys that have signed up for Salonika, and have been chosen by Randau, will leave tomorrow. Unless something miraculous happens my chances of going to the Balkans are nil. I may get to Paris in a few weeks when the new men come to fill up the section and if Dr. Gros sends out my pass, in which event I will begin my course in aviation. Now, to set your mind easy about the danger:

In the first place there are very few accidents as in America. The machine is very stable, inherently so, and unlike the planes in America, they practically automatically remain on an even keel. There have been practically no losses or injuries due to so called accident. All losses are due to being brought down by enemy avions. Secondly, according to figures and statistics that have been recently compiled by the French government, aviation is safer than the medical branch of the army, the infantry or the artillery. The proportion of fatalities is greater in those three branches than in aviation. Third, if a man is careful and does not seek trouble with two or three Boche at once, he is pretty safe. Most machines have been lost by impulsive men reck-lessly engaging in combat with superior enemy forces; example, staying aloft in an

observation or bombing plane when a fighting machine approaches. So don't worry
on that score. Now that we are at war I must fight, and must enter decent work. If
I returned to America, I would be sent to the Trenches. If I stay an ambulancier, how
will I feel when my friends come over as troops?

Aunt Annie just sent me a birthday gift of $25. She wants me to buy sweaters.
She can't bribe me or buy affection. With love to you all; don't worry. Lovingly, Cliff.

As it happened, of the ten men from Section 14 who left for Paris en route
to the Balkans, two – Joe Eastman and Eddie Corden – returned to their
home unit within days, apparently dissatisfied with the organisation of the
detachment going there or their roles within it. But with regard to most of
the others who continued on their way, the straitlaced Clifford professed
himself glad to be rid of a group he considered 'a dirty mouthed lot' who
could be heard 'swearing and cracking dirty jokes all the time and are
continually talking about houses and prostitutes'.

In their place would come fifteen new men 'probably from Eastern
universities' who would represent 'a decent type'. The one drawback of
the new arrivals, though, was the fact most of them did not know how to
drive. He and others would have to teach them, but in the meantime there
would be an extra workload borne by those already in post. His regular
driving duties and hours would have to increase in the short term. These
duties continued as before, but he also made other discretionary trips with
the medical officer. He recounted one such to the forward trenches on the
front line, high up on the hill beyond the Constantine *poste de secours*:

The Germans are firing few shells and so it was quite O.K. on the way to the top
of the hill. It was much further than one would think, looking at the hill from the
village. We followed a piste used for transporting supplies, etc. This is defendu in the
daytime, because the Germans can see from the observation balloons, but at night
it is all right, and when we started the ascent at about 2.30 A.M. it was still dark.
Men move in trenches during the day. On all sides and occasionally in the middle of
the piste were shell holes and craters. The ones in the valley are all, comparatively
speaking, quite small; that is, ten or twelve feet in diameter, and three or four or
five feet deep. But on the side of the hill, where the shells have been falling for so
long, there are holes twenty and thirty feet in diameter, and some as deep as twelve
feet. In the very front lines they dig connecting ditches, and use these big shell holes
as trenches. You have probably read how opposing forces will fight for possession
for one of these, and then get blown out of them later on. Then, nearly at the top

Trench diggers of the French
55th Infantry Division.
(Kimber Literary Estate)

A communications trench.
(Kimber Literary Estate)

of the hill, enter big communicating and supply trenches. Once in a while we could get out in the open, this when the position was fairly sheltered and concealed by little crests or trees.

The Med. Div. stopped in several of these really advanced 'postes de secours' and talked with the doctors there. These postes were well covered with logs and sand bags, yet we were shown one that a shell had hit. It seems as if they need fifty feet of earth above and then the Germans are apt to use mines. These postes are all small and have a table, a chair and shelves crowded with bandages all done up in neat little rolls. They are lighted by candle or inferior lamps. All said and done they present a very dirty, musty dingy and rather unpleasant appearance. To think of a doctor used to modern luxury living in caves like that, is very hard, till you see it.

There were not many soldiers to be seen on the way up. Most of them were asleep in dugouts. Occasionally we would see a sentry or a brancardier. My, but it was awfully gloomy in the early morning. Daylight was gradually breaking and it showed up the country round about, torn up by shell holes and trenches. Trees were all stripped of their branches; there was even little grass. Now and then we would run across a little patch of green or a group of wild flowers. Such a place to find flowers. As it grew fairly light, our guide pointed out what looked like a big settling or washout. 'That is where they mined several hundred soldiers,' he said, and then we were introduced to the type of dugout in which they were mined.

Emerging from an *abri*, on the front line. (Kimber Literary Estate)

We entered the first line trenches (not the advance shell holes etc.) and every 50 feet or so was a silent sentry. A little earlier they had been hard to make out in their light gray blue uniforms against the gray chalk walls of the trenches. There were many holes in the trench walls. They were about 3 feet high and 3 feet wide. They were the entrances to the famous dugouts. A leaning shaft extends from the dugout proper to these entrance holes from the trenches. These shafts are about 40 to 50 feet long and about every three feet have a board across the bottom to keep men from slipping. These acted as shelves or beds for soldiers, for on each stage or step was a dozing poilu. It was very hard to keep from stumbling over them and jerking them all to the bottom of the shaft. The dugout itself is simply a passage way or tunnel of unknown length in which men sleep on the floor, and hang their belongings, guns, canteens, etc., on the dirt walls.

Of course such a dugout may have several exits, but usually, once the trench is captured, any one left in the dugout is doomed. It was all right visiting a few of these caves, but to climb in and out of many on an empty stomach, was sickening, for they were very close, and had practically no ventilation at all.

In one of them the Med. Div. introduced me to the commandant. He was stretched out upon his stretcher, and looked very comfortable, in spite of conditions which to me seemed unbearable. He chatted in a most friendly manner, and seemed to enjoy the talk immensely. My position was anything but comfortable, for I had to stoop all the time to keep from bumping my head on the beams above, and it was impossible to get a decent breath of air.

Believe me, when we got back to the poste de secours that we serve, and where my ambulance was waiting, I was mighty glad to get in and drive those men back to M. But we had a splendid trip. Not a boy in our section has been to the front line in such an active front as this except myself. When I was way down in the dugout, I could not help feeling how helpless we would be in case of a sudden German attack (gas especially).

And those 'no prisoner' rumours are again confirmed. An officer said the other day that 51 Germans were taken prisoners; that 50 were shot outright, and one kept for information. There have been several attacks here quite recently, yet we have seen no prisoners brought back, or in the prison camps. Lovingly, Cliff.

On 4 July, American Independence Day and a month on from the presentation of the flag, the unit was to take part in another ceremony. French commanders, wanting to mark the work of Section 14 and mindful of the significance of the day in the calendar, arranged another set-piece event to mirror that of Tréveray. But this ceremony was to award a number of *Croix de Guerre* to the unit in recognition of its service.

SSU 14 prepares to receive the Croix de Guerre, 4 July 1917. (Kimber Literary Estate)

The flag is decorated with the Croix de Guerre by a representative of the French Army. (Kimber Literary Estate)

After the ceremony, 4 July 1917. 'All the men "lit up" and the jokes flew thick and fast.' (Kimber Literary Estate)

Four companies of French soldiers, veterans of recent fighting around Téton in Champagne's so-called Battle of the Hills, were lined up and a colour party from the section approached with their flag. One medal was pinned to the flag by the ranking general and another two awarded to individual members who had served in the American Ambulance from 1915: the French-American member of the unit, Pierre 'Peter' Fischoff and a second one later in the day to the section head, Allan Muhr.

Muhr's career, in particular, had been a noteworthy one to this point. Born into a prosperous Jewish family in Philadelphia in 1882, he had moved to Paris as a young man in the early 1900s. There, forging something of a career for himself as a translator and sports writer – although perhaps also supported by private income – he had devoted more of his time to pursuing his twin passions of rugby and tennis. Joining and playing rugby for the capital's Racing Club de France, he went on to represent France in their first ever international rugby test match against New Zealand's All Blacks at the Parc des Princes stadium in Paris on New Year's Day, 1906; and he subsequently played two games – home and away – against England, scoring France's first ever international try in the first of them.

A knee injury later put paid to his playing career, but he found an active role in sports management and administration, going on to chair France's rugby selectors and also act as France's Davis Cup tennis captain at different times from 1912. After the war, he was also involved, with International Olympic Committee founder Pierre de Coubertin, in helping organise the 1924 Paris Olympics.[24] But whilst in the ambulance service he had helped organise a number of rugby matches between French soldiers and American service personnel, and his award that day in July 1917 was at least partial recognition for this and other services to sport.

The ceremony marking his and Fischoff's Croix de Guerre was followed by what even for peacetime would have been considered a lavish feast: a ten-course meal, accompanied by wine and by the very drink which gave the area its name, champagne. Only the surroundings might possibly have given the game away that these were not normal circumstances, taking place as they did in a barnyard under a shed. The American Ambulance volunteers offered their toasts to Muhr and Fischoff, to the newly arrived members of the group, to the French officers, to their whole section. They felt suitably honoured by the day, but were also focused on another prize fast approaching: some weeks *en repos*, in rest billets away from the front. It couldn't come soon enough for Clifford; as he confided in his letters, he had not seen a bath in a fortnight.

17

EN REPOS

Early the following morning, when a number of the section might reasonably have been expecting a lie in, Clifford received an early morning visit from their French sergeant asking if he would report for duty at 9 a.m. with the staff car. The Med. Div. wanted to go on a tour of inspection to villages ahead of the division's *repos*, which was to begin the next day.

The officer wanted to head south in the general direction of Troyes, and would, with a police *gendarme* captain, inspect a number of possible villages and billets on the way to gauge their suitability as a base for the men. He was anxious to avoid any area with known *malades* or any contagious diseases and check on villages' basic sanitary arrangements.

They travelled on and off all day, until 7.30 in the evening, a long shift behind the wheel, but one which Clifford found exhilarating. The weather was beautiful and the driving conditions perfect, their car alone on the road for the most part and without any dust thrown up by other vehicles. But it was the countryside which captivated him. He was driving through what he had been told was the 'prettiest part of France', that region 100 miles to the east of Paris, and yes, he concluded, this was the prettiest country he had ever seen, the US and England included: 'Why should men fight to kill in this beautiful country? It is because it is so beautiful that it is worth fighting for.'

But he also enjoyed the company of the medical officer, who had taken an interest in him. He made a point of asking Clifford to dine with him and the captain at lunchtime – something Clifford was gratified by, given that he was dressed in a private's uniform – and was enthusiastic about

Clifford's attempts at learning French. He was, they told him, '*très gentil*'. That evening the officer even went so far as to argue on his behalf that he be given a good quality, officer-class room. Clifford accepted gratefully and settled into his luxurious new surroundings, marvelling at the old ornate room he found himself in, complete with lace curtains, carved wood and rugs strewn around. It was a far cry from the mattress and rough blankets he had grown used to. 'It was necessary to climb on a chair to get into bed,' he said, 'and then I sank down a foot it seemed into the downy mattress.'

The tour of inspection with the medical officer continued the following morning with the section eventually settling in camps in and around villages near Arcis-sur-Aube, north of Troyes. The *repos* was to last three weeks and Clifford was determined to keep up his correspondence with home. His mother and brothers might worry if they didn't hear from him, he thought. That said, and as he cheerfully admitted, he had so very little to say because they were on fewer hours.

It wasn't leave, but the work load was much lighter. There was a river a mile or so from their camp and another stream close by, and having gone so long without bathing, he and his section whiled away enjoyable

Washing the ambulance at Pouan, near Arcis-sur-Aube. (Kimber Literary Estate)

hours diving into the cold waters. Chores were carried out – the washing of clothes, the cleaning of their vehicles, occasional calls to driving duty. But it was time spent largely idling and he relaxed into it quite happily.

The one tangible thing that had emerged from the first part of their time away, though, came in the form of a frank conversation he was able to have with his friend Alan Nichols. Alan had recently returned to the section, temporarily stymied in his efforts to join the Lafayette Flying Corps. Dr Gros in Paris had accepted him for aviation, but his permission had expired before the French Government signed his acceptance papers. He would have to wait and try again. He and Clifford resumed their friendship, but it was, in truth, a friendship which had been under strain of late. Alan wanted to put that right and determined to be direct – but also, he hoped, helpful – in his advice to Clifford. It was advice for which Clifford was grateful and took to heart, much to his eventual advantage.

With S.S.U. par B.C.M. July 13th '17

Dear Mother, John and George,

Alan was so good and kind in the way he explained. I feel he is the best and most understanding friend I have of my age, outside you three of course. I don't know what he thinks of me; I know he likes me, but I certainly admire and almost love him for the really decent way he has always treated me in spite of my many faults, and, yes, I feel I ought to confess, disagreeable conceit.

Alan cleared up a lot for me; gave me reasons why other fellows do not take me up, and why most of the men in this corps have been so cold to me. And it has been, or at least most of it has been, my own fault. I see it now.

He admits that in all probability Randau wanted to slip me from the second corps because he didn't want anyone to share the honor of starting it. That is why he was so enthusiastic about my leaving early. He sacrificed the honor of himself taking the flag and gave it to me in hopes of shipping me out of his way etc. But he didn't think how big a thing I was going to make of the flag; and to tell you the truth the honor of carrying and presenting that beautiful banner is ample compensation for any troubles or unpopularity that I may have suffered. I maintain that although my head may have been turned to a great extent, at the same time lots of the beastliness of the others was prompted by jealousy, and Alan thinks so too, to a certain extent.

Then that Examiner article queered me with the boys, both of the 1st and 2nd Stanford Units.* It was a terrible mistake; I began wrong. It was partly the reporter's fault, and I suffered greatly at his hand but I must have said too much in my enthusiasm, etc. Yes, I was thinking partly of the honor I would get by decent publicity, but honestly I was thinking most of the flag, and was trying to get the flag recognized. Of course the article was sent ahead of me and the boys didn't like it. Alan says some of them remarked at that time that it might be a good lesson for me if they simply coolly accepted the flag without any ceremony and a short thanks, and then showed me the bunting flag that the section was already flying. But, thank the Lord my initiative smeared that possibility completely. By the time I entered Piatt Andrew's office in Paris, anything but a public presentation was impossible.

My second big mistake was to write the second unit about the attempt of the U.C. men to steal the flag and how I frustrated it. Alan says it sounded like I and me and myself all the time. Prompt action saved the day, but I should not have been the one to write about it. That should have been left to others, but where were the others? I think I had a right to be proud of how I got it back, but that was where I got it wrong the second time.

Then when I got in Paris, I suppose I tried to hurry Mr. Andrew too much; but as one of the boys, Gibson? says, he got as much honor and publicity out of it as I did, but after finishing with me I was a used tool and to be no longer considered. So he forgot his gentleman's agreement and promise and coolly ignored my request to transfer me when my unit arrived.

After I arrived at the front I tried to be quiet and unobtrusive. Alan remarked that he noticed a big change in me, an improvement, and he was glad. He said my speech was excellent, and didn't sound egotistical, etc. Now whether or not the fellows just took a dislike to me because I could not mix with them in the bar room, café, smoking, or 'chasing' (they call it kite-hunting or tail-hunting, most disgusting) or whether they were jealous, is a different question. At any rate they felt, Alan says, that I was stuck up after doing a big thing and could not come down to their level. Be that as it may I know I have been sadly at fault in more than one way, but I do feel above that bunch.

Then Carl Randau was given the chance to select the men from section 14 that he wanted to go to Salonika under his captaincy. You know the dirty way Randau

---

* This was the interview he had done with a reporter from the *San Francisco Examiner* in which he had been quoted, to his embarrassment even at the time, as making much of the rivalry enjoyed between Stanford and Berkeley, and about his carrying the flag first to the front.

unfairly excluded me, Alan said he wouldn't have gone under Randau for anything, but that gives me no satisfaction – they didn't want me; it was not a case of my not wanting to go. Why? It must have been my undesirable or obnoxious personality.

They went to Paris; Alan went on his permission about the same time and saw Jack [Alan Nichols' brother] and the others. Some of the members of the second corps openly said For —'s sake keep Kimber out there; we don't want him here. Now we are rid of him don't let him in again. In other words they didn't want me. Alan only told me last night. No wonder Andrew did not give me my transfer if he had talked with those outspoken fellows (but of course that was no excuse for his breaking his personal word of honor).

Well, now, why all this? To be sure part might be attributed to jealousy on the part of others; to the feeling that my head might have been turned, or to the way events molded themselves on the trip from Palo Alto to France. But Alan said, 'think it over, see if you are not at fault some way'. Then he was good enough and kind enough to talk it over with me. He said that when I started south last summer to sell books, he thought I would come in contact with people; that I would rub up against the hard world and learn the value of making many friends rather than relying so wholly on myself, etc. But my success only strengthened my self-confidence; it only made me realize that I could rely on myself and ignore the help of others. He was disappointed, for he said that having gone out against that tough proposition and succeeding only strengthened my feeling of isolation and satisfaction in the same. He said my year and a half in England in a strange school helped also to develop self-reliance and self-satisfaction too strongly.

Again, my trip across the world alone, doing all my own passport and ticket work, going thru England by myself, independent and self-dependent, and in such a successful way also, contributed to strengthen me in the fort that I had built up against the rough and cruel and more inconsiderate world.

He feels that it is a fine thing for us boys to pull together and so like a team, but that it has its bad effects also of making us, me especially, not appreciate the value of making friends many and often outside my own personal circle. He said that this indifference to the value of the association of others, etc., was just what college and travel was supposed to remove.

He says he doesn't feel at all friendly with about half the fellows, but he appears so. He says use tact. I told him if I took a dislike to a fellow I couldn't and wouldn't even try to cover it up; I hate two-sided fellows. He said that was not being two-sided – it was TACT.

Now mind you, he was not giving me a sermon or a lecture, but was just suggesting as I had asked him to. He was being perfectly frank as I wanted him to be.

He is a mighty well liked and popular fellow, his head is not at all turned, and he is as bright as a dollar. He is in a position to help me, and yet know what the other fellows think and say of me.

Well, I dare say Alan is right; it is harder now and the medicine is very distasteful, but thank goodness I am having it; it is worth money. But I don't regret the experiences I have had which have strengthened my self-confidence. Yet life is an awfully hard struggle some times, especially when one does not know just what is wrong.

I have had a wonderful lesson pointed out to me, and now I must learn it. Nor do I regret having carried the flag. In years to come that will be a bigger thing than now, I hope. But it is necessary to have respect for the opinions of others. Every man has a right to his own ideas, and I to mine but no one has a right to enforce his ideas on others. No, I believe I will profit by Alan's talk and the realization that I must be or have been at fault, and I will try for the future. This has been a most valuable experience.

I have been somewhat lengthy in discussing a subject which I am afraid won't interest you much, although it may, but which I desire to record, so that, say a year from now, I can compare my thoughts and see if there has been any change for the better. I have few enemies, they are simply not friends. Friendships are necessary for broadmindedness and character building.

He was clearly both grateful for and chastened by the talk with his friend. He continued to reflect on what Alan Nichols had said and specifically what he could do about it, and resolved to try to modify his behaviour or attitude to fit in better with those around him. He did not want to change his personality or principles, he decided, but he could at least make efforts to be more approachable to his colleagues. The results were noticeable. Within weeks he was happily able to confide in a letter that he had 'kept my mouth shut and as a result I am one of the boys', and noted that he was, for the first time, being properly included in their activities and socialising.

It was now 14 July and to celebrate the national holiday in France, the French soldiers of their regiment organised an athletics meeting to pit themselves against their American *ambulanciers*. Clifford donned vest and bathing tights as a makeshift track outfit and entered himself in the 100m and 400m. The event was a great success, the American volunteers taking most of the honours, and that night they sat down to yet another multi-course meal with champagne. The irony was not lost on Clifford that such celebration and plenty was on offer such a short distance from

Sports day at the 14 July celebrations. Snook with his new Graflex camera. (Kimber Literary Estate)

Sports day at the 14 July celebrations. The long jump. (Kimber Literary Estate)

Sports day at the 14 July celebrations. The sack race. (Kimber Literary Estate)

the privations and agonies of the front. But these same soldiers of the French 55th Division to whom they were attached would soon be returning there.

The next day Clifford and a number of others were allowed a temporary leave of absence from the camp, being given a forty-eight hour *permission* to travel to Paris. It was an opportunity to see the sights – Sacré-Coeur, Notre Dame, Les Invalides, the Louvre and the Tuileries – and to visit the cinema, all activities gladly indulged in.

But Clifford's first task was to see Edmund Gros and to press upon him his case for the flying corps. When he went to see him at the American Ambulance base after lunch on his first day's leave, Gros had both bad and good news for him. No, he said, Clifford's main aim of joining the Lafayette Flying Corps was not to be. But a lot of other men would be enrolled as US aviators and trained by French flying officers, and he thought the chances were very good that Clifford would be accepted. Accordingly, the medical director gave him a letter of introduction to bring along to US Air Staff at the American Expeditionary Force in Paris.

On his arrival at the Air Service offices the following day, he and another younger man, a student from Harvard, were interviewed by a number of officers and given partial medical examinations. They appeared to have

Repairing Mourmelon's streets (as seen from a staff car). (Kimber Literary Estate)

been well received and were informed that they would be summoned at a future date for further examinations, physical and mental.

A buoyed-up Clifford returned to the section, happy that he had progressed this far, and his determination grew once he learned that his friend Alan Nichols had now finally been accepted into flying and was to leave the camp a few days later. Yes, he knew that his mother did not want him to go into the Air Service, and he daily wrestled with his conscience and his desire to see her financially secure, worrying continually that she would sell the house in Palo Alto to make ends meet.

He would see her comfortably off once he returned from France, as he earnestly hoped was the case. However, in the worst-case scenario, any money owing to him, including that part of his inheritance from his father in trust and being looked after by his Aunt Annie, would go to her in his will. His decision to become a pilot was a final one and it wasn't born simply of a desire to seek adventure, but based on duty:

August 5th, 1917.

I must think of your feelings, Mother dear, and what worry is apt to do to you. You know how I love you; there is no need to speak of that; and also how I hate to see you worry, but you must put that aside. I have balanced up my duties; I have a duty to perform to my country – the country that has protected our family these long years – that will protect us in the future. I am the only one in our family fit to and in a position to give military service to my country. EVERY FAMILY SHOULD SEND A REPRESENTATIVE.

It is not fair that some poor family sends all their sons and some other family none. You have two boys left and, besides, the chances are you will have three. Richard [his cousin, son of Clara's sister Kate] has gone; he will soon be in Europe. Can anyone say that his loss would still leave two boys just as able and loving as I? No. George Zabriskie writes that he expects his regiment to be ordered to the trenches soon. Both the Braunsweiger boys have gone; the two Nicholses, and others right and left. No, I have a duty to perform not only for myself but for my family. Yes, if I wanted to I could ambuscade,* could stay in this fake service or could come home next spring and avoid being conscripted at least for the present. But how would I feel after the war, when friends who had served say, what did you do for your country?

---

* Clifford appeared to use this word not only in its meaning of 'to ambush' or 'lie in ambush' but also in its more colloquial sense, 'shirking or evading responsibility'.

I am not going to wait for them to come after me, I am going to step forward and say 'Ready.' I have done it.

Aviation is my chance; none of the services is without danger. Aviation is no worse than the rest, and not half as bad as infantry, artillery, etc., and then it is a pleasure. You said in your last letter, Come back to a position where you can use your brains. I can do that here. But did not Roosevelt, our greatest living leader, take up arms in the Spanish American war? What about Washington? Love to you again, Mother dear, don't worry, I will do my duty. Send this letter to the boys if you like but let no one else see it. Cliff.

Clifford's spirits were dampened somewhat by the news that the 55th Division to which his section was attached had been reassigned to the front. The American Ambulance would have to await word of their next posting and there was as yet no sign of that. For the first time in recent weeks he began to feel restless. Time suddenly weighed heavily again as he and the men whiled away the hours as best they could. But their life in the camp was neither one thing nor the other. It wasn't leave – they couldn't travel to any meaningful extent, and the work when it came was scarce and piecemeal. They were stuck where they were, awaiting orders, and looking forward once more to the prospect of seeing action in the field and being useful and busy again.

Yet another week passed and news finally arrived that the section would be divided up, with his portion being sent north-east – and east of where they had previously been stationed – to do evacuation work near the town of Sainte-Menehould. Their work duly arrived in the aftermath of what is sometimes referred to as the Second Offensive Battle of Verdun, north-west of Verdun. This was a geographically limited French offensive to capture strategic heights around the hills, including Côte 304 and Mort-Homme, scene of some of the battles which had raged through 1916 around Verdun.

The new offensive began on 20 August 1917:

With S.S.U. par B.C.M.
August 21st 1917

Dear Mother John and George,

Getting down to the hospital we were ordered to evacuate several hundred to the train. Car after car was loaded and hurried over to the station. With the assis it was all right, because they could get out and walk into a large shed where they were to wait. But with the couches it was awful. The night was cold; they were lying on the stretchers without any covers or blankets; only their big blue overcoats. And the six brancardiers who were supposed to be at the station could not be found for an hour. Think of only six brancardiers. With this system I don't see how the French ever succeed.

About three o'clock the train was loaded and we returned to the barracks, and piled back again into bed. Breakfast was late; I did not get up for it, but at about 9 A.M. another call came in; and as I was still in bed and it was my turn I dressed faster than ever before. In ten minutes all cars were ordered out again; another train had to be loaded. By dinner time believe me we were tired and hungry.

The attack was a tremendous success. The French according to present reports, and full returns are not yet in, captured over 5000 Boche, and broke thru in places 2–3 kilometers over a 22 kilometer front. At the moment of writing the success is beyond expectation, and this morning's paper announced that the Italians had captured 7500 prisoners and the English another 1200 and the Russo-Roumanian forces are holding the enemy. Such news is very encouraging. It seems as if the Allies had the Kaiser going now; he doesn't know where to expect the next blow. He is vainly guessing. Old Hindenburg is getting licked; each new blow comes hard and at a new point; and the Allies now seem to be cooperating. Look for the fall of Lens soon and a second strategic German retreat. There is still half a fighting year left before winter and then the Russians will hit again. The Germans nearly got to Paris between this time in 1914 and November. Let us hope the Huns get kicked out of France and a big part of Belgium this year. Next year will see their finish I hope.

The following week Clifford was asked to drive a French priest – a *padre* – and another captain to join the division to which he was attached. This involved travelling to the scene of the recent fighting around Côte 304 and Mort-Homme, driving through Montzéville and Esnes-en-Argonne to see for themselves what remained of these ravaged hillsides, churned up by the recurring battles of 1916 and 1917.

But as he prepared to embark on the trip with fellow SSU 14 volunteer Malcolm Law, Clifford vowed privately to himself that, if at all possible, they would round their journey off with a visit to Verdun itself, the city at the heart of all this fighting, and of which he had heard and read so much over the previous two years:

August 30th 1917

Montzeville, the town just before Esnes, was completely razed. When I was in the Champagne section and saw Prosnes, Constantine and Baconnes and part of Mourmelon knocked to pieces I thought I had seen fair examples of the Hun's ruthless destruction, but seeing the destroyed villages in the vicinity of Verdun was certainly a great eye opener. Imagine every village like San Francisco after the big earthquake. As we approached Esnes the roads began to get very bad. The driving was bad, too, for due to recent rains the road was muddy and slippery. Esnes is in a little valley with Hill 304 on the side toward the Boche. Where the road curves around the edge of the other hill makes a good target for the Germans. We didn't get fired on going into Esnes, but coming back it was quite exciting.

Esnes is another mass of ruins. The church tower still stands but it might better be down; it seems out of place up. The French have not yet had time to clean up the streets and huge rocks from nearby ruins block the way. To avoid all of these was impossible, so we just bumped over. In places the road was flooded. The road, or rather piste, leading up 304 is just 'lousy' with French batteries recently installed. They are most cleverly concealed by wire screens covered with grass and leaves. We saw several of the famous French 75s and also some of the heavier guns.

Road screens to provide some protection for road traffic from aerial strafing. (Kimber Literary Estate)

A concealed gun carriage with camouflage. (Kimber Literary Estate)

While the generals, Capt. V., the priests and the other officers were talking, Law and I seized the opportunity of investigating the leeward side of 304. Off to the right was le Mort-Homme. It was the most barren kind of a waste. Torn and cut up by shell fire, not a bit of vegetation remained. Hills nearby had bits of green, but Mort-Homme not a thing. And the strange thing to me is that the Germans threw so many men away in trying to take this one hill. Of course Mort-Homme has a strategic importance, but even if the Boche took it and many others there would still be hundreds of hills left for the gallant French to defend. The advance to Paris at that rate would have cost the Germans many more million men than they have.

I cannot describe all we saw. We simply stared around and wondered. Occasionally as the wind blew from the lines and 'No Man's Land', it carried a sickening odor. Other things equally horrible don't bear mentioning. While we were waiting on hill 304 the Germans began to shell the road on the hill opposite and on the other side of Esnes. First we would see a huge cloud of dirt and smoke near the road, and then we heard the whizzing sound of the speeding shell and then the explosion. The shells did not explode so awfully far away but they went so fast that each time we could see the explosion before hearing even the whistle of the shell. Nor were the French slow to reply, for their guns kept barking away quite regularly.

Dead French soldiers
in the field after the
2nd Offensive Battle of
Verdun. (Kimber Literary
Estate)

In a former German
trench on Hill 304 (Côte
304). (Kimber Literary
Estate)

A general view of Hill 304. (Kimber Literary Estate)

On Hill 304 after the 2nd Offensive Battle of Verdun. (Kimber Literary Estate)

Leave-taking ceremony, San Francisco Civic Auditorium, 24 April 1917
(*The First Flag*, © Kimber Literary Estate)

*Good luck to
Arthur Kimber!
Theodore Roosevelt
May 11th 1917*

'Allies Day May 1917' by American artist Frederick Childe Hassam.
(Courtesy of the National Gallery of Art, Washington DC)

Daily Mirror, 12 June 1917. (©Mirrorpix. With thanks to the British
Library, London)

L'ILLUSTRATION

Prix de ce Numéro : Un Franc.   SAMEDI 9 JUIN 1917   75e Année. — N° 3875.

PRÉSENTATION OFFICIELLE DU DRAPEAU AMÉRICAIN AUX TROUPES FRANÇAISES

Voir l'article, page 546.

Front page of *L'Illustration*, Paris, 9 June 1917. (*L'Illustration*, serviceclient@lillustration.com)

A doctor and priest from the French 55th Division with Walter Malm of SSU 14. It was Malm who, with Harold Blote, brought the first flag back to Stanford in 1919. (Kimber Literary Estate)

An anti-aircraft and gun crew. (Kimber Literary Estate)

'At last' – Fischoff, Nichols, Tucker and Spears: *permissions* start at Mourmelon. (Kimber Literary Estate)

An AEF despatch rider at Châlons-sur-Marne, July 1917. (Kimber Literary Estate)

'Loading a *couché* into my ambulance'. (Kimber Literary Estate)

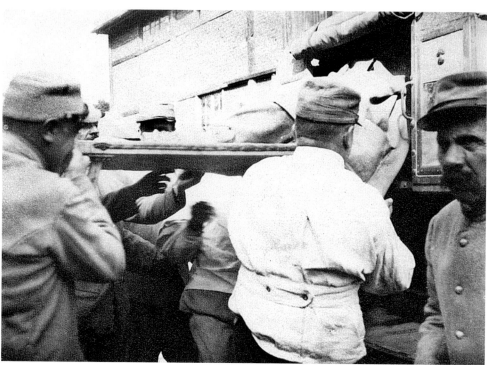

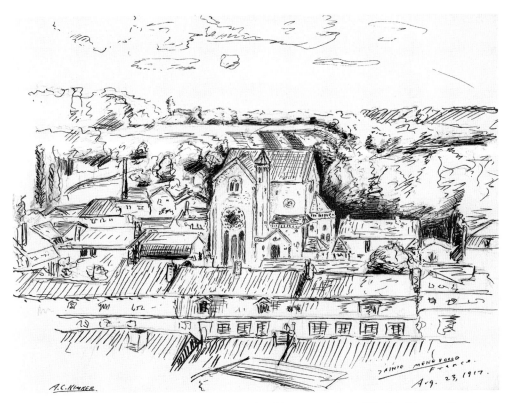

A sketch by Clifford of the town of Sainte Menehould, August 1917. (Kimber Literary Estate)

SORC First Lieutenant Arthur Clifford Kimber in his US Air Service uniform. (Kimber Literary Estate)

Clifford pictured in an airfield on service with SPA 85, July/August 1918. (Kimber Literary Estate)

Clifford at Cazaux gunnery school, March 1918. (Kimber Literary Estate)

Clifford poses beside his plane at Cazaux. (Kimber Literary Estate)

Clifford with first 'Nick' plane, a Spad VII, with SPA 85. The plane bears the escadrille's original Taurus logo. (Kimber Literary Estate)

Clifford with 'Nick 2', a Spad XIII. This plane was the first to sport Escadrille 85's new Joker logo. (Kimber Literary Estate)

Clifford (third from right) with J. Leroy Johnson and other US Air Service colleagues, posing with a young French woman, June 1918. (Kimber Literary Estate)

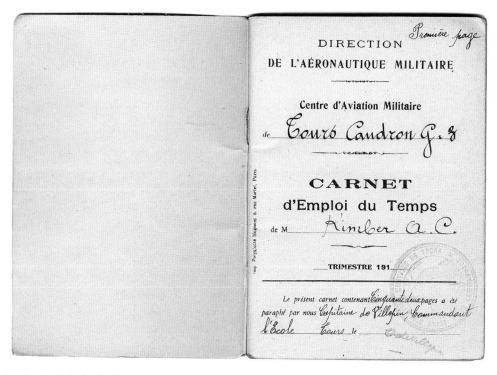

Clifford's flight logbook, September 1917–September 1918. (Kimber Literary Estate)

While we were watching all this and snapping our camera shutters as fast as we could load films, one of the orderlies called us and said the priest and captain were ready to go and wanted the machine turned around. We could not go up the hill any higher and the road was muddy and broken with shell holes, besides there were lots of shells and grenades lying around, and quite a bit of barbed wire. So we not only had to be careful not to slip into shell holes or skid off the road, but also to avoid running into or over shells, grenades and barbed wire. Honestly, I have never driven a car on such a bad road before. The General wanted to see the Captain, and if the latter had not been wounded and weak (he was hurt in the attack which carried 304), he would have walked from Montzeville and the car would have been left at the ambulance station there.

I wanted a picture of the church at Esnes; the priest stood next to it for me; it came out fine. It was surely exciting when we climbed the hill back of Esnes and rounded the corner which the Germans were shelling. We had to go on low, and it seemed as if we never would reach the top. Just before we arrived at the summit a big shell went off to our left, making an awful noise. It was followed almost immediately by a smaller one about the size of a French 75. It did not make such a sound, but a piece of éclat glanced off the car and more landed near us. Around the corner we nearly ran into a shell hole in the middle of the road. The car skidded around it, and bouncing and swerving, we made our way down the hill to Montzeville and out of shell fire.

Throughout it all the priest remained absolutely calm and silent. He sat on the front seat with me and never even budged when the big shell went off; but it certainly was great to get around that corner. The trip back to Bethelainville was without incident except that traffic was thick and we had to dodge around a lot. Oh, one thing, a convoy of trucks had passed a certain crossroad and had to turn back. They were turned sideways and blocking the road. It was necessary to crowd way over on the edge to pass them. After a short delay we got by and having arrived at Bethelainville, the captain, priest and orderly got out (the others had been left on 304), posed for a picture and bid us goodbye. At last Law and I were off for Verdun proper.

The main road to Verdun is perfect and with the throttle opened wide the old Ford ambulance rattled right along. Half an hour of speeding and we crossed the bridge over the moat and rumbled under the Porte de France. One of our most cherished dreams was realized. We were actually in Verdun, and driving down the main streets or rather what was left of them.

The city of Verdun is surrounded by a huge wall outside of which is a deep broad moat. The French have placed barbed wire entanglements in the moat and along

A street scene in Verdun, August 1917. (Kimber Literary Estate)

certain streets of the city evidently determined to protect it to the last ditch. Verdun will never fall to the Hun. Our stay in this world-renowned city was very brief for we had 42 kilometers to go in an hour and a half. But it was long enough to get the everlasting photographs and at least one thrill. The streets were absolutely deserted except for an occasional camion rolling through with its load of shells. Every now and then we would pass a guard crouching in a little abri set in the wall of some wrecked building. When we came to the place where we could look down on the church, I suggested that Law pose for a picture with the church in the background. The light was very bad so it was necessary to give the camera a 4 opening, maximum shutter and a 25th of a second, the slowest snap we had. Suddenly a big shell went whistling overhead and as the camera clicked Law turned quickly. The picture blurred as we found out last night when we developed. That was the only shell that landed while we were in Verdun, but it was enough. Nothing could have added to the picture of that ruined and dismal city with its houses wrecked and its streets blocked by debris. We had seen all of Verdun we wanted under the circumstances. One did not relish the idea of a house or wall falling over him. We turned the car around, went out the same gate we had entered, and started the long and tiring journey back to Sainte Menehould.

It was very late when we finally pulled in and climbed the hill to the barracks. The cook had saved some dinner though, and the fact that it was a little cold did not matter, especially when we were so hungry. All the boys agree that since coming to France their appetites have been tremendous. Why, no one knows. The food is good and wholesome and there is plenty of it; we don't work all the time or so awfully hard. There may be nothing to do for several days, and then we are rushed all night and the next day. But we are ALWAYS ravenous. Afterwards we developed the films. Although the light had been very bad, eighteen of the pictures turned out excellent. The ones of Morte Homme, Hill 304, the generals and priest, the church at Esnes with the priest, and two of Verdun, are exceptionally good. The night was well along when we finally turned in, but the 30th of August, 1917 was SOME DAY for us. Enclosed you will find two maps on which you can pick out the scenes of the trip.

Love to you all, as ever, Cliff.

News had reached the American Ambulance detachment a few days previously that their service was soon to be subsumed into the US Army proper. It did not come as a complete surprise to the men, but it now faced them with a choice of what to do next. Should they stick with it and sign up for ambulance work full-time until the end of the war? Or withdraw now while they had a chance and return to America? With the latter came the risk, the increasing chance, of being drafted later. Were that to happen, it might well mean returning to France as infantrymen.

For Clifford, if for no one else, that proposition was a desperately unattractive one, so it was more important than ever that he succeed with his entry into aviation. As luck would have it, that chance, that moment, arrived only days later. He received a letter from the US Air Service. It was his summons to Paris. A relieved Clifford caught the train to the capital on Sunday, 2 September, where the following day he passed his physical and mental examinations for piloting. He was in.

18

ON THE MOVE

Before taking up his new duties Clifford had ten days owing to him, a *permission* he had been saving up. It was a proper period of leave, time which he could call his own to sight-see at decent length and explore the country, rather than the snatched days he had managed up until now. He decided in the end on a trip to the south of France, but before setting out allowed himself a couple of days to attend to some tasks in Paris. First, he wanted to open a bank account with Morgan, Harjes & Co., into which he could put his aviation service salary as and when it materialised; and he also wanted to spend some time in the company of a young fellow *ambulancier*, James Leopold, a Princeton graduate, with whom he had travelled to Paris and who was due to return to America.

The pair visited the Palace of Versailles together, something Clifford could now check off his to-do list, but more importantly he wanted to help him pack up his belongings for the return journey to the States. Leopold had agreed to bring a number of articles back with him to send on to Palo Alto: an uncensored letter with more details of place names and movements which he had had to excise from other letters; a number of photographs taken at the front; and the coat he had borrowed from George in the spring, hoping that he would soon be issued with an army overcoat of his own.

That completed, and after bidding farewell to his friend, Clifford set off early on the morning of 5 September for the Gare de Lyons and his train to the Riviera. He still had happy memories of the European holiday he had been on with his father and brother all those years before and he wanted to recapture a little of that feeling: to get away for a few days, not to think of the war or plan his future, but just be a holidaymaker again, enjoying the simpler pleasures of sun and swimming and exploring the Côte d'Azur.

His first stop was Marseilles, and then Nice, enjoying the countryside en route; and all the while taking a childish pleasure in evading the attentions of ticket inspectors on the way:

The train was about 30 cars (short cars, though), and as all the third class ones were in back they all had to be passed. And everybody was running to get seats. A big crowd of officers and civilians. First class was hopeless, so I climbed into a second class compartment. And dropped into a reserved seat, and here I am on the train in motion. Either the owner wasn't here or I have scared him away. The conductors never come around to collect tickets, all a man needs is a little nerve and a third class ticket, and he can travel first or second, whichever is most convenient, and in case anyone says anything, 'comprends pas'. So far I have ridden 300–400 miles 1st class on 3rd class tickets. This is a 2nd on a 3rd class ticket, and may be 1st later on. (It was 1st from Marseilles to Nice.) One thing struck my attention immediately – the different kinds of people on this train. Of course the trains going east carry very many soldiers and officers, and only a few civilians. On this train nearly all are civilians with only a small proportion of military men. And it seems as if these people going south were different from those we have been meeting heretofore. I am going to watch the people in this car just for fun; also we are out of Paris, and I want to look at the scenery.

He befriended various groups of people and individuals on the way as well as a British colonial officer named March, who served in West Africa, and a group of Canadian soldiers. But once he got to Nice, it was enough just to sit and watch and listen and enjoy simply being there:

Hotel O'Connor, Nice, France
Sept. 8, 1917

Dear Mother, John and George,
I am writing this letter amidst undreamed of surroundings. I am seated on one of the benches along the Quai des États-Unis. This is a grand boulevard running along the waterfront of Nice with the beautiful Mediterranean bordering it to the south. The day is beautiful; a fresh and delicate breeze is just stirring. There is hardly

a ripple on the sea. It is just the way the Sound used to be, absolutely still; and to right and left are beautiful points stretching out like long arms, making the Bay of Nice what it is.

And for the first time in months I am hearing a band, a real concert band. They are in the building across the boulevard and are practicing for some concert, probably for tomorrow and which I must get the particulars of and attend. A yacht is slowly steaming by and there are lots of little boats on the shore; and everything is so quiet and peaceful. One can hardly believe the whole world is at war.

There goes the 'Stars and Stripes'. It has not got all the pep I like; French bands don't play it right. They have already played the British and Russian anthems. I guess this is going to be a patriotic Sunday concert. I got into Nice the day before yesterday, late Thursday afternoon. Some Canadian soldiers who rode down on the train with me told me about the Hotel O'Connor. For 12 francs a day they give you a nice room, lots of air and light, clean and attractive, and with running water and your three meals a day. Can you beat it? And for Nice.

He enjoyed the café culture, eating an ice cream and having a cold drink, watching the world go by, looking at the mix of passers-by on sunny afternoons. But as much time was spent swimming in the Mediterranean or hiking with his friend March in the coast's majestic background, the Alpes-Maritimes, and exploring the coast, seeing what was on offer.

One day he caught a local train as far as he could along the Riviera up to the Italian border. On another he went with March to Monaco to the Casino at Monte Carlo. He was given a tour of the latter by a guide:

He showed me where the Prince of Monaco sat in the concert hall with his royal retinue. France has certain laws against regular forms of gambling, but as it wants to allow it in at least one place, it permits Monaco to remain independent so all sporting Frenchmen and people from all over the world go there to gamble. Of course, as the Prince practically owns the Casino he gets a wonderful income. The Casino takes in nearly $7,000,000 a year. We saw the Prince's yacht which has not ventured out of Monaco Bay since the war began. It is a beautiful white boat, very much like the millionaires' yachts we used to see on the Sound. They gave me this paper, etc., in the Casino, and I told them I would go back after the war. I have never seen such magnificent rooms even in the most expensive New York hotels.

Mr March waited for me outside. As soon as I had rejoined him we hurried to the station of the log railway up the mountain. We ascended about 2,000 feet and walked back to Nice, about fifteen miles, having lunch at Èze, about 1500 feet above sea level and with a wonderful view over the Mediterranean. After lunch we went up to the old Roman castle where we basked in the sun for about an hour. We walked around the ruins of a huge Roman tower at La Turbie about 2,000 feet up at the end of the log railway before starting the hike back to Nice. Those two old castles were very interesting. We got back to Nice at about 7 p.m. after one of the most interesting days I have ever had.

This morning, Tuesday, I had my third dip in the Mediterranean; it was the best yet. Please excuse this writing but you know what it is to write on a moving train, and I was writing up to this point on the way to Mentoni. This afternoon Mr March and I went to the Italian border. We took the train to Mentoni, an old Italian village but now a French possession. It is very, very pretty and has a great charm; still, the buildings are in bad shape and in some places look like east side tenements, only the coloring blends and seems to fit in with the beautiful surroundings. We walked to the border and tried to prevail upon the French sentry to let us cross and stand on Italy, but he refused. We stood at the stream that marks the border. The sentry looked upon me with great suspicion because I had a camera. He refused to let me take any pictures at all. I pointed the camera at him and snapped without his knowing it. As he was about 30 feet away he won't be very big, but he wasn't anyway. The mountains come right down to the sea and are magnificent. Never have I seen such a beautiful land and water scene before. I must come to southern France and Italy again, and you with me.

On his return to Paris Clifford was given an early release and an honourable discharge from the American Ambulance. He did not have to return to his unit for an interim period prior to beginning his new duties, as he had initially thought. So, a few days later, on 14 September 1917, he was formally enrolled as a trainee pilot at the US Army Air Service (USAS) in what remained of the AEF office presence in Paris.

The main offices, General Pershing's General Headquarters, had decamped only the previous day to their new centre at Chaumont, 170 miles south-east of Paris, closer to the front line where the first American troops would be deployed in due course. Clifford, though, was to be trained much further away from the front, south-west of the capital at Tours on the Loire River. He was given his papers and enlisted as a private on a salary of $33 per month: a rank and salary he would keep until he passed his flying tests.

Until news of mobilisation came and the move to Tours, he continued to eat with others at the American Ambulance Headquarters at 21 Rue

Raynouard, staying at the Field Service Hostel in the nearby Rue Lekain. Over the next week, he and his new colleagues began work at the Air Service offices, busying themselves with whatever clerking duties were required as they awaited their call-up for aviation training camp.

They worked in their old American Ambulance uniform or civilian attire for the moment, but were issued with new AEF uniforms – soon to be used – of shirt, breeches, puttees and boots, along with the Expeditionary Force sombrero (the latter headgear had become a common sight on the streets of Paris in preceding months). There were even supplies of standard issue army underwear, and extra kit would also be issued to him at aviation school. So, Clifford had to work out which of his belongings to put in storage and which of them, once he got his trunk sent back from the front by the men of SSU 14, he could take with him to flying school.

The new recruits ran errands, waited on officers and sorted the mail. They gradually began, as Clifford noted, to get into a new rhythm of military life. Here it was 'necessary to obey the slightest word', in comparison with the volunteer service of the American Ambulance, where there was a danger of everyone feeling equal. 'Here we learn the difference between a Private and a Com. Officer.'

It was not all to Clifford's liking, of course. New censorship restrictions had been imposed on what he could and could not send in the mail, restrictions which included not enclosing any of his precious photographs with letters home, something he felt 'preposterous'. But the time for quibbling was at an end: he was in service now and that service was just to begin.

On 21 September came the order to travel down to Tours:

September 21st 1917

Dear Mother, John and George,

This morning we all caught the early train for T— where the aviation school is located. Really it was a tremendous relief to leave the great French metropolis. Life there gets so tiring after a week or ten days. We arrived at the grounds about 1 P.M. and had a regular old dinner. In P. one has to pay so much for a full 'pot' and here we get full for the taking.

We all lined up for inspection and orders. The new men form the beginning of the 4th platoon. I am No. 1, 1st row, 2nd squad; regular military drill and formation you know. While we were standing at attention and responding to the roll call, whom

200

should I see but Snook. He had a broad smile on his face and was incidentally much amused with us. We were temporarily dismissed and the first man I ran into was Joe Eastman, then Cady, and then I had a talk with Snook. All seem delighted with the school and the life as student aviators. The grounds are wonderful; there is a great open stretch which makes the largest aviation parc I have ever seen; and it should be large for students, for from early morning till late in the evening, machines are constantly in flight. The motors continually buzz, and everything has an air of business and actual accomplishment. Two or three machines start at once, and as soon as they are clear and away, three or four more follow. It seems as if there were always fifteen or twenty aeroplanes in the air at once. As they pass over your head they are very close to the ground, and you can see the wheels still running from the contact with the ground.

I don't know how many machines are in this school, possibly 50 to 75. Most of them are Caudrons (tractors)* and carry two persons. There are a few Farmans but they are used by Frenchmen. There is also an assembling plant on the grounds; one might almost call it a semi-factory.

The work here is all dual control; French instructors teach us the game. Men fly with them until they can turn and land properly. Then they are sent to a neighboring field where they are given solo and other flying. I don't know where acrobatics are taught, but we get them after several months before going to the front. I don't think we will get to the front for many months; six or seven or maybe more, but you never can tell. Learning to fly is just beginning the game. A man must learn to shoot a machine gun, observe, telegraph his observations, direct artillery fire, etc.

Alan Nichols is in the foreign legion flying corps. I have not seen him yet but expect to soon, as the foreign legion barracks are right next to ours. But right now he is at the other field and may not be back until after 7.30 P.M. The other five of us are in American aviation proper and are all recommended for First Lieutenant's commissions which we will get as soon as we pass the flying tests. This is given after we have spent a certain number of hours in the air, besides landing and taking off etc., and making decent turns; it consists, I understand, of remaining over a mile high for at least one hour. Some class.

---

* Clifford isn't referring to a farm tractor, but means that the plane had a tractor configuration: the engine was mounted with the propeller in front of it so that the aircraft is 'pulled' through the air. Some configurations had the propeller behind the engine and 'pushed' the aircraft forward. In the early years of powered aviation both tractor and pusher designs were used, though by this point in the First World War, pushers were largely obsolete. Today, propeller-driven aircraft are assumed to be 'tractors' unless otherwise stated.

Our barracks are the best we have had yet. They look like huge brooder houses. We have a large mess hall and from what I have seen so far we are going to have a great old time. We have beds and what do you know about it in war time – SHEETS.

By the way I was very lucky to get out of the American Field Service when I did. In the first place I got out before I was kicked out; several boys had received dishonorable discharges and punishments for taking rides in their ambulances without permission, or going out of their proper way. Certainly that Verdun trip* was 'out of the way', 25 kilometers and return. And if I had not received my honorable discharge when I did, if not punished comme-ca, I would probably not have gotten out for months, for the U.S. has now taken charge and not only cancelled all permissions, but suspended discharges and transfers, even in the case of those men whose terms are over.

About an hour after lunch today the sergeant in charge sent McMurray** and me into T— to get the baggage for the bunch. We went in a great big Packard truck and had a great trip. I seem to be always lucky; he just landed on our names haphazard.

The country here is very flat, ideal for aviation but not so wonderfully beautiful. But the trip into town was very interesting to say the least. The city is quite a place. It has a beautiful Cathedral with exquisite carving and sculpture all over the front and doors; have not been inside yet. What's more, we can buy ice-cream there and I hope soft drinks.

You are probably wondering about the dangers of learning to fly. Well, the following facts may interest you: there are very few accidents, no doubt due in great part to the fact that that Caudron machines are used in teaching at the start. The Farmans have an added safety factor, namely, long strong skids in front so now they can't turn over in landing, and in the history of this school which is a large and important one, and has turned out many pilots, only two men have been killed, and this is due to carelessness. The French pilot lost his head and ran into another machine. One thing that I am glad about is that the U.S. Govt. is so careful about venereal diseases; they are not tolerated. Men are examined every two weeks. Today we were all lined up and our penises examined carefully; all O.K. Fine. Don't know whether I will have access to a typewriter or not for future letters. In the meantime goodbye and love to you all.

---

* He is referring to the trip he had made three weeks earlier, driving the French *padre* and captain to Côte 304 and Mort-Homme. He had later driven on without permission to the town of Verdun to look around it. This was considered off-limits. He had since heard that the SSU 14 leader Allan Muhr was extremely angry about the trip and, had Clifford returned to ambulance duties, would have demoted Clifford.

** Ora Richard McMurry, from Preston, South Dakota, was awarded the *Croix de Guerre* for his service in SSU 17. He would later fly Spad XIII planes with the 49th Aero Squadron, 2nd Pursuit Group, USAS, credited with three victories and awarded the Distinguished Service Cross.

19

BEGINNERS' CLASS

The Tours aviation school which Clifford had joined was still a French military facility. It would be some months before it would be officially reclassified as an American Expeditionary Force Air Service base as the 2nd Aviation Instruction Center. But irrespective of its name it was already turning out, and would continue to turn out, French-trained American pilots, either from the last intake of the 'Foreign Legion' Lafayette Flying Corps, with which his friend Alan Nichols was flying, or new trainees for the US Army Air Service. Indeed as head of the AEF, Pershing had requested in the summer of 1917 that 100 cadets per month be taken into Allied schools, some British and Italian as well as French, in order to meet the demand for pilots.[25]

The air arm of the United States had had a challenging time in the five months since America had entered the war the previous spring, undergoing a logistical baptism of fire. Still in its infancy as a branch of the armed forces, its role was downplayed and what was still officially called the Aviation Section of the US Army Signal Corps found itself chronically underprepared and under-resourced at the outbreak of the war, with few pilots and fewer planes.

On 6 April 1917 it could boast only 131 officers, chiefly pilots and student pilots, out of an enlisted staff of 1,087 men. Of those 131 only twenty-six were deemed fully trained.[26] Worse still, no one serving had had combat experience and, aside from the 1st Aero Squadron, which had had a less-than-stellar career supporting Pershing's 1916 Mexican expedition in a reconnaissance role, no unit had been trained for combat

– all the stranger, given that Europe had been at war for three years. The groundwork had not been laid, or preparation made, and the Air Service now faced a steep development curve if it was ever to mount a credible threat in the skies over Europe.

The very number of planes available to the service was testimony enough: a total of 132 craft, obsolete even at that.[27] Having been pioneers of aviation only a decade previously, America now lagged some way behind Europe in terms of the kind of technical aircraft development and design forged in the heat of conflict.

A race now ensued to obtain suitable funding from Congress to finance a wholesale modernisation drive. A rapid production effort was needed to ensure a steady supply of new planes and engines for the service along with a rapid programme for the training of new pilots. All of this required determined political drive and an effective plan of implementation.

A notable spur in this direction came, helpfully, from an external force: a cablegram sent to the White House by the French Prime Minister Alexandre Ribot in May 1917. In it, Ribot requested a greatly increased aviation effort from France's new ally, and was quite specific in his shopping list: 4,500 aeroplanes, 5,000 pilots and 50,000 mechanics, along with the necessary equipment to be ready by the following spring.[28] The cable had the desired effect. President Wilson forwarded it to the Joint Army and Navy Technical Board which quickly approved its content, pushing it through both the main board and its respective departmental hierarchies, before it was signed off by Secretary of War Newton Baker. By July, Congress had approved an appropriation bill for $64 million.

While this process was worked through at a political level, some of the necessary planning processes got under way to determine as quickly as possible what specific aircraft should be made, where they should be made, and by whom. A commission of investigation, the Bolling Commission, was set up, led by Major Raynal Bolling. The commission travelled to Europe to study Allied plane design and the production methods currently being pursued in Britain, France and Italy. The commission was tasked with obtaining the rights to manufacture any aircraft it decided to put into production in the United States, to purchase aircraft in Europe, and to prepare for the training of American pilots there.

After some weeks of consultation, it was eventually decided not to go down the route of developing and manufacturing a new generation of purely American pursuit/fighter planes. Rather, attention was focused on producing trainer planes like the Curtiss JN-4 ('Jenny') and a licence-built version of the British-designed De Havilland DH.4 reconnaissance bomber, powered by a newly developed American engine, the Liberty. Other combat types, the majority of them pursuit/fighters, would be purchased outright from the Allies.[29]

A new supervisory body was set up to oversee the production efforts in America. The Aircraft Production Board, later renamed simply the Aircraft Board when given official status by Congress, was handed the task of leading the manufacturing drive. Civilian led under the chairmanship of Howard Coffin, one of the founders of the Hudson Motor Car Company, its brief was a difficult one. It was necessary for the board not only to co-ordinate the might of American industry in all its competitive complexity, but also, through the Secretaries of War and Navy, to satisfy the varying requirements of military and air leaders anxious to get their hands on whatever craft they could, whether American-produced or bought in Europe.

Ambitious targets were set for the effort by the Aviation Section which outstripped anything suggested by Ribot: among other things, the raising of 345 combat squadrons, 263 of them scheduled for use by the end of the following June. These were heady targets indeed, captured in the mood of the time by the enthusiasm of Brigadier General George Squier, Chief Signal Corps commander, who spoke of building an army in the air with 'regiments and brigades of winged cavalry on gas-driven flying horses'. In order to help meet these targets Pershing signed a joint accord with the French Air Ministry – the 'Agreement of August 30 1917' – for the French to supply 875 training planes and 5,000 service-type aircraft by June 1918. These included planes which would go on to form an important part of the American air effort in north-eastern France and elsewhere the following year – Breguets, Nieuports and Spads.[30]

It was not all plain sailing, though. Coming up with a plan of action and writing a shopping list was one thing, but it was another to realise those ambitions. While the order books in US factories were now full, practical difficulties began to emerge in the American production effort. The design and manufacture of some engines, like the new Liberty, proved a notable success, but problems were encountered with other models like the Hispano-Suiza engine, to be used in a number of other craft then in service, and there were delays in the delivery of the American built DH.4 reconnaissance bomber.

For their part, the gargantuan order taken by the French authorities proved overly ambitious and would only be partially fulfilled. Only a quarter of the planes ordered arrived by the due date in June 1918, and were still shy of the target even at the war's end in November 1918.

Having said all of that, the industrial effort was properly underway some months into 1918 and by the time of the decisive American-led campaigns of the late summer and autumn of 1918 the supply chain was ensuring that more and more planes were reaching the front just when the German war effort was beginning to falter.

Part of the problem encountered by the service as it adapted to its new role, and to its greatly expanded size, stemmed from its curious origin within the military firmament. Still a junior member of the armed forces, and officially only an adjunct of the Signal Corps, it needed to carve out a place for itself in Washington as well as staking a place in Pershing's plans for the American Expeditionary Force now being assembled. With few men or machines at its disposal, its co-ordination was further hampered by a disparate leadership that saw different Aviation Section staff with different responsibilities scattered across Washington. It was an evolving process and a confusing one for a young service trying to establish itself within a military structure that still prided itself on its land and sea power and which was, at this time, preparing to concentrate most of its effort on land-based warfare in the European theatre.

Even the name of the junior partner changed from one minute to the next – a clue to its uncertain status. As General Henry H. Arnold recorded some years later, it was known by a variety of titles by different parts of government and the armed forces: the 'Aviation Section', the 'Aeronautical Division', the 'Airplane Division', the 'Air Division'. All were terms used to describe what was still officially the 'Aviation Section of the Signal Corps'. Only in time would it evolve into its longer lasting title of US Air Service, yet even that was a soubriquet only really enjoyed with the American Expeditionary Force in the autumn of 1917.[31]

With this confusion of names came the problems of clarification and evolution of meaningful leadership roles and responsibilities. It took time for a new, larger force to gel together. In fact, even when the Air Service of the AEF was constituted in France, it took several restructurings to manage its role within the military configuration there and for it to find its feet.

In Paris and at the AEF Chaumont headquarters, new service chiefs were allocated different areas of responsibility, among them training, supply, personnel, and aircraft technical requirements. Some key leaders of the Air Service now began to emerge, figures who would come to dominate the aviation war effort for the Americans in 1918.

Major (later Brigadier General) Benjamin Foulois, the former commander of the 1st Aero Squadron in Mexico, began the war as the senior flying officer in Washington but came to Europe initially as Chief of the Air Service, AEF. Another famous soldier, Brigadier General Mason Patrick, was later put in charge of the whole service by Pershing, and one of the most celebrated of all the American air leaders at the front, Colonel (later Brigadier General) William 'Billy' Mitchell, an energetic if at times spiky officer, took command of all air combat units in France in the latter stages of the war and was an early proponent of 'air power' as a major offensive tool.

But if that was the overall picture of what was happening above him, at his level far below in the autumn of 1917 Clifford was beginning to settle into his duties and training rosters at his new camp outside Tours. This was done under the tutelage of French instructors, in whose hands he and the others would find themselves for the next six months. Given the time of year in which they were beginning, the autumn wind and rain and the reduced hours of daylight would mean a slower pace of training for the new cadets than might have been hoped, but they got down to the new life with enthusiasm, settling into the camp's routine.

A typical day began, as Clifford recounted, with an alarm at 5.45 a.m., and after a quick breakfast he and the other cadets would report for duty at 6.30, ready to be marched out to the flying fields around them. However, Clifford reported that the punctuality and work ethic of some of the instructors left something to be desired:

With American Expeditionary Air Forces, Sept. 24th, 17

The life is exceedingly healthy and all the boys are in fine condition. We are outdoors nearly all the time. There is a great deal of loafing and wasting of time while we wait for the machines, but I have found every branch of war service I have been in so far, just the same. We will have lectures on the theory of the aeroplane too, but so far the hours have not been announced.

There is one feature about the service I don't like, and that is our French instructor keeps us waiting so long, and for needless reasons. For instance, the last two days our squad all reported at the appointed field, and both mornings and afternoons our monitor for some reason or other failed to appear. Today we waited and waited: the French instructors made a few hops with some pupils and they played children's games of jumping around, and 'cat in the corner' etc., with some pretty girls who turned up from nearby chateaux. And when they did go up they would turn their avions so the full propeller blast blew on the ladies with the results that their skirts rose like balloons and exhibited really graceful ankles and legs. And once in the air, the gallants would swoop down, just skimming over the fair ones' heads.

Very interesting indeed, but a useless display of tricks, for they were supposed to be teaching us and not showing off themselves. A French pilot instructor would scold or lecture a pupil for doing something wrong in the air, and then peep out from the fuselage and smile at his ladies. Oh, yes, great stuff.

This afternoon our monitor failed to appear, so we spent our time watching the others fly and teach. One learns an awful lot watching others, especially in regard to landing. About 7.30 C. landed. He was a monitor for yesterday, and failed to appear. Today he was free and had just landed for a mechanic to tighten a wire which had loosened while he was making a voyage or 'joy ride'. In desperation I went up to him and asked him to carry me back to camp, which he did and I had my first aeroplane ride since joining the U.S. service. I kept my hands on the levers, and believe me, it was all kinds of fun. You see there are several large fields in connection with this school. The auxiliary fields are several miles from the main field and camp and hangars. We, the pupils, go over in auto trucks, and they the instructors fly over when they get ready. As C. was alone he readily consented to carry me back, and as it was about time to return anyway, it was O.K.

When he next took up his pen a few days later Clifford was in a less sunny mood. It was, he noted, five months since he had set off on the train from California, and the memory of it caused him to reflect on that and on his future in his letters home.

As Clifford saw it, he had a duty to fulfil and he would carry that out to the best of his ability. He would fight in the service of his country. But, and not for the first time, he did not leave it at that, restricting himself to his own situation. He reflected on what he deemed the shortcomings of others, in particular what he believed was the shirking of responsibility by contemporaries from California.

The subjects of his ire, happily unaware of his censure and busily engaged in service of their own, were two fellow Stanford students, recent graduates and notable athletes, the Murray brothers, Feg (Frederic) and Bay (Francis). Frederic – who would go on later to find fame as an illustrator and broadcaster – was, like his brother, a Quaker and had gone to France with Francis as part of the Friends' Reconstruction Unit, a humanitarian effort to help rebuild war-torn France. The pair would later go on to join the AEF proper in varying capacities, with Francis working as an army engineer.[32] But news of their initial pacifist role, when he learned of it, went down badly with the outraged Clifford:

United States Air Service, September 27 '17

During the past few months I have felt many times a longing to come home, almost a certain homesickness, but as long as the war lasts my duty is here and that must be first. Oh, if the war was only over. However, you must all realize that if I had not come over when I did I would never be satisfied, nor would you.

Alan told me the other day that Feg and Bay Murray were to come to France connected with an organization to rebuild destroyed French towns. They are taking advantage of the fact that they are Quakers to get out of serving their country. I did not know that they were over-religious, although the old man is or pretends to be. But do they think for one minute that it is any more against their religion than ours to kill and fight, or what is more to the point, to risk their lives in the defense of their honor and their country's honor? And all that is just and right?

All war is against Christian teaching but when it is absolutely necessary do you think Christ would excuse Quakers quicker than Episcopalians or Catholics? He gave His life for the world; now we are all asked to risk ours, not necessarily give them, and these Quaker-professing people can't stand the test. It would be worse for us all to refuse to kill or harm our enemies and in turn have all Christian principles blotted out and humanitarian ideals crushed by barbarism and Teuton tyranny, than to fight in defense of these principles and possibly kill others in defense of what is right.

Alan says that if the news which he has received is true, he is disgusted. I feel the same way. Think of those two big husky athletes absolutely fit and able, both talented and with ability to lead others and become officers, slacking, and coming over to help reconstruct ruined French towns, men with that kind of spirit are not needed or wanted here and are scorned and looked down upon by practically everybody who is doing anything at all. I used to admire the Murrays; if that news is true I have lost all respect for them. I admire more and would quicker welcome as a friend, some weak hackney-type Tommies whom I saw in Liverpool. They have the spirit, and though not gifted with athletic bodies and perfect minds, they are the goods and overshadow the slackers. I do not want to seem like a hypocrite, etc., and I want to get home and have the war over as soon as anybody else, but there is one thing that will give both of you and me satisfaction, which, if I had stayed home, or in a position that persons unable to fight could have held down, you would not get. It is this: Whether or not I am killed, you will know I was ready to do my duty and did it. If I am killed, you will be proud that I did not hesitate, and if I am not killed, and I hope I won't be, you will be prouder of me; but in all events I know you would rather have me out of the way than me a 'slacker' and I would rather die than show a yellow streak. And an aviator is no ambusque.

John and George both want to come over I know, but their eyes handicap them; their spirit is right, though, and I am just as proud of them as if they were here. Besides it is harder for those who stay at home than for those who come. But for able bodied men like the Murrays, to choose an ambusque job, is more than I can stand. It would be harsh justice of fate if they never reached France. This is no place for slackers. I wish you could hear the fellows talk about Sayre, Pres. Wilson's son in law in the Y.M.C.A. He is a big joke here and so is the Y.M.C.A. Under the guise of a great and noble name it houses thousands of slackers. WHY DO SUCH HUSKIES MAKE OTHERS FIGHT THEIR BATTLES FOR THEM? I did admire them, but now no longer.

Last night I had a very amusing dream. I landed in Germany with engine trouble and was taken to the Kaiser's palace. He entertained me and introduced me to the Crown Prince. I was having a great time and he was entertaining us with most fascinating talk. Suddenly everything switched to an outdoor Court in one of the King of England's palaces. Everything was fitted up in a magnificent fashion. The king was sitting on his throne and I was standing talking to him. Unexpectedly, it grew dark and explosions, bombs and shells were heard on all sides. Several Boche avions buzzed right over our heads and started dropping aerial torpedoes. Everybody scattered in different directions. The king lifted a trap door in front of his throne and jumped down. I tried to follow him but the queen grabbed my arm and said that was for the king alone, a private bomb proof. The confusion was awful. Buildings and walls began to fall over; bugles sounded; the guard rushed around. I woke up and heard the last notes of the French bugler's rising call.

Yesterday I had my fourth aeroplane flight. After rising several hundred meters the instructor let me drive it alone. He kept hitting me on the back because I let it climb all the time. That meant move the lever forward. I watched the wing tips *and their relation to the horizon. If the right wing went up a bit I moved the lever toward that wing and the machine assumed an even keel again. It responded at the slightest touch. The whole secret is to keep cool and not jerk the lever or move it too fast. It is simply a matter of applying pressure gradually and waiting for the response of the planes.*

Controlling an aeroplane is very easy once you are in the air and if the air is not rough. Getting off the ground is not so hard, but landing is really difficult.

Contrary to what one would think there is little sensation in ordinary flying in an aeroplane. Even when taxiing on the ground you do not seem to move so fast. Once in the air things seems to float by as slowly as the shore passes from a ship or distant hills appear from a railroad train. There is no 'elevator feeling' in landing, no dizziness at all.

But progress was slow. The autumn days were getting colder and the winds stronger, and frequent rain as well as the numbers of students being trained, meant that time in the air was limited. After three weeks at Tours he was still stubbornly stuck at the fifty-five minute mark of air time. Twenty-five hours would be necessary before he would be able to graduate from this primary flying school to the more advanced schooling he would need prior to going to the front.

He knew that his hours would increase once he was allowed to fly solo but that was still some time off and he began to chafe at the 'tremendous inefficiency', as he saw it, not only of the French but also of the American war effort. So, and as was normal, he found another outlet for his energies:

At last I have found a good way to spend my extra time, and an interesting one too. Of course I try to get in all the French study I can, but that and other reading is now only getting second place. I am making a careful and very serious study of aeroplanes. So far I have collected many valuable tables regarding the leading aeroplanes and motors both the European and American; have secured and traced plans of all the leading machines, American, French, English and German and have collected data regarding their weight, speeds, surface lbs. per ft. and horse power and accomplishments. I have access to a very interesting series of lectures delivered by a French officer and translated into English; besides will soon study the theory of the aeroplane in class as part of the school work. Again, having visited three of the big French factories, Caudron, Voisin and Nieuport in Paris, and having the privilege of hanging around the shops and hangars here, I have been able to study methods and ways of construction etc. Of course I am taking copious notes and making drawings and doing all in my power to perfect my knowledge of the aeroplane. There are several types of motors in the lecture room and it is extremely interesting to examine them and the opened parts. I was absolutely surprised the other day when I picked up a cylinder of an Anzani motor to find how light it was.

You know one of my big ambitions for 'after the war' is to put on the American market an aeroplane which will sell cheap enough and yet be strong and safe enough to create and meet a popular demand which is sure to come. 'The Ford of the air.' That, and ranching with the boys are my two dreams.

20

DREAMING ALOUD

Flying and ranching were indeed Clifford's principal interests of the time – two recurring themes of his letters home from France. The latter in particular took up a great deal of his spare energy and imagination. To him, 'ranching with the boys' represented a realistic opportunity for the future, a financial anchor for him and his family in post-war California.

'Ranching' – or to be more precise chicken farming – along with the interconnected theme of money, were matters discussed by Clifford at almost every turn in his letters, pursued with relentless energy and enthusiasm. Restless, he wanted to look ahead, to plan for the years after the war, to secure the future financial stability of his mother and brothers. Clara in particular was never far from his thoughts. Her health, indeed her wealth, and happiness were paramount.

There had developed in the years since the death of the Reverend Arthur Kimber something of a siege mentality in the family – the family versus the world, with their put-upon mother as its principal focus. Now, whatever money could be gleaned from whatever source, from Clifford's wartime savings, money which his brothers could earn, money which might be unlocked from the wider family resources, money from a share-offering – any and all of it could be put towards a united family effort, a joint business enterprise on the land in California. Happiness and security would, in Clifford's view, surely result.

From the summer of 1917 onwards, barely a letter was written without some passing reference to Clifford's savings or farming ambitions, or indeed his worries about Clara, before he would turn to news of the war and his work or training. At times his musings would have a wistful edge as he dreamed of home, but for the most part he could be found elaborating on his latest farming thoughts and issuing detailed plans of action to those back in California.

Finding the opportunity to write these long letters seems to have been easiest in his first six to eight months in France, when he found himself with the most time on his hands. It was the downtime which caused him to constantly complain. Not a natural mixer, most obviously in his first months away from home, he could not have been the easiest of companions, especially to some of his more laid back colleagues. They might have been irritated by his attitude towards their relaxation, inactivity which he deemed laziness or timewasting.

Clifford had determined to fill his spare hours as profitably as he could, improving his French by reading French literature and studying French grammar, catching up with English classics, and practising his various hobbies. But he had also contracted with himself to write in detail his experiences on the front, intending to publish some kind of memoir in years to come.

So the steady stream of letters Clifford sent home was a mixture of all these thoughts and reflections and experiences; and those thoughts increasingly involved the idea of farming with his brothers. Chicken farming was a bit which he now got well and truly between his teeth, adopting it as his eventual goal, for which he was to be personally responsible. He was determined to take a lead in forging a secure future for his family as once his father had, a dream which would grow as the months passed.

His interest – the Kimber boys' interest – in chicken farming had actually originally stemmed from the time they had spent on the smallholding bought by their mother when they first moved to the Palo Alto area. Set outside the town in Santa Clara County, 'Kodina' had offered the family a period of stability and relative comfort after the three nomadic years following Arthur Kimber's death. There they finally began to put down roots in the West and, although in time the need to be nearer school and university drew them into the town of Palo Alto itself, they looked back at their time on 'the ranch', as they called it, as the real start to their new life, preparing for the future. 'Heaven' it was to be there at the time, remembered Clara. 'I have never seen happier boys.'

The boys busied themselves with a multitude of tasks and interests on the ranch as they set about trying to enhance the family coffers.

In Clifford's case the tasks included money-making opportunities, both to contribute to the family pot and to buy materials for his beloved gliders. One such enterprise consisted in selling the blackberries which he found growing in abundance by the sides of the roads nearby. To keep them fresh, he set up an ingenious water-cooled store using the family water tank.

John was already getting down to his first early experiments at chicken farming. The farming was a hit-and-miss affair at first, but the chickens came to capture their collective imaginations, both then and in the longer term. One early failure saw John misjudge the effect of the high temperatures of a California summer, realising only too late that the baby chicks in his carefully constructed huts were slowly being baked alive.

But rather than being put off, the disaster seemed to act on John as a spur to bigger and better chicken rearing methods. To the amusement of classmates at his local high school, he even began to draw up elaborate plans for a million-hen ranch, complete with a breeding plant, and started talking loftily of 'scientific farming'. He interested himself in new methods of egg production, including the so-called 'Hogan' system of selecting and breeding poultry being talked about at the time.

Although interrupted in his early pursuit of farming by the family's move into the town of Palo Alto – and by his own university studies – it was the germ of an idea whose time would eventually come because he had also sparked something in his brothers, Clifford in particular. The latter decided it was a surefire way to riches. Thus began the recurring theme of Clifford's letters from France.

He set out the stall, beginning by addressing how the business might be financed: family money might be used as seed capital and their father's fortune could be unlocked. Held in trust by the much maligned Aunt Annie, Clara's sister-in-law, the money would be prised from Aunt Annie's grasp at the earliest opportunity upon his return. Financial worries would be a thing of the past:

There will be quite a lot of capital to start us boys in the chicken business and at the same time give you a comfortable lump. Speaking of the chicken and egg business, one of the most encouraging bits of news came in George's last letter. If only we boys unite in that enterprise it will mean wealth for the four of us. We can become millionaires by selling eggs free and above board without using any crooked methods. I think George is right; ranching is the best line of work for him and for

John and me too. By uniting together we can have all the advantages of big capital and big business and lots of chance to use organizing and administrative ability. As for letting others in on the deal, it would be best to wait. I don't advocate it. We can get more out of the work by running all the risk and reaping all the gain and keeping entire control and say. George asks me if I don't think it would be wise for him to specialize in agricultural courses and possibly go to Davis. [University of California, Davis, the agricultural college and offshoot of Berkeley, established in 1909.] *YES BY ALL MEANS. Farming and farm management are a new line of work, and one with tremendous possibilities and opportunities. If we boys go in together, and I don't think there is any question but that we will, it will be necessary to have someone who understands the technique of farming and crop raising and stock. John and I have taken few courses along those lines; we have spent our college courses and time in other lines of work, though I hope equally profitable. In such an enterprise as I am dreaming of now it will take more than mere organization, business ability, experience in marketing goods, and buying etc. etc. The success will depend in great part on the production, and WE MUST KNOW HOW TO PRODUCE. It is my ambition to go into the chicken business. If we all go in together, think of the advantages of pooling our interests; one well, the same buildings, houses, etc., all the advantages of large scale work, and the consequent saving of waste and duplication. Let us not worry now as to where we will locate our ranch; but of course keep your eyes open. The main prerequisites are of course proximity to a good market, good roads, and good climate (men must not only labor, they must play). It is necessary to enjoy the work. Good morale is necessary and that comes from environment as much as anything else; but that is a question to work out later on. LET US DECIDE ON UNION NOW. If I am not mistaken John is equally enthusiastic about egg production. And can any of you think of a nicer thing for Mother than to all be together on a beautiful little estate with Mother queen, and a large and growing income all pulling together with the same reward of success?*

Precisely where their farm would be located was a discussion point for the boys, although they did not want to think beyond California. Their experiences as older children and teenagers, first in Hanford and then near Berkeley and Palo Alto, had made the California countryside an important part of their lives. It was the Santa Clara Valley, where they had their little Kodina ranch, which had most captured Clifford's heart:

Every place I go, the more I think you are located in the paradise of this world, the Garden of Eden, all its perpetual glory. Just to think of the beautiful Santa Clara

Valley and Coast Range mountains, with their charm and scenic beauty, makes me yearn for California; and I will welcome the day when I return, as I sing, 'Once more, dear home, I with rapture behold thee; and Greet the fields that in glory enfold thee.' (I know the last line is wrong.) Try not to worry, Mother, the best is yet to come.

The letters criss-crossed between Clifford and his brothers and their mother as he tried to bulldoze them with his relentless enthusiasm. His family had perhaps grown wary of some of Clifford's more fanciful schemes over the years, inured to what Clara referred to as his 'bizarre' ideas. When growing up, she said, he was 'so bright, irrepressible and fearless that he would take notions which no other boy would have the wit or the desire to think of'. But Clifford was now quite serious, and persistently working on each brother in turn if they expressed any reserve either about chicken ranching per se (George felt there was room for other types of farming include arable farming) or whether the practicalities of family life made a joint enterprise really such a good idea, as it appeared John had suggested.

In the case of his younger brother, George had just reached the stage when he was making his course choices for university and he had run his ideas, including those of arable farming, past Clifford. The latter did not give them an entirely ringing endorsement:

The course you have mapped out is fine but rather uselessly long, it seems to me; however, that is your affair. I am glad you are going to major in botany and have decided to become a farmer. But please get the idea of raising grain out of your head. This sounds funny and ambiguous; your head sprouts many ideas, but pas de blé [wheat, in French].

There are several economic arguments I will advance to you on that score. More of it later. However you are making no mistake in learning all you can about life etc. And slip in a course of 'chicks anatomy' if you can. I do not underestimate the importance of such knowledge but think on the contrary that it is of the utmost value.

But, in any case, irrespective of anyone else Clifford had already set his heart on his scheme. He would pursue his dreams without his brothers if necessary. His plans would 'make people open their eyes':

About the chicken business; my heart is set on it. I am going to be a rancher, whether the boys are or not. It would be nice to do it all together. This is a safe game and a pleasant occupation. It is somewhat slow at first but a man is his own master, and his chances of getting rich and comfortable, moderately wealthy, are excellent if he sticks. And what could be nicer than a country home in the Santa Clara valley in close proximity to San Francisco and good schools and STANFORD UNIVERSITY? With all our friends in that vicinity University people, not plain farmers. The climate is ideal; the people are nice; there is a great demand for eggs, a growing demand. And a sure supply if one goes at it right. ME FOR THE CHICKEN BUSINESS. The boys will follow. Together we will be a grand success.

As the months wore on, Clifford's letters showed his increasing commitment to this post-war idyll. It was not, John and George realised, only a passing phase, a mere diversion nor one of Clifford's pipedreams. Gradually, and perhaps in spite of themselves, they found themselves being won over. The length and detail of his letters from France kept up a brisk transatlantic trade with the brothers replying as and when, George a notably more frequent correspondent than his elder brother.

Clifford outlined his thoughts on everything from how their business might be financed and projecting what they might earn in the short to medium term, to making suggestions on the size and location of the farm and its buildings, accompanying the letters with detailed sketches. He even began to draw up some putative rotas, thinking how they might best manage their time and duties. He also suggested that they might continue to live at the family home in Tennyson Avenue, but commute out daily in the little Ford touring car he had earmarked as an early purchase. He believed their farm location should be ideally situated no more than 5–10 miles away from Palo Alto, perhaps in Sunnyvale or Mountain View. There, on the ranch, they would take it in turns to carry out various tasks and to do early morning deliveries of eggs to depots and groceries as far up as San Francisco:

The local trade would be sufficient the first year or two while we were starting. So deliveries could all be completed in about an hour.

I advocate starting very simply as follows: purchase of five or ten acres, depending on the capital we will have or will want to invest in the enterprise. Putting in of a well tank or tower and electric pump for a two to three inch steady flow. The erection of an office building where a nightman would stay and sleep; of a barn for two horses – only one would be bought first year – and storage of hay and straw. A garage and shop attached, and an egg house, incubator room and grain room combined, according to plans enclosed, and a brooder house and whatever number of laying houses we see fit to erect at first. It would also be necessary to purchase certain implements, and tools, plows etc. These would be bought second hand if possible and would be picked up by individual bargaining. New incubators and brooders would be bought, and more brooders modelled after bought ones.

John will have saved by that time at least $1000 and will have his Ford. I will have $1000 saved up. Our net assets together will be about $2500. I feel absolutely confident of our ability to sell $2500 worth of shares [in addition] on that; say 50 shares preferred stock, redeemable means 50 shares. I'll bet right now I could raise that in Palo Alto alone. We could then have enough to buy five to ten acres and put on certain improvements and buildings, the ones I have already mentioned. At that point we would want working capital etc., a mortgage would raise another $2500 at least. Let other people's money help you out. We would not of course incur any big liabilities that were not covered entirely by the property of the company and there would be limited liability.

If George gets a good job next summer and is very saving, he ought to have $250 to $300 to invest and possibly more. In 1920 we would all put in thousands if the project proved to be successful, and would buy back or let stand outstanding stock. Of course if we should go before George finished college, he couldn't give so much time to it as John and myself until he finished college, but he would be an active partner just the same. We would not have to adopt the above plan for financing if we did not start till 1920, although we would want to proceed just as carefully regarding outlay until we saw whether or not the thing was to be a real GO. With proper management the plant ought to expand rapidly and prove a quickly growing success. The main points to observe would be caution and consideration; but a great deal of initiative and guts and forethought would have to be shown.

By now the three young men had got into their stride, earnestly discussing everything from grain supply for feed – Clifford wanted to buy in whatever they could, cheaper and better quality than anything they could grow – to ideas on staff training and labour issues. In the case of these latter they had assumed by this stage that they would need some older and more experienced hands on the farm alongside them.

John had given up thoughts of Harvard Law School in 1918. What had begun as a summer job in mid-1917 selling aluminium pots and pans as a travelling salesman had carried on. He had grown used to the income it was bringing in and decided to continue with it for the time being, building up his reserves of savings before branching out into the field they were now discussing.

He was cautious about some of Clifford's more optimistic predictions of future earnings, thinking it might be difficult to expand beyond the point of making more than $10,000 per person a year. However, he had now fixed on a longer term future in chicken farming if he thought it could pay. He toured some chicken farms in California, including one owned by Walter Hogan, the man whose methods of poultry selection and breeding he had studied years before in high school. At college he had taken some courses in agriculture and he now wanted to get more specific and detailed training in this, his new chosen field. He duly did, eventually moving up to Oregon for a period to carry out graduate work in the poultry department of Oregon State College under Professor James Dryden, the head of poultry science.

Meanwhile Clifford was determined that a proper commercial go could be made of their putative business, given his brothers' agricultural knowledge and himself in the position, self-appointed, of 'business manager':

If the work was subdivided properly a man [employee] would not have to know very much in order to perform successfully the task assigned to him, it would be pure labor and work. I would not mix the jobs. I would not run the plant as a series of complete units; I would run it rather as a combination of departments and we would be the all-powerful combining influence. I would have a man at the head of the feeding; another to supervise the cleaning; a third for raising green food; a fourth for egg sorting, gathering, packing, etc.; a fifth for marketing; a sixth for purchasing grain etc., another for building or construction, again yet another for the machinery – an engineer for the pumping plant who would also be the mechanic etc. We four would be at the head in our respective positions: administration, marketing, purchasing, advertising, production, breeding, etc. Of course these departments would grow gradually and would not be started all at once. There would be three of us and it would be necessary for each one to know the entire business through and through to such an extent that in case of labor trouble in any one department one of us could step in and act as foreman till it was again straightened out. The labor would be specialized and more or less unskilled. It would be well and fairly paid and excellently treated. I would establish profit sharing. I would see that during the noon hour, for instance, that the men got a warm lunch or a supplement to their own and a rest room where they would have books and games etc. I would try to get them to take a pride in their work and would make an effort to unite them as a TEAM. There would be no labor problems till the affair got really big.

I would try and make the work in each department, that is the labor, so simple in its standardization that the men would realize if they left, others could easily be gotten to take their places and THEY would lose, not WE. Ford* has handled the labor problem well; others have too, why shouldn't we? Do you think the labor problem on a chicken ranch is anything like that of a big factory or manufacturing concern?

I know the thing will succeed. I only hope God grants us each other so we can try.

They could invest slowly and deliberately, growing the business up bit by bit and gaining experience on the way. They would succeed, he was certain of that. It was the bull-headed optimism, the restless energy of a 21- or 22-year-old talking. No grey areas. Yet, as matters turned out, Clifford was to be proved right. The business did see the light of day in post-war California, although events would intervene to ensure that the day dawned without him.

---

* This reference to Henry Ford shows Cliff's interest in new labour arrangements and techniques for labour saving in factories. His description of how his employees would work gives more than a hint of the assembly line. His suggestion of profit sharing and facilities for recreation and rest for workers, on the contrary, shows he was also influenced by new social ideas, however imperfectly understood. Interestingly, both George and John admired Henry Ford to the extent that until after the Second World War neither would buy anything but a Ford car.

21

BIRD'S EYE

United States Air Service
A.E.F Oct. 24th '17

Dear Mother John and George,

I can now call myself an aviator, for yesterday I had my first solo hop and everything came off all right. Am now operating the machine alone. You feel so much like a bird and look down on everything. It is great.

There was practically no wind. One man preceded me on another plane. He went too far to the left. The chief pilot gave me final instructions. 'Do what I tell you' said he, 'and don't mind the advice that everybody else in the class is giving, for they don't know any more about it than you.' My mind was made up and I inwardly smiled, for I knew what I was going to do. And Mr. De Haven's last words were 'don't go above the roof of the hangars, then peak and coupez' (cut off contact). It was all planned out, and I was going to climb, climb, climb.

'Contact' called out the mechanic. 'Contact' replied I. With a swing he turned the propeller over and in a few seconds it was whirring full speed. Other members of the class were holding the plane. I watched Mr. De Haven waiting for the signal to cut and then shoot on again. He waved his arm: 'Coupe'. Everyone jumped clear. 'Contact' – the machine leapt forward with the revolving Gnome 80 H.P. roaring full speed. In a second the tail was up high above the ground. The machine leapt and bounded and the ground rolled by lickety split. A slight pull back of the marshal ballet (controlling stick) and I rose alone in the air with my life in my own hands.

Higher, higher, higher I climbed, quickly too, for the lightly equipped Caudrons mount very fast, much more rapidly than the heavier Anzani Dual Controls that we have been used to. The hangars on my rig were below me. I was already to Mr. [F.W.] De Haven's limit, 15 meters. The machine kept going up. I wanted to go on; so free, so independent, so joyous. In the moments that I was up an awful lot unfolded itself before my eyes. Thirty meters. The hangars were now far below; I was too high. A slight push forward and the machine peaked. A click of the contact button and the engine stopped sputtering and began to slow down, the propeller gently turning. The wires stretched tight as those of a newly tuned piano, hummed and seemed to sing as the wind rushed by them. The ground was now approaching. At first slowly and steadily, then faster as I got nearer. It was time to redress, five meters high. The machine responded instantly and resumed its flying angle, gently settled. Back with the lever, the tail went down still more and then, altogether, the four wheels and 2 skids touched the ground. A slight bounce; another touch; a very insignificant shock or bump – call it what you will, and gradually the speed was reduced and I came to a stop.

A perfect landing. My first solo hop was over. I sat there in the seat high above the ground breathing heavily and with a tremendous feeling of satisfaction. It was not so hard after all. Much like a young bird that has just gotten back to the nest after the first successful attempt at flying.

Suddenly I woke up and cut out my daydreams; the motor had stopped. Upon landing I had forgotten to switch it on again, and it was necessary to taxi back to the starting point to give another man a chance at his first hop.

I stood up and yelled 'mechano, mechano'. There were several at the hangars a hundred yards away. They did not answer, paid no attention. I thought they did not hear. I yelled louder and louder they looked up and laughed and pointed in. Ah, then I understood. There in the distance were two mechanics hastening toward me. They were the men that had cranked the car several minutes before. It seems as if there are two or three mechanics to each machine and other mechanics do not encroach upon the rights and duties of their comrades.

Finally they arrived; cranked up again, and then making a wide detour to the right to avoid other hoppers I slowly taxied back to the starting point.

'Are you satisfied?' asked the chief pilot. 'Yes' I replied, 'I still have my neck, no broken bones and an intact machine. Are you?' 'No,' he ejaculated. 'You went too high and climbed too fast. You will break your neck yet.' ENCOURAGING.

That was early Tuesday morning. Monday was also an interesting day. In the morning it was foggy and there was absolutely nothing doing. We all just sat around the fire and loafed. Several of the boys, in want of a better amusement, got out their combs, put a thin piece of paper over them and started a comb band in opposition to Joe Eastman's banjo orchestra in the adjoining barracks. This latter is by the *way very good and consists of Joe who plays the banjo remarkably well and three other boys with a guitar, 2d banjo and a ukulele. Our men soon drowned them out, they played all kinds of tunes, chiefly popular airs, but including a few hymns and Y.M.C.A. drolls [waggish songs]. At first the music was a little discordant. But gradually they all got together and now we have a band that rivals Sousa's. Funny that college men revert to children's amusements at times.*

As I say, we were all lying around in the barracks, crowding in front of the fire or sprawling on somebody else's cot, reading a little, some of us writing and trying hard to concentrate above the din of our jazz band, and of course 'bulling', when suddenly one of the boys ran in and joyfully yelled out: 'No lecture for the 4th platoon today, fellows. Hamilton's gone to Paris.' Immediately all was bustle and increased confusion. I did not wait to see what the other were doing. Having dressed in my town clothes when I got up, I simply slipped on my coat, grabbed my campaign hat, made sure that I had my purse (very important indeed) and beat it out the door with a bang off to the city – off to [Tours] for dinner and sightseeing, till the afternoon's flying.

Already dressed in his town clothes, Clifford made it out of the door ahead of the other cadets. He walked the few miles into town from the aviation parc, past the nearby fertiliser plant (which caused him to gag), walking on through the town's northern suburbs and reaching the banks of the Loire. He crossed over the St Symphorien suspension bridge into the centre of Tours and, pausing only to check the opening time of the restaurant he had decided on, then made his way down Rue Lavoisier towards the cathedral.

He had made a number of brief visits to Saint-Gatien cathedral in the weeks before, but he had wanted an opportunity to explore it properly on his own, and he now walked around the outside of the building, trying to take in its various aspects before going inside. There, his attention was held by the magnificent sixteenth-century organ in the south transept, raising itself aloft to the stained glass rose window above, which poured its light into the interior, softening the sun's rays as the mellow light fell on to the pillars and seats and floor below. He moved around the cathedral taking in the delicacy of the arches in the cloisters and the nave before curiosity got the better of him and he decided to explore beyond the ground floor. He noticed a door in one of the two towers that dominated the cathedral's front and began to walk upstairs to a balcony:

There I was on a narrow balcony in the left wing, and half way to the vaulted roof. Here the smell was very musty and the air warm. In spite of my pretending to be an aviator I felt a little dizziness looking down on the vacant chairs, stalls and pulpit. To see a cathedral's interior from half way up the wall is an interesting experience. I stood at least ten minutes on this narrow ledge. The balcony was not more than two feet wide. And then suddenly I espied another small door at the opposite side of the wing. It was necessary to go slow. The adventurous instinct was upon me. My hobnailed military shoes kept grating on the stones. A soldier was kneeling below and praying. It was imperative to keep silence. Fearing each moment that I disturb him from his prayers I gradually worked my way around the balcony to the door opposite. It made an awful creaking noise as it swung on its hinges.

Ha. Another spiral stairway. Slowly and as noiselessly as possible, I ascended. It led to another balcony just under the highest gables of the wing, only this time the balcony was outside. Thank the Lord it had a rail. A network of scaffolding rested on this balcony; a man was working above me but did not discover my presence. Far below were the rooftops and the barracks. Beyond was the river. In back was another door. I peeped in. A great surprise awaited me. I was looking into the attic of the cathedral. Standing on this arched and vaulted ceiling and walking along its center was very much like tramping on a big cement aqueduct. This was the most novel thing in its way that I have ever done.

After many minutes of wandering in semi darkness, I reached the bell tower. There was no way to go higher. To the right was a ladder going down 10 or 15 feet to a landing or room with open arches for windows. This was the observation tower. Before descending I opened still another door and looked out on the square below on which the cathedral faces. A man glanced up; he saw me. Was it right to exhibit Uncle Sam's uniform on top of a cathedral? Hastily I withdrew, hooked the door and descended the ladder. And still another stairway presented itself. It was next to the last. The steps were in terrible condition, so that in places they were cracked, and covered with planks for the safety of climbers. I will not burden you further. At last I took the last step and attained the observation balcony as high as it was possible to go without a rope and poles.

The view was wonderful. In spite of the rather hazy day the river crossed by its three bridges slowly wound its way ocean-ward. People crossing the bridge looked like ants. On its further shores were the best houses of [Tours], and every now and then a beautiful home, ages old, almost a chateau standing out in all its grandeur, the center point of interest in magnificent grounds. Off in the distance the aviators' school, barracks, hangars and grounds.

Directly below were the soldiers' quarters and an old fort. Soldiers hurriedly scurried across the court to the back of the cathedral beyond the choir. I could see the canal connecting the two rivers which border [Tours]. To the right was the station – a fine building; boulevards and the main arteries of thoroughfare were quite easily traced. Other streets made a regular network. The Hotel de Ville stood out above the buildings around it. I could see several other fine looking churches, but the tips of their spires were all below me. Straight in front was the square. An important street led from it past the Municipal theater (which by the way I am going to next Sat. night) and which is indeed a building for T. to be proud of. And off quite aways rose Charlemagne's Tower, another old and famous building which I still have to see and which has considerable historic interest.

What I saw I cannot describe for I have not the powers of writing that I would like. THE VIEW WAS GREAT. The whole city was stretched out below.

Going down all those spiral stairways I really got dizzy. 349 steps. Who wouldn't have been affected? But I am going up that tower and next time will take some pictures to send you.

I had dinner at the café Lyon and then made a few purchases, including a pair of goggles for flying. The truck back to camp was just on the point of leaving and was in fact a little late, so speed was necessary. I just got into my aviation clothes and out on to the field in time, for Mr. Dubois had just cranked up and was preparing to leave for the landing field. He picked me up. A great treat awaited me; we climbed to about 500 meters (about 1800 feet or ½ of a mile), and then flew over T. to the other side. Well, you can see a whole lot more of a city from a moving aeroplane than from standing still on a cathedral tower. But both experiences are worthwhile.

We spiraled down to the landing field and the landing practice began. At the end of the day's work Mr. Dubois lacheed me, that is promoted me to the solo class.

22

TAKING WING

The logistical effort involved in training a completely new cadre of pilots like Clifford was a big one indeed. A new structure of academies and training facilities had to be created to deal with the avalanche of new recruits. Tours was one part of this and an important piece in the jigsaw puzzle, especially in the early months.

Initial responsibility for co-ordinating the air training programme had been entrusted back home in America in 1917, not to a member of the War Department but to an academic, Hiram Bingham. A Yale history professor, Bingham was in many ways an odd choice for the role: a man seemingly as at home in the jungle as the classroom, a bundle of energy who combined intrepid exploring with academic prowess. In 1911 he had been credited (although others had also laid their claim) with uncovering the Incan mountain citadel of Machu Picchu in Peru: the spiritual home and final refuge of the Incas and the settlement of tombs and temples to which they had fled to escape the plundering advances of Spanish Conquistadors. Having put Machu Picchu on the archaeological map for a world outside, Bingham led missions back to Peru in subsequent years, bringing back thousands of artefacts to the United States for study.

However, by 1917 this man, likened to an 'Indiana Jones' type figure by his biographer, had other concerns.[33] A member of the National Guard in Connecticut, he had developed an interest in aviation and begun flying himself. He was commissioned as a major in the Signal Corps and established a network of ground schools to instruct trainee pilots in basic aviation theory. Bingham would go on to command the advanced flying school, the 3rd Aviation Instruction Center (AIC) at Issoudun in France, but in mid-1917 the ground schools he founded were dotted around the US at eight universities: from the University of California to the universities of Texas, Illinois, Ohio State, Cornell, MIT, Princeton and Georgia Tech.

These ground schools were useful primers, able to put willing cadets through their paces in eight- to twelve-week courses, cramming the recruits with the principles and theories of flight, engines, radio, codes, photography and weaponry.[34] But the next stage, the practical matter of training pilots in planes, was still being put into place. Flying fields were built and training planes acquired. By the end of the year fifteen fields were in service. Nearly half of them in Texas, with Kelly Field and Brooks Field in San Antonio among the more celebrated, and others springing up in Illinois, Michigan, Ohio, Virginia, Oklahoma and California.

As has been seen, however, not all primary flight training could be done in America. The Allies were asked to soak up as many as they could manage and, indeed, training was undertaken by them. But by the autumn of 1917, given the Allies' other needs and due to a combination of poor weather conditions and the situation on the Italian Front, that number fell short of what was needed. The school at Tours, with its throughput of 100 cadets per month, was the only American school where primary training could be undertaken in France at the time, and numbers of would-be cadets far outstripped that capacity.[35]

But whether in an American-based school or a training facility in Europe, tutors put their charges through their paces, requiring a set number of hours of flying experience before they could be given their wings and sent on to a more advanced training facility to learn the deadlier pursuits of aerial combat and the acrobatic manoeuvres which accompanied such warfare.

The instructors at Tours, predominantly French, could be exacting in terms of the time they expected their trainees to devote to their new craft, which became a prolonged and iterative process. A good many of the instructors were combat veterans not long back from the front, and if their methods were at times painstaking, their approach was, they believed, one which could produce both good and safe pilots. A deliberate progression was required through different planes and different techniques and all done at a pace which they hoped, while slow, would be a better investment of time and lives.

Not all the Allies concurred, however, with the British in particular placing much more emphasis on brisker training methods. They had their own approach, which included the use of the so-called Gosport system: a tube which ran between the cockpits of instructor and student that allowed the two to communicate during flying lessons. Students were advanced quickly, fast-tracked through the various classes of planes.

Over time American schools gradually fashioned the best of these training regimes into their own model, leading one observer to remark, as quoted by former American air commander General Henry Arnold in his memoirs, 'The British tell them to go North, the French tell them to go South, the Italians tell them to go West, so they usually do what they think best and go East'.[36]

Through late October and into November 1917 Clifford and his cohort worked their way doggedly through the drills and flight patterns laid down by the instructors. Other cadets from the Ambulance Service had already graduated, including his friend Alan Nichols, who had attended the Foreign Legion school on the same complex, and he was determined to join them. Reaching the coveted twenty-five flying hour mark would be necessary to see him off to advanced training school and onwards to the front.

Clifford graduated from his original 'Gnome' class quickly to another, '*Anzani tour de piste* class'. There he learned spiral training and was taught how to manage his plane through a series of dips and sharp turns. Even during these drills he found occasional moments of delight high above the ground:

U.S. Air Service A.E.F. via N.Y.
Nov. 3d 1917

Yesterday morning the clouds were 250–300 meters and it was all kinds of fun, rather thrilling too, in plunging through them. I would be flying along and would see a foggy or smoky looking bank ahead of me. Suddenly the earth faded from sight, roads and all landmarks disappearing and I found myself lost in a cool chilly vapor like a dense fog. Mr. de Haven said in case we ran into clouds, dive, and I did. Gradually the mist thinned and roads and buildings appeared again, and I continued my tour. Some sensation though. I have often wondered just what clouds were like; they look so white and soft and fleecy, and now I can go right to them and find out, playing hide and seek with the world.

In his letters home Clifford was at pains to stress how 'safe' the whole endeavour was, to make light of the risks encountered in training, mindful that his ever anxious mother was wary of the manoeuvres he and fellow trainees were undertaking; being carried away doing what she termed in one her letters as 'dare devil stunts':

U.S. Air Service A.E.F. via New York
November 7th 1917

In acrobatics there is safety. These European aeroplanes are built so strong that there is absolutely no danger of their breaking in the air. When a man is high up he is safe; for if he falls he has lots of time to recover his line of flight; the danger is in landing. Each time we come to the ground we run more risks of accident than in any kind of flying up high. And a man well fastened in his a seat is quite safe, even if his machine does turn over and smash or wing slip or anything else. This has been demonstrated here. Every day nearly two or three machines come to grief, wing slip or turn over, but the pupil is seldom hurt, even though the plane is smashed all to pieces, provided he is well fastened in.

It is the funniest thing in the world to see an aeroplane hit the ground too steep, raise its tail high and turn over on its nose with the student, just one of us, dangling helplessly, quite excited and waving his arms and legs in a vain hope that someone may see him quickly and let him out by undoing the strap; even Mr. de Haven laughs. He just lets the pupil hang in his seat upside down, kicking his legs and arms, while one or two of the boys take a leisurely walk over to undo the strap. After an accident interest nearly always centers on the machine, not on the operator, for he is usually just excited and quite whole.

No one had been hurt out of the 300 cadets who were currently in, or just through, their training at the centre since Clifford had arrived. He had now reached the fourteen flying hour mark and so was able to graduate to the next level, one where he would be allowed to go on cross-country *voyages*. On these, the trainees would be given certain fixed courses to fly, increasing in distance and duration, flying between points or covering an area of terrain in a triangle. As time progressed and when the trainees were sent on longer trips – or indeed if they encountered bad weather or had technical problems – they were told that they might also put down for the night, something that very soon happened to Clifford:

U.S. Air Service A.E.F. via N.Y.
November 20th 1917

Dear Mother, John and George,

I am on my first voyage and have just finished the first lap from T. to V. [Tours to Vendôme, where there was a Royal Flying Corps training school]. This is a petit voyage. Later on I must make two big triangles, each side about fifty miles.

The machine I have is a Rhone Caudron. I don't like these revolving motors. You have to push your right foot forward all the time and, as the pedals are very close to the seat because Frenchmen have short legs and these are French machines, you get very tired. Besides the revolving motors are very delicate, and hard to regulate and choke easily. However, cross-country flying when you rely entirely upon your map is all kinds of fun.

After getting about half way and while over a forest at 600 meters altitude, my wonderful motor choked and pooped. I peaked the machine's nose over and made great endeavors to keep the sputtering motor from dying out entirely. After falling about 150 meters, the speed of the machine keeping the motor spinning, and the drop giving me several seconds to try my experiments on the tricky machine – more gas, less spark, vice-versa, more air, less essence, etc. – it caught again and picked up to 1200 R.P.M., but for the rest of the voyage it went badly and in spurts and jerks.

Among other things, I sailed over and through clouds. It rained a little on the trip. Rain feels very funny, like so many needles sticking the face. It blurs up the goggles too. It only lasted a couple of minutes but it necessitated a drop of 50 meters to get out of it. I passed over one very large and magnificent chateau. The grounds were very formal and beautifully laid out. A long narrow pond looked like a lawn. In most cases however, bodies of water shine very bright.

When I started, a little gas was dripping from my gas tank. It had just been filled, so I took no notice of it, thinking it was simply overflow. Upon landing at V [Vendôme], the English camp, it was leaking pretty fast, so I had the English mechanic look it over. He removed the boards around the tank and discovered a split seam causing a thin four-inch slat. As soon as he removed the board the essence simply poured out. He drained the tank and saved all he could (gas costs $1.25 per gal. in France). He said the tank would have to be taken out for repairs and that it would be impossible to fly back to T. that day.

[Raymond] Estey and Hamilton were there after having a forced landing the day before. They were on the way to C. Had started very late and landed at V., half way, at dusk.

There were a lot of Curtiss planes which we looked over. The English like them for training machines, saying they are a good step between the Caudron or Farman, and the fast battle planes. But they are not used at the front. They are said to stand a lot of punishment and all kinds of hard knocks.

We met Cowell, one of the last Foreign Legion boys at our school. A Farman plane, in taxiing along the ground, had cut the tail of his Caudron off. The English were awfully nice to us. We had cakes and chocolate at the canteen. So different from the dirty French canteen at our Camp or the Y.M.C.A. Eleven French student pilots had landed at V. that day. The English kindly sent a special truck into town with them and us.

We secured rooms at the Hotel Commerce. Only 3 f. apiece, and meals about 3.50 francs. Quite reasonable under the circumstances. And then a sixth member to our party turned up. John Hurlbert, who has been trying to make a triangle for the last two weeks was on his way to camp by train. He had smashed another plane and said he was all ready to start again. He told a very amusing story of how his propeller dropped off while he was about 200 meters high. He said he watched it going till it landed, and that it did not break; then he landed.

A pilot flew down from Tours with a replacement plane for his Foreign Legion colleague, but the work to Clifford's plane took a further three days. What should have been a routine training trip turned into an unexpected mini-break. It was an unusual little interlude for him and for those who found themselves there at the same time, although it was expensive. The understanding had always been on overnight stays like these that the expense would be borne by the trainee; and hotels, meals and incidentals soon mounted up for Clifford.

That said, he determined to make the most of the opportunity, even if it was late November. He went sightseeing with his colleague Bill Lindsay around the historic old town of Vendôme, taking in the castle and main church and talking to the locals, even being invited into the house of one of the older residents, a local justice of the peace who gave them a tour of his home and gardens. The following day a group of them hired a car to explore the surrounding countryside, visiting the château at nearby Rochambeau, historic seat of Jean-Baptiste-Donatien de Vimeur, the French nobleman, Count of Rochambeau, who had led French troops alongside American revolutionary forces at Yorktown in 1781.

Clifford returned the next day to Tours to recommence his training. He continued his 'totalizing', chalking up the remaining hours he needed to graduate. He and colleagues continued on their *voyages*, sometimes flying up to 200 miles a day in spite of often freezing conditions. But with the flying came bonuses – further stopovers whenever they could be managed:

Hotel St. Louis

R. Chandivert

41 rue d'Orleans, Chataudun.

Yesterday was a wonderful day for voyage and altitude; that is, it was clear although cold as the dickens, and quite windy. The monitor gave me a machine with a new Anzani motor and told me to try to make my altitude on one of the legs of the triangles. It is very difficult to make altitude with our Anzani engines because they are in such poor condition; but with a new one it is easy. The machine had just been rewired and restrung in the shops, so it was necessary for a monitor to test it out first. He made a petit tour de piste and said it had a tendency to tip a little to the left. The mechano soon fixed this. I got in my 'Teddy-bear' suit and fur overshoes etc., etc., got in the appareil and started out.

You would think that a man so well wrapped up and in a big fur teddy bear and fur overshoes would be warm. I had a pad of leather gloves and woolens underneath; Mary Lee's neck muffler, wristlets, etc. but I felt nearly frozen before I got thru. The first leg of the triangle to Portlevoy was easy. I flew from 600 to 800 meters and had no trouble in finding the way, although the strong wind carried me four or five kilometers south and I had to back into it to make the hangars. It is lots of fun to go by a map; you can't depend on the roads for they all look alike, nor the railroads for they do not show very clearly. Rivers are good course determinators, but the best things to go by are cities and woods. Forests look just the way they are on the maps. The shapes are the same, etc., etc. It took me about forty minutes to fly over Amboise, cross the Loire and reach Portlevoy. The chateau at Amboise looked very beautiful; I must make a special trip there some day or 'forced landing' to look it over; ditto Blois.

There was a very strong wind blowing from the direction of Chateaudun towards Pontlevoy. I figured it would take an hour and a quarter or more to buck it and cover the distance. So I had mechano fill up my tanks and started off on altitude and the second leg of the triangle. Before I reached Blois and crossed the river I had climbed to 2100 meters – over a mile high, and above a layer of clouds; but there were open spaces, so I could get my direction. I could see 50 or more kilometers and pick out woods as my marks. I got my direction by compass and map and began bucking a thirty mile wind. It was awfully cold and the wind driven back from my propeller went right thru everything; the teddy bear, two sweaters, my uniform, flannel shirt and woolen underwear. Next time I shall wear my leather aviation coat, too. My hands were like ice and my feet were chilled through and through. Thank goodness my altitude is over. Next time I go that high for so long I will have an electrically heated suit.

The only parts of my face that were exposed were my cheeks, chin and nose. They got so cold they seemed to burn. I drew the muffler around and held it over my face; it helped a great deal. Hereafter we will be given leather masks. If it hadn't been for Mary Lee's muffler and wristlets, I believe I should have been forced down by the cold. As it was I almost gave it up.

It took half an hour to reach the 2000 meter mark with the old Caudron; they are slow climbers. The altitude requirement is to maintain a course over 2000 meters for an hour. In the winter on the 26th of November, a mile is pretty high. I cut and started the long glide down. It took about 15 minutes. At 1000 meters it began to get warmer, and at 200 almost pleasant in comparison with 2300. But the wind was very strong and gusty and the old plane bumped around and tipped. The landing was good. Have not smashed yet and hope to finish school without an accident.

But this sightseeing and touring France in an aeroplane is all kinds of fun. We pick out what we want to see and then land and see it, staying as long as we like or as long as we think we have excuse for not flying back to camp at T–. The regular tourist asks somebody what to see and is then not always satisfied. There are 11 of us aviators here now. Most of us landed at the grounds and got into town before 3 P.M. There was lots of time to get home but we were all tired; 11 makes a party and we decided to stay. In numbers there is strength. The major telephoned up to ask how many American planes were at Chateaudun. At that time there were seven of us. He said to come back. We were tired and took rooms at the hotel instead. He phoned up a little later and when the mechano said there were now 11 and all were going to stay he went wild. Well, there is one thing about aviators. They individually know whether or not they ought to fly and if they don't want to they don't have to go up; their life is their own. A lot of Frenchmen landed later on and as they are staying too we have lots of excuse. Two hours and a half on a cold day in a Caudron is enough for anybody.

But just imagine the wonderful time that 11 regular Americans, all college men, and all able to get around in France, having served in the Ambulance, etc., and meeting Frenchmen under French conditions, can have when they go sightseeing in the chateau district of France, in aeroplanes. I will never forget the times we are having, as long as I live. Alan's talk did me good. I am much happier and treated decently; feel easier too.

Clifford completed his primary flight training late on the afternoon of 30 November 1917, an end-of-month goal he had privately set himself. Now that the base had become an official US Air Service facility, a new set of regulations was due to come into effect and he did not want his records confused, straddling two systems.

He had reached the required flying total and was now deemed to be a qualified pilot. It was time to move on to the next stage of his training, advanced flying in newer, combat-ready aircraft. He was to do that at the new American flying base, the 3rd Aviation Instruction Center, further to the south-east at Issoudun in central France. He was to report for duty the following week and travel there via Paris, being granted three days of official *permission* en route in the capital. A proud young man visited the camp tailor before he left and stepped on to the Paris train sporting his new brevet: silver-white US Air Service wings with a shield bearing the US initials in gold lettering. He was a pilot.

23

ADVANCING

The Issoudun camp to which Clifford and his fellow officer cadets were now moving was still taking shape in the early days of December 1917. Work on the facility had begun in the late summer but it was the autumn before major construction work was properly underway. It was a gradual process, although in time this base – the 3rd Aviation Instruction Center, some 65 miles south of Orleans – would mushroom into a vast complex: seven camps and eleven training fields spread over 3,000-odd acres, the largest airbase then in use. The Issoudun camp would see many hundreds of pilots through its doors and become home to many future squadrons and celebrated wartime pilots.

Little time was lost when Clifford and his cohort arrived. There was a new training regime to get used to, and quickly. New practice drills were set, and new planes and skills introduced to get them ready for the deadlier tasks ahead on the front. Suddenly the planes were faster and manoeuvres more demanding; and the young cadet officers were also brought out to the fields for shooting practice. Some of the men were already proficient with a shotgun, others like Clifford had never handled a weapon before. But either way, hours were spent out on the ranges trying to get their eye in and reactions honed, the round clay discs springing from their traps and flying high above them. It was a taster for the more advanced gunnery training they would need to complete before going into combat.

Christmas came a few weeks later and with it, in this part of central France, plunging temperatures. They were grateful for the sturdy and warm barracks in which they were housed. 'Hardly a camp,' Clifford recorded, 'more of a city of well-built and substantial buildings.' Better still, the food was the nicest he had had in France.

The men made the most of their first Christmas away from home. A tree was chopped down from a nearby wood and decorated inside their hut. Socks were filled with little gifts and with fruit, cake and nuts. Christmas parcels were distributed, gifts from anonymous donors back home via the YMCA. At three o'clock on Christmas Day the men sat down to a meal of roast turkey, mashed potato, turnip and gravy, apple dumplings, mince pies, cheese and coffee. It was a happy reminder of the homes they had left and of the families who would be sitting down to a similar meal thousands of miles away.

But it was a brief interlude for the men, as the demands of war set in again almost immediately. It was back to the flying fields and some bitter weather outside, the temperatures made worse by the fact that the warm flying uniforms and equipment they had been used to in Tours had not yet been replaced at Issoudun:

U.S Air Service A.E.F. Dec 29th 1917

Dear Mother, John and George,

Yesterday and the night of the 27th it snowed real hard with the result that the ground was covered with a blanket of white 3 to 4 inches deep. There were drifts six inches and a foot. An icy wind has added to the already cold enough weather.

I took a walk in the snow yesterday just to get an idea of what a snow storm feels like. Believe me, I'm strong for California. Never before has nature seemed so cold and bleak and miserable. It makes a man feel wretched, and yet mighty thankful for access to a warm fire.

Thank goodness my cold is over except for a little sniffles. My great mistake was to let my feet get wet. You see, the snow gets in the shoe some way, the heat of the feet melts it and as water it seeps right through; result, wet socks and cold feet, alors grippe. I now keep three pairs of shoes going full blast, two pairs always before the fire, and change wet socks twice and thrice a day; result: dry feet – healthy boy.

The morning's flying was the coldest I have ever been through. One boy froze his nose and another his right cheek. The former rubbed snow on to thaw it out and took the skin off. If you have a slight cold, flying in weather like this makes your nose run like a fountain and that provides lots of freezable matter.

My feet were like ice. On the ground they were first cold, then felt warm; a bad sign so I had to jump up and down till they got cold again. In the air they were numb. It is high time Uncle Sam supplied us with the promised flying clothes.

Training began at Issoudun on the so-called *rouleurs*, or 'penguins', small monoplanes, often French Morane models, with clipped wings. The idea of the *rouleur* class was not to attempt to fly the machines but to try to drive them very fast over the ground, to learn to handle them and tack them sensitively. Too sharp a turn left or right and they ended up in what Clifford learned to call a *cheval du bois*, an uncontrolled manoeuvre which saw a wing tip dragging on the ground and where the pilot risked careering off the runway and smashing his plane. Others, used to their earlier and more manageable older craft at Tours, allowed their craft to gain flight briefly before crashing to earth in a heap.

Clifford witnessed crashes from the outset which, if not frequent, were not uncommon. In the first, the occupant of a *rouleur* was dragged from his plane with a torn and bloodied face. But worse was to come, the first casualty was on 20 December when a lieutenant in a more advanced class was unable to arrest his plane as it spun uncontrollably to the ground.

Clifford kept his nerve and within three weeks had been promoted to the next class up. A week later and another class: each step up meaning smaller, faster craft. By early January he was issued with a 15m wingspan Nieuport, an *avion de chasse* – a fighter plane – of the type which had seen service on the front.

With the increased speed and manoeuvrability of these planes, though, came added danger. Injuries around him mounted. One colleague was involved in a particularly bad crash, and was lucky to get away with his life, with only his arm and shoulder splintering. Another escaped with just a hospital visit when he went into a *vrille* from 150m.

Clifford was aware of the dangers that he and the men faced in the small craft, although he maintained in his letters home how he was particularly careful when flying under 300m. That altitude represented some level of safety to him, a point at which the pilot had the ability to correct any mistakes made. Indeed he had taken great care up to this point, with his clean record to prove it. But all presumptions of safety, any complacency, could be undone in an instant, as he soon discovered:

U.S. Air Service France, Jan. 19th 1918

Enclosed is a souvenir. It is a piece from the propeller of the chasse plane I wrecked today, my first smash-up and a mighty good one, take it from me. But I was not hurt, so DON'T WORRY. You may be interested to know what it is like to be in an aeroplane wreck. Got in the plane this afternoon and made three flights with fair landings. These chasse type planes land very fast, 40 to 50 miles per hour and faster, and as I said before are very, very sensitive and quick to respond. In fact sometimes we are too brutal with the controls, as the French moniteurs say. We forget ourselves and handle these highly sensitive machine birds as we handled the lumber wagons we first flew in, planes like the Curtiss, Farmans, and Caudrons; that's what I did today.

I came down pretty fast, a little faster than I thought, like a 'bat out of H.' to use the generally accepted expression over here, and I didn't redress, pull back on the stick, quite soon enough. Result: the plane hit on the wheels and bounced way up in the air; this would have done nothing if I could have kept even, it would have ended in a 'pancake' or three point landing, but I tipped a little to the right. I corrected, but was too brutal, for instead of shoving the stick to the left just a little, I threw it over all the way as I should have done with a C. Up went the right wing; down went the left; and in the twinkling of an eye the left wing hit the ground, crumpled up like paper with a cracking sort of sound and the end strut dug in. The machine hesitated a second and then with a swing and a sudden jerk it reared up on its nose splintering the propeller into bits (only a matter of a couple of hundred dollars or so; thank heaven I don't have to pay a cent; it is on Uncle Sam and you good old taxpayers at home), and burying the revolving motor a foot in the ground.

I expected to go right on over on my dome but, wonder of wonders, the machine remained standing on its nose with me perched way up above the ground, feet on a level with my head and looking at the mud below. My belt held very tight and as I was in a rather cramped position I had a job undoing myself.

Gasoline was running out of the gas tank opening, like water from a fire hydrant. There was no stopping it. Castor oil, which is used a lubricant and makes the motor run better (please don't repeat this), was also leaking out pretty fast.

It seemed as if everybody was running toward me to see if I were hurt. Well, I wasn't, and I demonstrated this fact pretty well by the way I jumped out after I finally got the strap undone. My, but the old plane was a wreck. Unlike Alan when he smashed at T. only doing a half way job, I did a complete one.

But it was a shame, and tonight I am feeling awfully sore at myself for my hith-erto perfect flying record has been broken. Still, good luck can't last forever, and my lucky streak has lasted quite a while. Now my bad luck has come and gone, for it has gone I hope; I have a new lease on another lucky streak (maybe).

The French moniteurs have a very good system. They don't punish you for smash-ing. You are a little shaken up so they let you wait about ten minutes; then before your nerve is gone and you have had a chance to brood over your bad luck, they send you up again; in that way if you have not been hurt you get your nerve and confidence back. The moniteur waited for about ten minutes and then sent me up for another four turns; my landings were all good; now I feel like an aviator again.

It is wonderful to fly these fast little one-seater planes. You feel so like a bird and have such control in the air. You look out at the wings and there are only four wires on a side holding them, two ground and two flying wires and only one V strut on each side. Great stuff. The world is below and you are in another world, challeng-ing the eagle in his domain. Cut your motor and you float silently and feel perfect peace and absolutely safe. Zigzag banking at 60 degrees or ride up and down as in zooming and diving. It's the greatest sport yet. You are free to do what you want; you are alone; the Avion de Chasse is a fiery Pegasus and you learn to love it and care for it like a comrade.

The following week, comrades with whom Clifford was training were not so lucky. Clifford hesitated over what to say in his next letter home, aware of the likely effect on his mother, but ultimately decided to be as candid as possible in this, as in future letters:

U.S.A. Service France Jan. 24, 1918

I have something sad to tell you; I don't know whether I should or not. It may set you worrying; but please try not to. I keep nothing from you and this has been such a sad thing for us all and has made me look at things in a more serious way.

We all know what it is like to have a friend die, but to talk to a comrade one minute and have him gone the next is very, very hard. This is just the beginning of the war for us and thousands and thousands are going to die all around us if not we ourselves. The fact that two of my friends were killed from accidents that perhaps they could have prevented if they had thought and acted right at the right second, has driven home this war to me more than anything else.

Monday [21 January 1918] our class and another were working together on chasse planes. I went up in machine number — and made my several tours de piste; the plane was in perfect order, controls and motor absolutely O.K.; another fellow took his turn and then Leach.*

Poor Leach rose on his last flight, his first in this smallest type plane and made his tour. He had climbed way up to about 300 meters and it was evident that he would overshoot the field a great deal. He passed over us at about 150 meters and put on his switch again, but did not speed his motor up. It was going about 800 R.P.M. instead of 1100 or 1200. He should have speeded up. He was evidently rattled. Then he foolishly started to climb, at any rate he headed the plane up and seemed to turn to the left as if to come back. He fluttered a moment in a stall, and then wingslipped going into a nose dive, dropping to about 50 meters. We gasped, for it looked like the beginning of a vrille. He pulled her out and started away again. We thought he was safe. He did the same thing twice and next time dropped a hundred meters in a vrille to the left which he entered from a wingslip; three or four turns and he crashed.

We ran over but, it was hopeless and he was unconscious. It was some minutes before we could chop him out of the machine which was a total wreck; he must have hit with four or five tons force. Both legs, his left arm and nose were broken, his forehead and mouth cut open, and he had a terrible cut in the abdomen which killed him. He died a minute or so after the doctor arrived and we could not save him. He did not suffer, thank the Lord, to him it was simply a sudden drop and then lasting peace.

One good thing about aviation is that you are killed instantly or not at all; there is no lingering death. But I hope and pray that if I meet death in the service of my country I meet it at the front at the hands of the Hun, and fall like a shot eagle. But to be killed in training or through an accident your own fault that could be avoided, seems such a pity in comparison. It seems as if you had not yet struck a blow for the cause of right and humanity and democracy.

Today I had just come in from one of the ground classes when I heard that Jack Wright** has been killed. He went through the school at T. with me, was in my class a short time ago and I knew him quite well. He was spiralling; fell because he attempted a turn too near the ground and without speed. He should have peaked more; thus we learn through the mistakes, sometimes fatal mistakes, of others.

---

* Ernest Hunnewell Leach, born in Hanson, Massachusetts, on 4 November 1895. He had previously served in American Ambulance SSU 18 from April to September 1917.

** Jack Morris Wright, born 9 July 1898 in New York City, in the Transport Section 526 of the American Field Service, 28 April to 16 August 1917. He died aged 19.

Both Jack and Leach were fine fellows. Leach cracked a joke just before he went up and as he put on his goggles. Wright was very well liked and always had a broad smile and a cheery word. We may speak to a comrade one minute and the next may see him killed. It is sad.

I was talking to some men in the Lafayette Escadrille when I was out at the front, and they said the hardest thing of all is to wish a friend good luck as he starts out on a patrol and then hear of his death some hours later or not know his fate for weeks. But c'est la guerre. We must not let those things rest on our minds or brood over them. We must keep our nerve and think of happy things and times.

Personally I sort of believe I have a guardian angel and that it will be the other fellow that will get killed. You are going to see me home when this awful war is over, and we shall have many happy years together and shall have a most wonderful home of four, and a great time on the farm. But I pity the poor fellows in the trenches. They are the men who will win this war; they suffer more than any of us and live in a regular HELL. Hats off to them. THEY hold the line.

Clifford redoubled his efforts to complete his advanced training, practising his acrobatic training, spinning and twisting at altitude. He learned vertical turns and *renversements* – performing an aerial about-face, turning the plane over and coming in the opposite direction – and he learned to cut his engine at 1,000m and spiral down at a near vertical angle before gliding his plane into the landing circle on the field below.

In fact, the latter technique proved useful almost as soon as Clifford had perfected it, when one day his motor did actually cut out for real. He was on altitude training, maintaining a flight path just under 4,000m when his engine cut out 7 miles from base. After some manoeuvring he managed to glide his plane home, parking safely near the aerodrome hangars.

By mid-February Clifford and a number in his cohort had nearly finished their advanced schooling, all but combat work (gunnery) and formation flying still to be completed. But before he left Issoudun Clifford and a group of other pilots were asked to travel to Paris to ferry back a new consignment of the latest model Nieuports. As before, the delivery of new planes was lagging behind. More were needed to train the increasing numbers of pilots now coming through. They travelled up by train, and as so often was the case made full use of the opportunity to enjoy what the capital had to offer. Even in wartime that meant a chance to dine out, visit the theatre, a show or an opera, and the luxury of an overnight stay in a hotel.

But his visit to Paris also afforded Clifford the opportunity to load up with new flying equipment. Although by now issued with a 'teddy bear' suit, he still needed a new lined helmet and gloves and new goggles to keep the cold at bay. Once fully attired, he set off to the air depot with the others to collect the new consignment of planes. They were to begin flying in stages south-west from the depot outside Paris to Issoudun, via the town of Étampes:

This delivering planes is some job. We left Paris for the aviation field about 1.30 and arrived there 2.15 or thereabouts. I have never seen so many hangars in my life; several hundred like a great wall, entirely around the field. There were thousands of planes ready for delivery to various parts of France, the front and the many schools; dozens of types too. We each had to sign up for a certain plane, absolutely new machines and two-seaters; the motors all worked like a charm. We watched our chance and took off as we could, as near together as possible. I left the field about four p.m.

It was very hazy and therefore very hard to pick out points to steer to. All the planes became separated. Nine out of 12 reached Etampes; I was second to land there; none of us had maps or compasses or any instruments but the revolution indicator. Considering the haze, we were lucky to get as many machines there as we did, especially without maps. I was told the general direction, got my angle with the sun, kept the course, and finally saw the Etampes field below. There is a big French school there. I guess the other three are lost and 'somewhere' in France.

My, but the French Caudron pupils went wild over the new Nieuports we drove in. They are pretty classy machines, but they seem so big and lumbering after the little 15 meter chasse planes we have been flying.

When he eventually returned to base a pleasant surprise awaited him. There was news that an appeal he and others had lodged had been upheld. It was a request they had made to be upgraded from second to first lieutenants, something they had taken issue over some weeks before when their initial commissions had come through. They had argued that, on the basis of an official order they had obtained, anyone passing either the Reserve Military Aviation tests in America or their own French *Brevet* before 5 December past should be eligible for the higher office. This they had done, and it was a point of principle they wanted to uphold, not only for the prestige and rank represented by the office, but also because it meant a material increase in pay. At that stage, first lieutenancy carried with it a government salary of $186 a month, a respectable wage even allowing for the fact that they had to pay for certain clothing as officers, and contribute nearly a quarter of it to the officers' mess.

So it was as First Lieutenant SORC (Signal Officers Reserve Corps) that Clifford now proceeded to his final tranche of training, hoping all the while that he would see action before the war's end.

24

FINISHING SCHOOL

The last days of training at Issoudun were intense and tiring for Clifford and his class, devoted to aspects of combat work and formation flying. The former would, of course, be the bread and butter of the fighter pilot – the *chasse* pilot – he was to become; a necessary ability not only to manoeuvre a plane but to be able simultaneously to fight at close quarters in the skies. By this time it was no longer enough to think in terms of the dexterity and bravura of the single pilot, with the aviator as hero, the glamorous lone fighter criss-crossing the heavens. Increasingly, as the lessons learned on the front proved, it was important to practise not only the skills of close combat but also the defensive drills of formation flying. This was necessary both for the job of shepherding observation aircraft and the mutual protection of fighter patrols who were carrying out that role.

In union and in numbers lay strength, and the importance of formation flying was being drummed into the new pilots. The journalist Heywood Broun, who travelled to France with the American Expeditionary Force in 1917 and who spent six months observing the war at close quarters, noted how the French had adapted to the new circumstances:

> The air policy of France ... was in a state of great fluidity at this time. They were not prepared to lay down the law, because they were in the very act of giving up their own romantic, adventurous system of single man combat, and were borrowing the German system of squadron formation. They were reluctant enough to accept it, let alone acknowledge their debt to the Germans. But the old knight-errantry of the air could not hold up against the new mass attacks. And the French are nothing if not practical.[37]

This lesson was now being drilled home to them by their French instructors. Clifford and his class spent eight hours in the air each day learning to lead or follow, maintaining discipline at altitude, speeding along at 110 miles per hour and keeping the formation and shape of the groups in which they were flying, heightening awareness of the comrades around them. This drill was followed by basic combat techniques as the cadets would break off, swooping down to 10ft above the ground, diving at sheep, horses and cows in the field.

It was a good grounding for them, but it was now time to marry these skills with the shooting practise they had begun trying out weeks before in the fields around Issoudun. For this they were going to have to move to their final camp, a gunnery school in the south-west of France at Cazaux, south of Bordeaux. The French authorities were wary of situating any gunnery facility in a populated area and had set up the École de Tir Aérien at Cazaux back in 1915, followed later by a similar school at St Jean de Monts further north on the Vendée coast.

It was only at the turn of 1917–18 that Cazaux had been earmarked as a training camp for American pilots. Empty stretches of the nearby Atlantic coast and the tranquil lake, the Étang de Cazaux et de Sanguinet, made the base an ideal training ground. The forest-fringed lake was a quiet and controlled area for the young pilots to practise their shooting skills. It was an excellent training ground; but what appealed to Clifford was the wild beauty and remoteness of the area they found themselves in:

March 3d 1918

Dear Mother John and George,
    Today I got a view of the broad body of water that separates me from home, the Atlantic Ocean. We are in SW France now and about seven kilometers from the sea. The country between is covered with pine trees, not very large to be sure, but lots of them. Most of these trees are notched and a tin can tied just below the notch so the resin from which turpentine is made can be gathered as it runs out. There is also some chapparel and a great deal of heather like that in our back yard at home; only this heather is in places way over your head. It is very pretty now even if it is not in blossom. Oh, it felt fine to get out by myself and walk thru this pretty country. I started out right after lunch and plunged right into the woods, working my way westward and keeping my direction by watching the sun thru the tree tops. After a little over two hours I smelt the ocean and then the sand dunes came

in sight. Everything reminded me of Carmel and home. My time being limited I had to hurry and could only spend a few minutes at the beach. How I wanted to go in swimming; but being alone and seeing that it is March 3d and it snowed yesterday and last night, I denied myself that pleasure. As I stood on the dunes looking across the broad expanse of water, it was very calm, my thoughts went homeward. It is hard to be so far away and for so long.

The target practice they now carried out was intended to develop more mobile and versatile skills. They were still to practise trap shooting to improve overall accuracy, but the idea now was to learn to use a greater variety of weapons and to fire while on the move from positions on land, on the lake and eventually in the air, although their aerial gunnery practice was hampered in the first week by poor weather:

We started out by shooting at stationary water targets from fast moving motor boats; this is wonderful sport. The lake is large and we can get in a full hour's run going and returning. Four or five men stand up and shoot at once and believe me those poor old targets get many a broadside. Quite deafening for the shooters too, for the carbines have an awful report. From the stands we shoot out at targets anchored in the lake. Every now and then they send up a bunch of little balloons for us to aim at. Few escape the Americans. The Frenchmen all think we are wonderful shots and, indeed, on average we have it over them 2 to 1; but why shouldn't we? For all the men in aviation, pilots and observers especially, had to pass very hard eye tests. We get in quite a bit of trap shooting with a shotgun and even the little 16 millimeter, about the size of a 22 caliber cartridge, comes in for its share at target practice. The machine gun is being drummed into us hammer and tongs and indeed it should be. By now all of us can strip it and assemble it tres vite and we are getting quite familiar with the jams. About every fourth and fifth bullet is a tracer bullet and you can see it leave the barrel and go whizzing past or through the target. It is fine for helping you correct your aim in case the sights are a bit off so you allow enough for the deflection of a moving target.

He enjoyed the busy routine, the hours spent learning the new skills of weaponry and manoeuvring his plane to fire on targets on the ground and in the air, and he devoted many pages of his letters home to diagrams explaining the art and science of shooting at a moving target when he himself was speeding towards it. But above all it was finally a sense of purpose that buoyed him, a sense that he was preparing for a day which would now finally arrive, that he would see service on the front:

We are getting wonderful training in flying and shooting and will be equal of the average Boche flyer. Personally I feel very confident and am sort of longing to get to the front again and do a bit of fighting. I want to get in at least one blow for Leach and Wright, Hoppy, Wilson, Philipiteaux (old Phil was a fine chap. I wrote you how he and Bill Lindsay worked hard all last Xmas eve to help give the fellows a Happy Xmas) and Hagadorn, all friends of mine who have fallen before ever reaching the front but nevertheless for the cause we are all fighting for.* The training is nearly as dangerous as flying at the front. Thank the Lord my training is practically over and I know how to fly. If I fall now it shall be at the hands of a Hun and death at the front would be glorious if I must die. But I have as good chance of living through it as anybody; why worry? If I wasn't doing my bit I wouldn't be satisfied nor would you all, Mother, John and George. I am not at all afraid to go to the front; I want to fight.

A funny thing happened in class yesterday: Quentin Roosevelt, 'Hot Potatoes' Converse (we call him H.P. because that is his favorite expression and uses it so much) and Bigelow** came in late. In the meantime we took a barrel out of a Vickers machine gun and when those three came in Turner, the instructor, asked Roosevelt to inspect the gun. He pronounced it O.K. Converse found fault with the safety seal; Bigelow said the recall or fuse spring was too loose for perfect action. Of course the barrel is hidden in the Vickers gun by the water jacket case and muzzle piece etc. When the instructor told these three inspectors that there was no barrel they were nearly knocked over. You should have heard the class roar. Q.R. is a pretty good sport and has lots of life. He is absolutely democratic and very well liked. I imagine that if this bunch all goes chasse as they probably will (but there's no telling in the army), that we'll be in the same escadrille.

Quentin was the youngest son of former president Theodore Roosevelt. He and his three brothers, Theodore Junior, Kermit and Archibald, were all serving in France, although Quentin was the only one to have gone into the Air Service. He joined shortly after the outbreak of war, signing up with the 1st Reserve Aero Squadron in his home state of New York and

---

* Hoppy – Charles Alexander Hopkins was born on 24 October 1895 in Newark, New Jersey. A member of AFS *Camion* Sections 526 and 184 from 5 May to 6 August 1917, he was killed on 30 January 1918. Arthur H. Wilson was killed on 23 February 1918. Leland James Hagadorn was killed on 23 February 1918.

** First Lieutenant Robert R. Converse was assigned to the 13th Aero Squadron, 2nd Pursuit Group, only to be shot down near Jaulney on 13 September 1918 and taken prisoner. Donald Asa Bigelow was born on 30 September 1898 in Colchester, Connecticut. He was in AFS SSU 17 from 12 March to 30 August 1917, and was killed in a crash on 3 June 1918.

training on Long Island. But even after arriving in France he had initially acted as a supply officer at the Issoudun base, helping to get it up and running before turning his attentions to piloting proper. He would go on to join the celebrated 95th Kicking Mule Aero Squadron, one of the first in active service on the front. He was killed in service, shot down some months later in July 1918.[38]

The three weeks he spent at Cazaux represented a 'glorious' time for Clifford, 'like a three-week *permission*', he told his family. It seems to have been one of the happiest periods of his time in France, enjoying his surroundings and the increasingly spring-like weather in the south-west of France. It is also clear from his letters that he was becoming increasingly clubbable, less aloof or reserved, and was enjoying the camaraderie of classmates like Donald Bigelow and, especially, his friend Jerry Jerome with whom he spent increasing amounts of time. He was easy in their company and relishing the training they were doing together:

We are flying about twice a day. The idea of the course is to practice aiming the airplane at a target and shooting at it over the Lake. We have finished practically all of the ground shooting. This kind of flying is pots of fun; first there is the parachute chasing, then uncontrolled and controlled firing at little balloons and sausages anchored over a certain spot and lastly, firing at a huge stocking about the size of an aeroplane fuselage pulled in back of an old G.4 Caudron. The parachute practice consists of climbing to about 1200 meters, making a vertical virage and throwing the parachute out in the midst of it and then diving and zumming at the parachute all the way down until it settles to earth.

The other day I went up 200 meters and set the parachute adrift. By the time I had glided to the required height of 1000 meters I had run into the parachute so had to continue gliding to earth. Yesterday morning I went above the clouds and had a lot of fun; finally the parachute disappeared in the clouds. I dived then and circled around below where I thought the parachute would be coming out, but I never saw it again, poor thing.

Shooting at the balloons is great sport, too, because we have tracer bullets that make a flare all the way, look like a shooting star and we can see if the aim is good. Every fourth or fifth bullet is a tracer. Yesterday out of 100 shots I saw one tracer go through the balloon, the others went all around it.

I am writing this letter from a rowboat on the canal going into the lake. Austin is rowing; I am in the front seat and Bigelow is smoking a big fat cigar in the stern; he looks like a general or somebody. The day is fine and when we get out in the lake where the water is clean and near the shore where the water is warm and the bottom is sandy we are going to take a swim.

March 14th 1918

I am sure you are beginning to think now that it will be impossible for me to ever bring down a Boche. Maybe, but the consolation is that it is going to be just as hard for him to get me. Two combatants may maneuver around each other for an hour and a half, use up all their ammunition, 500 shots or so, and all their essence, wave their arms at each other, smile, scowl, nod, swear, or shake a fist, and fly home to their respective camps. According to McConnel, Major Lufbery* had this kind of fighting acquaintance with a big German 'ace' and it was not until after three or four duels with this same man, each on a different day to be sure, that Lufbery finally brought the Hun down.

A man must calculate instantly, too, for chasse planes going full speed will pass each other at about 300 miles per hour and the effective range is only 600 to 700 yards and the most common 200 to 300. Of course, in maneuvering for shooting the planes are not always passing, but may be chasing each other or diving, one at the other's wings or tail.

To aid the pilot in his shooting tracer bullets are used. Every third or fourth bullet leaves a streak in back of it and looks like a shooting star. Thus if a man is quick he can correct an error by watching the tracer bullet. Skill in flying counts as much as skill in shooting. A man may be a wonderful shot, but if B can outmaneuver him or dodge him every time he is just ready to shoot, A's shot goes wild or he never shoots. To win a fight is very hard; to lose is stupid if there is only one plane against you and the planes of both combatants are about even. To get away is not easy but possible. I'm going to stay right in the middle of my formation. The big danger is in falling out, and then being alone; being picked off by three or four Boche. The idea is always to catch the straggler. In union is strength. Formations seldom fight each other; they maneuver around the sky and each formation tries to pick off the other's stragglers. And all this takes place miles above the earth in the kingdom of the air. Scraps are staged 15000 to 18000 feet high. Do you find this interesting or blood curdling? Don't let it worry you; I'm going to be very VERY VERY CAREFUL.

---

* Raoul Lufbery was an air ace who had served in the Foreign Legion Lafayette Escadrille before joining the US Air Service's celebrated 94th Hat in the Ring Aero Squadron.

March 19th 1918

Dear Mother John and George,

A funny thing happened tonight. It proved that I am beginning to 'comprende un petit peu de francais.' Tonight I had dinner at a little hotel near camp. The madame gave me a little table all my own. I asked her what kind of vegetables she had and she said none, only salad. I told her I was very disappointed, because I had been looking forward to pommes de terre frites, a favorite dish with Americans. Some French officers came in and sat at the large table in the middle of the room. They asked for some potatoes also but the lady again said there were none. Suddenly I heard 'Mericain' and pricked up my ears. The madame had just entered the door and was bringing me a huge plate of French fried potatoes when stopped by the French officers. They were arguing with her and insisting that if she had spuds she ought to give them some as well as the American. She sat them on my table and I glanced up and smiled at one of the Frenchmen. He asked if I understood what they were saying and I replied in fair French, 'Ah oui, j'ai compris. Mais je suis un seul et vous etes beaucoup.'

Of course this was nothing; only a trifling incident, but it took the Frenchmen by surprise; few of the Americans here speak French. Most of them are R.M.A.s and haven't had the chance to learn yet. But the French have gotten into the habit of talking a lot about us in our presence thinking we don't understand them. It's really lots of fun to be the subject of a conversation and then politely drop in a word or two. It nearly knocks them over.

Clifford and his class had finished their training at Cazaux the day before and had just completed a final examination the same day, Tuesday 19 March. Their training was now over and the next step was waiting to see to which squadrons they would be assigned, which way the war would turn and where they would be needed. But before learning where they would be posted some, like Clifford, opted to take some leave they had built up.

In Clifford's case he was mindful of the opportunity this represented, a last chance to relax before, as he expected, he would finally see service on the front. He did not want to be separated from his friends for long, he confided, but after months of intensive living, eating, sleeping and training together it would be a nice break for a week. Besides, it would be good to be away from the persistent roar of plane engines and the vibrating bark of machine guns, a chance for a quiet time on his own. He had decided to return to the south of France, to walk and take the air there, and he began by taking a train from Bordeaux to Marseilles, and from there on to Nice:

49 Ave. de la Care, Nice, A.M. France,
Friday March 22d, 1918

The streets of Marseilles are mostly cobblestoned. That and hobnailed trench shoes make dangerous walking. More than once I felt myself wing-slipping or skidding, but by being quick with my controls I kept out of a vrille, nose dive and tailspin. A rather broad avenue runs straight to the quai. It is bordered with several fine buildings, among them the Bourse, a truly magnificent house of business, and of course the finest cafes in the city.

You see all kinds and classes of people. Many of them are from the French colonies across the Mediterranean, that is the uniformed men. Some are dressed in gorgeous uniforms with huge bagging pants like balloons drawn in at the ankles. These may be, say, rich blue although colors may vary. Add a flashy red tunic or small coat and a big turban or Turkish hat, like a huge inverted flowerpot. Stick a lot of service ribbons or medals on the fellow's chest and give him a good set of mustachios; give him a gun or not as you choose and you have one kind of French soldier. Or he may be a ZOUAVE* with a simple brown suit looking very much like the American soldiers' outfit except for the hat and other fittings. Of course he'll have puts (spiral puttees) not leggings; a brown fatigue cap instead of a sombrero and his face may be dark and tanned. Then there is the well groomed French officer in his tasty blue uniform or loud red pants with or without a black stripe and a black coat; or black pants with a red stripe and a red topped hat. French officers, you know, wear just about what they want, and it is hard as the dickens to find two uniforms exactly alike; there is always something different. The poilu is generally present with his huge pack, long overcoat and gun and toujours ils semble contents mais fatigue. Usually you can pick out Canadians, for they have a habit of coming to Nice via Marseilles on their leaves of absence. And you see dandified English officers; many of them young swells, with thin legs, slender waists, a classy cane

---

* In fact, Clifford's previous description of the uniform he had seen French Colonial soldiers dressed in most commonly resembles that of the *Zouave* fighter. Originally a term used for French infantry regiments composed of Algerian recruits, they were noted for their bravery and colourful uniforms. The uniform often included a short, dark-coloured jacket worn with baggy, brightly-coloured pantaloons, often red, and a turban or fez as headgear. In the American civil war self-styled *Zouave* volunteers formed units to fight in the Union Army.

under the left arm high off the ground, it may be a swagger stick, turning circles and doing imitation acrobatics, a cigarette hanging from the mouth and possibly a glass in one eye. Boots and leggings are shined to perfection; spurs glitter; brass buttons and insignia almost twinkle and dazzle one with their brightness. And along comes the crack snappy looking U.S.R. with his gold and black hat cord sparkling; his new Sam Brown belt at just the right angle and shoes like mirrors. He has a fine cut on the uniform, yes, but in all he looks deucedly uncomfortable in that high tight-fitting collar, especially when you compare it with the English or Canadian open turn-down kind. But the American dress hat is undoubtedly the classiest, most military looking head cover in the world.

On the train from Bordeaux Clifford had met a French lieutenant on his way home to Menton, further up the Riviera coast. The young Frenchman had recommended a room in a private house in Nice where he could stay. It was comfortable and reasonably priced – 3 francs a night – and Clifford was able to eat in another nearby home. It was a boon for him as he was beginning to find prices rising ever faster, at a time when he was trying to concentrate on saving what he could from his salary for after the war while sending some money home to his mother in California.

He arranged to have dinner with the lieutenant a few days later in Nice and when they met up they began by strolling down the Avenue de la Gare, lined with its cafés and restaurants, and then along under the palms of the Promenade des Anglais on the seafront. His companion told him of a private club for American officers that he had heard of and suggested going along for a visit. Clifford agreed, although he felt self-conscious about what he was wearing. He had ordered and would soon collect his new lieutenant's uniform, but for now he was still in his old private's uniform, even if it was partially set off with the officer's Sam Browne belt and correct officer's shoulder bars and insignia:

The host and hostess were two very wealthy Americans with a charming and talented daughter of marriageable age. They dropped insinuations that only American officers were invited there and so at once the Frenchman who speaks English fairly well became uncomfortable. And they eyed me very exceedingly politely and if I had been alone or with another U.S. officer and in dress uniform, I should have enjoyed myself immensely. In fact if I ever come to Nice again I am going to call there and look decent. But by that time the daughter may be married and the Club will have done its duty.

There were several classy looking Captains and one of them, a very well educated and refined gentleman who spoke French fluently, seemed to have a monopoly on Miss Blanche. They all looked at me from head to foot as if I was standing inspection and if I had been I should have been sent to the Guard House for a week, for it was not exactly right or befitting the dignity of an American officer for me to appear in the uniform I had on. But I bore the scrutiny well and without flinching and showed them that I was a gentleman in action and knew how to behave. And at the same time I felt a certain defiant satisfaction, for I was the only aviator there and they knew it, and personally I would rather have my wings on my chest than any number of bars on my shoulders. I intend to be a fighter rather than a parlor ornament.

Our host was very polite and polished and asked us in to tea. The tea room was charming. Really I wish I was in a better position to avail myself of such an opportunity as that of visiting the place oftener, as the host asked. There are billiard rooms and reading rooms and everything has been done to make the officers comfortable.

One thing made my blood boil. Milk is very scarce in France. Babies are dying for lack of it; and yet these people could fill a saucer with the precious liquid about every five minutes and put it on the floor for a pretty little parasite of a dog to lap up. After half an hour or so of forced politeness on both sides, for to tell the truth I felt a little embarrassed and almost angry that hospitality should be so forced and insincere, we bade adieu to the hosts and bowed ourselves out. A soldier is a soldier and ready to make the supreme sacrifice whenever called upon, and if he is true to his colors and neat and clean no matter how mean is his dress he should be respected and treated like an equal, especially by persons who are not called upon to make any great sacrifices. ACH. Maybe I was more embarrassed than I was ready to admit and things are not half as bad as they seemed. The world is still a long ways from Utopia. I know I did the wrong thing to go in with a Frenchman, but he insisted and also I should have worn my good uniform etc. Ha. Ha. We should worry.

Clifford left Nice a few days later, travelling back via Paris to rejoin his class. He celebrated his 22nd birthday there, taking care before leaving the capital to collect his precious new officer's uniform. From Paris he was to return to the advanced training school at Issoudun: a temporary base while he and colleagues waited to see where they would be posted.

However, if he was expecting any imminent deployment Clifford was to be disappointed. The wider course of the war, and the American role in it, was still being defined, determined by outside forces as well as by the organisation of the Americans and their Allies in the field. It would take some time yet.

25

GETTING READY

Early 1918 found the battlefields of Western Europe in an almost static position following three and a half years of fighting – a stalemate of muddy trenches and wasteland. The last of a great series of set-piece offensives in the Third Battle of Ypres, the Battle of Passchendaele, fought over four months in Flanders, had ground to a brutal and inconclusive halt the previous November. Similarly, no headway was made by an assault further south in northern France at Cambrai, notable mainly for the fact that it had been the first time a massed tank assault had been employed on the battlefield.

The winter that followed these conflicts had been bitter, with temperatures plunging deep below zero. Tunics and coats, balaclavas, woollen hats and any form of padding were used by men to try to keep the bone-chilling cold at bay. A terrible broken landscape lay frozen between the two warring lines, cutting off thoughts of advance or any imminent conclusion to Europe's war.

However, the situation was to change suddenly and dramatically over the months to come. It was clear to both sides that each would have to mount last titanic efforts to oust the other from their positions. Yet precisely how or when those offensives would come about in the spring and summer of 1918 remained to be seen. The Allies knew that there were still parts of their positions which needed shoring up before any advances could be made in the north closer to the coast, and further south near the Somme where British and French lines met.

They had also accepted, through the formation of the Supreme War Council at the end of November, that more would have to be done by way of a united and co-ordinated war effort; and in that regard the French General Ferdinand Foch was now appointed Supreme Commander on the Western Front. A part of Foch's task was also how to integrate Pershing's American forces on the front, to help him get men and materiel into Europe in numbers and on to the front line.

For his part, Germany's General Erich Ludendorff was more advanced in his planning for a massed attack. Over the preceding months he had pieced together a strategy which would, he hoped, finally break Allied lines, and he wanted to do so sooner rather than later. Ludendorff wanted to take advantage not only of the more favourable weather afforded by the spring thaw but also of the scores of German divisions now being freed up by the collapse of the Russian war effort on the Eastern Front. Not only that: he wanted to ensure that German forces would make these numbers count before equal legions of American forces finally made it to the front.

Time was critical, and so it was that on 21 March 1918 there began a series of offensives, five in all, which would stretch from March to July – from Flanders in the north to the banks of the Somme and the Marne – and in that time troops of the American Expeditionary Force would become more and more involved in the fierce and often bloody fighting.

The task of assembling AEF troops – the so-called 'doughboys' – and fashioning them to into a proper fighting force had proved a trying one for General John Pershing over the course of the autumn and winter. It was a long journey, a long road travelled, to bring American troop levels and training up to the standard he wanted to see on the front. At the outbreak of war the total strength of the American Army only hovered around the 200,000 mark, Regulars and National Guard reservists combined. This figure was dwarfed by the 4 million men still committed to the field by the Allies on the Western Front, and where they were faced by 2.5 million Germans.

When planning began for the war effort in Europe, and when it was handing Pershing the responsibility for assembling the American Expeditionary Force, the War Department had been working on the assumption that around 500,000 men would need to be taken under arms. Pershing, however, had his own ideas. Almost from the outset, and with the help of his newly appointed Chief-of-Staff Major James

Harbord, Pershing set a goal of twice that figure. It was an ambitious target, but one he felt was justified and necessary. Yet an upgrading on this scale would mean difficulties of both organisation and supply.[39]

The first division to arrive in Europe in June 1917 was, fittingly, the 1st Division. 'The Big Red One', as the 1st was known, was made up of regular troop, as was the 2nd Division which arrived some time later, although the latter was comprised of units which had arrived in Europe separately and assembled in France. To their number were added two National Guard divisions: the 26th, known as the 'Yankees' and the 42nd 'Rainbow' Division. But that troop level was where numbers would stay until the early part of 1918. Those four core divisions, the 'big four', represented the sum of the American combat presence in Europe until the arrival of men from two further divisions, the 32nd and 41st.

But it was not just a question of finite numbers of men being available to Pershing. There was also, necessarily, a considerable run-in time before any of the units would be properly equipped and trained and brought up to speed with the requirements of the front. It was to be the second week in October before any Americans were put into front-line service, one battalion from each of the Big Red One's four infantry regiments, serving under the French 18th Division. The first casualties, the first Americans killed in combat in an American unit in the First World War, came some weeks later. A corporal and two privates were killed on 3 November 1917.[40]

By mid-January the 1st Division was operating as a whole unit in its own right, stationed in the Ansauville Sector, a relatively quiet area near Toul in north-eastern France. The area nearby, around the St Mihiel Salient, a bulb of German-held territory which protruded into the French lines, was a part of the front which had lain virtually static since the early weeks of the war in 1914. It would be the scene of fierce fighting involving American forces later in the year, but for now this sector was the only one where Americans found themselves in an advance position.

Different factors were at play in the slow build-up of force numbers. The logistics of getting a large and well-equipped army into the field of course involved proper training and organisation, but the pace at which this was being done was also caught up in the wider politics in play. Repeated pressure had been brought to bear on Pershing from political and military leaders on the Allied side to prioritise the transport to the front of manpower over materiel; to be done in such a way that these men could then be deployed alongside British and French forces, with American battalions plugging the gaps that were beginning to appear in Allied lines.

The British Permanent Military Representative to the Supreme War Council, General Henry Rawlinson, put forward a plan to restrict American troops being brought to France to infantry and machine gun units; not, as Pershing wanted, to create a transport chain which included the necessary complement of artillery, engineers and support services that could round the American numbers off into self-standing divisions. But eventually compromise was reached, with US Secretary of War Baker and President Wilson involved in the discussions. 'Preferential transportation' was to be given to infantry units, although these units would be under Pershing's direction as AEF commander-in-chief and would only rise to a certain ceiling.[41]

Pershing wanted to stick to that letter of the law, the instructions with which he had originally been tasked the previous May by Baker:

'In military operations against the Imperial German Government', the instruction read, 'you are directed to cooperate with the forces of the other countries employed against that enemy; but in so doing the underlying idea must be kept in view that the forces of the United States are a separate and distinct component of the combined forces, the identity of which must be preserved.'[42]

Pershing would not give up on the idea that the United States would form a fully-fledged army. He would maintain his army's identity as an independent fighting force even if that took more time, while at the same time giving his and the AEF's backing to Foch as Supreme Commander to plan and direct military action.

By April 1918 the time had come to deploy AEF units in greater numbers and in a more acute manner. Ludendorff's first 'great offensive', breaking through the British 5th Army around the Somme and threatening, though not capturing, Amiens, had been followed by a second offensive in Flanders in April, between Ypres and Lens. But the Americans were now ordered to deploy to that first area where fighting had raged the previous month. They were sent to the Montdidier Sector some 25 miles south-east of Amiens where Ludendorff's advance had been stopped. It was decided to take the town of Cantigny there, straightening out the salient bulging into Allied lines, an action scheduled for the end of May. But just as the assault got underway – one which was ultimately successful, if costly in terms of casualties for an arguably limited objective – a third German offensive began to the south towards the Marne. It, too, led to American involvement.

Ludendorff's 3rd Offensive on 27 May 1918 was originally meant to be a feint, not an all-out offensive. It was intended to draw French units eastwards, to split them from British units around the Somme and further north and make a later attack easier. But the feint was unexpectedly successful. Ludendorff had originally intended that his armies move south across the Aisne River and stop at another, the Vesle – a distance of only a dozen miles. But such was the weakness of the resistance from three French and two British divisions there, in what had mistakenly been considered a quiet sector, that German forces ploughed on towards the Marne. By 3 June they had taken a bridgehead over the Marne east of the town of Château-Thierry, only 56 miles from Paris.

With the American 1st Division committed further north at Cantigny, Pershing was asked to commit other units in the line to stop the advance. He called on the 2nd Division and elements of the 3rd, which until this time had been in training. Over the next four weeks American forces fought a committed and bloody ground war in an area north of the river, around Belleau Wood. It helped stem the German advance and demonstrated, alongside Cantigny, that AEF troops were capable of fighting in the European theatre. Yet, as the former military commander and historian John S. D. Eisenhower argues in his *Yanks: The Epic Story of the American Army in World War I*, while American forces had performed well in their first exposures in battle, their overall contribution in stopping Ludendorff's 3rd Offensive had been minor. The German attack had been stopped principally by logistical failure rather than military action. Be that as it may, it marked a beginning for the American forces. A more substantial contribution would come later.

For the American Air Service, meanwhile, a combination of internal distractions and problems of supply had dogged their efforts to prepare themselves more fully. At the time of the 1st German Offensive in March the only real operational squadrons – and flying old planes – were the 1st, 12th and 88th Observation Squadrons, and the 94th Hat in the Ring and 95th Kicking Mule Pursuit Squadrons. Even then, their readiness would have been questioned had Pershing's offer of immediate help to the Allies been taken up at the time.[43]

Several months on from the arrival of Benjamin Foulois as chief, jeal-ousies and divisions continued to hamper the service's progress. It was fuelled by the superiority felt by those with direct aviation experience over those 'ground officers' who had been brought in, many of them from civilian life, and further fresh organisational action was needed to rectify matters. That action arrived in the form of Brigadier General Mason Patrick, a senior Corps of Engineers officer, as the new Chief of the Air Service. Patrick refashioned the whole of the administrative structure, eventually making his predecessor Foulois his assistant chief, after Foulois had spent a spell in the so-called 'zone of advance', leaving the forceful and charismatic Billy Mitchell to take up the main role there.

However, the service was still beset by difficulties of supply, both of qualified pilots and machines. By early 1918 the throughput of pilots ear-marked for air training programmes in Europe was backing up, not helped by the paucity of aircraft in which to train. But that same supply chain was also causing problems for the service in putting together a proper fleet of aircraft for those pilots already qualified. The order books, so optimisti-cally filled the previous summer and autumn, had yet to bear fruit at the pace required by the air chiefs, and the planes took their time in arriving.

It was a complex supply process which stretched, in the case of US man-ufactured planes, from the production lines of America through the US base ports in France and the work of the AEF's Supply Section to assembly plants like the Production Centre No. 2 at Romorantin, before eventual delivery to the Zone of Advance. This was also true for those planes originating in Europe, through air depots like Orly near Paris, where they would still have to be fitted out with armaments and accessories being sent in the same supply chain. As General Patrick and Edgar Gorrell concluded in their *Final Report of the Chief of Air Service* following the war:

> owing to the many technical problems which had to be solved, to the many
> difficulties connected with the procurement of equipment which had to be
> overcome, and to the considerable time that it takes for training, it has been
> shown that it requires longer to place an efficient Air Service in the field than
> is the case with any other arm of the Service.[44]

The service had been assigned the area of Toul in the north-east of France near Nancy: a relatively quiet sector in combat terms, where the untested American pilots could cut their teeth and make the transition from training school to active units. Bordered on the west by the heights of the Meuse River and on the east by the main Metz–Nancy road, it was another of those fronts which had been established early in the war. Yet it was of strategic importance to the German High Command, with coveted coal mines and iron deposits near Metz and the important railway systems at Sedan and to the south-west.

As a combat zone it would assume greater importance later in the year, but for now, in this period of spring into early summer of 1918, the new squadrons were just beginning to take wing. The 95th and 94th Aero Squadrons took up their positions in February and March respectively, but it was a slow start. They and other units were forced to move base on more than one occasion; and although a fresh and much needed consignment of new planes had arrived in the first week of March – three dozen Nieuport 28 fighters – other teething problems presented themselves. Some from the 95th Squadron actually flew on the front without guns because the weapons had not yet arrived; others had yet to even receive the necessary gunnery training. It was only in mid-April that the first 'kills' for the American Air Service proper were recorded, Lieutenants Alan Winslow and Douglas Campbell of the 94th bringing down two enemy fighters on their aerodrome at Gengault near Toul.

Only gradually would the US Air Service establish itself; and only over time would the pursuit and observation squadrons, the reconnaissance and bombardment units, the balloon companies and their army of engineers and ground staff assert themselves. In the meantime, many young fliers had to learn to bide their time, including First Lieutenant SORC Arthur Clifford Kimber.

THE WAITING GAME

Back at the Issoudun training camp in early April 1918, Clifford was waiting. It had been weeks since he had last flown at the gunnery school at Cazaux and there was still no news of any imminent deployment to a service role. Time was beginning to pall, so his mood cannot have been lifted by a letter he received from his old friend Alan Nichols. In it, Nichols detailed the action he had seen while serving as a Lafayette Flying Corps pilot, flying with French Escadrille No. 85 and recently having chased down a German reconnaissance plane. This was the kind of action Clifford wanted for himself. He was getting itchy feet.

Duties at Issoudun, such as they were, were light and so Clifford was delighted one day when he and a colleague were asked to take two planes from the testing department to deliver them to one of the nearby fields in the complex. His was a fast and sleek plane, 'a dandy,' he recalled later, 'the best and niftiest chasse plane I have ever fastened myself in'. He took off, enjoying the sensation of flying once more, the thrust of the engine, the sudden release into the air. He began a series of S-manoeuvres and climbed heavenward to start a series of acrobatic displays.

Then suddenly – a rush of blood. He banked his plane and dived in, plunging towards the ground, scattering those below him:

The next crazy thing I did was to dive at the dual control classes and crowds of waiting students. Each time I would dive I would make a glorious chandelle or quick side turn on the Zumm and look down at the commotion I was causing. Three or four dives and an officer ran out with a red and white flag and called off flying while

I was there. What a fool I was. Oh that I had known that the Major was on that field and that I was scaring him 'peeless' as well as the moniteurs and students. But how they must have been cussing me. To make matters worse I had a great big 308 on the fuselage so there was no trick to identification of the culprit.

I side-slipped from about 1000 meters down to the new field where I was to deliver the machine. Of course this was not one long slip but a series of several, broken by occasional tight spirals. The landing was perfect and 308 taxied in the direction of the hangars.

An orderly on a motor cycle with a side car was waiting for me. He had orders to drive me to the main field and Major's office tout de suite. Before I had landed, three fields had rung up head-quarters to report 308, and beside that the Major had been one of my targets. POOR ME. What should I do? I decided to make a clean breast of it and ask for leniency, put myself on the mercy of the powers that be.

I told the Major that I was sorry, that such a performance wouldn't happen again; that I hoped he would dismiss me with a reprimand. I was thoroughly ashamed of myself to have acted such a fool. I told him I had learned my lesson and I had. If anybody had been frightened before, I was actually scared stiff now, but I had to face the music. The Major who was really angry, and with just cause, sent me up to the colonel for sentence. I told him the same thing and I believe he saw how sincere I was in my repentance. He asked me my age. I said 22. He said I should have known better. He added: 'You ought to be canned but you have been through C. and the Govt. has spent too much money on you. Why can't you fellows coming back from C. behave sensibly?' (So there had been others before me, Hobey Baker and Capt. Rickenbacker, I presume).* Without exception if you come back here to await orders before going to the front and you are lucky enough to get out a good machine, you raise merry hades. Remember this is a training school. It may be all right for you fellows to do these things because you can fly and can get away with it. But by so doing you set a bad example to the beginners. They think that is the proper way to fly as soon as they get their single-seater and therefore may kill

---

* Hobart A.H. Baker – a celebrated amateur ice hockey player and American footballer, later an accomplished fighter pilot with a number of squadrons including the 103rd Aero Squadron, comprised of many pilots from the Lafayette Escadrille and Lafayette Flying Corps. Edward 'Eddie' Rickenbacker entered the war as one of America's top race car drivers having competed in the first Indianapolis 500 and setting land-speed records at Daytona. Flying with the famed 94th Hat in the Ring Aero Squadron, Rickenbacker ended the war as America's Ace of Aces with twenty-six confirmed 'kills'.

themselves. There is no danger to you, but by setting this bad example you endanger the lives of others. I will see what I can do for you.' If ever I felt cheap, I felt cheap then, absolutely humiliated.

Clifford was not officially grounded by the commanding officer, although invitations for him to test-fly or ferry planes were notable by their absence over the next fortnight and more. That said, few chances existed for others either.

It was a waiting game. Rumours circulated from time to time of impending moves to the front but subsided just as quickly, so Clifford did what he had done before during periods with the Ambulance Service or while training, and learned to bide his time, settling into a routine. He pursued his various hobbies: continuing to learn his French grammar; reading voraciously; playing chess; writing back home to friends and family and expanding on his and his brothers' plans for their family farming business after the war. He even attempted, for a period, to combine language study and letters home by writing to his family in French, although the experiment did not last long as whatever stories he wanted to tell outreached his French vocabulary. He wrote for the most part from the comfort and warmth of a new officers' club which had been established and was then largely maintained by women volunteers from the Red Cross, something for which he was immensely grateful.

A week passed. He began to wonder whether there was any hope of ever seeing action on the front. If they could not fly here, 200 plus miles from the fighting, what chance of them being drafted to the Zone of Advance? He pondered whether or not to consider positions that he had previously dismissed: a plane tester's role or that of a 'ferryman', delivering planes on a full-time basis to other schools or to the front, and not actually holding out for a combat role:

I am still hanging around and haven't been in the air since my circus performance, but neither have the others, so I should worry. We all have hopes of getting in the biggest battle of history. We evidently aren't needed very badly or else aren't very good, or they would have sent for us. Well, those American aviators who are at the front are distinguishing themselves, so there is the satisfaction of knowing that the good old U.S. air service is going to be more than dreaded.

He took to writing short stories of his flying experiences to date and compiling a glossary of various aerial manoeuvres, explaining to his family how pilots accomplished their twists and turns. But he was restless; he needed to be on the move again. He started exploring the countryside around Issoudun on foot with one of his friends, James Beane, and they combined some of their walks with routine chores, taking their dirty laundry with them. There was a laundry service at the camp but women in the local villages who needed the money would wash the laundry for some of the young men at the base. He enjoyed the opportunity to get away from his military life for a few hours, to sit in a French home while the women worked around him, chatting to their families, the bustle of domestic life going on around him. He happily recounted these visits in his letters, sending his mother and brothers descriptions and sketches of these 'typical French peasant homes' and families. It seemed to fill something of a gap for him after so long away from home.

As diverting as these home visits were though, flying opportunities when they were gradually restored a fortnight later came as a great release. True, his air time for the most part involved ferrying planes in short hops from one aviation field in the Issoudun complex to another, but there were now also occasional deliveries of planes to bases further afield. At every opportunity he used the flying time to explore and reconnoitre areas of interest; and he now extended his roaming – and visits to families – to grander settings:

> Lately I have been making a habit of singling out good-looking chateaux and circling over them. If I like them, I stunt a bit. Friday morning I flew over one about ten kilometers from here. Several 'fair ones' came to a second story window and leaned out to get a better view of my plane 'No. 37'. I was delivering it to one of the neighboring fields from the main field and was taking in 'les beautes' of the country as incidental to my work. So when I saw these 'charmantes' I decided to hold an inspection; and therefore flying very, low, I zigzagged into position and skimmed over the trees in front of the 'loges'. Ah, tres bon. I repeated the performance and waved a 'bonjour', bucking my No. 37 like a bronco to emphasize my good spirits. They all replied and seemed DELIGHTED.

The following Sunday he decided to try to effect an introduction to the girls he had seen and to visit their château. As he set out from camp that morning it began to rain and by the time he reached his target, what had started as an April shower had turned into a downpour. His prized new uniform was now a little bedraggled, and worse, when he arrived it was to discover most of the family were out at church. Luckily for him, though, there were at least some signs of life in the great house. The owner of the house was sick in bed and some of the domestic staff were at home with him. When Clifford knocked on the great door he was ushered into the château's hallway by a sympathetic housekeeper who brought him downstairs to dry out in the warm basement kitchen and to wait for mother and girls to return from Mass.

Clifford was as engaging as possible with his new saviour and began to calculate, or hope, that the family might show similar hospitality when they came back – at least, if he made an effort, put on a suitable show of embarrassment and good manners and smiled his broadest smile. This he duly did when the time came and soon he found himself sitting down to lunch in the château with his new hosts, an extended Sunday contingent of the Rouget-Belletour family. Then, after the meal it was entertainment time as they retired to the drawing room for a music recital. He was in his element, his cares evaporated for an afternoon. A young 22-year-old, fed, entertained and feted by his hostess, a lady in a French château who professed what an 'honour' it was to have this American officer aviator in their midst. Better still, to be enjoying the attentions of the Rouget-Belletour daughters, chatting eagerly around him and escorting him for a walk in the extensive grounds:

I told them at dinner that I flew over the other day. They said they had been tremendously interested and said they saw me wave, waved back, and remembered my number, asking me if it wasn't No. 37? 'Oh, oui'. The girl who had been to England told me about her trip there. She seemed delighted that I knew all the places she mentioned and told me about Oxford, London, Folkestone, the 'regatta' on the Thames, etc. etc. The whole family wanted to know how I knew so much about England. I told them about KC [Kent College in Canterbury where Clifford had been at school] etc. They thought it was fine. Out on the walk we looked for good landing fields near the chateau and found one exceptionally fine. I said if I could get a two-place machine I would come over and take them up. You should have seen them jump and skip for joy. They didn't disguise it any. They asked me to come over with a friend some day this week and play bridge and take tea. I told them I didn't savez bridge, but they said it didn't matter, they would teach me, and their mother pressed the invitation when we got in the house again. I promised to *fly over early this week and drop a message in a parachute, telling them what day we will be over. I think I'll ask Beane because he speaks French fine. Also I expect to buy a box of candy at the YMCA and tie it to the parachute too.*

Indeed, Clifford did see the Rouget-Belletours again and even visited some of their other relatives whom he met at the château. He also held good to his promise to deliver a note with accompanying sweet treats to the girls by makeshift parachute.

But the day arrived just over two weeks later when he and his cohort were told to get ready to leave Issoudun. Work was at hand. He gathered his belongings and prepared to make his goodbyes:

May 15th 1918

Dear Mother John and George,
    Today we are off. In half an hour the train leaves from this center and then we'll be on our way. They may make us ferry for a while, I don't know, but soon there will be beaucoup d'action.
    This morning I was awakened, very early for me, 5.30. Orders had come for us to leave today and baggage had to be ready by nine. We left camp about 10.30. Well, I had quite a lot of packing to do so I was glad to be awakened early. My laundry I had left in Paudy several days before so I had to get that. I went to the transportation office and secured a Harley Davidson and sidecar. The driver, at my behest, went over slowly at a comfortable speed. You see I didn't want to get messed. I saw the wash-woman and told her to wrap my laundry up and I would be back in a few minutes. Then I directed the driver to go to the chateau of Mme Rouget-Belletour. It was too bad to call there so early, about 8.30, but I wanted to tell her that Beane and I couldn't go there for dinner tomorrow, Friday, and I also wanted to say au revoir to my new friends, especially Mlle Jeane to whom I have taken a considerable liking. She and her sisters are tres agreeable. As a matter of fact, I am awfully lucky to know these nice people. Madame R-B has been so nice to me too.

From there, he and a group of colleagues set off by train to Paris. But here their journey was to end. He had had a hunch that it was to be yet another false dawn and his instinct was to be proved right. Paris was another halfway house. They were not destined for the front, not yet anyway, but to work at the distribution depot for American planes at Orly, south of Paris. He would be a ferryman for now.

27

DELIVERY MAN

The Aviation Acceptance Park No. 1, as it was officially known, had come into being barely a month before at Orly, the result of conversations between the French Government and leaders of the US Air Service. It had been the original plan for French aviation suppliers to deliver planes to the French facility at Le Bourget, north-east of Paris. But after German bombing in March had destroyed a consignment of Spad fighters which had been awaiting onward delivery to the front line, the government asked the AEF to establish their own acceptance base. The new facility was operational in record time, from the identification of the patchwork of land in the southern suburbs to the first planes landing on 6 April. In time it would grow into a complex of nearly eighty hangars with scores of barracks and miles of cinder road, home to 2,500 officers and enlisted men.[45]

But for now, in spring 1918 this base was Clifford's new workplace and new challenge. He and his colleagues would have to learn to fly whatever planes came their way, new or old, and be able to deliver them wherever and whenever was deemed necessary. If nothing else, it was a good grounding in flying:

Grand Hotel 12 Boulevard des Capucins, Paris
May 19th 1918

Dear Mother John and George,

    It has been some time since I wrote you a real letter, but I hope you got the cards I sent you the other day. A great deal has happened.

    In the first place I am doing ferrying work. Our bunch has done all possible to go chasse; it is simply a question of machines and so they are having us ferry until our planes are ready. I don't know how long this will be; maybe a month, maybe three; but the ferrying is good fun all the same and as I have done all in my power to get to the front QUICK, I am now resigned to my fate, satisfied that I have done my best, and in this work I find myself quite happy and content.

    We left I. Wednesday noon, Wednesday the 15th. I put up at the Grand which although expensive is so admirably situated that the difference in price is well worth paying. You know it is over the Café de la Paix and fronts on the Place D'Opera. At 8.30 next morning our bunch left for O. on the Seine.

    When we got out there they had nothing for us to do except go through the necessary formalities of registering etc., so we took the fast Fiat truck back to Paree. I went to the bank, Morgan Harjes & Co, deposited about a hundred dollars, got a shave and hair cut at the Grand Hotel, a real shoe shine and then went to the Opera House and got a ticket to Rigoletto. Oh dear. 16 francs. Weep.

    Some time ago we old ambulance men received notifications from 21 rue Raynouard that the old Chateau there was being fitted up for old ambulance men who happened to be in Paris and that they were welcome to stop in for their meals and room and only 6 fr. a day. They have the old place fitted up fine with several club rooms, a billiard room and a reading room etc. The Chalet is fitted up with beds etc. and they have a dormitory in the chateau. Carpets are laid; everything is swell, and so different from when I struck the place this time last year. Only the grounds are the same and they are beautiful, to say least. Everything is green. Incidentally, the trees along the boulevards are well leafed out. Indeed Paris is the most beautiful city I have ever been in. And whom do you think I met at 21 rue Raynouard? JACK NICHOLS . . .

    Can I tell how glad I was to see him? It was like meeting a brother. I felt so delighted and in the last two days we had a wonderful time together. We had dinner together at rue Raynouard and then, as the Opera began at 7.30, I had to beat it in the middle of eating. But we had talked some time before supper and I told him I would try to arrange to take him up.

    On the 17th of May after getting back to O. I had a flight in one of the fastest types of machines in the world, the Nieuport 28, which it is claimed can out-manoeuvre, out-climb and out-speed the Spad. I don't know how true this is, but it sure can travel. It is the fastest I have ever been in my life and just to think that I was all alone in this speedy little bird going 135 to 140 miles an hour opened up, and landing at about 80. Gee, but it was GREAT STUFF. I cut some virages, felt her out, chandelled and dove a bit and then came down with a good landing to let the next fellow have his turn.

Bigelow and I played catch a while and then we had dinner (supper). I was just getting ready to turn in when a Lieut. came up from headquarters saying they wanted five men to go to C. [Chartres] to fly Sopwiths. I immediately volunteered.

We left for C. the next day, May 18th at 7 a.m. We just caught the train in Paris. We arrived at about 10 and it was raining. I went out in the rain and got wet but saw the cathedral. I was in it for several hours, it is wonderful; they were holding mass and I heard the beautiful organ of which I sent John a picture. I sat in contemplation and prayed for my dear ones at home and for the success of our armies in this war against the Hun. I am awfully glad it rained.

We left C. for the aviation parc about 1.30. I was third off in my Sop., a big two-seater affair. I flew by the river and saw chateaux etc. Had a beautiful ride of 45 minutes. The country was awfully interesting. I landed according to the direction of the T which happened to be pointing right across the wind and I side stepped and bounced like a circus horse but didn't smash anything at that. So you see I am learning to fly everything. It is lots of fun and I believe the experience is going to prove invaluable. I have now flown six types of planes and been up in nine.

Clifford began to get into his new role, bemoaning only in passing his and his colleagues' inability to get to the front line in a *chasse* (fighter) role. There was variety in what he did and a freedom. He enjoyed flying over Paris when the opportunity presented itself, admiring the gardens of Versailles, circling the Eiffel Tower. He enjoyed the ability to criss-cross France in different directions, notching up air miles in Caudrons and Farmans, Nieuports and Sopwiths, delivering to schools or the front and bringing planes from other bases to Orly. It was frequently tiring, with little downtime in between deliveries and returning to base on long and slow train journeys. But when he was back in Paris he and his colleagues, a mix of people he had known through Tours and Issoudun, and indeed from ambulance days, had the run of Paris any evening they had spare.

There were some problems along the way – one trip to eastern France ending prematurely for Clifford with a forced landing and a burned out engine – but each day was different and held its own excitement. But more importantly, Clifford felt at last that he was beginning to do something meaningful. Never before, he said, had he been in such a responsible or exciting position:

June 6th 1918

Dear Mother John and George,

Since writing you last I have made another long trip to the front. I really had a close call the last part of it, too, although no forced landing.

About ten minutes before I landed at my destination E. [most likely Épernay] my left foot began feeling funny and sort of tingling. For a while I thought nothing of it as often the vibration of the rudder bar makes one's feet feel sleepy and numb. But about four or five minutes before I landed my foot got really uncomfortable. It felt cold and wet and as if being pricked by pins and needle. So I ducked my head down under the cowl of the cockpit and looked at my feet. Horrors. It was drenched with gasoline. My leg was wet half way up to my knee. The shoe and puttee were spongy. A veritable stream of essence came pouring down. The gas pipe from the gravity tank to the carburettor had cracked and half the gas flow was escaping.

Immediately I began thinking of what it would be like to burn up and of other aviators who had come down in flames. You see the bottom of the fuselage was drenched with essence and the gas fumes were awful. A backfire and away we would go. If the gas worked to the magneto and was sparked off it would be GOODNIGHT.

E. was about 10 kilometers ahead and the only field on which I could make a good landing. At the moment I was about 1000 meters high. I risked running the motor a little longer and peaked in a straight line down toward E. It seemed to approach quickly. I didn't care how I got down as long as I got down without burning up. Didn't even make a tour de piste. Bounce, bounce, bounce. Crack went the tail skid; I should worry ... I was safe on terra firma. GOODNIGHT. If there is anything an aviator dreads it is burning up. But except for a broken tail skid the plane was OK. I got a receipt for it and went to the barracks to rest a while. My foot had started to blister so I got off my shoe and sock as quickly as possible and bathed my foot and put on some blister powder that one of the boys had. I met a lot of friends and they were very nice and put me up overnight. We went to the YMCA movies and spent quite an enjoyable evening.

The next day I got in the train for Paris. Yesterday we went to the funeral of Dan Asa Bigelow, one of our boys who fell three days ago. I had known him ever since we enlisted in US aviation, and well. We trained together at T. and I. and C. We ate together, slept near each other, and came to O. together. He used to be in the

ambulance but not in my section. Lt. Bigelow was a fine fellow and a true and faith-
ful friend. We boys get to know each other and love each other almost. It is hard to
lose a comrade but c'est la guerre. Each time I lose a friend I want to sail right at
a Boche, and yet we are held here in ferrying. Well the day will come.

The funeral was very touching and beautiful. The boys contributed over three
hundred fr. for flowers and there were some beautiful wreaths. They buried him
in a new little cemetery near Paris recently bought by the Americans on a high hill
overlooking the wonderful city. An American flag was draped on the coffin. Bigelow
didn't die in action fighting the Hun, but he died a hero's death just the same and
will be remembered and avenged. After the funeral I took Jerry to A—M—to meet
Jack Nichols. We all had dinner together. Jack is certainly a magnificent boy. He
gave me news of Alan, but says he doesn't hear from him much as he is too busy
fighting Huns. Only six of his escadrille are left and he is one. I have all kinds of
confidence in Alan. Give him any kind of luck and he'll be an ace.

The next ten days saw Clifford make a clutch of other trips: south-west
to his old base at Tours; east towards the front, experiencing some trouble and a little shock there with a smash-up on landing when one of the
wheels on his plane collapsed; and he also headed due south on a longer
voyage towards Clermont-Ferrand, a trip he regarded as a plum job.

He had heard that a number of two-seater Nieuport planes needed to
be ferried and that a pilot had just dropped out. Volunteering immediately
he rushed down to the hangars to select one of the two planes which were
ready and began to test the engine. He made a head start on one of his
colleagues on the trip, Weir Cook, and set off for his first stop and the
airbase at Avord:

It was hazy and sort of difficult to see, but as I'm a believer in no delay in getting
started, for fear of having contradictory orders find their way to me before I'm off, I
opened up my motor and took off with a rush. It develops that I got off an hour before
Weir. Naturally enough I was the first to arrive at Avord where Alan received part of
his training. You see I had to stop there for gas and oil, for the Nieups only hold about
two hours' fuel and the trip was of three and half to four hours. On the way down
I passed over Sully (Loire) and its famous chateau. I circled around it several times
to get a better look; I'll take a stop-over from the train and have a decent look at it.

At Avord I had lunch with some American flying ensigns stationed there for some
temporary work. One of them named Sayre had never been up in a Nieuport
and wanted to know if it would be possible for me to give him a ride. No question

about, it; besides he had been awfully nice to me and had insisted on my being his guest at lunch.

On the way to the hangars we met Cook and a Lt. S. whom he was carrying down to Clermont to join his command. He asked if I wouldn't take S's valise the rest of the way to Clermont and of course I was 'delighted' being the only response possible under the circumstances. You see I had no passenger for Clermont.

By the time that I was all ready to start again Cook and S. were in their machine. I took off and circled above waiting for them to try out the motor. Five minutes more and both machines were pointing south, I watched Cook for a while and kept close to him for company's sake. But it soon developed that he was headed straight for Clermont which would take him over very hilly country, awful for forced landings and also over a range of mountains. That may have been all right, but a forced landing in mountains means a smashed plane. (You know it's really quite simple to smash a plane to save your life. That's what the Frenchmen say. But what under the sun is the use of taking a chance that may make you break a perfectly good aeroplane even though you do get away with your neck.)

So I headed SE to pick up the Loire [the tributary of the Loire, the Allier] *and left our Lt. Cook to his fate which happened to be losing his way and having to land to inquire where he was and ask how to go to Clermont. It was wonderful flying. The valley was beautiful. After I got over Clermont I did some mountain flying of my own, but within gliding distance, really doubtful gliding distance of the Clermont field. I played around the top of the highest mountain (about 1500 meters high, a mile I should say). I got down about 200 meters over its top and enjoyed myself immensely just like an old hawk over Grizzly Peak, Berkeley. It was fun doing semi-contour flying in the foothills, too. Clermont is a very attractive town in that the people are so nice. So different from Paris, but then the impressions one gets in Paree and the judgment he forms from it are apt to be wrong. After a year in France I am just beginning to see the good side of the French people and now I am really beginning to appreciate them. My great handicap was ignorance of their language. Now I can talk to them more or less intelligently and interestingly. My French is none too good but it is improving and I think I am getting a real grip on it. Cook got in while I was eating dinner with some old friends who had trained with me at T. and I. but who had wound up as instructors etc. at Clermont instead of ferrymen at O. or pilots at the front ... the height of our ambition. BUT I'LL GET THERE YET AND AS A CHASSE PILOT. Ten of our boys just went out in a French escadrille, and I am simply awaiting my turn which may or may not come. I have almost given up trying to get anywhere; I simply go where and do what I am told and let fate decide my destiny or destiny my fate whichever way you want to put it.*

But less than a week later came two pieces of news. The first provoked a reaction of excitement among Clifford and his group. They were, finally, moving to the front.

But the second piece of news profoundly shocked him. It was 15 June 1918 and he was at Rue Raynouard. He picked up a copy of the *New York Herald*, its Paris edition. His best friend from Stanford days was dead:

June 15th 1918

Alan has died of wounds. I went up to headquarters to find out about him for I heard he had been shot down in the French lines and they said he was severely wounded having received a bullet in the back, abdomen and leg. I can't make myself believe the paper. Am making to headquarters today to see if it is really true.

Poor brave Alan. No words of mine can do him justice. I mourn him not so much because of his being, as I believe, my best friend, but because of what he was, the man, the hero. He was always there, ever ready to volunteer, never complaining when he got the raw end of a deal, constantly cheerful and always pure good and noble to live up to. He saw his duty in this war and hesitated not a whit. Although serving and fighting with the French armies he died for our cause and for his country, the US.

Thank the Lord I am going to the front now and in a chasse escadrille. With any kind of luck I am going to avenge dear old Alan. Already in this game of flying I have lost many friends; but Alan was my best. If I don't succeed in making the Hun pay dearly for his death, may I fall for the same cause that he gave his life for, and in the same way – in action.

This sad news does not make me hesitate or feel timid about going to the lines. On the contrary it makes me yearn to be there. Don't worry about me. 'To every man upon this earth death cometh soon or late.' What if I am killed? Could any other form of death be more glorious? And I may survive. Now I'm after Boche blood and I'm going to get it. It may be some months before I down my first Hun, but I'll get him or he'll get me.

I am awfully glad I took out that $10,000 insurance. That means that you, dear Mother, will not need to worry as to finances. It might be some months before the payments start regularly, but see Mr. Buchan, 1st Nat. Bank, and he'll tell you how to write Washington DC to hurry it up. My affairs here are in pretty good condition, too. But why talk this way? I believe I've got a lucky star. A certain percentage survive, why shouldn't I be one of them? Honestly, something within me tells me there is other work cut out for me when I come home. Fighting Huns is just going to be an incident in my life.

But dear old Alan. He has been a lot in my life. He has stood by me and encouraged me when I felt nearly alone in this world over here, and he has cheered me when I felt blue. He has often stuck up for me against tormenters. Ever since I first knew him in Palo Alto and Stanford he has become an influence and an ideal for me. To be like Alan has been one of my ambitions. He will always stand a landmark in my life and when I start on the wrong course he will appear and set me right. I loved him like a brother.

How his folks must feel, and poor Jack. But they are brave too. To win the war sacrifices are necessary, and they shall not have sacrificed Alan in vain. I shall write them immediately this newspaper article is confirmed. Oh that it isn't true … The blow must be a hard one on Jack. He possibly feels alone in this world now, this world across the ocean I mean. If I can cheer him I shall do my best. But now let us try to pass over this sadness. It will remain ever in our thoughts. We must remember, however, that this is no time for brooding over misfortunes. Action counts; words weigh little beside deeds; I shall avenge Alan or die in the attempt.

28

THE 85TH

Clifford was indeed on his way to the front, but it would actually be to fight with a French unit in the first instance: the build-up of the US Air Service in mid-June 1918 was still a work in progress. The 1st Pursuit Group had only been brought to full strength at the end of May with the addition of two units, the 27th and 147th, joining the combat squadrons of the 94th and 95th already in service near Toul.

The Toul Sector had been comparatively quiet in terms of front-line fighting thus far, but useful for all that. New pilots, those who had not seen previous service, were afforded the time and space to cut their teeth and learn their craft; although that was not to say that it had been a complete backwater. The skies above had claimed their fair share of casualties, among them the feted Major Raoul Lufbery, commander of the 94th Hat in the Ring and former star and ace of the American Foreign Legion Lafayette Escadrille. The sector would also soon experience an escalation in its importance as a theatre of war.

In addition to the combat units in the area a number of balloon companies and observation squadrons were also in service. These units were tasked with a variety of intelligence and monitoring activities, from short- and long-range reconnaissance to photography, artillery adjustment and location targeting. The 2nd Balloon Company had actually been the first American air unit to go into service on the front, in February, moving into position near Royaumeix, north of Toul. Similarly, by June squadrons like the 91st Aero were carrying out valuable visual and photographic reconnaissance flights for the 8th French Army, flying deep behind enemy lines into areas around Étain, Conflans and Metz.

But even then, units like the 91st or the 1st and 12th Observation Squadrons – the latter pair having recently formed into what was known as the I Corps Observation Group – were attempting to carry out their early work in old planes: planes they grimly referred to as 'ARs' – not *Avion Renaults*, their real name, but 'Antique Rattletraps'. It was only gradually that these relics were being replaced by new craft coming into service, planes like the state-of-the-art Salmson 2A2.[46]

The organisation of American air forces and where they were being placed was thus a gradual process. The training, supply of craft and deployment of pilots would shift as the summer went on and change as the war took its different turns.

So for now, Clifford and the others would not find themselves assigned to an American squadron, but assigned to fly with their Allies. Somewhat irritatingly, at first he and his twenty strong group, including colleagues James Beane, Remington Vernam, Jerry Jerome and John Aiken, were not handed an immediate combat role. They would be billeted for a two-week period some way back from the actual front line. French commanders wanted to assess the capabilities of their new charges, both American and French, before deciding where they would be posted. Clifford realised that he needed to accept the situation, that it would be for the best.

June 27th 1918

Dear Mother John and George,

Tonight I am feeling in high spirits, for now I am one step nearer the front. Really it has been my impatience; and I find myself ridiculous for constantly announcing to you all that I'll be there right away. You see, in my youthful anticipation and exuberance I am always going too fast and the French are so slow and there has been so much red tape in getting us connected with them. It is only a temporary connection, too, by the way. They can't be hurried; everything must go along the regular channels and seemingly by mail – nothing by dispatch.

During the last ten days we have all had six hops. One on a Nieup and five on a Spad. Just to show the French, I suppose, that we could fly chasse planes; purely a formal demonstration. Our boys flew rings around the French pilots and had crowds of them standing on their feet watching us acrobat their old planes, something unheard of at this particular post. One of our boys did a loop and they called him an 'ace'. I did some virages and renversements and ended up with a couple of vrilles. When I landed the French Lieut asked me if I vrilled accidentally, that the Spad was a trick machine, etc., etc. All I could do was to laugh. Vernam did some renversements and barrels, awfully pretty too. It was a real good exhibition; the newly trained French pilots stood open-eyed. I guess they took us for experienced veterans and yet we're only novices. The front makes the veteran.

Tomorrow Aiken, Vernam, Fish and I leave for X via Paris for Escadre No. I French front. I don't know. We are dreading another week or two delay. Who knows? We should worry. Every step leads in that direction – the front – and it's only a matter of time. But the route is not the quickest in time or distance, we think. But we don't know and we are simply pawns and will prove good ones I hope. Have confidence in superior officers; obey orders; ask no questions; be always cheerful willing and ready; that is the only attitude to take; so – we should worry.

An *escadre* was the name for a larger formation or 'wing' of planes, a collection of groups, themselves each comprising three squadrons. In his case, and as luck would have it, the unit Clifford was being transferred to in Escadre 1 was Groupe de Combat 19, Escadrille Spa. 85, the same squadron his friend Alan Nichols had flown with; and there he met Stephen Tyson, Alan's roommate and someone he already knew of by reputation. Tyson was a veteran both of American Ambulance Service work, having served on the front from 1916 – earlier than Stanford units – and working with ambulance unit SSU 1 on the Verdun Front before joining the Lafayette Foreign Legion Corps.

Although he had not met him before, Clifford had read about Tyson in articles published in the *Palo Alto Times*, from pieces sent home by Alan. Clifford's family had sent him copies of the *Times* at various points. Now, meeting him, he was able to tell his family what a 'fine fellow' he was and how lonely Tyson had been since Alan's death:

It seems like awfully hard luck that I wasn't ordered out to escadrille Spad 85 before Alan was killed. Just one month earlier and I would have seen him.

Absolutely nothing had been done with Alan's baggage or personal effects. Tyson had no authority to go ahead and besides he didn't know what to do. I was really rather surprised in that Alan had left no instructions as to what to do in case he should be killed. So Tyson simply gathered the things together and locked them up. In due time they were going to be taken care of in regular military channels and you know what that means. I talked the matter over with Captain Laurent, the commander of our escadrille. He was awfully nice and told me to go head and use my judgment and that what I decided and did would be OK. So yesterday afternoon I got Tyson to help me and we went over the baggage, sorting it into two groups. One was of war apparel etc. that Jack might be able to use; the second was the remainder, which we placed in the trunk. The photos and films I am going to send to the Nicholses in installments of about 50 a week so at least they won't all get lost.

The Captain gave me permission to come into Paris to fix things up. Am leaving the duffle bag at American Ex. Co. for Jack to call for next time he comes in to Paris. Of course it is impossible and impracticable to try to send it to him. You know he is in the US army now, the tanks; the trunk I am sending home to his folks. Of course I have to take considerable liberties and go ahead and act as my judgment dictates. There is no use loading Jack up with all Alan's baggage. He's a private in the US army now and of course I am in a position to know what that means. Was a private myself for some months, so I speak from experience. To leave things to the military would be inadvisable and to let them wait till I heard from Jack would be inexpedient. I might even bump off while waiting for a reply and then things never would get fixed.

Alan had two Boche officially, one alone and one with Tyson, besides several unofficial. He had been cited twice and proposed for the Medaille Militaire but he died before it could be granted. As soon as his second citation arrives with his Croix de Guerre and 2 palms the Captain is going to give them to me to send to his folks by registered mail.

Alan's loss is felt by everybody in the escadrille from mechanics up. He was loved and admired by all his comrades. Never before have I heard so many good words for any man.

Thank goodness I have in Lt. John Aiken a man and a friend who will do all this for me in case anything should happen. He has a sealed letter in case of an unexpected event and he is giving me the same for him. It might be well to write the Nicholses now, so I'll quit. Have already written Jack asking him to second what I do. It is just luck that I found myself in escadrille Spad 85 and Tyson is going to be a wonderful help.

Clifford had by this stage been allocated his own Spad fighter, a Spad VII model, but even so it was necessary to bide his time. The unit moved camp from time to time and he was still required to drill and practise combat manoeuvres, waiting for the right moment.

On the front the 3rd and 4th Offensives initiated by Ludendorff's German forces were in the process of being stopped. The initial drive down to the Marne, to Château-Thierry, was reversed in June. The bloody mopping-up operation on the ground and fighting around Belleau Wood continued, only winding up at the beginning of July. During this time American Air Commander Colonel Billy Mitchell, in charge of American units in the Zone of Advance, had fashioned a new air operation to aid the effort.

The new 1st Brigade, made up of the four squadrons of the 1st Pursuit Group and I Observation Group, plus a number of French squadrons, was deployed. It was a baptism of fire for still relatively inexperienced American pilots against tough and experienced German air units, including Hermann Göring's Jagdgeschwader I, the notorious 'Flying Circus' formerly led by the late Baron Manfred von Richthofen.

On the ground there was a pause in the area where American forces had been fighting. But it was brief. Ludendorff was coming back for more. A fresh onslaught, his 5th Offensive, was unleashed on 15 July. Again his armies descended on the Marne, towards Château-Thierry. The plan was to flank Reims in the Champagne area, cutting the cathedral city and its defenders off to allow a clearer path to Paris. He needed to seize the valley of the Surmelin River, running into the Marne east of Château-Thierry.

The German 10th and 36th Divisions bore down on the American 3rd Division. But the 3rd held firm, the 30th and 38th Infantry in particular taking heavy casualties. Its objective was achieved and the 'Rock of the Marne' protected its base. There then began a counter-offensive on 18 July to drive home the advantage, one that had been at the planning stage for some time. Supreme Commander Ferdinand Foch knew that he needed to reduce the salient in the Aisne-Marne area and had waited until he felt his German counterpart's effort had been sufficiently spent.[47]

Attached to the 85th Escadrille, Clifford's time had nearly arrived:

Escadrille Spad 85, July 16th 1918

Dear Mother John and George,

I may rightly say that I am half in, half out of this big battle. The Captain wouldn't let me go out when it first started because the clouds were very, very low, necessitating dangerous low flying and the fighting was exceptionally violent. He said he wanted his new pilots to have a little more experience before sending us into such a fiery furnace. Now that the battle has been in progress a couple of days he is going to let me out. In half an hour I am going out on a patrol and will probably see some real excitement.

∽◌∽

July 17th 1918

It certainly was an interesting patrol yesterday. Am going to tell you all about it. I was second off and circled about the appointed spot waiting for Lt. Menard who was going to lead. Six planes were scheduled for the patrol but Tyson, [Félix] Gohier and I were the only three that got off at the right time. We circled around for fifteen minutes and then as the rest didn't come up Gohier took the lead and we sailed off toward the lines. A strong wind was in back of us and in ten minutes we covered the 35 kilometers and were over the lines. And just to think that we started our patrol over the same town and sector that I was in in the ambulance world last August. Everything looked so familiar.

On the way out we passed over a couple of Breguet bombing planes. We are to patrol the sector at 2000 meters. There were supposedly other French formations above us at 5000, although I'll be darned if I saw any. Gohier, leading, made big zig-zags over the lines. Sometimes we were three kilometers in Boche territory and sometimes the same in our own lines. Tyson on the right and I on the left in back of and higher than Gohier kept swerving and zig-zagging sharply looking over our shoulders for Boche and anything else in the kingdom of the air. Occasionally I found time to look at the trenches. For a width of about five miles the ground was simply sliced with zig-zag trenches and dotted with shell holes. Talk about barren desolate waste. That brownish yellow bare smoking ground is the worst I've ever seen. Every now and then there would be a puff of smoke, a shell going off in the trenches throwing up dust and dirt. We could hear no report. It just so happened that there was not much artillery action in our sector yesterday.

Inside and below us were a lot of French saucisses or observation balloons. In a corresponding position across the lines were the Boche balloons. They do most of the observing and we chasse pilots guard them against attack.

We had been cruising around for quite a time when I saw a fourth Spad. It was Lt. Menard who had gotten another machine and came out to join us, so now we made four. At the moment there was a lot of white shrapnel near us. I remembered Alan's explanation. The French anti-aircraft were notifying us of the presence of Boche. As a matter of fact, we had all seen them a few minutes before. Constantly S-ing and looking over your shoulder while slightly turning gives you a complete view of everything and so if you keep your eyes open you won't get surprised.

I counted nine Boche. They were all the latest Fokker biplanes, really quite easy to recognize. Gohier and Tyson later said there were sixteen. At the same moment, looking way off to the left over Hun territory – we were flying in an easterly direction at the time – were many black puffs of smoke. Boche anti-aircraft, and right *in front of them beating it 'hell bent for election' to use a vulgar phrase but what always appears to me as a funny one when I hear it, was a small group of Spads. The German Fokkers, their latest chasse plane, had a wonderful position; they had altitude and were right in the sun. I was absolutely expecting them to attack; but, strange to say, they didn't worry me at all. I wasn't a bit excited but was just as cool as I could be, which fact surprised me not a little. I just increased my S-ing and zig-zags and watched those Huns like a bull-dog.*

They bunched up ready for the attack and started to dive at us from about 600 meters distance. We bunched too and waited. I was sort of hoping for a scrap although odds were against us. I think the Boche were trying to drive a wedge between the other group of Spads and our formation and cut us off from each other. But seconds count in this game and they weren't quite quick enough. The other Spads made a dash to the right, we a sprint to the left and just as the Boche started peaking we were ten. Still, even then they had the advantage of numbers and position. But way above us were two R-IIs (R-onzes) the latest bimotored three-place Caudron. (Not one has been brought down yet and they cruise way back into the German lines and are never even attacked. They are faster than any two seater on the front, equal in speed to many chasse planes and so well armed fore and aft that they are a sure bet in attack or in defense). And for some reason Fritzie changed his mind and stopped diving and did not attack. Maybe he feared a counter, for he started climbing and re-crossed to his own lines.

What a sense of security one feels when he is patrolling in such a large group. And what a thrill. What a branch of the service to be in. Cavalry of the air. It's wonderful. And I am really looking forward to a general mix-up some of these days to a free for all of about 20 against 20. Individual combats are great stuff but they have got nothing on an aerial battle. Really it was the prettiest aerial sight I have ever seen. The way those beautiful little Spads wove in among each other diving and plunging and turning like a flock of birds.

Naturally we didn't attack, for our orders were to patrol at 2000 meters and give our attention to protecting the spotting planes, reglage machines [observation planes used for artillery adjustments] and sausages and not to go off on any wild goose chase which might take us miles into German territory and away from our beat. And besides the odds were too much against us.

Over the A. [Argonne] forest two Spads engaged a Boche; Gohier saw part of the combat. Tyson says he saw the Boche fall in flames at 6.45 PM. A few minutes later Tyson developed motor trouble and headed into the lines. Gohier and I fol-lowed him for a ways and saw he was going to make a good landing at a French aerodrome. Gohier watched his atterrissage [landing] while I looked over some

French sausages. Our patrol was over at 6.45. By that time we were well within our own lines; another French squadron had taken our place and beat and it was safe for us to separate, each man for himself. I chased an A-R or Dorand, the same kind of a machine I had my first ride in in June of last year. My, what a slow clumsy bus it was. By 7.15 I was over our field and after making a renversement just for ducks, landed. Really it was the most interesting two hours I've had yet in the air. Tyson got in later. Not having fought we had no losses and all our machines returned safely.

We had a fine meal last night out under the trees. It was very hot yesterday; Hugues [Marcel Hugues, celebrated French pilot], the French 'ace' with 12 official victories, came to dinner in his white pyjamas, socks and slippers. Another French lieut in shirt sleeves and suspenders; some were all slicked up in their black coats with gold and silver trimmings and medals and scarlet pants; our captain had on his khaki uniform; everybody was happy and gay. The French never seem to crab. The clean tablecloth seemed awfully white in contrast to the green around. The poilu waiter served dinner just as if we had been at the Astors or the Vanderbilts. Can you imagine such a scene with such contrasting combinations? And then you must remember all the wine bottles on the table, for the French are great but not intemperate wine drinkers. (I have seldom seen a Frenchman drunk.) The evening was wonderful.

On the ground the counter-offensive to reduce the Aisne-Marne Salient continued. The cathedral city of Soissons on the Aisne was retaken north-west of Reims, in what was seen to be something of a turning point. German forces were on the retreat and Clifford was on the move. He and his fellow men woke at 3 a.m. on 18 July to move camp again, the earliness of the hour necessary to allow the trucks laden with tents and equipment to make a start for their new base early enough to arrive before nightfall at the other end. Appreciable distances were covered and the roads were difficult. It would, Clifford calculated, take a truck around twelve hours to accomplish what he could manage in an hour's flight.

Given that, he waited behind after the trucks left to see if there were front-line patrols to do on the way:

Just before lunch the newspapers came. In Le Matin was an article to the effect that Capt. Quentin Roosevelt had been killed at the front, having been brought down in flames in the course of an aerial combat. He had evidently been promoted since last I saw him at Orly. 'Quentin' as we all called him, never Lieutenant Roosevelt, was a very likeable fellow and his death is felt by everybody. He wasn't a brilliant flyer, just average, and I think was inclined to be a little too reckless. Really, in spite of his fine physique and abnormal bodily development, he was only a boy, no older thinking than the average boy of his years (21 I believe).

So many that I knew well have bumped off and the process still continues, so that now I am getting quite used to seeing my friends go; and only in exceptional cases such as Alan and Bigelow do I think much about it. C'est la guerre. A certain number, a rather high percentage it must be confessed, are killed in this game. Losses are to be expected and, while to be regretted, come as a matter of course. You may think I am getting quite cold-blooded; I am. How can a man be otherwise? Worry in this game is fatal; and brooding or thinking too much about accidents gets a man's nerve quicker than anything else in the world. As soon as it happens, forget it, except for the lesson it teaches.

From what I can gather, about 30 per cent of aviation deaths are accidents in school. Possibly another 20 per cent are killed in accidents at the front. Many flyers try to show off near the ground. That makes ½ the deaths thru accidents. The other day a French lieut tried to show off for some soldiers. He fell in their midst, killing himself and three poilus. They may get by for a while, but they get it in the end. You can't tempt and flout death all the time and never get scratched. Some pilots think that just because they are at the front they are 'finished' and can do anything. Others get careless and fall; and many get rattled and so get killed, whereas if they kept cool they might get out with a whole skin.

The rest of the deaths we will say occur in action. And of these, at least half could be avoided. Many are due to carelessness and conceit and others from recklessness and fool daring against unequal odds. For instance a man will say, 'Oh I'm going to be brave. There are four Boche. I am only one but I'll attack anyway and show 'em I'm game.' This has been known to work but it fails more times than it succeeds. If he runs up against poor flyers such an attack may demoralize them; enable him to shoot down a couple; get away and earn the DSC. But if they are good cool flyers as all men at the front should be, this daring boy will be 'easy meat'.

Or again a man may be lucky and get a couple of Boche. Instead of attributing it to luck or to the other pilot being exceptionally poor, he conceitedly thinks he is a wonderful pilot, much better than the average and so practically invincible. He gets careless and over confident and sooner or later gets bumped off when by exercising judgment and care he might have lived to serve his country more and might have become an ace.

(As a matter of fact I don't want this repeated to anybody but from what I can gather from Tyson, the Captain and others, Alan was a little over-confident. He got a Boche officially and several unofficial. He liked to leave the formation with Tyson and go way back into the lines and look for trouble. You really will get all the fighting you want without trying to beat up double your number. Well, one day Alan got just one bullet and that finished him.)

Exercising judgment and caution is not cowardice. I know four French aces in our Groupe de Combat pretty well. These men have very much surprised me. They are not daredevil reckless pilots; they are cool quiet calculating men. They patiently wait their chance and, seizing it, always win out. They are the least confident-acting and talking men in the crowd; and from looking at them I should say they were all over 25. They are brave men but not reckless youths. The daredevil wins out several times but generally 'gets it' in the end. The other man does his country just as much good, possibly a little slower at first, and he lives to tell the tale. Which is the better to be? Both deserve praise and admiration for their bravery and daring, but we simply say that one used more judgment because of his years and the other was a brave but impetuous lad. The rest of the pilots brought down die in fair fight, either brought down by a better man or in carrying out some perilous enterprise ordered by the CO, or simply have hard luck which, in the law of averages, has to come to a certain number.

Incidentally there is still some individual stuff, but it is being displaced by team work. A man may do his duty in his formation and never get a Boche. Individual work is being discouraged. A man seeking glory will rush off from his formation to get victims. Generally he is brought down and doesn't do his country a bit of good. Often he gets some Boche first; then he is got.

There are two big things that chasse pilots are used for: first to protect their observation and spotting planes and sausages, the 'eyes' of their generals; they beat off attacks; that is their main duty and they get all the fight they want as a squadron as a formation. And here it is a squadron accomplishment rather than that of the individual. The soldier who fights with his company doesn't shine, perhaps, but he fights just as hard as the individual who prowls around No Man's Land alone and bombs some Fritzies. For that reason the English idea of not disclosing the names of the pilots who bring down the Huns is good. They believe that just as much honor should go to the observation pilot who never fights but often gets brought down in flames, as to the chasse pilot who, because he has a single-seater machine with which he can bring down Huns, often stars. They cut out the starring by cutting out the names; all run the same risk.

The other work of the chasse pilots is to hunt Boche observation planes. This is often done by big fleets of planes or attacking squadrons and sometimes by individuals. When a squadron goes hunting it runs up against a protecting enemy squadron and that is why chasse pilots fight chasse planes; but every time they get a chance they attack something easier. And that is why the individual attacker generally gets brought down. Luck may be with him for a while but it doesn't always last. He goes out looking for trouble, looking for an easy victim. Suddenly he gets more than he was looking for, for an enemy squadron drops down on him and he is 'finis'. Sometimes 'decoys' are used. These are slow, heavily armored planes. They look easy; they tempt a few chasse pilots over the lines. These drop for the attack. Suddenly 15 or 20 Huns dive out of the clouds and the 2 or 3 attacking planes are up against it. But the poor decoy pilot, in spite of his armor, is often brought down and made a sacrifice. I would hate to be a decoy pilot; he sure has to have guts. As a rule, though, he isn't a very good pilot; all he has to do is to fly in a straight line and obey orders.

All the above will probably be interesting because it throws quite a few sidelights on this game of aviation. Don't let it worry you at all, though. Just always make up your minds not to worry for worry never did anybody any good; it won't help you and can't help me.

29

ON PATROL

The whole of Clifford's Escadre No. 1 had pitched camp in the country-side north of Troyes, a new temporary base from which it could patrol the changing front lines as the Allied armies advanced north. It was the same part of the country in which Clifford had found himself a year before while serving with the American Ambulance, when he and his erstwhile colleagues had been *en repos* with their French division. Back then Clifford had been complaining in his letters home about time wasted, time spent idling as war raged on elsewhere and impatient to be part of it. Now things were different: he was in an active combat role, part of the war effort at last.

There were still periods of inactivity, of course, time spent waiting for the next operation to materialise or the weather to clear. The only differ-ence now was that the next operation, any operation, could turn in an instant and become something altogether more serious. Either that or, as he learned, some odd episode might be thrown up, a quirky interlude to puncture the deadly weight of the war around them.

One such episode came the day after they had arrived at this new temporary base. It was 19 July and Clifford and his fellow pilots waited around for news of their next work. They whiled away the time as best they could, dozing in the shade under some trees or reading or chatting. In Clifford's case, he was attempting a mix of all three while beginning a letter home. Anything to occupy himself while remaining aware that they could be called on to take to their planes in short order.

The situation had remained this way throughout the day. In fact, the young pilots had all but assumed they would be standing down, their thoughts beginning to turn to dinner and the evening ahead when suddenly the languor was broken. An orderly rushed from the airfield by car. It was 6 o'clock – a rush patrol was on. They followed him back to the field and within a few minutes had scrambled into their cockpits and were airborne. Their orders were to head north-west towards the Marne River to patrol the front between Château-Thierry and Dormans; and they were to do so, as the highest of a number of patrols in the area, at an altitude of 5,000m.

But things did not go exactly according to plan for Clifford:

Chateau de Vaux, Fouchères-sur-Seine,
Dept. d'Aube, France, July 20th 1918

There were a lot of Boche but they didn't start any trouble, and as we were a protecting and not an attacking patrol yesterday, we didn't attack. You mustn't leave your beat or your poste unless you go to the rescue of another Allied plane, but we had to stay in a group. Danger lies in getting separated, for then you are apt to get picked off singly.

In making some sharp virages after being on the lines about an hour and a quarter, my motor suddenly pooped; we were over Hun territory, too. I began losing altitude with my motor only turning at half speed. There was only one thing to do. I put her on 'nourrice'. That is the reserve tank which lasts for ten minutes. And pointed south and at full speed and alone and at 5000 metres.

I must confess I was quite excited. What with trying to fix the motor and straining my neck for Boche, I had my hands full. Before the nourrice had run long, I got the motor going again from the reservoir. Something was wrong in the feed pipe. When I get back to camp the mechanos will have to look it over. By that time I was back of the lines and beating it south. It would have been foolish to try to find the patrol. Besides, two planes were following me rather suspiciously, and with my motor running as it was I didn't feel like taking a chance against them. Under ordinary circumstances I should have investigated.

By the time I had entirely shaken them, I had lost my bearings. Was safe enough to be sure, but too far south, and I had no map of that district. Besides, it is hard to read a map well at such an altitude. I opened my map to try. Whiff. A puff of wind tore it in two and the important half blew out, so I had nothing. I thought I knew where I was, and so kept flying, thinking I recognized some landmarks ahead. But each time I looked too far ahead, and when I got over the particular woods or river, it looked unfamiliar. The funny thing was I had passed several aviation parcs where I could have landed to find out where I was. So it was really my fault that I kept on getting lost, worse and worse, but always in a straight line south. Finally as my essence was nearly gone, I decided to land anyway. I glided down to 2000 meters when the regular tank gave out entirely and I had to switch on nourrice again. Ten minutes now. The only decent grounds that I could see were those of this chateau. They and the chateau looked fine. There was a large flat field from which the grain had just been removed. I s-d and slipped and spiraled down over the chateau and glided into the field. It was bisected by a barbed wire fence straight ahead. Didn't see it till a couple of seconds before I reached it. 'Gave her the gun again' and jumped the fence making a perfect landing on the other side. A beautiful field to land in. I cut the motor and looked at the essence guage. Three minutes only left. Breathing a sigh of relief I undid my strap, unloaded the mitrailleuse [machine gun], monkeyed with my many levers and jumped out. The first thing I did was to take a long needed and very relieving leak.

The occupants of the chateau had all rushed out to the steps thinking I was falling. They said afterwards they expected to have to pick up the pieces. Monsieur de Fontenay told me that when he saw me heading straight for the fence he turned his eyes away from what he believed was going to be a tragedy. Ha. Ha.

M. de Fontenay is a very old man, a veteran of the war of 1870 with a long white flowing beard and whiskers and a beautiful moustache. He asked me if I was hurt but I told him no, only perdu and then explained my predicament. He played a noble part, insisted I stay to dinner and sleep at his chateau and in fact live at the Chateau de Vaux until I received orders from my capitaine or was able to get essence and a mechanic to fly back to our terrain. His little grandchild Kate loaned me her bicycle to go to Fouchères-sur-Seine to send a telegram to Capitaine Laurent. He probably thinks I was shot down over the lines. Won't Aiken worry …

On the way in a French Colonel overtook me. He had rushed out from the town in his car thinking there was an accident; he sent the telegram for me; that done, he said when the reply came he would phone out to the Chateau and for me to go back there and take a much needed rest. Everybody still thinks an aviator is a different kind of human being and must be handled with delicate care and every consideration. So here I am the next day after my adventure at the wonderful chateau of a French millionaire 60 kilometers south of Arcis-sur-Aube living a royal life and waiting for orders and instructions from the capitaine.

Clifford confessed that he felt bad finding himself where he did, aware that his escadrille needed all the pilots it could muster at the time. But having notified Captain Laurent, he was to bide his time at the château until the necessary mechanical help arrived to make his plane airworthy. Clifford needed little more encouragement. He embraced the opportunity enthusiastically and, with his hosts' blessing, began to make himself at home in the château and to explore the 200-year-old house and its extensive grounds:

The grounds include thousands of acres, woods, forests and much arable land. Before the war and now when Capitaine de Fontenay comes home en permission they hunt deer and wild boar. The chateau itself is very large and wonderfully furnished. Dozens of fine oil paintings adorn its walls. Half way up the magnificent stairs is a knight in full armor. I must close this to get the one o'clock mail. That is the time the postman calls for the letters. Will write describing the place and my time here first chance I get. So goodbye, good luck and lots of it. And all kinds of love as ever. Cliff

Escadrille Spad 85 July 21 1918

Dear Mother John and George,

Under a separate cover I am sending you a picture of the Chateau where I stopped and you can Judge for yourself of its size and magnificence. And M. de Fontenay was fine. There was a huge canopy and very rich stuff over my bed; I felt like King Louis himself. The ceiling was about 16 ft. high. Beautiful oil paintings hung on the walls; rich carpets covered the floors; rare ornaments and fine old furniture adorned the chamber. I had a special garçon to tend to all my wants.

I had dinner very late eating all by myself in the grand dining room. Opposite me at the table sat M. de Fontenay; Mesdames de Fontenoy 1 & 2 and Mme de F. and sister. They had dined earlier but they were so anxious for news from the front that they made me do more talking than eating.

I am very much surprised in that I can carry on a fairly decent conversation in French and evidently interest my hearers and when they talk a normal pace I can get the drift as a rule. The little grandchild Kate, 12 years old, spoke English very well. She had an English governess so no wonder she was learning so quickly.

The French Colonel in F. [Fouchères] offered me his car to go to T. [Troyes] to get essence and a mechanic. Just as we started out, having gone about 2 kilometers, we met Capitaine Laurent, John Aiken and one of 85's mechanos coming full speed in our car. Result was I called off the trip and we all went back to the Chateau.

While we were waiting for the mechanic to fill up my tanks John and I accepted the hospitality of Monsieur and tasted some very refreshing and excellent white wine. I got off in a very, very strong wind. It was so bumpy that I called off the promised acrobatics. But anyway the Captain said not to do any till I got over our own field again. In 35 minutes at 130 miles an hour and with the wind at my back I got back to escadrille Spad about 2 hours ahead of Aiken and the Captain.

When he arrived back at the base, however, it was to more bad news. His new friend and colleague Stephen Tyson, Alan Nichols' roommate, was dead:

TYSON HAS BEEN KILLED. He met his death the same day I got lost. About ten minutes after my motor forced me south Gohier, leading the patrol, started an attack on eight Boche. He said he only intended to scare them back to their own lines by diving a short way and then pulling up. He did this, but Tyson very recklessly kept on diving.

None of us can understand why he kept on going as he did, straight after one particular Boche regardless of the others whom he passed. Then the two first Boche pulled up and swung down in back of Tyson. He was easy prey and fell in flames. He made a terrible mistake and violated all rules of aerial warfare when he passed Gohier, the Chef de la patrouille, and dove on by himself. All should watch the Chef and do what he does; dive with him to the attack, but redress with him and not pass him.

Tyson and Alan were, according to the other flyers, excellent pilots and no one can question their bravery and daring; but both were young and impulsive; too anxious to get Boche too quickly and become aces; and altogether too reckless and over confident.

I had a long talk with Gohier, who is the best pilot now in our escadrille. He says it is very hard for all young and new pilots to begin the game in the right way. They always want to get into a fight quickly and long before they have had enough experience. He says a man can really be of more service to his country by going slow at first, than hitting the line hard, than by being over-anxious and throwing himself away. He cites the cases of practically all the French aces who well illustrate his point. The pilot's big school is the front and he should go very carefully until he has mastered all the lessons it has to offer. Again, he says, young pilots cannot realize why the chasse patrol doesn't start a fight with every Boche patrol it meets or why it is bad to separate from the formation. The discipline of the patrol and staying with it is hard, very hard. There seem to be so many chances to get a Boche by leaving it. Sometimes you succeed for a while as did Nichols and Tyson, but you are nearly always brought down too soon; really much before you have the chance of rendering the service you might render if you went slow at the start. There is an ace in 94 who flew as a chasse pilot for 19 months without getting a Boche but now he has eight; has never had a bullet hole in his plane and his fellow pilots say he always surprises the enemy, and due to his 19 months experience he can easily get away if the odds are against him. Well now you have simply got to hand it to the other fellow for being brave beyond words, but you have to take off your hat to the clever ace. And which is of most service to his country?

He picked up as many tips as he could from the different experienced ace pilots in his own escadre and those pilots he came across from other units. Some were older, some surprisingly young, like 19-year-old ace Pierre Marinovitch of the 94th Escadrille who was already highly decorated. He was impressed by the modesty of those he spoke to, by the fact that they were for the most part quiet and retiring, not talking in the first person about their solo achievements but rather about the common goal and tactics of the flights undertaken with colleagues.

As if to prove the point about the need for the newer pilots to learn their craft slowly and obey collective orders, there were still only certain missions that Clifford and others were asked to undertake. One they were not allowed to join came the day he returned to the base. Laurent, as captain, wanted to send his most experienced charges up to harry retreating columns of German forces on the ground, issuing a crisp 'nothing doing' when Clifford attempted to press his point.

It was, Clifford reflected later, perhaps the right course of action, judging by the reception given one of his more experienced colleagues who did go on the patrol. That pilot had had to manoeuvre fast and outrun a group of ten German Albatros planes who swooped on him during the mission. In order to escape, his colleague had first raced his Spad into enemy territory before climbing into the clouds and doubling back for a further 50 or 60km and ending up landing way off course to the south-west.

Escadrille Spad 85 July 25th 1918

We have a new Escadrille commander, a lieutenant. The Captain was promoted to command a Groupe de Combat. He seemed very glad to go and we were as glad to have him. He was an old soldier with 19 years' service and had many fine soldierly qualities and was a good organizer. But he was not an exceptional flyer and had no Boche. Our New CO has four official, is young and a good mixer, and is very well liked by all. He is a splendid example and goes on nearly all the patrols as the commander of an escadrille should do; and we have absolute confidence in him.

Today I went up with a new Lieut. for a practice combat. He wasn't very good, a novice to the Spad, and if he had been a Boche pussy, he would have needed all his nine lives nine times. I was rather rough on my machine and dove and plunged and made renversements like a wild Pegasus. Lieut. Dumas was rather pleased yesterday and today, and today before sending us up he said to Pellet, 'Lieut. Kimber n'est pas un mauvais pilot'. When I got down this afternoon he said 'FORMIDABLE'. He said he should not have sent me up in that machine which was as I thought a perfectly strong plane, but that Mardi, five days off, I should have the new 220 HP Spad that had just arrived. He said 'il faut pour l'aviateur Americain un avion tres solid'. Well you can imagine I nearly went wild. Just think of it. I had thoroughly expected to serve an apprenticeship on an old machine. I shouldn't really say 'old machine' because none of the front line planes are old. After only a few hours in the air they are sent back to the schools etc. Am going to name my new plane NICK after Alan.

Clifford's new higher powered 220hp plane, a Spad XIII, duly arrived and he took great delight in putting it through its paces in practice. He also enjoyed the signal honour of having his new 'Nick' plane decorated with a new symbol, that of the Joker. As was customary on the Western Front, each squadron had its own adoptive symbol and the 85th was no different. But the 85th's men had recently decided to change their insignia from that of their old Taurus bull to the new Joker and he was to be the first recipient.

Yet Clifford took greater pleasure still from the praise of his new commander, Lieutenant Paul Émile Dumas, who had flown with some of the celebrated French aces of the war, like Georges Guynemer, René Fonck and Albert Deullin. Dumas was, he felt, an inspirational leader who could get the most out of his men: more effort and sacrifice, but also mixed with a dose of realism. He had been wounded in the head the previous year, learning what he said was the most valuable lesson of his career: not to leave the formation to attack the enemy.

Accordingly, he asked Clifford to be 'prudent' in his approach. If he was, he told him, Clifford could expect to shoot down 'many' enemy aircraft before war's end:

Escadrille Spad 85 August 4th 1918

We are all very optimistic. The taking of Soissons is not the climax. It is only a step or a happening in the sequence of events. Personally I believe Foch will keep the offensive from now on to the end of the war, although, of course, I know nothing. Today we are out of the tangle of the jungle of petty rivalry, indecision, and lack of unity, and we are on the high road to victory with one purpose and one guide FOCH to lead us to our goal. Our resources are unlimited and our spirit indomitable. But let us not 'go easy' to what is now sure victory; but let us redouble our effort, as Baker says. Let us hasten everything and bring the finish of the war so many years earlier.

The rain for the last two days has somewhat held up flying. Three days ago I got in a very good patrol in the morning. It is very interesting flying 4000–5000 meters above a front constantly moving northward. In the afternoon I had motor trouble again. We hadn't gone more than 30 kilometers along the battle front when one of my magnetos [electrical generator using magnets to produce current] broke. With my motor running at reduced speed I couldn't hold my place in formation and had to wiggle up and down a bit to say 'motor trouble' and then leave the patrol. At the time I didn't know that the trouble was but upon landing the mechanos discovered that the gears in one mag. were all ground to pieces. Incidentally I have the same mechano that Alan had. I am very well pleased with him.

The other day I saw a most horrible accident. Something that may happen to any of us any time but which is all in the game and which we must NOT let unnerve us. One of the flyers in 96 was doing practice acrobatics at about 2500 meters. I was not looking at him. Suddenly there was a BANG, a report like a cannon. I looked up; it took some time for the report of the breaking wings to reach the ground and by the time all eyes were turned upward the poor pilot was in his final plunge. The wings on one side had come off and were floating hundreds meters above the now spinning plane. The motor was going full speed and that and the shrieking wires as the plane vrilled made a horrible noise that could be heard for miles. There was no looking away. In such a scene your eyes are glued to the victim and his plane. The fall seemed interminable; would he never hit? He disappeared behind a clump of tress. I could see dust and wreckage fly in all directions; three or four seconds came the report of the smash and the motor stopped roaring. He must have hit at about 300–400 miles an hour. He was probably dead or unconscious at 1000 meters so he did not suffer. Ah, what a relief. To know that if you get killed in aviation death is instantaneous. Seldom is there lingering pain. It is not often that you are just hurt. The plane was kindling; the motor scrap iron and the poor pilot chopped meat, pieces of his body being thrown 20 and 50 meters.

Escadrille Spad 85 August 10 1918

Every day the Allied lines go forward and the Boche lines go back. Now they are on the old front of 1916 and still on the run eastward. I don't think they'll stop either for some time. Our work is very interesting. We go out with the line drawn on our map and when we come back we have to move the line a little, giving the Allies so many more villages, woods, hills etc. The clouds have been low and for the last few days have kept us under 2000 meters, most of the time at 1500. But even at 1000 it is hard to distinguish who's who in the smoke on the ground. Our mission is to protect our observation planes and balloons. Today we started to dive on three Boche but they were far off and when they saw us coming they scampered off so quickly they were out of sight in no time. One of the Boche saucisse balloons that was near M. [Metz] yesterday today had moved back about ten miles. Hun aeroplanes are very, very scarce.

We had a very interesting patrouille this afternoon right after lunch; a little time to rest after returning, tea and a general hashout of events with the Frenchmen; a sprawl on my bed; this letter started and another patrouille right away at 6.30 before dinner. It is very tiring and the strain, noise and smell of the oil and gas make one very sleepy. Sometimes the alert is at 5 AM and you have to be ready all day after making the patrouille. I have little time or inclination for reading. Our camp and field is about 12 kilometers from a fairly large city [Bar-le-Duc]. Naturally none of the trucks or autos arrived when we did, in fact, not until long after. So at noon we sat down to our lunch of a sandwich apiece and a glass of wine. Breakfast had consisted of a couple of cups of coffee and hard boiled eggs. You see everything, kitchens, utensils, stove etc. etc. had to be packed on the camion the night before. And so they could pack the tent, we had to get up at 5 AM.

Certain practical issues were thrown up from the fact that Clifford and his colleagues were continually on the move. One was that mail was slow in arriving or, to be more precise, in finding him wherever he was. In the course of the year he had been billeted in different locations with the American Ambulance and French Army. He had been based variously at Tours, Issoudun and Cazaux, and returning to Issoudun, then in Paris and Orly, and now latterly moving up the lines as the front changed in eastern or north-eastern France. He had tried asking his family to mail him at different times via the American Field Service or the American Expeditionary Force, US Air Service AEF, or more recently via his bank, Morgan Harjes, in Paris. There were periods when nothing arrived for up to six weeks, causing him to feel a little disheartened and lonely, anxious for news from home and from friends.

But by late July and early August letters were once more beginning to get through in fits and starts, even if posted some weeks or even months before. However, a more immediate and practical concern over preceding weeks had focused on accommodation. Often they would be called on as officers – depending on availability of barracks or beds at camp or whether the new camp had been pitched in the new forward position – to find accommodation in hotels in nearby towns and villages, especially if they had arrived, as was usual, many hours ahead of their colleagues. Even then, and as had happened already on a couple of occasions, the reservation of rooms or tables to eat at the hotels was no automatic guarantee of success. French officers from other squadrons arriving later would pull rank and place their own baggage in rooms previously earmarked by the young Americans. The latter's luggage would later be discovered stored unceremoniously somewhere other than their supposed bedrooms.

But Clifford increasingly learned to shrug off episodes of this type. While once upon a time they would have enraged him and offended his sense of fair play, he now preferred to see them as odd and funny – even the furious reactions of some of his colleagues. There was no point in getting mad any more, he mused. There were more serious concerns in the world around them:

US Air Service AEF August 16 '18

Dear Mother John and George,

C'est la guerre. By now I have reconciled myself to anything. Orders are orders and there must be reasons, good and sufficient for them, even if they are beyond our powers of penetration. About five days ago orders reached the escadrille to 'send the American pilots back to O. [Orly] where they would report to the American officer in charge.'

GENERAL CONSTERNATION. Altho it was a general order for all American chasse pilots with the French, our French superiors were not in a hurry to give us *our traveling papers until they could investigate, so Lieut. Dumas and Capt. Le Fevre got in touch with Capt. Deullin (eighth best flyer in France) and he in turn saw Commandant Minard, 'boss of the whole escadre'. He phoned the French head of aviation and he in turn the American Headquarters where it was decided, 'nothing doing'. Our French comrades sure wanted to hang on to us.*

Really I shall be awfully darn glad to get with the Americans again, and I sort of welcome the change. The change of grub in the first place sounds so good; nor will living expenses be so high; I can save more, I hope. But I am very thankful that I had the opportunity to spend another two months with the French. I feel I know them now so much better; they're not a bad bunch at all. Again I have learned an awful lot about flying at the front from real masters; from men who have gotten Boche and who know all the tricks of the trade. Now I can go out with the American flyers armed with real experience and I feel much more confident in being able to take care of myself. But really isn't it nice to serve with one's own countrymen? About eight days ago I got another dose of dysentery or diarrhea. It was much worse than last year at Arcis except for one redeeming feature: I had no fever. I flew as long as I could safely. For the last three days with my escadrille I had to lie around like a sick man and live on a diet self-imposed of eggs and milk; and naturally I began to get better.

The only thing that I am really afraid of is that I'll lose the bunch. You see, the recalled pilots are nearly all of my friends and I'd love to go out to the front with them. Knowing each other well gives pilots much more confidence; but, even so, practically all the American pilots are a splendid type of fellow and they can be counted upon in a pinch. This hospital is really a delightful place; the few days of rest are so nice. Clean, white sheets and soft beds; no rush; you couldn't hurry if you wanted to. In my ward are a lot of infantry artillery and engineering officers who were in the Chateau-Thierry scrap. Their stories and deeds of daring are awfully interesting. They are addressed as Lieut. X. or Captain M. or Capt. L. but the nurses, doctors and everybody simply call me the aviator or Mr. Aviator. It is very amusing. Four officers came in last night; one blinded by gas. It's horrible. Thank the Lord I fly. With me the chances are I'll get off scot free or be killed instantly. It's a great consolation after seeing those wounded and maimed heroes, incapacitated for life. WHAT WOULD LIFE BE WORTH LIVING WITHOUT LEGS OR EYES? NOT FOR ME ... I am very anxious to get back to the front; will probably have my wish granted in a few days. I want to get into some good scraps and get some of those darned Boche – at least avenge Alan. It seemed too bad to leave Escadrille Spad 85 so soon just after getting so well acquainted with all the pilots and getting my fine new plane NICK. Dumas promised to take the name off so I can name my

new American plane NICK. We are practically positive of going out again as chasse
pilots; thank the Lord for that. Now for another month I don't' suppose I'll get any
more letters from home. That is the hardest thing of all, but c'est la guerre. Again
you had better send all my mail c/o US Air Service AEF.

Uncertainty still hung over where he and others would be posted. In spite
of what he said in his letter, he feared that he might not only be separated
from his colleagues but that the new posting might involve a step back from
the front. Either taking on ferrying work as some had already been asked to
do, working as an instructor or being assigned to an observation squadron.

His illness had struck at an awkward moment, wanting as he did to put
himself in the shop window down at Orly, to make his case for inclusion
at the earliest opportunity in a fighter squadron. But on reaching Paris,
as he had alluded in his letter, he had considered that the wisest course
of action was to seek proper treatment to rid himself once and for all of
the dysentery he had contracted, so that he could report for duty in a fit
state. Accordingly, he had checked into hospital, the American Red Cross
Military Hospital No. 3 in the Rue Chevreuse in Montparnasse, a short
walk from the Luxembourg Gardens. After three or four days' bedrest,
the symptoms began to clear. He was well enough to leave the hospital
during the day to report to the aviation park at Orly before returning
there in the evenings:

No orders have come for us to go back to the front yet with an American escadrille.
We are still waiting and in the meantime supposed to be ferrying. I go out to O.
every day to get the dope or 'keep on the boat', for I want to get in the first bunch
out. It has hit our fellows hard to come in from the front as chasse pilots (on Spads)
and be asked to ferry while waiting to go back to the front. It's really an awful come-
down and riles us up a bit. There is only one ferrying trip I would sort of like to take;
that is, flying an old bus back to England from France and returning in a new one.
But I'm afraid if I take that trip which I could get easily, I'd miss getting back to the
front with the next bunch out. To a person not understanding all my motives my
queer actions would undoubtedly appear like a highly complicated mystery. Send
me back to the front, Chasse to fight the Boche, and try to avenge my many friends
and I'll be the happiest little bird alive.

You remember my friend Lieut. Jerry Jerome whom I have written you so much
about? Poor brave Jerry, he was one of my best friends, but he is no more. Over the
lines with a Frenchman he was attacked by four Huns. The Frenchman got away

and Jerry was left to his fate, last seen one against four. 'Failed to return; probably killed.' Such is the report issued over a month ago. Jerry was one of the most admirable characters I have ever known. He and I were close comrades and he took me into his confidence. His life history is wonderful. The way Jerry surmounted natural handicaps was great. I will tell you about him some time, but strictly confidential. Jerry was a hero all right. And so it goes. Our bunch, we who went through T. and I. and C. together, is getting smaller and smaller. Accidents and bullets are thinning it out. C'est la guerre. C'est l'aviation. I'll be a wiser sadder man after this guerre.

But do such things discourage me? NOT AT ALL. JAMAIS. They harden my determination and will. My hatred for the German increases. Kill a man's friends and comrades and if the man's a MAN you've got something to reckon with. Germans say of our drafted men they won't fight well because they were drafted against their will. Is that so????? As soon as the Germans have killed a few comrades and friends of those 'drafted men' those drafted men will fight like Merry Hell. Do the high percentage of casualties in my game worry me? NOT AT ALL. Nor should they worry you. By now I am an absolute fatalist. Destiny rules all; the Gods; the earth; spirits; men; the universe; ALL as it is written in Siegfried, which I have just finished reading. But right now my idleness makes me wretched. My whole frame and body seem quivering with pent-up desire to get back to the front and after the Hun. Why must we wait here in and near Paris? Yes, the work behind the lines must be done; we can't all fight. However my mind is not easy; I can't be at rest here. Many of my friends have been killed by the Hun. Alan must be avenged.

It may seem almost ridiculous for me living this uncertain life to always write about my plans for the future for 'when I come home.' But I always think of 'after the war' and I dream and dream; yes, I live in the future. It is my tobacco; my nerve soother. And the more I think of it the more delighted I become at the thought of our ranch in California. We boys must absolutely get together on that. Personally, I want several years of that kind of life after the war before doing anything else. The life will be pleasant and healthy and I believe there will be lots of opportunity. If we go at it right we'll have success.

More days passed as Clifford travelled back and forth to Orly. There was still no word about what would happen or where they would be sent. Still less were there any tasks for Clifford to throw himself into. There was no ferrying work and only one opportunity for the briefest of practice flights in a Spad. He began to fret about flying pay which had not yet come through and chafed at the attitude of some of the ground staff at the Aviation Acceptance Park.

But eventually came the news he had been waiting and hoping for. He was indeed to go back to the front, and as a fighter pilot. He and others, including friends Remington Vernam and 'The Baron' James Beane, were to join the 22nd Aero Squadron of the US Air Service.

30

THE 22ND

The Air Service had proved a valuable asset to American and Allied ground forces in the summer's fighting. The surviving young recruits of the 1st Pursuit Group, near novices only a few months before, had by August honed many of the skills in the air that would stand them in such good stead in the remaining months of the war.

Their development had come at a price, however, in the midst of often fierce fighting against the experienced and tactically astute German Jagdstaffel thrown their way, but the pilots saw some notable successes during the Aisne-Marne campaign in late July and early August. In particular they had enjoyed success at Soissons, hitting German forces on their western flank near that town as the French 10th Army, aided by US 1st and 2nd Divisions, had advanced on the ground. The group's air units had flown hundreds of escort and patrol missions destroying thirty-eight enemy aircraft with the resultant loss of thirty-six of their own pilots; and the 1st Corps Observation Group had lost eleven men in the same period.

The figures were necessarily dwarfed by losses on the ground. The AEF had suffered as many as 50,000 casualties of one sort or another, out of a contingent of 300,000. Yet the Air Service was finally beginning to establish itself as a necessary feature of the AEF's overall combat capability as the Americans began to play their part in the fighting. Ludendorff's 5th Offensive, the final offensive of the spring and summer, had been successfully repelled. German armies had retreated to areas of high ground north of the Vesle River to the north-west of Reims. Although still short of the line of the Aisne River, Foch suspended any further northward drive in the area after them. Momentum was with the Allied and American armies, yet Foch wanted to pursue other objectives.[48]

One of those objectives lay further east in the area where American forces were now being concentrated, the Toul Sector south-west of Metz. The prize in that area was the breaking down of the St Mihiel Salient, a part of the front created back in the autumn 1914 when the invading forces of Crown Prince Wilhelm and General von Strantz had made an early attempt on Verdun. The former's army had been held in the north while von Strantz had captured the ancient town of St Mihiel on the east bank of the Meuse River. The resulting right-angled bulge created in the lines had remained in place in the years following, marked on the west by the densely forested heights of the Meuse River before turning sharply eastwards into the plain of the Moselle River. What was at stake was the protection by the Germans of the strategically important railroad centre at Metz and the iron and coal areas around it.

In order to get at those areas it would be necessary for the Allies first to storm the heights of the salient, a task which would now fall to a newly created entity, the US 1st Army. With this army, Pershing had finally got his way. A fully rounded and self-contained battle complement of US forces had been assembled. The army, three corps of Americans bolstered by a further corps of French troops, now had the wherewithal to take to the field.

Plans for yet further expansion – a 2nd Army – had been put into abeyance for the time being, but the 1st Army was ready and could now take to the field under the direct command of Pershing. The general duly drove down from his Chaumont headquarters on 10 August to take up his formal command and to begin his preparations for the attack on the salient.

Colonel Billy Mitchell began at the same time to organise his own greatly increased Allied air effort, a necessary part of which was an expanded US Air Service. In order to achieve this, the 2nd Pursuit Group was formed in late July at Toul, a group of four squadrons under the leadership of Major Davenport Johnson, a former commander of the 95th Kicking Mule. This was quickly followed by the advent of the four-squadron 3rd Pursuit Group under Major William Thaw, one of the early members of the original Lafayette Escadrille of American foreign legionnaires.

Together, these two new groups – 2nd and 3rd – were in turn formed into a larger entity still, the 1st Pursuit Wing. In this wing they were joined by the bombers of the 1st Day Bombardment Group.[49] It was into this newly reorganised and expanded force that Clifford and colleagues arrived in late August. In Clifford's case he was to join one of the squadrons of the 2nd Pursuit Group, the 22nd Aero*:

22d Aero Squadron 2d Pursuit Group
August 29th 1918

Dear Mother, John and George,

At last I am fixed permanently I hope. Please send all my mail to above address – that will be quickest. I wrote you how I was sorry and yet glad to leave the French. With them I had an invaluable experience; but here are the associations; at present I am happy indeed and the bunch is fine.

In the 2d Pursuit Group are many of my friends, fellows I know real well and with whom I have trained since September 1917. They are a splendid crowd, too. Oh there is nothing like being with your own countrymen in a foreign country and fighting by their side. The French are all right, too, but now with the experience I had in Spad 85 I am delighted to be with American boys in an all American chasse escadrille.

I have just about as good a machine as I had in 85 and the same make too. Yesterday I took her up for a few minutes and put her through a little test. Certain things in the alignment etc. didn't suit me, so today the mechanics made changes for me. Just before dinner I tested out my two machine guns and sights. Personally I object to the possibility of any experience like Alan's, namely where he fired 500 shots at a Boche only to miss him and to find out upon landing that his sights and guns didn't agree. Be prepared.

Now everything seems to be well adjusted. Hope to go out to reconnoitre the new American sector tomorrow and then BUSINESS. Really I feel very confident. Never can I be too thankful for that wonderful experience with the French under the direct tutelage of French aces, the men who KNOW and are the masters of Hun-hunting in the clouds.

Aiken and Fish are not with me, being in the First Pursuit Group. An American Pursuit Group corresponds to a French Groupe de Combat except that the four squadrons composing it are about one and a half again as large as the French escadrille. But Vernam is with me and also the Baron minus two fingers. He says he stuck his thumb to his nose at a German ace and the Boche shot off his fingers for

---

* The other members of the 2nd Pursuit Group, 1st Pursuit Wing, were the 13th, 49th and 139th Aero Squadrons.

it. All said and done, the Baron was mighty lucky to get away with his life. He was up against 7 or 8 and his escape was nothing short of miraculous.

Beane and Vernam are my two roommates. Mac and Bill L., Bill Backus and other friends are all in the same group. Really things have turned out better for us than any of us could have hoped. My mechanics are a good bunch of boys. Fine, clean, intelligent young Americans. They are great to have around. They work twice as fast as my Frenchman did and are just as careful, interested, and proud of a job well done. Crippen, my head mechanic, says that with all the pottering around they are doing for me I must get the first Boche in the squadron. As the squadron is absolutely new and hasn't got a Boche yet (some of the members have, of course, but that was before the squadron was organized) it seems that I have at least an even chance of doing what Crippen wants. I'll try my best and do my darnedest. VOILA ...

This is a beautiful country we are in. Hilly and wooded, it is great to look at but I hope and pray I never have a forced landing on the graceful hillsides or fuzzy looking tree tops of the forests. The other night several of us went to N. [Nancy] near here and had dinner. We had a wonderful time. This section of the front is certainly different from anything I have seen before, that is of the lines. Already I have seen over half the lines.

Who do you think I had dinner with? TUCKER. He is a Stanford man and was a member of the SSU14. He got into aviation when Snook and Cady and Joe Eastman joined up. Isn't it a coincidence that we are in the same American chasse squadron?

I saw Joe Eastman the other day, too. He is in the 1st Pursuit Group and we ran across each other at O. just before I left. Cady, another of our SSU14 boys and a Stanford man flying with the British, has recently been cited for bravery and decorated with the Distinguished Flying Cross. Snook is still in charge of an American training field.

There are so many things I want to tell you but I can't. I am more than ever careful now that I am censoring my own mail again. It is hard to control this pen but you'll just have to wait until after the war and then night after night at home at 666 Tennyson Ave I'll let loose my many tales. You know it is very hard to be so far from home and for so long, for us all, you as well as me. But all said and done I don't regret a thing I have done in the last 18 months. None of us could have been satisfied had I stayed home. By coming to France when I did I have seen a great deal more than if I had waited. There is all the satisfaction in the world in having been a volunteer. And in my mind for me there is no branch of the service like being a chasse pilot in United States aviation. It's a great old game and makes a man of a fellow. For a long time I never believed I could face bullets and fight to kill. I doubted my nerve. That was over a year ago. Today I realize that there is something to me *after all. Hunting the Hun is a thrilling and exciting game but there is no terror to it. Acrobatics are nothing now, but a year ago I dreaded the thought of them. Once I jumped when I aimed and shot a gun, but now behind my two crackling machine guns and roaring motor I never blink nor flinch nor do I shudder when I find myself upside down a couple of miles high.*

The war has done a lot for me, and I feel I have 'guts' after all. You may rest assured your son and brother is not afraid and will do his duty for the honor of our name and country. I must quit; it is getting dark. Goodbye, good luck and lots of love. As ever, Cliff.

The 22nd Aero had been formed more than a year before at San Antonio, Texas, its arrival heralded by military decree – Special Order No. 34, on 16 June 1917. The new squadron's home base was Kelly Field, one of the first of a wave of flying fields that had come into service at the beginning of America's involvement in the war. Yet the unit had enjoyed something of a peripatetic and disjointed existence in the intervening year. Although the new recruits carried out some initial work at Kelly, primary training for the 22nd, as for some other squadrons, had actually taken place that summer in Canada under the guidance of the Royal Flying Corps (RFC) – in the case of the 22nd, in Toronto. Following that spell, the squadron returned to finish its training at Fort Worth, Texas, in the autumn of 1917 before moving on to Garden City on Long Island in January 1918, preparatory to setting sail for Europe.

Almost as soon as it arrived in Europe, however, docking in Britain in mid-February, the squadron had found itself split. Some of the enlisted men were sent on to Dunkirk in France while others, pilots, were afforded further training at schools run by the RFC working on aerial gunnery, scout bombing and observation work. Some of the men saw early service in what was then the newly created British air arm, the Royal Air Force, following the merger of the old RFC and Royal Naval Air Service in the spring of 1918, and the group experienced a number of early casualties both in training and on the front. The squadron was finally reunited in France in June 1918 and sent first to Issoudun and then to the base at Orly for retraining work. That retraining work was to transform the unit from a De Havilland bombing squadron, their original brief, into a fighter squadron.[50]

It was a transformation not without difficulties for pilots and mechanics alike, but the new unit duly went into service. The first patrol of the new squadron, made by Lieutenant John Sperry, took place immediately before Clifford arrived on 21 August and the first credit of an enemy plane for the squadron came a fortnight later. But it was low-key work at first as the men got used to their new surroundings and new role and equipment as they prepared for the big assault to come:

22d Aero Squadron Sept. 2d 1916

Dear Mother John and George,

Life with this squadron seems to be pleasant and normal. So far there has been nothing exceptional or exciting. My machine is having the motor changed, so it is at present out of commission, but Lieut. Vernam is going to lend me his for this afternoon's patrol. I am very anxious to get down to real work and see if I can't do something; but I suppose we must go slow and take our time.

September 3rd

Well, it was some patrol; three of us made it. My bus, or rather Vernam's, wasn't even ready; everybody else got off and they were still loading my guns. I held one end of a long belt of incendiary cartridges while the armourer slowly passed it in the ammunition box. Then I climbed in and in my haste neglected to pump up pressure until the mechanic was tired out cranking. Finally I got off. At 1500 meters I picked up the others on the way to the lines. Two had been forced down with motor trouble, so we had only three in the patrol. We were supposed to patrol at 4000 meters but there was nothing doing at that altitude; nothing even in sight. So Lt. Sperry the leader started to climb to see if we couldn't pick off a Boche observation plane. These creatures have a custom of crossing over at about 6000 meters, snapping what they want and beating it back to Boche air before an Allied plane can climb to their altitude to attack them; but sometimes they are surprised.

We saw nothing, so Sperry decided to go out for an altitude test. Hudson and I followed and went just as high as Sperry did, the highest I've ever been in my life. At 6700 meters Sperry's altimeter broke and as our gas was getting real low it was necessary to go home. 6700 meters is about 20,770 ft. We could have gone higher I am sure, but it was AGONY. In the first place I had gone out with only a 4000 meter patrol and so only had on a light cloth combination to keep the oil off my clothes and not the cold. The side doors at my feet were open and let in a cold stream of air. My wind shield had been fixed for Vernam and was too low for me, with the result that the icy propeller blast blew straight into my face cutting it like a knife. I was awfully glad when we started down. But I suffered no ill effects from the rapid climb and speedy descent (15min. only, gliding down), a little over an hour climbing and half an hour up there. No dizzy feeling; no sick feeling; only a slight pressure on my ears. It proves one thing, and that is that I'm fit for high work.

22nd Aero Squadron Sept. 10 '18

Four of our pilots, including [1st Lt. Jacques Michael Swaab] Schwab, out on a patrol the day before yesterday. The clouds were very thick and rather low and a strong wind was blowing eastwards. Flying by their compasses above the clouds they soon passed north of the lines; and then diving through the clouds they were horrified to find themselves over M., some 30 kilometers or so in the German lines. They knew it mighty quick, too, for the archies or anti-aircraft began shelling them right and left making their life miserable. Each man for himself, they again climbed into the clouds, this time entirely separated.

An hour or so later three of them landed on our field. Many holes were in the planes from anti-aircraft fire. Schwab failed to return. So it appeared that the squadron of which I am a member had lost one of its pilots. Yesterday came a phone message from way South near a neutral country. It was from Schwab, 'Wounded and crashed'. The Captain, a 'prince', had the Cadillac out toute de suite. He is always on the job. This morning we got the details. Separated from the others, lost in the mix-up and the clouds, S. had flown south by the compass hoping to cross the lines where he originally went over. But the strong wind kept blowing him eastward, so instead of coming south to us he went southeast and remained in Boche territory. He knew he was lost but after a reasonable time he decided he was in France, and so came out of the clouds to land and find out where he was.

Voila un aerodrome. Down he went to land. Suddenly he saw a machine start to take off. It was a Hun chasse plane with black crosses on its wings. S. peaked, shot a burst of incendiaries at the enemy, saw him burst out in flames, and then realizing where he was, namely over an enemy aerodrome, he pulled up again and beat it in a straight line west.

Before he got into the French lines he ran into a patrol of ten Boche. Surrounded and hopelessly outnumbered he was still game. He attacked two, sent one down out of control and saw the other start to spin helplessly toward the ground and then by luck and skill he outmanoeuvered the others and got across the lines. But he had received a bullet in the head during the course of the combat and as he entered cloud on our side of the lines he fainted. In sort of a daze he crashed, but luckily was not hurt apart from the fact that he had already been wounded. His aeroplane *was riddled with bullets. So, we are not short of one pilot after all but instead have a hero to welcome after he gets out of the hospital. The Captain is tickled to death.*

The weather has been rotten lately and there has been very little aerial activity. In a sort of way I am glad because my motor has been out and so with the bad weather I really haven't missed very much flying. They got the new motor in yesterday and are mounting the two guns today. I hope to test her out this afternoon.

The bunch is fine. I couldn't ask for better comrades. Of course I would like to be home, that is if the war was over, but as long as it lasts I want to be here, at least that is my present wish. Sunday afternoon three of us, Hall, Richter and myself took out the new Dodge limousine for a trial spin. We were delighted. The trip was glorious, through very pretty country. We called on a lot of our friends in the 3d Pursuit Group and I saw Johnnie Aiken and Fish.

Incidentally Group de Combat 19, our old French group, has moved up near here. In a couple of days, after they get really settled Vernam and I are going to breeze over in the brown Dodge limousine and say hello to Dumas, Fanquet etc. They certainly will be surprised. Tomorrow my new uniform will be ready and if I can get over to Nancy to try it on etc., I shall do so.

News from the battlefront is still mighty bright. I am perhaps a little too optimistic, but I look for a very decisive battle to commence in the next ten days and when it is over the German's fate in France (in France I say) will be decided. We still have Belgium and Alsace-Lorraine to take and must carry the war to Germany before Germany will admit she's licked, and settle the eastern and Balkan questions right; but this year I look to see the Huns driven out of France.

The time was approaching for the assault on the St. Mihiel Salient. A mighty ground force had been assembled, the U.S. First Army bolstered to a combined strength of sixteen American and six French divisions with a sizeable array of heavy weaponry gleaned in large part from the Allies. The Allied cooperation was also evident in the force which had been assembled by Billy Mitchell, the largest aggregation of planes to engage in a single operation in the course of the war. The U.S. Air Service mustered a dozen pursuit squadrons, three-day bombardment, 10 observation and a night reconnaissance squadron. Seventy other squadrons from France, Britain and Italy brought the combined total to 1481 planes.[51]

In the first recorded use of the term in American military circles,[52] Field Order Number 9, 1st Army, dated 7 September 1918 stated simply that, 'The First Army will attack at H hour on D day with the object of forcing the evacuation of the St Mihiel Salient'. That day was fixed for 12 September.

31

ST MIHIEL

The offensive began in the early hours of 12 September, a heavy artillery barrage across the length of the front heralding an all-out assault. The guns then lightened, as scheduled, at 5 o'clock, as the first ground troops began their move. Troops of 1st Division led the way as forces began the drive up through the rolling countryside towards the town of Vigneulles: an advance which they found surprisingly good going with the Germans' old and rusting barbed wire on the front easy to trample over.

At the same time as their advance, the first of the aerial cover began, with the 90th Aero Squadron taking to the skies. The 90th and its fellow squadrons in the IV Corps Observation Group had prepared for the day for the previous two weeks, studying maps and photographs, with each team of pilot and observer assigned specific tasks. It was, they knew, a big test for all of them. They had waited impatiently for the day, a day which now dawned wet and grey over their base at Ourches.

The Final Report of the Chief of the Air Service noted:

September 12 was marked by the worst kind of weather for flying ... a terrific south-west wind made formation flying extremely hazardous, and a low ceiling of fast moving clouds reduced the visibility to two or three kilometers. The heavy rains of the previous week had made the Amanty airdrome so muddy that the propellers of fifty percent of the airplanes were broken while taking off ... it was rare that half the airplanes left the ground.[53]

As the 90th Observation wondered what the day would yield, a short distance to the east of them Captain Ray Bridgman's 22nd Aero Squadron was likewise waiting to carry out its early morning mission. Bridgman was himself a veteran of the conflict, having arrived in France two years before. He had served in a French squadron, No. 49, and spent nearly a year with the original American foreign legionnaires' squadron, the Lafayette Escadrille, forging a reputation as an aggressive pilot and winning the Croix de Guerre with star. In February 1918 he had received his captain's commission in the US Air Service before taking up a flight command with the 103rd Aero Squadron, a new US unit, but one made up largely of experienced pilots from the old Lafayette.[54]

The difference between his command with the 103rd and the task which now faced Bridgman cannot have been lost on him at dawn on 12 September. A unit of talented yet still largely new pilots would have to contend with the elements on this foul morning before they could even think of the enemy fighters they might encounter. That said, would they even manage to take to the skies from the soft mud of their Toul airfield? Moreover, would they be able to see anything when they were up there? After half an hour of early morning rain the downpour gradually began to ease off. A wind started to blow to the south-west and visibility improved slightly. They were hardly ideal flying conditions, but it was enough for the 22nd Aero's first mission to attempt a take-off.

At 5.45 a.m. First Lieutenant Vaughn McCormick taxied out on to the airfield and was soon airborne, leading a patrol of four other colleagues into the heavy skies, and within the hour Bridgman was in the air after them. If he could gather enough of a first-hand picture of conditions in the Moselle River valley area, the commander believed, he could better advise his young pilots still on the ground, including Clifford, who would be taking off later in the day. Clifford recounted the events of the day in a letter home:

22nd Aero Squadron Sept. 13 '18

Dear Mother John and George,
My machine NICK is now working fine. At 1.15 four of us started out on a low patrol to keep a clear space ahead of the advancing lines for our reglage planes to work in. Two had motor trouble, so just as four French Spads came along I flapped my wings as a sign to Baron Beane to come along, and we joined them. They happened to

be 96,Vernam's old escadrille, and I imagine [Lt. Pierre Fanquet-Lemaitre] *Fanquet*, whom I saw last night, was leading. That's the beauty of knowing insignias.

We went 9 or 10 kilometers into the Boche lines; the clouds were awfully low and we had to fly at 500–800 meters only. There were lots of Allied planes but not a Boche machine in sight, but they made up for it by peppering us with anti-aircrafts. Today those archies were awful. Crack-bang, loud and distinct above the roar of the motor, and then a puff of black smoke would appear dangerously near. They had us squirming all the time and, believe me, it was no joke. Shrapnel at such close quarters gets on our nerves. They were machine zumming us from the ground, too. Every now and then I could see an explosive or a tracer bullet go flashing by me. They look just like shooting stars.

A man seeking excitement or thrills gets all he wants in this game. Darn the clouds. I hope tomorrow they are not so thick so that we can climb up way out of range of those cussed anti-aircraft batteries. There were a lot of fires in villages and towns and forests which the Hun vandals are evacuating. But I was really surprised at the comparative quiet on the roads in Boche territory. I guess it was there all right. I just had my hands so full I couldn't bother to notice it. While the six of us were flipping about we had to look out for each other and scan the skies. You can't do everything at once.

On the way back to the aerodrome I saw a Liberty plane on the ground; left everybody; dove down and looked it over. It was evidently one of the planes belonging to a squadron near us Spad men. The fellow had had a forced landing and had hit a shell hole. Result: he turned over and smashed, but neither he nor his observer were hurt. I skimmed by at about 90 miles per hour and waved to the doughboys guarding it. Couldn't see a number. Upon landing at our field I gave the exact location of the plane so a wrecking party could go after the remains. At the office they had heard it was down but didn't know where to look for it.

About an hour and a half ago we saw some of the fruits of this brilliant American advance. About 2000 prisoners passed our camp. I can only guess at the number. All had been taken by one division. They came along in fours guarded by a few doughboys and cavalrymen. WHAT A SIGHT. The youth of Germany is certainly nothing extra; and there are lots of rickety old men; but to be truthful I must admit there were a lot of fairly strong-looking soldiers. But they had nothing on their guards. A lot of us stood by the roadside and watched them. When they stopped we studied their faces and some of the boys questioned them. On the whole they seemed indifferent. In fact so tired were they from walking, or rather tramping, hour after hour that they didn't seem to care one way or the other. Some said 'three years of war – me – too much – over now.' To hear a Boche try to talk English is very funny after hearing

French attempts. Well it certainly does seem good to know our boys are pulling in the prisoners. The surprising thing is to what a large extent the Boche have been deceived by their leaders. Some of the prisoners said their officers told them the Americans were not over in force, but that the soldiers in the lines opposite them were Englishmen dressed like Americans to deceive the Germans. WHAT RUBBISH.

I know you would like to have me keep on writing, but I can't do it. I'm hungry as the dickens, and it's dinner time. We wait and wait and wait at the hangars and stand on call about all day. If there is no patrol there is a lot to have done about the machines. Since the offensive has started I have not even been able to go to Nancy to get my uniform. If I ever have a forced landing in Germany, I want a good suit of clothes on my back. I always wear my big boots on patrol, for leather is scarce in Allemand. Next to my machine, my most important possession is a Colt 45. If I'm ever forced down in Germany and the Huns get too curious I'll explain the mechanism in a practical way.

Well goodbye I must quit. Love to you all and the best kind of luck. Maybe we'll all be together again next year. Comme toujours, Cliff.

The speed of the first day's successes on the ground exceeded expectations. By lunchtime, the 1st Division had achieved its initial ground objectives for the day, but the decision was taken to press on, and to press home the advantage. Joined by fellow divisions of the IV Corps, the 42nd Rainbow and the 89th, and aided by the two corps flanking them, they continued the advance. Gradually, with the help of the 26th Division coming in from the west, they closed in on Vigneulles.

In the air, the huge armada of Allied planes enjoyed similar dominance; yet the lumpen skies still held danger, and the reconnaissance mission that Ray Bridgman had begun on behalf of his young pilots had proved to be far from smooth. As he patrolled the front from east to west, Bridgman could see little sign of the formation led by Vaughn McCormick that had gone up ahead of him, and now out of the clouds appeared a German Hanover plane, seemingly oblivious to his presence. Closing in on the enemy plane, Bridgman fired a barrage of rounds sending it towards the ground.

Five minutes later another enemy plane had appeared, escaping almost as quickly, and ten minutes after that Bridgman spotted a group of five German Rumplers. It was time to head back to base. Turning his plane, he headed south towards Toul, but he was about to run into some difficulties. Some way into his flight a shot from the ground, most likely from the American lines, hit his plane damaging the engine. He was still 20 miles or so short of his home field and Bridgman had to land, bringing his Spad to rest near the recently recaptured village of Remenauville.

On touching down, he immediately commandeered a car and raced back to his squadron's base at Toul to fetch one of the squadron's mechanics. But on getting there it was to discover that his patrol leader of the morning, Vaughn McCormick, was dead. McCormick had crashed on landing back at base, possibly having been hit while leading the patrol.

Other casualties of the 2nd Pursuit Group on that first day of the St Mihiel campaign included the group's leading ace and flight commander of its 139th Squadron, First Lieutenant David Putnam, who was shot through the heart in a dogfight as he attempted, with a colleague, to come to the aid of an observation plane. Indeed, planes were lost from a number of units – pursuit, observation and bomber alike – but overall, this first day had proved a notable success for the legion of pilots above the salient, as they bombed and harried the retreating columns of German soldiers in the burning fields below.

Operations continued the following day, Friday 13th, another dank and difficult one for flying, but the cloud cover did not prevent a busy schedule. Observation squadrons worked effectively with the rapidly advancing infantry on the ground, and pursuit flying, while largely confined to low-altitude work, concentrated most of its efforts on the strafing and bombing of German troops and convoys. Indeed, bombing for the pursuit pilots was a new facet of their role in the campaign. In addition to the main work of the bomber squadrons, these fighter pilots were now equipped with a small rack on the outside of the plane to hold a small number of 'Cooper' bombs which could be released and dropped from a height of 250–300ft.

Even though the land war was nearly finished by close of play on the second day, aerial warfare continued unabated for the next few days. On Saturday, 14 September, the third day of the campaign, the sun came out and in spite of a degree of cloud scudding across the sky visibility was good. Morning and afternoon patrols were carried out across the sector, including by the 22nd Aero, and it was around 3 o'clock in the afternoon that the first fully fledged encounter took place between a formation of the squadron's planes and a group of enemy Fokker aircraft.

A detachment of the squadron's planes was to fly out over Mars-la-Tour, west of Metz, to meet a Salmson observation craft, there to take photographs of the battlefront. The orders were to clear the sky of enemy craft in advance of the front lines. Clifford recounted the episode the following day. It had been a notable one for him:

22d Aero Squadron Sept. 15th '18

Dear Mother John and George,

It has always been my policy to be perfectly frank with you and tell you everything. If anything should happen to me you would be glad to know of all my experiences. This is war and war is in itself dangerous. Everybody knows that. Yesterday I had the most thrilling experience in my life. Now I am going to tell you all about it, but don't allow yourselves to worry. It will do no good. We chasse pilots run many risks daily and they are all in the game.

One of the boys says I shouldn't write home about our harrowing experiences because it causes unnecessary worrying. He says it is thoughtless and cruel. I take the attitude that you want to know and that you are sensible enough to remain cool-headed and not to worry. So here goes.

On the anniversary of my enlisting in the US aviation I had the biggest fight of my life; September 14th 1917 I joined up in Paris. Little did I dream then what a chasse pilot goes through; now I know. Yesterday I found out. But in addition I learned something that I am very glad to know — I don't wilt under gun fire nor do I lose my head in even an unequal fight with bullets shrieking and whistling all around me, hitting my plane NICK, and just missing my head. That is one satisfaction.

Yesterday afternoon eight of us started on a patrol with the C. [Captain Bridgman] leading. Our mission was to create a safe zone for our observation planes five kilometres ahead of our advancing forces; and to do this we had to fly 8–9 kilometers north of our most advanced lines.

Because of my having had a little more experience than some of the boys, I was placed on the left end to bring up the tail and cover the others. Rear man has the worst position in case his patrol is attacked, for he is the first victim picked upon, and in case his patrol attacks he gets little glory, for it is the leading men who shoot at the enemy first.

So when the nine Fokkers attacked us six (two had returned home earlier because of motor trouble) Little and I were the first victims. About four of the red-nosed blue-bodied bastards jumped on me. They had height and were in the sun, and all I could do was to wriggle.

At that moment I looked below and saw that five or six other Fokkers had come up and were attacking the rest of the patrol. In a dogfight like that it soon develops into 'each man for himself and the devil take the hindmost'. Well, I was the hindmost, but at the same time I didn't like the idea of being easy meat for the devil Huns. We were about 5200 meters high and 10 kilometers into the Boche lines.

I watched my tail like a cat and saw the enemy come on. One especially attracted my attention and he was only about 75 meters off. He flew prettily and I moved like mad to get out of his sights. But he wasn't my only worry for there were three or four picking on poor me alone. No sooner would I avoid one than another was firing at me. Rat-tat-tat-tat. What a sound. And then a streak of pale sickly whitish blue smoke would whish by over my head as the bullet flew by. I'll bet a hundred bullets came within six inches of my body. Nick was absolutely riddled. I didn't even have a chance to fire a shot. I had to look in back of me all the time; and, with me, I don't like to fire unless my beads are on the other man's head. There's no use firing bullets wildly if they are not going to hit something. This is not a 4th of July celebration just for noise sparks and smoke. And yet through it all I never thought so quickly or so clearly in my life. My head was just as cool as could be. It was a game to outwit the Huns and get away.

With motor racing full speed I swung into a fast steep right hand spiral dive; going down almost vertically and yet turning enough to keep the other fellow's sights off me. Really, to tell the truth, I've never seen such a pretty sight as those traces and incendiary bullets flying past leaving their trail of smoke; but that smoke smells awful. The rat-rat-rat-tat-tat is bad, but the whistle and crack as the bullet hits home in your machine, ripping the fabric and breaking the woodwork, is awful. For 1200 meters those streaks and bullets kept flying past me, then the Boche seemed to pull out of their following dives, evidently convinced that they had sent a Spad down out of control. I let NICK dive vertically for another 800 meters just for good luck and then gently pulled him out toward our lines. Looking up and back I saw the Huns circling around like hawks over their prey. In the air was considerable wreckage. Evidently a plane had exploded. We lost a man but our crack little pilot Brooks thinks he got two Huns, so that evens us up a bit. As I crossed the lines the Boche kept archying me with their black archies, but I couldn't help laughing, their shots went so wild. My altitude then was about 3000 meters. That 2200 meters was the fastest I've ever dropped. Giving NICK the once over, I decided it was best to make for our aerodrome and land. My landing was terrible and bouncy because among other things the Boche had shot off my left tire. As I taxied up to the hangars, a great crowd of pilots and mechanics gathered round my plane; and of course they had to have the story and congratulate me upon getting away. NICK and I certainly were lucky; there's no question about that.

He had been lucky this time, but as he knew, another colleague had not. When the remainder of the patrol returned Clifford learned that the Spad he had seen exploding was that of his fellow lieutenant, Philip Hassinger, a tall New Yorker who had enlisted the previous summer. Hassinger and another member of the squadron, First Lieutenant Arthur Raymond Brooks, had downed two planes in the mêlée, yet the former was now officially listed as 'missing in action'. No one could definitively say that they had seen what happened to Hassinger's plane once it was hit. Indeed, in spite of work after the war led by a US Air Service investigator, the tenacious Captain Fred Zinn, to trace Hassinger or any sign of a grave, nothing was ever found of him. First Lieutenant Hassinger remains one of the war's missing aviators.[55]

Meanwhile, on the ground on that day, 14 September, Clifford inspected the damage done to his own plane. It had had been 'unreasonably shot to pieces', the official historian of the squadron and his colleague, Ray Brooks, later recorded, '[Kimber] himself surviving by several minutes':

My machine was so badly shot up that I'll probably have to have a new one. The motor was untouched so I'm going to ask the captain if I can't have that in my new plane. There were nearly 70 holes in my machine, mostly in the fuselage and body. The three vital parts, my engine, the gas tank, and I were untouched, although bullets smashed some struts and wires not three inches from me. The rudder control wires were nearly cut in two, ditto one aileron control and the left flying cables. The tail was nearly shot off; the rudder was perforated, and the left lower wing was a wreck with the longerons nearly cut away. Three struts in the fuselage were smashed and many wires were severed. The prop. had two holes in it.

Well, now it will be my turn next time, and I certainly do hope to have better luck with the Hun than he had with me. Gee, but I wanted to go right up again after a Boche. But this is no game for the single hunter, the Hun flies in formations of 15 to 20 and the man who flies alone in an offensive is a fool. No, my chance will come and I hope it won't be in a dog fight but in a duel. I went up this morning in another fellow's machine but it developed motor trouble so I had to land. But I have all my nerve and I've smelt a lot of powder. I'm a wiser and more experienced pilot. [God] was merciful to me. I hope I can prove myself worthy of his mercy in this war and in later life. Well I must quit; goodbye good luck and lots of it and much love. God bless you all. As ever, Cliff.

Theirs had been one of a number of savage dogfights that day, with several fellow squadrons of the 2nd Pursuit Group particularly active south and west of Metz. The Germans had taken to the skies in numbers and in concentrations of aircraft to bring the fight to the Allied pilots, one large formation of Fokkers from Jasta 18 swooping on the 13th Aero Squadron and bringing down four of its planes.

The fighting continued into the following day, a Sunday, but overall the Germans were outnumbered. The Allies had finally achieved the air supremacy they had sought. In the four days of the campaign, American squadrons alone had flown 3,300 sorties, downed more than sixty German aircraft and a dozen observation balloons and carried out over 1,000 bombing raids.[56]

On the ground, American and French forces had achieved their objectives in a speedy campaign. Yet, as John S. D. Eisenhower notes, by what he calls the 'cruel accounting' of war, the 'light casualties' still stretched to 7,000 Americans dead or wounded – and even then St Mihiel was to be seen as a mere dress rehearsal for what was to come.[57] Foch and Pershing, aided by the air capabilities of Billy Mitchell, had their eyes fixed on a push north into the forests of the Argonne. The Meuse-Argonne Offensive – one of the last great drives of the war – was at hand.

32

MEUSE-ARGONNE

Having conducted the St Mihiel Offensive where they had, Pershing's forces might now reasonably have been expected to follow a different course of action from the one they were to take in the days that followed. The fact that they did not gave them something of an initial edge, and provided a surprise in their next assault.

At St Mihiel, the American 1st Army had tackled the German lines by pushing up from positions in the south – south-west of Metz and south-east of Verdun. It had been a campaign fought to the east of the Meuse, the river which ran through Verdun and onwards north towards Belgium. Ludendorff and his generals in the field expected the American focus to remain in that area. It was possible to imagine the Americans turning their attentions further east towards Metz or to continue north as before, but in both cases staying on the eastern side of the Meuse. What Ludendorff did not know, however, was that Pershing had already agreed with Foch and General Pétain on a different course of action.

A full ten days before St Mihiel had even begun, it had been decided that American forces would later concentrate their effort further to the west, something which was now addressed. Division after division was moved to the west of the Meuse, a feat achieved, crucially, without German suspicions being aroused. From there the 1st Army would strike northwards up towards the German Hindenburg Line to the River Aisne, to link up with the French 4th Army.

In this manner the Allies would be attempting not only to break the German stranglehold in that field of operations but to bring pressure to bear on them in an area of great strategic and military importance. The main railway line, running through Sedan, was one of the two principal supply and evacuation routes for German armies in northern France. The railway had, as its vital section, the line which ran between the towns and cities of Mézières, Sedan and Carignan, which in turn linked on to Luxembourg and Metz.[58]

The plan laid out by the Allied commanders called for the American forces to advance through some difficult terrain, bordered on the west by the dense and steeply banked Argonne forest and on the east by the heights of the Meuse. The far shores of the latter were studded with German observation posts and gun positions, which would make progress hazardous. The elevated forest to the west likewise held the danger of strategically placed artillery positions and lookout posts.

It would be necessary for American troops to deploy themselves in a manner which not only dealt with these hazards to left and right but also allowed them to advance down the middle, through a ridged corridor itself fortified at careful intervals with German battle lines. None of the progress would be easy: whatever could be gained by way of surprise had to be weighed against the dangers they had to overcome. Either way, speedy progress was imperative to allow for advance before the German lines could be reinforced. The objective set out by the Allied leaders was to break through the *Kriemhilde Stellung*, the name given to the eastern section of the Hindenburg Line, further up this corridor.

As Pershing moved his command headquarters to Souilly, south-west of Verdun, in preparation for the ground assault, Billy Mitchell, soon to be promoted to the rank of brigadier general, was putting the final touches to his air plans. Mitchell knew he would not have the same array of air assets available to him as two weeks before, given the spate of co-ordinated Allied attacks now being planned up through the line on the Western Front. But that air armada would still number 820-odd planes, three-quarters of them American, and he now assigned his different groups separate jobs.

The 1st Pursuit Group was given the task of clearing the skies of enemy balloons and taking on low-flying battle planes. The 2nd Pursuit, including Clifford's 22nd Aero Squadron, and the 3rd Pursuit Group were to give high cover for these operations and escort the planes of the 1st Day Bombardment Group. The Spad XIIIs of these latter two groups were now additionally fitted with bomb racks to carry two 25lb bombs intended to harry German infantry on the ground.

In the week before the new offensive, and prior to being moved to a new base closer to the proposed drive, Clifford's unit continued operations from its base at Toul. Events on the ground had temporarily quietened down but the skies above were still busy with enemy planes. In between operations Clifford sat down to write home, to talk as ever over a range of subjects which he hoped would be of interest to his mother and brothers back in California. He spoke in detail of his finances and his saving plans for the months ahead. By January 1919 he hoped he would have put aside over $1,000. He had also sent his mother $450 in the course of the year which, Clifford said, he hoped she had 'spent and not tried to save'.

He then talked about letters he had recently received from his two brothers and recounted some events, military and non-military, of the past days:

> That uniform I ordered at N. [Nancy] was going to be a dandy; but when I went to get it they had mixed it up with a 2nd Lieut's order and it wouldn't fit. As we are moving, the tailor had to give me back my deposit and cancel the order. He was very nice about it, but as it was his mistake, why shouldn't he? Today he is wiser and sadder. I was sore at first, but now I don't care. Am going to have present uniform cleaned and pressed and will go without a new uniform till January; don't need it anyway.
>
> Well, they managed to fix NICK up again with a new left lower wing and tail (all except vertical pin) and prop and wheel and 3 fuselage struts from the captain's wrecked plane. But NICK has acquired a very bad habit and wants to dive all the time. In other words, he has been poorly groomed or lined up. This afternoon the engineering officer Davis is going to superintend the lining up. NICK has got to want to climb before he carries me 10 kilometers over the lines again.
>
> Yesterday we went out on a patrol at 6 pm. As usual there were altogether too many damned Fokkers and they dogged us about wherever we went, but didn't attack. We were ten kilometers in their lines part of the time and they had altitude on us, too. But four French Spads flew way above us all and I guess that sort of scared the Hun airmen.
>
> The beastly anti-aircrafts or Boche archies are the most annoying pest of all. Fritzie was firing all the time right into the middle of our formation and we were S-ing, etc. to keep out of the way of those cursed shells. They go off with a crack right near you, and then you see a big puff of black smoke. Sometimes the concussion rocks the machine. In spite of the roar of the motor they are easy to hear. Sometimes they shake one's nerves quite a bit. Darn it anyway; an aviator has lots to get his goat. But c'est la guerre; it is our daily work. Time flies and winter is getting

close, it seems. I'll be glad when it really starts again. In the meantime, goodbye,
good luck, and lots of love. As ever, Cliff

Four days later the 22nd Aero was on the move up closer towards the front. Pilots and ground staff of the 'Shooting Stars', as they now called themselves, were to relocate some 35 miles to the north-west, to an airfield at Belrain between Bar-le-Duc and Verdun. The new quarters the men found on arrival were not all they might have wished for, a theme taken up by Clifford's colleague Ray Brooks in a history of the squadron after the war. He peevishly remembered:

> Removal to the Verdun drive took away much of the joy that came from inhabiting a reasonable dwelling place. At Toul, the quarters were comfortable and convenient, transportation was adequate for mind-saving trips to such palaces of the epicure as Nancy or Toul afforded (when not interrupted by bombs dropped by unsympathetic Boche). The main satisfaction of being an aviator, on account of the charm of living outside the muck of battle after the day's fighting, was taken away and the real conditions of warfare indulged in for the next month. Billets in Prie-la-Brulée, and Belrain were offered, supplemented by shacks on the field. Liaison was difficult to establish in many instances. At all events, with many trials in camp, much fighting in the air, and the tremendous drive of the Armies after the forcing of Montfaucon after September 26th, the Squadron, from the worried Operations Officer to the mechanics who worked all night with a searchlight, felt all that the war seemed to lack up to the time of Verdun.

But it was now the night before the Meuse-Argonne Offensive was to begin, and Clifford used what time he had in between duties to write home. As was often his custom, it was only part of a letter. He wrote whenever he could, in fits and starts over a number of days, and so long as he at least started the letter now, he thought, he could always continue it at a later date and with more up-to-date news:

22 Aero Squadron, Sept 25th 1918

Dear Mother, John, and George,
   Today I feel very guilty for it has been nearly a week since I last wrote. Much
has happened in the last few days, not especially over the lines, although I have

been on quite a few patrols lately; but in and around the camp. Among other things, we have moved. Only those in the US Air Service know what it means to move an aerodrome. I am afraid you can't exactly appreciate all that it entails. We had been told we were going to move a week ago and so we got ready. And for all that time we lived in a packed-up condition which is anything but pleasant. And the day before yesterday, or Monday the 23rd, we were all awakened about 3 am. It was raining and a miserable day. Pas de petit dejeuner. A cup of coffee and a piece of bread eaten in true French style sufficed. At 5.30 all our baggage was loaded on the trucks; and then we simply hung around till about 5 pm waiting for good enough weather to fly in. For dinner we had gone to town.

The trip took about forty-five minutes and was over rough, rugged hilly yet very pretty country; no incident of importance. Nothing was ready; half enough hangars for the place; poor quarters; no rooms for us; someone came up with a list of addresses where we were to be billeted. We took the Fiat truck to the little village to look at our new homes. My, what dirty dusty mouldy rooms, and what a wretched little village. Pas pour nous. About ten of us lieutenants got back on the truck and made for B. [Bar-leDuc], near where I first joined SSU14. After an awful job looking all over town in practically all the hotels we found some rooms. Hudson and I bunked together in the big French bed and the others all paired off likewise. But, best of all, we had a very good dinner.

The captain had asked us to be back at the field by 7 am the next morning. Orders are orders, so at 6 moins 15 we got up. The ride was cold. A thick heavy damp fog which chilled to the bone went right through us. And at the field we spent most of the morning standing around miserably. About 10.30 someone hinted that there was a barracks up on a hill near the town that was empty. Anything is better than a dirty French room and a lousy French bed in a sloppy muddy filthy French village; so Henry Hudson, Paul Richter, and I investigated. The old wooden barracks wasn't much, but it was good enough. It is one of the collapsible kind, leaky and drafty and full of holes. It reminds me a little of our brooder house on the ranch KODINA. We got the orderlies to clean it out and straighten it up. The mess was awful, but now it is fixed very well.

It was the last letter Clifford wrote.

33

FINAL FLIGHT

A few hours after Clifford penned his letter the big guns opened up, lighting up the late September sky. A 'violent artillery fire of preparation', as Pershing described it, a precursor of the assault to come.

The assault began at 5.30 a.m. Three corps of troops – each of the corps was three divisions strong – went into action, men and armour rolling into no-man's-land. On the left, into the Argonne forest, went Lieutenant General Hunter Liggett's I Corps. On the right-hand side, tackling the hazards presented by the German emplacements near the Meuse, went III Corps, commanded by Major General Robert Lee Bullard; while through the middle, a comparatively inexperienced three divisions of soldiers in the shape of Major General George Cameron's V Corps. Meanwhile an additional body of troops, the French XVII Corps, was holding the front north and east of Verdun, as Pershing kept a total of six divisions in reserve.

The battle plan as set out by Pershing called on his men to push quickly up the territory he had identified with Foch and Pétain. At the top of the corridor through which they would pass lay the main German line, the Kriemhilde Line, running west to east between the three villages of Grandpré, Romagne-sous-Montfaucon and Brieulles-sur-Meuse. In order to get there, though, American forces would need to fight their way through a number of formidable obstacles and positions, with an almost continuous series of positions manned by the Germans stretching out over 10 miles and more.

Dominating the landscape early on, and a focus of American attention, stood Montfaucon, the Mount of the Falcon. The capture of this hill was set by Pershing as an early objective on day one. In spite of more sober assessments and predictions from his French allies, he hoped not only to have secured Montfaucon but seen his forces well beyond it, attacking the Kriemhilde by the end of the day, before German reinforcements could be brought in. However, the ground to be covered in getting there was to prove a problem in itself: the soil underfoot was spongy and only four badly damaged roads crossed the zone, a challenge for the engineers in the days ahead.

At 4.00 a.m., halfway through the opening salvo of the big guns, and as the ground troops were mustering in preparation for their assault, the first of Billy Mitchell's planes took off from the west. Their mission was to make German observation of the coming attack more difficult to monitor. As the lights of cannons illuminated the front lines below them, eighty-one Spads of the 1st Pursuit Group flew out in search of enemy balloons, using the murky dawn light to cloak their mission. Within an hour six observation 'sausages' were in flames and the group had claimed the first of its ten kills that day. Pilots of the other groups readied themselves for action.

The 22nd Aero Squadron's pilots took off throughout the morning in different groups and on different missions. One four-man patrol, including lieutenants Henry Hudson and Bernard Doolin, was attacked by a much larger force of German Fokkers but managed to bring down one before escaping to safety. Clifford's friend James Beane brought down another enemy plane after being separated from his colleagues at altitude.

In the latter part of the morning it was Clifford's turn. 'Nick III', the third plane he had named in honour of his friend Alan Nichols, and which he had been flying since joining the squadron the previous month, was still not airworthy after the squadron's dogfight on 14 September. So, when Beane returned from his mission, Clifford borrowed his friend's plane and took off on a patrol with their squadron commander, Ray Bridgman.

They were headed north to the top of the German lines. Their task was to strafe roads along and north of the Kriemhilde from Grandpré to Dun-sur-Meuse, the latter a railway centre on the train line identified by Allied leaders as strategically important. One group led by Bridgman flew down to 200m near the village of St Juvin, east of Grandpré, scattering German forces on the ground; and while Bridgman did this, Clifford continued to lead two other colleagues on a raid, following the line of the main road up from Grandpré towards Dun-sur-Meuse looking for German positions.

Halfway along the road stood the village of Bantheville, a crossroads held by German forces and guarded by anti-aircraft battery No. 721 of the German 5th Army. Whether the battery was his main target, or whether he was intending to continue up to Dun-sur-Meuse, is unknown.

It was around 11.30 a.m. and Clifford nosed his Spad down out of the clouds into a dive towards the ground. A bullet or shell from the ground hit one of the bombs he was carrying. The plane exploded. Clifford fell to his death.

34

AFTERMATH

Who fired what from the ground was never really established. A bullet? A shell? From which side? Differing suggestions were offered from different sources as to what had happened to Clifford. One account just after the war, from Ray Brooks in his official history of the 22nd Aero Squadron, suggested that Clifford may have been the victim of friendly fire, 'hit by a direct burst from the American artillery barrage through which his formation was flying'. The Deutsche Militär Kommission, meanwhile, stated their belief that it was the anti-aircraft battery in Bantheville that had brought him down.

Clifford's own commanding officer, Colonel E. C. Whitehead, was perhaps closest to the truth when he wrote in his report to the Chief of the Air Service that it was 'unknown whether the shells of artillery from either side, or a bullet from the ground into the bombs, caused the tragedy'.[59] The only thing thing they could agree on was that Clifford had indeed died, that his plane had exploded and that the wreckage of man and machine had been seen smashing into the earth of the little village below. Yet no one could precisely say what subsequently happened to Clifford's body.

What is less in doubt is what happened on the front in the six weeks that followed. The Meuse-Argonne Offensive, and the simultaneous drives up the Western Front by British and French forces, proved decisive in the prosecution of the war, although it was slower going for the Americans than Pershing had hoped or planned for. Montfaucon, his early target, was taken not on day one but halfway through day two, an early indication of the scale of opposition they would encounter as they fought their way up the difficult terrain.

Overcoming the multiple German positions established in the central theatre of attack proved problematic as Ludendorff ordered more and more divisions in to defend the region: four divisions by close of play on the first day, a further six by 30 September. But if the frontal, central attack was proving difficult for the Americans, progress on the left up through the Argonne forest was equally painful and bloody. The I Corps commander, Hunter Liggett,[60] had compared the Argonne to something akin to the shape and dimension of Manhattan. If that were the case, the tackling of the forest by his men was not far short of street-to-street fighting within it.

A temporary halt to the attack was ordered by Pershing at nightfall on 29 September, in an attempt to regroup and augment his forces. Other divisions were now drafted in from the St Mihiel area, among them his trusted 1st Division, The Big Red One, to tackle the Argonne. On 4 October, all-out assault was rejoined as the American forces pressed on with renewed purpose. By the middle of the month the Kriemhilde was finally breached and German forces began to retreat in the face of a pincer from the joint American and French armies, the latter advancing on the west.

As the fighting raged on the battlefield, however, behind the scenes the first tentative moves were being made towards peace. The new German Chancellor, Prince Max of Baden, began to explore the terms of a possible armistice in the first of a series of letters to and from President Woodrow Wilson and Secretary of State Lansing in Washington. Wilson and Lansing, aware of the sensitivities of British and French Allies, were initially circumspect in formal replies, unwilling to commit to specific detail or negotiation without proper consultation with the Allies and their military commanders. It would take some more weeks for these processes to work their way through, but the first straws of peace were in the wind.

Meanwhile, unaware of, or unwilling to be distracted by such manoeuvrings, Pershing continued with his campaign in the field. The British had broken through the Hindenburg Line up in Flanders, taking control of the Belgian coast and now, having made the breakthrough of his own on the Kriemhilde, Pershing's 1st Army in the Meuse-Argonne, now under the new command of Hunter Liggett, took further German-held territory north of the Kriemhilde on the Barricourt Ridge. US forces continued their march towards Sedan and the prize of the Mézières–Sedan–Carignan railway line so prized by Pershing. As they did so, the recently formed American 2nd Army under Robert Bullard swept east towards Metz and the Briey iron region.

In the air, Mitchell's forces played an ever more prominent part, his pilots providing not only reconnaissance and observation reports and dealing with enemy aircraft but taking on an increasingly offensive role, bombing German positions and supply sections in major set-piece initiatives. A notable example of the latter involved a series of raids by French, American and British planes on Damvillers, east of the Meuse, with hundreds of Allied bombers, backed by pursuit planes, dropping a payload of 80-odd tons of explosives on enemy forces below.[61] It was, felt Mitchell, a portent of military aviation in the future, a glimpse of air power with a wider and more strategic brief.

The end came soon enough. As the pace of war increased and the Allies advanced, Germany now found itself isolated. Austria, already shorn of the Hungarian part of its dual monarchy, sued for peace. On 7 November German emissaries led by Matthias Erzberger arrived by arrangement inside French lines to begin thrashing out the full terms and conditions of an armistice. It would take another four days before that armistice would be realised and peace declared, during which time fighting would continue and the 1st Army would breach the railway line through Sedan.

But peace did come on the eleventh day at the eleventh hour. The guns suddenly stopped, soldiers came out of their trenches and the skies above no longer hummed with the angry noise of warplanes. Quiet descended on the war-ravaged land below.

The role of aviation had changed much in the course of the war. A war which was fought so heavily on the ground in an attritional series of encounters had nonetheless during that time seen a new service grow to assist military commanders in the field, increasing their reach and vision.

The technology and doctrine of aviation had evolved greatly in the past four years. Pilots had learned new techniques in the art of flying and pushed the boundaries of their machines' capabilities, and air commanders had developed a new understanding of what could be achieved by means of aerial warfare. The US contribution to that change was necessarily limited, given their short time operating on the front in 1918, yet the US Air Service had come a long way in the nineteen months since Washington had entered the war, and only seven months or eight months on from the first tentative combat flights by US Air Service pilots.

The Chief of the Air Service, Mason Patrick, was sober in his overall assessment, acknowledging that the service had had a lot of ground to make up even before reaching France:

> One fact stands out most prominently, one common source of all of our difficulties becomes apparent; these failures were the unavoidable result of our unpreparedness and of the necessity for actually preparing for war while hostilities were in progress.

Yet alongside his criticism he was able to record in his Final Report:

> On the Marne, at St Mihiel and in the Argonne our air forces were pitted against the best which Germany could produce and the results show that the enemy more than met his match.[62]

In all, American fliers were credited with the destruction of 776 enemy planes and seventy-two observation balloons for the loss in action of only 290 American planes and thirty-seven balloons. The tally of those killed, captured or missing in action may have been higher than those figures suggest – some 466 men, with more wounded and killed in accidents besides, or those who died of other causes.[63] Yet the skill these men had acquired in such a short period of time was still testimony to their courage and resilience.

Before hostilities had ended, seven more of Clifford's colleagues had been killed, among them his friends, First Lieutenants James Beane and Remington Vernam. The two, both officially air aces by the time of their deaths with eleven victories between them, had left on the same patrol together on 30 October 1918 but never returned. North of Buzancy, as the 1st Army advanced on the ground towards Sedan, Beane had found himself outnumbered by a force of the reorganised 'Richthofen Circus' of the late Red Baron and was shot down. His grave was located after the war by the US air investigation officer Captain Fred Zinn.

Vernam, meanwhile, was wounded in action and crashed, being taken as a prisoner on the ground and brought to a nearby hospital. There he was initially treated but later abandoned by retreating German forces and, although rescued by the Red Cross when the area was liberated a few days later, he died of his injuries shortly after the Armistice.

But the squadron they had all served had, in those few short months, achieved a remarkable record. In spite of its late start to the campaign, only being operational on the front from late August, it had scored the fifth highest total of victories – forty-three – of all the US Air Service pursuit squadrons.

35

AT REST

It was not the end of Clifford's story, though. Not quite. That last chapter finally came to be written long after his friends had gone to their rest.

Most of the young men who had fought bravely beside him and who had died in the service of their country had also, in death, enjoyed small monuments to their lives, graves that might be properly visited by their friends and family in years to come. In Clifford's case, that had not been possible. In spite of the best endeavours of his brother George and those of his mother from 1918 onwards, there was no marker of his passing, nothing left except the memories of those who loved him. Attempts to trace his body had proved fruitless. But that all changed one day in the autumn of 1921.

George had returned to America, resigned to the distressing thought that he would never find his brother. It was three years since Clifford had been shot out of the sky, a long time, and even George's relentless optimism was crumbling. It was a bitter feeling. George truly thought he had found the right location in that French village a year before, or as near as he could properly gauge it. All the evidence pointed that way. But identifying a rough location was not deemed good enough; his determined drive had not proved to be sufficient. Persistence had been met with dead ends and brick walls. The vigour with which George had begun his quest had subsided, replaced by the unhappy acceptance that he would never have the opportunity to stand at Cliff's grave.

George had finished his studies under Professor Rutot in Brussels in June of 1921 and had spent the summer down in Switzerland as planned with his friend Fernand Chodat's family. He travelled down with Fernand in July, joining a summer course at the University of Geneva. There he worked in the university facility in the Alps run by Fernand's father, Robert. From there he, Fernand and fellow students at the Alpine Laboratory in Bourg St Pierre would go for long hikes in the mountains, accompanied as often as possible by Fernand's sister Isabelle.

Isabelle used the opportunity on those walks to sketch the wild flowers around them. George would study the same vegetation, comparing what he found with the plants of his own native Sierra Nevada in California, determined to see what he might learn and use back home in terms of agricultural enterprise. He and Isabelle became close during these summer months. In time they talked of marriage, but before he could think of asking her to commit to him he first resolved to sort out his future back in America. He wanted to pursue the dreams of farming that he, Clifford and John had all mapped out – whether it was to be together as a big family unit or individually. John had bought land for a chicken farm in the southern part of the San Francisco Bay Area and George wanted to find his own land for more agricultural purposes.

He returned to America in the autumn, having been offered a job at a high school in Hughson, near Modesto, east of Palo Alto. It was the post of agriculture teacher and was one that would give him some financial backing while he began looking for his own farm.

It was shortly after he had returned and was settling into his new job that Clara received an unexpected and joyful letter back at the old family home in Tennyson Avenue in Palo Alto. Clara contacted George and John as soon as she could – there had been a breakthrough.

A letter had arrived from Captain Charles J. Wynne of the US Army Cemeterial Division:

> This office is pleased to advise you that the investigation which has been conducted for some time with a view towards locating the grave of your son ... reveals the fact that the body of the deceased is interred in grave #4, row #2, north-eastern corner of the French cemetery at Bantheville, Department of Meuse.

A letter with the same happy news, though from a different source, was arriving at George's old flat in Rue de la Loi in Brussels. The retired chaplain who headed up the Information Branch of the American Graves

Registration Service in Paris, Joseph Kangley, wrote to say that his brother's body had been 'found and identified, and is now in Romagne Cemetery awaiting permanent reburial'.

So, George had not been so far out after all. Clifford had been in Bantheville all along – but in the cemetery, only a few yards from where George had been searching. His prayers had been answered, yet almost at once his elation was tempered by nagging queries about how exactly his brother had come to be found and how exactly he had died. What had happened? What condition was he in?

The latter questions had always haunted him. Did he die in pain? Was it over quickly for him? George went back to his typewriter to restart correspondence, beginning with the body's discovery in the graveyard – how did this tally with the message of a year before from German and American authorities that 'there is no grave there belonging to Arthur Clifford Kimber'? He wrote to the Cemeterial Division again to ask them for help to clear up some of these questions, and he enumerated a host of others: Was the body in a casket? What was its condition? What was the likely cause of death? What were the injuries? Was the whole body shattered, as from a direct hit and explosion of an anti-aircraft shell or was it a head wound or shrapnel or the fall to earth which was the main cause? Could anyone know if death was instantaneous or not? Was any personal property found on the body? What marks of identification proved the identity? Where was the body now?

George asked for any replies to be made to him and not to his mother, 'I wish to spare her as much shock as possible in this matter.'

On 17 November 1921, Captain Wynne wrote back to George with some of the details he had asked for, but which nonetheless would have been painful to read. Firstly, on the grave where he had been found – it had not borne his name, said Captain Wynne. The grave containing the body of Lieutenant Kimber had 'Unknown U.S. Soldier' stencilled on the marker and, he said, had been 'originally buried' in this plot – in other words, this was where it had always been, presumably buried by German forces three years before.

It had:

> ... the remnants of ... a regulation Officer's uniform of the Signal Corp ... body wrapped in airplane cloth, without shoes or leggings; very badly decomposed, features not recognizable, skeleton disarticulated ... color of

hair apparently brown; head shattered and upper jaw fractured; both arms broken above and below; both legs broken above and below.

Clifford's body had actually been exhumed from the church cemetery in Bantheville in June, identified by those dental records which Clara had sent months before.

So there it was. It was over. His beloved brother could now be buried, although, as it happened, it took longer than the American Graves Registration thought to rebury Clifford. The months passed from 1921 into 1922, as work continued more generally on the cemetery at Romagne. In June 1922 the quartermaster's office in Washington wrote to Clara saying that 'unforeseen obstructions' had temporarily delayed the work of completing the permanent American cemeteries abroad. But, the official went on, 'please be assured that the body of your son will not be lost nor will it be handled with anything but the respect due the remains of the men who gave their lives for their country'. The official assured her in a subsequent letter that a request she had made for a photograph to be taken of Clifford's grave when he was finally laid to rest would be honoured. It was, and Clifford was finally reburied in the late summer of that year.

In 1932 Clara joined other bereaved mothers on a visit to the cemetery, under the auspices of the American Government. Beyond that she lived another eighteen years, until after the next great conflict in Europe, long enough to see her other sons marry, settle and raise families.

George initially began to farm crops in Merced County in central California, starting with irrigated alfalfa plants. He returned to Geneva in 1927 to marry Isabelle, and she finally came with him to California to settle. George continued to teach in a variety of institutions there, branching out from his field of botany into the wider study of geography, and eventually earning a doctorate in education for work in the development of junior colleges in the state.

As for John, in 1925 he finally established the chicken ranch that he and his brothers had spent so much time talking about. Beginning in Niles, in the eastern part of the Bay Area, he pursued the scientific poultry farming that had so attracted him as a boy, introducing pioneering new breeding methods. Gradually, his small 800-hen farm grew into a large multinational company with a 300-strong workforce and stock farms and hatcheries dotted around Europe and the Far East. But Kimber Farms Inc.

only flourished until after John's death in 1970, ultimately being bought up by a larger company in the field of agricultural research.

Meanwhile, George's and John's brother lies at rest with over 14,000 other Americans, the largest number of American military dead in Europe, in the graveyard in eastern France close to where his plane fell nearly a century ago. The 130 acres of the Meuse-Argonne Cemetery at Romagne-sous-Montfaucon is as tranquil as it is spacious and manicured. An imposing entrance gives way to a careful layout spread out over a slight valley: a vast swathe of headstones edged by buildings and monuments, set white against the gentle and verdant landscape.

A memorial loggia, a chapel, a circular pool and a visitor centre are all dotted around eight large rectangular plots, each bounded by linden trees. Clifford's grave can be found in the last of those plots, in one of the final rows, towards the back of the cemetery. One of the first of his countrymen into France in the war, he came to be one of the last buried. A Latin cross in a sea of other headstones bears the simple inscription: 'Arthur C. Kimber. 1 Lieut. 22 Aero Sqdn. California. Sept 26 1918'.

The flag he brought to Europe still exists, kept at his home university of Stanford in Palo Alto, California.

NOTES

1   Jennifer D. Keene, *The United States and the First World War* (Pearson Education Ltd, 2000) p.15.
2   Robert Roberts, Scott Hammond, and Valerie Sulfaro, *Presidential Campaigns, Slogans, Issues, and Platforms, the Complete Encyclopedia* (USA: ABC-Clio, 2012) p.875.
3   Woodrow Wilson, Address of the President of the United States to the Senate (17 January 1917) wwi.lib.byu.edu/index.php/Address_of_the_President_of_the_United_States_to_the_Senate. (Accessed March 2015.)
4   Woodrow Wilson, Speech to Congress Regarding Unrestricted U-Boat Warfare (3 February 1917) www.firstworldwar.com/source/uboat_wilson.htm. (Accessed March 2015.)
5   Robert Lansing Papers, Library of Congress, in Arthur Link (ed.), *Papers of Woodrow Wilson* (USA: Princeton University Press, 1983), Vol. 41, pp.118–25.
6   Woodrow Wilson, Speech to Congress Regarding Unrestricted U-Boat Warfare (3 February 1917) www.firstworldwar.com/source/uboat_wilson.htm. (Accessed March 2015.)
7   wwi.lib.byu.edu/index.php/The_Zimmerman_Note. (Accessed March 2015.)
8   Woodrow Wilson, Address to a Joint Session of Congress: Request for Authority (26 February 1917) www.presidency.ucsb.edu/ws/?pid=65398. (Accessed March 2015.)
9   Arthur Zimmerman, Speech Regarding the Zimmerman Telegram (29 March 1917) www.firstworldwar.com/source/zimmermann_speech.htm. (Accessed March 2015.)
10 Mark Ethan Grotelueschen, *The American Army and Combat in World War I* (Cambridge: Cambridge University Press, 2007) p.11.
11 Ibid.
12 George J. Hawk, *History of the S.S. St. Louis also known as U.S.S. Louisville, 1895–1919* (1919, Library of Congress) pp.41, 46.
13 Ibid. pp.44, 46, 50.
14 Charles Affron, *Lillian Gish, Her Legend, Her Life* (USA: University of California Press, 2002) pp.109–10.

15 George J. Hawk, *History of the S.S. St. Louis also known as U.S.S. Louisville, 1895-1919* (1919) pp.44, 68–69 and 72; Richard E. Schroeder, *Missouri at Sea: Warships with Show-Me State Names* (USA: University of Missouri Press, 2004) p.80.

16 Dr Lindsay Krasnoff, Office of the Historian, US State Department, *The Role of the U.S. Diplomatic Community in France, 1914*, pp.5–7, PDF online via http://history.state.gov/departmenthistory/wwi. (Accessed June 2015.)

17 'Organizing the Field Service, April 1915: A. Piatt Andrew, Soldier, Scholar, Statesman', www.ourstory.info/2/a/Andrew.html. (Accessed February 2015.)

18 Stefania Chinzar & Roberta Ruffino, *Where the Border Stands: From War Ambulances to Intercultural Exchanges* (Ulrico Hoepli Editore, 2014) https://books.google.co.uk/books?id=dR7jBAAAQBAJ&pg=PT22&lpg=PT22&dq=piatt+andrew+alsace+neutral+ambulance&source=bl&ots=YjViIQkxuR&sig=UD1Gqyo5NhkzMSqNqtkOSZtsEAA&hl=en&sa=X&ei=6GjrVK_aLI2tPLyRgYAN&ved=0CC8Q6AEwAg#v=onepage&q=piatt%20andrew%20alsace%20neutral%20ambulance&f=false. (Accessed June 2015.)

19 Richard Van Ness Ginn, *The History of the U.S. Army Medical Service Corps* (USA: Library of Congress, 1997) pp.38–39.

20 Joanna Bourke, *An Intimate History of Killing: Face-to-Face Killing in Twentieth-Century Warfare* (London: Granta Books, 1999) p.256.

21 Niall Ferguson, *The Pity of War 1914–1918* (Great Britain: Penguin, 1999) pp.373–75.

22 Tom D. Crouch, '1908: The Year the Airplane Went Public, Air & Space, Smithsonian Institute', www.airspacemag.com/history-of-flight/1908-the-year-the-airplane-went-public-8791602/?no-ist (Accessed February 2015.)

23 Clara E. Kimber, *The Days of My Life*, 1938, p.89.

24 Huw Richards, 'The Remarkable Story of French Rugby's First Hero', http://en.espn.co.uk/france/rugby/story/251813.html (Accessed March 2016.)

25 James Hudson, *Hostile Skies: A Combat History of the American Air Service in World War I* (New York: Syracuse University Press, 1996) p.30.

26 Ibid, p.3.

27 The National Museum of the US Air Force, www.nationalmuseum.af.mil/factsheets/factsheet.asp?id=324. (Accessed March 2015.)

28 James Hudson, *Hostile Skies: A Combat History of the American Air Service in World War I*, p.4.

29 Arthur Sweetser, *The American Air Service* (New York & London: D. Appleton & Co., 1919) pp.188–92, in James Hudson, *Hostile Skies: A Combat History of the American Air Service in World War I*, pp.14–21.

30 James Hudson, *Hostile Skies: A Combat History of the American Air Service in World War I*, pp.21–22.

31 Robert Futrell, *Ideas, Concepts, Doctrines: Basic Thinking in the United States Air Force 1907–1960* (USA: Air University Press, 1989) p.21.

32 *The Stanford Daily*, 55.3, 17 February 1919.

33 Christopher Heaney, *Cradle of Gold: The Story of Hiram Bingham, a Real-Life Indiana Jones, and the Search for Machu Picchu* (USA: Palgrave Macmillan, 2010.)

34 Robert W. Christie, *Wooden Props & Canvas Wings: Recollections and Reflections of a WWI Pilot* (iUniverse, 2009) pp.20–21.

35 Maurer Maurer (ed.), *The US Air Service in World War I, Volume I: The Final Report and a Tactical History* (USA: Progressive Management, 2012) p.94.

36 Henry Arnold, *Global Mission* (USA: Tab Books, 1989) p.65.

37 Heywood Broun, *America in the War: Our Army at the Front* (USA: King Press, 2009) p.107.

38 Edward Renehan Jr, *The Lion's Pride: Theodore Roosevelt and His Family in Peace and War* (Oxford University Press, 1998) pp.138, 155, 191 and 197.

39 John S. D. Eisenhower, *Yanks: The Epic Story of the American Army in World War I* (USA: Simon & Schuster, 2002) pp.12 and 46.

40 *The Papers of George Catlett Marshall*, ed. Larry I. Bland and Sharon Ritenour Stevens (Lexington, Va.: The George C. Marshall Foundation, 1981). Electronic version based on *The Papers of George Catlett Marshall*, Vol. 1, 'The Soldierly Spirit', December 1880–June 1939 (Baltimore and London: The Johns Hopkins University Press, 1981) pp.123–25.

41 John S. D. Eisenhower, *Yanks: The Epic Story of the American Army in World War I*, pp.112–17.

42 Kevin D. Stubbs, *Race to the Front: The Materiel Foundations of Coalition Strategy in the Great War* (USA: Praeger Press, 2002) p.238.

43 James Hudson, *Hostile Skies: A Combat History of the American Air Service in World War I*, p.56.

44 Maurer Maurer (ed.), *The US Air Service in World War I Volume I: The Final Report and a Tactical History*, p.48.

45 Maurer Maurer (ed.), *The US Air Service in World War I Volume I: The Final Report and a Tactical History*, pp.117–23.

46 James Hudson, *Hostile Skies: A Combat History of the American Air Service in World War I*, pp.76–86.

47 John S. D. Eisenhower, *Yanks: The Epic Story of the American Army in World War I*, pp.142–63; James Hudson, *Hostile Skies: A Combat History of the American Air Service in World War I*, pp.91–94.

48 James Hudson, *Hostile Skies: A Combat History of the American Air Service in World War I*, pp.106–117; John S. D. Eisenhower, *Yanks: The Epic Story of the American Army in World War I*, p.173.

49 James H. Hallas, *Squandered Victory: The American First Army at St. Mihiel* (Praeger Publishers/Greenwood, 1995) p.19.

50 Arthur Raymond Brooks, 'A History of the 22nd Aero Squadron: Shooting Stars', *Cross and Cockade Journal*, 4.2 (1963), pp.109–113.

51 James Hudson, *Hostile Skies: A Combat History of the American Air Service in World War*, p.139; John S. D. Eisenhower, *Yanks: The Epic Story of the American Army in World War I*, p.184.

52 US Army Center of Military History, Combat Orders: The General Service Schools, Fort Leavenworth, Kansas. 1922–1923 (Fort Leavenworth, Kansas, 1922) www.history.army.mil/html/faq/ddayhhour.html. (Accessed May 2015.)

53 Maurer Maurer (ed.), *The US. Air Service in World War I Volume I: The Final Report and a Tactical History*, p.365.

54 James Hudson, *Hostile Skies: A Combat History of the American Air Service in World War I*, pp.145–47.

55 Blaine Pardoe, *Lost Eagles: One Man's Mission to Find Missing Airmen in Two World Wars* (USA: University of Michigan Press, 2011) p.108.

56 James Hudson, *Hostile Skies: A Combat History of the American Air Service in World War I*, pp.181–86.

57 John S. D. Eisenhower, *Yanks: The Epic Story of the American Army in World War I*, p.195.

58 Michael Duffy, First World War, www.firstworldwar.com/source/ meuseargonne_ludendorff.htm, and www.firstworldwar.com/source/ meuseargonne_pershing.htm. (Accessed March 2015.)

59 Arthur Raymond Brooks, *A History of the 22nd Aero Squadron: Shooting Stars*, pp.17–19; private letters of George Kimber, 12 October 1920.

60 Hunter S. Liggett, quoted from *Liggett's AEF: Ten Years Ago in France* (New York: Dodd, Mead & Co., 1928) in 'The Argonne', Gary J. Clifford, Robert Porter Patterson, *The World War I Memoirs of Robert P. Patterson: A Captain in the Great War* (USA: University of Tennessee Press, 2012) p.167.

61 Alfred F. Hurley, *Billy Mitchell, Crusader for Air Power* (Indiana University Press, 1975) p.36; John S. D. Eisenhower, *Yanks: The Epic Story of the American Army in World War I*, p.253.

62 Maurer Maurer (ed.), *The US Air Service in World War I*, Volume I: 'The Final Report and a Tactical History', pp.17 and 63.

63 James Hudson, *Hostile Skies: A Combat History of the American Air Service in World War I*, p.299, quoting sources from *Victories and Casualties*, Gorrell Histories, AS AEF, M, XXXVIII, p.3, and Arnold, *Global Mission*, p.49.

APPENDIX

LETTERS ORIGINALLY PRINTED IN THE BOOK *THE FIRST FLAG* BY CLARA E. KIMBER

(THE FRIENDS OF FRANCE, SAN FRANCISCO, 1920)

From US Secretary of War

February 18, 1920

I am interested to learn that the first American flag to go officially to the battlefields of Europe after our entry into the war has found its permanent resting place beside the altar of the chapel of Stanford University, from whence its unit started. The Croix de Guerre pinned to its folds typifies the successful termination of the career of high-souled adventure of its guardians.

As one of the officials of the Department, and as one of the citizens of the country in whose service Lieutenant Kimber met his death, I share your grief that the hands which carried this banner eastward across the ocean might not have brought it back. The Croix, with the flag, will stand as the most fitting memorial to those of its brave bearers who did not return.

Cordially yours,

[Signed] Newton D. Baker.

From the Chancellor Emeritus of Stanford University

An ardent believer in the ideals of democracy and peace, and willing, if need be, to give his life for them, Arthur Clifford Kimber left the United States in May, 1917, as advance member of the Second Ambulance Unit of Stanford University. On this trip he carried with him an American flag, presented by the 'Friends of France' to the First Stanford Ambulance Unit, already in service at the front. The details of the presentation on the battlefield are vividly recounted in these pages.

The character of this young man was typical of the best in America. Wise, resourceful, and resolute, yet at the same time gentle and idealistic. It was my fortune to know him well as a student, and to recognize his noble qualities.

That war insistently devours such men as Clifford Kimber is its final indictment at the bar of civilization.

David Starr Jordan.

From the President of Stanford University

Stanford University is very proud of its sons who gave an early answer to the great call that came to us from Europe. Particularly is this true regarding the ambulance units sent from the University to France before the official entrance of the United States into the war. It will be hard to duplicate in character and initiative these small but ardent groups of men. The incident of the flag described in this little book is symbolic of the spirit, the enthusiasm, and the wholesome youth of the men who so nobly represented Stanford on the other side. We take pride in the splendid record of Arthur Kimber, both in life and in death. We think of him as a high example of the type we take pride in calling the 'Stanford Man'.

Ray Lyman Wilbur.

From the Director of the American Field Service in America

The American Field Service, from the time of its inception at the beginning of the war, stood squarely for the cause of France. During the years when this country maintained perfect neutrality, its ambulances were actually serving at the battle-front. As its efforts became more widely known, contributions and volunteers flowed to France in steadily increasing numbers, proving that the loyal and intelligent citizens of the Nation had accepted the Great Cause.

This volunteer work, permitting immediate action at the front, appealed particularly to the youth of the Nation, whose vigor and idealism, fostered by fine training in truly American homes, impelled them to take up the active burden of service and sacrifice.

Among the foremost of these was Arthur C. Kimber, who volunteered as a member of the Second Stanford University Unit. To his care was entrusted an American flag, presented to the First Stanford Unit, then serving in France. This flag was accepted by the War Department, as one of the Nation's official standards. It was the first American flag officially carried to the front. As the bearer of this distinguished trust he may well have been anxious to see it unfurled in France without loss of time, and soon after his arrival in Paris he had the satisfaction of being sent out with it to Section 14. where the flag was received and officially recognized by the French Army at a splendid review and consecration.

When the Field Service was taken over by the United States Army, Arthur Kimber decided to enlist in aviation, and trained as a chasse pilot. This ambition he later realized, and during the heat of the great battles over the fields of France, in the summer of 1918, he was doing his share of the work as a fighting scout. It was while he was so flying, and after a record of splendid achievement, that he was killed within the German lines, September 26, 1918, at about half past eleven in the morning.

His death is equally mingled with tragedy and glory. It is the eternal epic of high-spirited and patriotic youth. The finest blood of a nation is always ready to give the fullest sacrifice. Those who are willing and fit to give the most to life are also willing to give the most to death. Though little may be said to lessen the tragedy of his loss, or to add to the glory of his death, it seems worth while to record a few of the words spoken by General Baratier, at the grave of Paul Osborne, killed in our service at the front, in 1917:

'My thoughts go out to your parents, who, over there on the other side of the ocean, will learn of the sorrow which has stricken them. I know that words have no power to lessen a mother's sorrow, but I know, too, that the thoughts of the ideal which she inspired in the heart of her son will be able, if not to dry her tears, at least to transform them. For it is through these tears, the tears of all mothers, of all women, that VICTORY will come--- that VICTORY which will assure the peace of the world, and which will be theirs more than any others', since they have paid for it with their hearts. 'Soldier, sleep on, in the midst of your French comrades, fallen, like you, in glory; sleep on beneath the folds of the flag of the United States, in the shade of the flag of France.'

With the same spirit that gave utterance to this stirring and tender tribute, will the memory of Arthur Kimber be guarded by his comrades and compatriots.

Henry D. Sleeper.

BIBLIOGRAPHY

Berg, A. Scott, *Wilson* (Simon & Schuster, 2013)

Brooks, Arthur Raymond, *A History of the 22nd Aero Squadron: Shooting Stars* (Cross and Crockade Journal, 1963)

Broun, Heywood, *America in the War: Our Army at the Front* (King Press, USA, 2009)

Christie, Robert W., *Wooden Props & Canvas Wings: Recollections and Reflections of a WWI Pilot* (iUniverse, 2009)

Eisenhower, John S.D., *Yanks: The Epic Story of the American Army in World War I* (Simon & Schuster, USA, 2002)

Grotelueschen, Mark Ethan, *The American Army and Combat in World War I* (Cambridge University Press, Cambridge, 2007)

Hansen, Arlen J., *Gentlemen Volunteers: The Story of the American Ambulance Volunteers in the Great War August 1914–September 1918* (Arcade Publishing, 1996)

Holroyd, Jack, *Images of War: American Expeditionary Force France 1917–1918* (Pen and Sword, 2012)

Hudson, James J., *Hostile Skies: A Combat History of the American Air Service in World War I* (Syracuse University Press, 1968)

Hurley, Alfred F., *Billy Mitchell: Crusader for Air Power* (Indiana University Press, 1975)

Keen, Jennifer D., *The United States and the First World War* (Pearson Education Ltd., 2000)

Kimber, Clara E., *The Days of My Life* (privately printed, 1938)

Kimber, Clara E., *The Story of the First Flag* (Friends of France, San Francisco, 1920)

Maurer, Maurer (ed.), *The US. Air Service in World War I Volume I: The Final Report and a Tactical History* (Progressive Management, USA, 2012)

Renehan Jr., Edward, *The Lion's Pride: Theodore Roosevelt and His Family in Peace and War* (Oxford University Press, 1998)

Reynolds, David, *America: Empire of Liberty* (Allen Lane, 2009)

Online Resources

www.firstworldwar.com/source – Primary documents relating to the First World War

http://wwi.lib.byu.edu/index.php – First World War document archive (Brigham Young University)

www.ourstory.info – A history of the American Field Service

INDEX

'A completely fresh and, at times, astonishing new light on what we thought we knew about the First World War; the under-reported US experience through the eyes and pen of a thoroughly admirable and thoughtful young American. A family tragedy and a national epic.'

Andrew Marr

★ ★ ★

'Revealing, absorbing and moving. This is the too often untold story of the First World War as seen through one man's eyes and one man's words.'

Nick Robinson

★ ★ ★

'Very few books take a reader direct into the First World War like this.'

Jeremy Vine

The destination for history
www.thehistorypress.co.uk